D1489934

The Faith That Moves Mountains

The Faith That Moves Mountains

By Lee Roberson
Chancellor, Tennessee Temple University
Chattanooga

SWORD of the LORD
PUBLISHERS
P.O.BOX 1099, MURFREESBORO, TN 37133

Cover Photography by Diane S. Parks
Chattanooga Area Chamber of Commerce

Printed in U.S.A.

Dedication

*Affectionately dedicated to my wife,
Caroline Allen Roberson,
my constant companion and inspiration
for forty-seven years.*

Introduction

Since preaching my first sermon at a small mission church in Jeffersontown, Kentucky, in 1928, I have preached many times on faith because I know the importance of faith. There is no salvation without faith. There is no peace of heart without faith. There is no solid accomplishment without faith.

"The Faith That Moves Mountains" is the FAITH we read about in Matthew 17:20: ". . .If ye have faith as a grain of mustard seed, ye shall say unto this mountain, Remove hence to yonder place; and it shall remove; and nothing shall be impossible unto you."

We all have some faith, but our need is for a faith that moves mountains! Every Christian faces mountains—mountains of unbelief, mountains of satanic doubts, mountains of inertia, mountains of indifference. Our Lord wants us to have the faith that moves mountains. The Word of God plainly says that God wants us to have a workable, moving, overcoming, peace-giving faith.

In hours of weakness, in times of great distress, I remind myself to have faith in God. I have known physical weakness and illness, economic stress, the opposition of unbelievers, the sarcasm of "baby Christians"; but in all of this I have found peace of heart by looking to the blessed Lord and believing His Word. Paul tells us in Romans 10:17, "So then faith cometh by hearing, and hearing by the word of God."

Lee Roberson
Chancellor, Tennessee Temple University
Pastor Emeritus, Highland Park Baptist Church
Chattanooga, TN

Table of Contents

1. The Shield of Faith

Above all, taking the shield of faith, wherewith ye shall be able to quench all the fiery darts of the wicked.
—Ephesians 6:16.

We are well acquainted with the Christian's armor as given in Ephesians 6. For successful warfare we must put on the whole armor of God, because ". . .we wrestle not against flesh and blood, but against principalities, against powers, against the rulers of the darkness of this world, against spiritual wickedness in high places."

I want to call your attention to one piece of the armor carried by the Christian—the shield of faith.

The shield that Paul had in mind here is not the small, round buckler, but the oblong, door-like shield, measuring 4' x 2½', curved to the shape of the body and carried by the Greek and Roman soldiers. When joined together, these large shields formed a wall behind which a body of troops could hide themselves from the rain of the enemy's missiles.

These military shields were made of wood, covered on the outside with thick leather, which not only deadened the shock of the missile, but protected the frame of the shield from the fire-tipped darts used in the artillery of the ancients.

So, faith is the shield of the Christian soldier, defending him from the fierce attacks of the foe from within and without.

The shield of faith is able to quench all the fiery darts of the wicked. This shield cannot be pierced or destroyed by the fiercest fires of hatred or malice. The arrows of the evil one, though flaming with cruelty, are stopped by the shield and extinguished.

By the help of the Lord, I want to strengthen your faith. I want you to go from this building feeling stronger in faith than when you entered.

There are so many things which work to destroy our faith in God. The skepticism and the doubts voiced by an unbelieving world are often used by Satan to shake the faith of the best of God's people.

Again, the unfaithful lives of Christians are often used by the Devil to wreck faith. Therefore, we need to know some very simple but fundamental things about faith and what it can do for us.

I. WHAT IS FAITH?

Simply defined, faith is belief and trust. It is believing God and trusting God. Both elements must be present to make faith.

It was a good answer that was once given by a poor woman to a minister who asked her, "What is faith?" She replied, "I'm ignorant, and I cannot answer well, but I think it is taking God at His Word."

Faith is the foundation of all Christian graces. Dr. Arthur Pink says, "The beginning of faith is faith in the beginning."

The Word tells us, "Through faith we understand that the worlds were framed by the Word of God, so that things which are seen were not made of things which do appear."

There is no true faith that does not begin at recognition of God as Creator. We must believe that before we can believe anything else.

After the acceptance of God, we must accept the way for coming to God. This is the blood-sprinkled way. No one can come to God except through Jesus Christ. This must be accepted by faith.

After salvation, it is necessary that we walk and work by faith.

Someone may be asking even now, "How can I get faith, and how can my faith be increased?"

This answer is given us in Romans 10:17, "So then faith cometh by hearing, and hearing by the word of God." The beginning, progress and strength of faith are by hearing. God gives faith, but it is by the Word as the instrument.

If we are to have faith, we must hear and believe His Word. It is not hearing the enticing words of man's wisdom, but the Word of God which will increase faith. And how must we hear it? We must hear it as the Word of God.

Believe the Word, read the Word, hear the Word is the way for faith to increase. Read His precious promises and rest upon them. There is no other way to get faith but this way.

II. WHAT FAITH DOES NOT DO

It is necessary that I discuss a negative aspect of faith in order that some difficulties be removed from your minds. There are disappointed and disillusioned Christians all about us because they misinterpreted the working of faith.

As an example, I heard a man say not too long ago, "Since I became a Christian, it seems that everything has gone wrong. We have had sickness and suffering. I have lost my job. We have had much trouble, but through it all God has been good and has helped us."

Notice some things that faith does not do.

1. *Does not shield from physical suffering.* The Apostle Paul wrote the text of my message for today, yet few men ever suffered as much as Paul. He wrote to the church in Corinth:

"Of the Jews five times received I forty stripes save one.

"Thrice was I beaten with rods, once was I stoned, thrice I suffered shipwreck, a night and a day I have been in the deep;

"In journeyings often, in perils of waters, in perils of robbers, in perils by mine own countrymen, in perils by the heathen, in perils in the city, in perils in the wilderness, in perils in the sea, in perils among false brethren;

"In weariness and painfulness, in watchings often, in hunger and thirst, in fastings often, in cold and nakedness."—II Cor. 11:24-27.

Paul suffered, also, from a thorn in the flesh which was doubtless a physical weakness of some kind. We read that he went to the Lord three times and prayed that it might depart from him. The answer of God was, "My grace is sufficient for thee; for my strength is made perfect in weakness."

Paul was a man of faith, yet it was not God's will for him to be free from this thorn in the flesh. He made that reply which every suffering child of God needs to make: "Most gladly therefore will I rather glory in my infirmities, that the power of Christ may rest upon me."

2. *Does not shield from loss of earthly possessions.* I firmly believe that God does bless those who believe in Him and are honest with Him. I have seen this proven many times. But we do not put our faith in Christ and serve Him simply so that we can prosper in a material way.

Some Christians seem to think that because they believe in God and Christ that they must prosper greatly; and if they lose their earthly possessions, they become rebellious and feel that God has failed. We can find the records of many great Christians who were stripped of every possession; for in it all, God had a definite purpose.

3. *Does not guarantee ease.* Turn to Hebrews 11, that great chapter of faith, and you will see that those whose names grace God's honor roll suffered much.

Moses, chosen of God, turned from the ease and luxury of Egypt, "choosing rather to suffer affliction with the people of God, than to enjoy the pleasures of sin for a season."

And of others it is said that they

". . .had trial of cruel mockings and scourgings, yea, moreover of bonds and imprisonment: They were stoned, they were sawn asunder, were tempted, were slain with the sword: they wandered about in sheepskins and goatskins; being destitute, afflicted, tormented; (Of whom the world was not worthy:) they wandered in deserts, and in mountains, and in dens and caves of the earth."—Heb. 11:36-38.

How did they do this? Through faith in God.

4. *Does not shield from grief.* We will have grief in life, for death is all about us. Our loved ones will be separated from us. God does not promise anything else, for saints and sinners come

to die. He does not say that we can simply have faith and live on in this life. Or that we can have faith and sustain the lives of others.

A person said to me, "I do not know how So and So could die, when I had such faith that he would live." Let us not think that our faith, though it be strong and steadfast, will shield us from having grief.

These are some things that faith does not do.

Now, may we turn to the positive side of the matter.

III. WHAT FAITH DOES

1. *Faith saves.* *"For by grace are ye saved through faith; and that not of yourselves: it is the gift of God: Not of works, lest any man should boast."*—Eph. 2:8,9.

Salvation is not by works; it is not by doing, but it is by believing.

God has put salvation in such a place that it can be reached by all men.

A lame man might not be able to visit the sick, but he can believe. A blind man, by reason of his infirmity, cannot do many things; but he can believe. A deaf man can believe. A dying man can believe. Yes, salvation is by faith in Christ; and it can be received by faith by the young and the old, the educated and the uneducated, the rich and the poor.

2. *Faith justifies.* *"Therefore being justified by faith, we have peace with God through our Lord Jesus Christ."*—Rom. 5:1.

When we are justified, we are made right in the sight of God.

3. *Faith stabilizes.* In the same passage, Ephesians 6, the apostle speaks again and again of standing, being steadfast in our warfare. It is faith that makes us steadfast when the battle is raging hot. It is faith that gives us the courage to stand when the flesh desires to run.

The Word exhorts us in many places to stand true.

In I Corinthians 16:13, "Watch ye, stand fast in the faith, quit you like men, be strong."

In Psalm 125:1 we find the result of faith: "They that trust in the Lord shall be as mount Zion, which cannot be removed, but abideth for ever." Stand back of the shield of faith and stand fast. The shield will be sufficient to quench the fiery darts of the wicked one.

4. *Faith strengthens.* Paul said, "I can do all things through Christ which strengtheneth me" (Phil. 4:13). When we have faith in God, no task is too hard.

God has the power for our lives, if we will tie on to Him. In ourselves we can do nothing; through Him we can do all things.

5. *Faith sings.* When I mentioned a moment ago the many hardships that Christians can expect in this life, I did not exaggerate one bit. That is the common portion of man. But I want to emphasize this: though we have physical suffering, loss of possessions, hardships and grief, we can have a song in our hearts in the midst of the darkest night.

It was faith that made Paul sing at the midnight hour. They were not singing because they feared the darkness or the hand of the Roman government. They sang because their hearts were full of faith and they knew that God was with them. Take this motto for your life: "Rejoice evermore." Rest on the promises. Rejoice in the Lord.

6. *Faith sends us out.* It is faith that makes us messengers and witnesses for Christ. What God has done for us, He can do for others. The same Christ who saved me can save any lost one who will come in repentance and faith to Him.

I have faith in the willingness of Christ to save anyone who will receive Him as Saviour. Whether that person be in the heart of Africa or in our own city, His promise is, ". . .him that cometh unto me, I will in no wise cast out."

We can have faith in the power of Christ to save to the uttermost. "For I am not ashamed of the gospel of Christ: for it is the power of God unto salvation to every one that believeth; to the Jew first, and also to the Greek."

In Hebrews 7:25, we read, "Wherefore he is able also to save them to the uttermost that come unto God by him, seeing he ever liveth to make intercession for them."

It is a joy to preach the unsearchable riches of Christ and to know that He is able to save. I would not want to preach if there

were a doubt in my mind regarding His power. Therefore, it is my faith in the blessed Saviour which sends me into the field to preach and witness.

"Above all, taking the shield of faith. . . ." Friend without Christ, His promises are true. He will save you now, if you will only believe. Not a fiery dart of the wicked has ever pierced the shield of faith. No one has ever been lost who has stood behind that shield. It is yours today for the taking.

By Faith

By faith and not by sight,
   Saviour, I walk with Thee;
Lead Thou my feet aright;
   Choose Thou the path for me.

Choose Thou the path for me;
   I would not if I could;
For only Thou canst see
   My highest, heavenly good.

My highest, heavenly good
   Lies in Thy will alone,
Designed and understood
   By Love upon His Throne.

By Love upon His Throne
   My life is planned aright;
Secure in Christ alone
   I walk by faith, not sight.

             —E. Margaret Clarkson

2. Adventuring Faith

...Launch out into the deep...
—Luke 5:4.

Almost everyone has at some time or other felt an urge to go to lands little known and far away. The call of adventure: to go to strange countries and see strange people, to see scenes entirely different from the scenes of home.

It is this sort of urge that possesses some people and makes of them world travelers. It is from their lips, their books, their pictures of far-away places that we get our knowledge of such places. As some youth looks and listens, often he is filled with a desire for adventure; and someday he starts out. Most of us quench all adventuresome ideas and settle down to everyday living. And, after all, we doubtless would not be willing to pay the price for an adventuring life in distant lands.

But this morning I want to fill you, if I can, with a real desire for adventure—adventure that will take you into little known lands—yet you will not have to leave this city.

To enter these almost unexplored regions will take "Adventuring Faith." You must have faith to spend and to be spent in order to learn the secrets of these God-given countries.

There is nothing compulsory about going into these lands. Your salvation does not depend upon it. You are saved by grace through faith—this is a matter of launching out into the deep.

Let me give you three almost untouched continents or lands, separate, yet side by side.

I. THE LAND OF UNSELFISHNESS

Most people are too selfish to enter this land; therefore, it remains unexplored. Many of the wonders and joys of this "selfless land" will never be known.

1. *Nations are selfish.* Name one nation of the globe which is not motivated by a selfish motive. Our own nation is. "Buy defense bonds to save OUR nation." "Help England to help ourselves." We openly state that we do what we do for our own benefit. Germany is impelled by pure selfishness. That can be said also for Italy, Russia, Japan, and all the others.

2. *Individuals are selfish.* Paul correctly sums it up: "For all seek their own, not the things which are Jesus Christ's" (Phil. 2:21).

We live by this motto: EVERY MAN FOR HIMSELF. We are so selfish we have lost our ability to "rejoice with them that do rejoice, and weep with them that weep." We have no fellow feeling for others. Romans 12 gives us strong lessons in unselfishness.

Let us be unselfish in our relationships of life. "Given to hospitality," losing self in service to others.

There was sickness in a home the other day. The neighbors were coming and going, giving all the help they could. A lady visiting in one home said, "I've never seen anything like the people of this street. They are so unselfish, so helpful." That was a worthy compliment.

This is a great but little explored land. Take a trip into it. Think of others. Seek the good of others.

3. *This "Land of Unselfishness" brings a vision of unselfishness toward others and toward the Lord.* When by faith you enter this land, you cease to think about how little you can give to Him, but **how much**. Anyone who enters this territory will not have to be persuaded to tithe because the tithe will be just the beginning of unselfish, willing giving.

> "Others, Lord, yes, others, let this my motto be;
> Help me to live for others, that I may live like Thee."

If you want adventure, try this Land of Unselfishness.

II. THE LAND OF BELIEVING PRAYER

Prayer is one of the mightiest forces in this universe, but so few have entered the Land of Believing Prayer. Some pray but have little faith.

But you say, "So many prayers are unanswered." That is true, and the reasons for unanswered prayers are not hard to find.

Sometimes we do not pray according to His will. God may have something better for us in His plans. We must pray according to His will.

Sometimes sin in our lives cuts off answers to our prayers. You pray but your heart is not right before God.

"Behold, the Lord's hand is not shortened, that it cannot save; neither his ear heavy, that it cannot hear:

"But your iniquities have separated between you and your God, and your sins have hid his face from you, that he will not hear."

Too many times we lack faith in prayer. This materialistic world makes us doubt God and prayer.

One of our greatest inventions is the radio. We can sit in our homes and listen to words spoken in London, Berlin and Rome, thousands of miles away. Understand radio? No, but I know it is so.

And we know something else: the same God who made and set in motion the forces by which radio operates can hear the prayers of His children when they call on Him. Christ told us to "ask" and "seek" and "knock". Surely He didn't say these things to mock us. Someone has said it is good, spiritual exercise to pray; and if you never get anything, it is still good for you. But surely Christ would not mock us in that way. When you pray, know that ye receive.

Adventuring faith is needed to walk into the "Land of Believing Prayer." Great and wondrous things have come from those who have adventured by faith into this land.

Lord Kelvin, without doubt one of the greatest scientists of the nineteenth century, said, "Every discovery I have made that has contributed to the benefit of man—He has given me in answer to prayer."

Professor S. F. B. Morse, the inventor of the telegraph, said, "Many a time when making experiments in my laboratory at the university, I would come to a standstill, not knowing what to do next. An obstacle would present itself that seemed to be insurmountable. A mental fog would cloud my mind that would not clear away. But during such times I always locked my doors, knelt down and prayed for light and help. And light and help always came."

Christian, why don't you try it?

III. THE LAND OF SOUL REDEMPTION, OR THE LAND OF SOUL WINNING

The other lands you enter will bring you hardships and a recompense of contentment and victory; but when you enter this field, your difficulties will be multiplied; but your joy will be beyond measure.

Just three important bits of equipment you need: (1) a love for the Christ who saved you; (2) a love for lost souls; (3) a Bible knowledge sufficient to point a man to Christ.

Christians can be divided generally into two groups:

Those who follow Cain who said, ". . .Am I my brother's keeper?" In this group are Christians who feel no burden for the lost, or if they feel a burden, cast it aside and live for self. The other group is that which follows the Apostle Paul who said, "Brethren, my heart's desire and prayer to God for Israel is, that they might be saved." (Rom. 10:1).

When we come to walk in this Land of Soul Winning, we bid self-interest good-by and concern ourselves with others and their salvation. We pray for them, live before them so they will see Christ, and talk to them at every opportunity about their salvation.

So few people have entered this land. So few want to enter. But when you do, be prepared for great and exciting adventure.

Some of you men like to fish. The thrill and adventure of fishing repays you for lost sleep, long trips, etc. But the adventure of fishing for lost men, bringing them to Christ, will exceed all joys of other things.

Dave Marbury said he called a preacher one Saturday and said, "Do you like to fish?"

"Yes, sir, I do."

"All right," said Mr. Marbury, "I want you to go fishing with me tomorrow."

"Oh, I'm sorry, but I never fish on Sunday. You must have the wrong number."

Then Marbury explained he wanted him to preach at the Southside Jail on Sunday afternoon and try to win men to Christ.

"I will make you fishers of men," said our Lord.

D. L. Moody adventured by faith into this Land of Soul Winning. He set as his goal to speak to one person per day about his soul. This he did. Many times he would walk the street at night in order to find a man whom he could talk to about his soul.

A crippled boy of the Louisville Seminary went into this land. He couldn't get around very much, but he wrote hundreds of letters to people about their salvation.

Old Dad Hall, Episcopal preacher, long ago entered this land. Called, "The Bishop of Wall Street," he spoke to men every day personally. When he was sick he took the New York City telephone directory and called people he did not know and talked to them about their souls. "Crazy," you say? If so, it is a wonderful form of insanity!

Why not set a goal for yourself to speak to one person each day? Venture by faith into this territory, unknown to so many Christians. Each day you will find a person somewhere, a person who says, "I'm not a Christian." Will you witness to him or her? Ladies, speak to friends who come to your home or someone at the store or get names from our recent church census. Men, speak to people wherever you find them—in the mill, at the lodge, in the civic group—anywhere. Young people, speak to other young people at school or in the social gatherings—ONE PERSON EACH DAY! I accept this for myself. Will you do the same?

Adventuring faith. Let it take hold of you now. LAUNCH OUT INTO THE DEEP!

Lost friend, the greatest experience of your life awaits you—when you come to Christ. The Christian life is an adventure that never loses its thrill.

Faith

Faith is not the blind outreach
  Of groping hand
That seeks some solid thing to hold
  Amid the sinking sand.

But faith is certain trust
  In One well known
Who in the Saviour's cross
  His love has shown.

And faith is sure repose
  Of quiet love
That knows each step is ordered
  From above.

It will not fuss or fret
  When things go wrong,
But in the valley dark
  Sing a song.

It knows that God is near
  When clouds arise,
And looks to Him to clear
  The storm-swept skies.

And should God's blessing fail
  For some short while,
It knows that somewhere round the bend
  God yet will smile.

—David B. Stewart

3. *Contending for the Faith*

> *Beloved, when I gave all diligence to write unto you of the common salvation, it was needful for me to write unto you, and exhort you that ye should earnestly contend for the faith which was once delivered unto the saints.*
>
> —Jude 3.

We have announced that this service is going to be different, and different it is. First, it is different because every person here has in his hand a copy of the Scripture to be discussed. Second, it is different because we are going to preach right out of this one little book.

There are many interesting sidelights in this book by "Jude, the servant of Jesus Christ, and brother of James" which we would like to discuss, but time will not permit.

We will tell you about the threefold position of believers, as found in verse 1:

First, sanctified by God the Father.

Second, preserved in Jesus Christ.

Third, called.

We want you to see the three eternal things mentioned:

First, eternal life (vs. 21).

Second, everlasting chains (vs. 6).

Third, eternal fire (vs. 7).

Then, the words "keep" and "kept" are mentioned several times.

First, the Lord's people are kept ones. The revised version reads in verse 1. . ."kept for Jesus Christ." Thank God, we have that assurance that we are kept!

Second, some angels "kept not their first estate," so they are "kept" in chains (vs. 6).

Third, we must keep ourselves in the constant full assurance that God loves us (vs. 21).

Fourth, He is able to keep us, not merely from "falling" but as the revised version gives it, from "stumbling," for stumbling precedes falling (vs. 24).

The key phrase of the book is "earnestly contend for the faith" (vs. 3).

We will make the following divisions for the facility of our study: First, the troublemakers; second, God's judgment against evil and evildoers; third, twofold exhortation to believers.

I. THE TROUBLEMAKERS

"For there are certain men crept in unawares, who were before of old ordained to this condemnation, ungodly men, turning the grace of our God into lasciviousness, and denying the only Lord God, and our Lord Jesus Christ."—vs. 4.

Yes, false teachers had come into the midst of certain Christian bodies who were turning the grace of God into filthiness and wantonness. These false teachers claimed that because they were free from the law, they were therefore free to indulge in all kinds of sin.

They were also guilty of "denying the only Lord God, and our Lord Jesus Christ." All false teachers are wrong about the person and work of Jesus Christ.

Watch out for "certain men."

II. GOD'S JUDGMENT AGAINST EVIL AND EVILDOERS

The Holy Spirit says, (verses 5-9) 'We are now going to illustrate God's judgment with a play in three acts.'

The first act shows God delivering the children of Israel from bondage.

We see the gracious mercy of God in preserving and caring for His people across the Red Sea and through the desert. But then instead of lovingly obeying God's command to take the land of promise, they refused. God's judgment came upon the disobedient and unbelieving. He decreed that not one of the unbelieving should enter into Canaan.

The second act of the play takes us into Heaven. Certain angels of Heaven are rebelling against Almighty God. Judgment falls; they are cast out and kept in everlasting chains under darkness unto the judgment of the great day. I agree with Scofield that this judgment of angels will take place when Satan is judged after the thousand years. The saints will have a part in this judgment.

Listen, friend! God will not spare sinners, whether in low or high places, for He spared not the angels. As soon as they developed an evil nature, He saw they were not fit for the holiness and joys of Heaven; so He cast them out. God deals first in mercy, but afterwards in judgment.

The third act of this play begins at once after the second. You have time just to see the awfulness of rebelling against God. And now, act three opens upon a scene of great hilarity and merrymaking. The cities of Sodom and Gomorrah are running wide open. Money is plentiful; wild parties and immoral orgies are held nightly. In the midst of it all, God speaks; and fire and brimstone rain from Heaven. Laughter turns to fearful screams. Sin and sensuality are paying off in tears and destruction.

Those who are not on God's side—beware! You can't go on forever in sin, despising God and God's Son and loving evil, without coming under judgment. That fearful day is coming. Don't be foolish!

But now the Holy Spirit comes to say still more about those troublemakers and filthy dreamers. They are like three men of olden days who also called forth the judgment of God.

They are like Cain who rejected redemption by blood. He wanted to do things in his own way. A lot of folks are like that today.

Also, like Balaam, who was a hireling prophet, anxious only to make money. He tried to tell God what to do.

And like Korah—his sin was denial of the authority of Moses

as God's chosen spokesman, and trying to come to God without the mediation of God's appointed high priest. The earth opened up and destroyed Korah and his company. The lesson for us is that we can only come to God through Jesus Christ, our High Priest.

Judgment is coming upon evil and evildoers, upon all who are not under the blood. It is coming when Christ comes in power and great glory (Vss. 14,15). Three thousand years before the first coming of Jesus, Enoch prophecied the second coming of Christ. The day of judgment is coming, and the only safe place to be is with the Judge.

III. THE TWOFOLD EXHORTATION TO BELIEVERS

"Earnestly contend for the faith which was once delivered unto the saints."—Vs. 3.

Earnest contenders for the faith are very few in this day. I am afraid the number is going to get less and less. The world is breeding a kind of tolerance for all religions and heresies until there will be but a few voices raised in the next few years for the old-time faith.

I believe in religious freedom. I believe in freedom of expression. Our boys are fighting for it now, fighting so that all groups may have absolute freedom of worship and expression.

In my own mind, they are not fighting for the spread of heresy. But heresy is being spread today; therefore, it is up to the saints who have been called, sanctified, and kept to "earnestly contend for the faith."

In all love I want to express myself plainly. Some of you sitting before me doubtless have an idea that just so a fellow has some kind of "religion," he is all right. It doesn't matter what kind he has.

That is the very kind of tolerance this war is promoting. I SAY, IT DOES MAKE A DIFFERENCE.

IT MAKES THE DIFFERENCE BETWEEN HEAVEN AND HELL.

It makes the difference between getting your prayers answered and just blowing words into the air.

It makes the difference between victorious Christian living and a makeshift farce of pious Sunday morning attendance at the "church of your choice."

There are so many "isms"—first, the Russellites. If they are right, we are wrong. They deny much of the Word of God. They do not believe in Hell. They do not believe in the Trinity of Father, Son, and Holy Spirit. Russellism would destroy every church in the world. Russellism denies the deity of Christ. They say He became divine only after His resurrection.

In contending for the faith, also shun profane and vain babblings; they increase unto more ungodliness. Don't allow the deceptive Watchtower literature in your home.

Second, Christian Science. We have been a lot kinder to the Christian Scientists than they have been to us. This group, originated by Mrs. Mary Baker Eddy, is an attempted combination of religion, science and philosophy.

She wrote a book called *Science and Health, With a Key to the Scriptures*. This book is placed above the Bible. Christian Science rejects the fact of sin, denies blood redemption. Since there is no reality to sin, it thinks, also, there is no reality to Hell and the judgment.

If Christian Science had charge of this country, there would be no hospitals, no doctors, no nurses, no vaccination. Christian Science cannot cure anyone, because, according to Christian Science, you have never been sick.

If you want the truth, unvarnished and plain, read *Religio-Medical Masquerade,* by Peabody. This book was printed ten times, copies running into the thousands. It was written during the lifetime of Mrs. Eddy. The author invited Mrs. Eddy and the Scientists to sue him for slander if he was wrong. He was never sued.

Christian Science is like a guinea pig, which is neither guinea nor pig; or like grapenuts which contain neither grapes nor nuts, it is neither Christian nor scientific.

Third, the Roman Catholic Church, said to be the strongest religious body in the world. I have no personal grievance against any Roman Catholic. But the Bible and Roman Catholicism both cannot be true. If we are right, they are wrong. If they are right, then we are wrong. WE HAVE ONLY ONE DECIDING AUTHORITY—THE BIBLE.

This copy of a letter recently came to my desk. Listen to some of it:

> This war time is giving the Catholic church a great advantage in many respects. Protestants and Baptists are gaining but little numerically and spiritually from the war. Catholics are gaining numerically in spheres of influence.
> Catholics are protesting against our missionaries being allowed in South America.

Yes, we are exhorted to earnestly contend for the faith. We are exhorted to "build" up our spiritual lives. Having laid well our foundation in gospel faith, we must build upon it, ever making progress in spiritual things.

We can build ourselves up by:

Praying in the Holy Spirit. He makes our prayers fervent. He makes them loving. He makes them believing, for a man prevails only as he has faith.

Keeping ourselves in the love of God. This will keep us from mistakes and worldliness.

We are to look for the Lord's return.

We are to build ourselves up by being soul winners. "And others save with fear, pulling them out of the fire; hating even the garment spotted by the flesh."

4. A Mother's Faith

> *Then Jesus answered and said unto her, O
> woman, great is thy faith: be it unto thee even as
> thou wilt. And her daughter was made whole
> from that very hour.*
>
> —Matthew 15:28.

The whole world honors faith. We pay homage to the man who lives by faith, moves forward by faith, attempts great things by faith.

The Word of God places strong emphasis on faith. Salvation is by faith in Christ: "He that believeth on the Son hath everlasting life. . . ."

Not only are we saved by faith, but we are exhorted to walk by faith and not by sight.

Victorious living is accomplished by faith: "For whatsoever is born of God overcometh the world: and this is the victory that overcometh the world, even our faith" (I John 5:4).

Jesus said great blessings belong to those who have faith: "If thou canst believe, all things are possible to him that believeth."

In our prayer life we must have faith: ". . .let him ask in faith, nothing wavering. . . ."

Yes, faith is the indispensable element in our relationship to God. The writer of Hebrews declares: "But without faith it is impossible to please him: for he that cometh to God must believe that he is, and that he is a rewarder of them that diligently seek him" (11:6).

The story of a mother's faith is before us in our Scripture

reading. Here is a divine record of the accomplishment of faith. The story is given in three parts.

I. A MOTHER'S TROUBLE

The trouble of a child is a mother's trouble. This woman of Syrophoenicia had a daughter "vexed with a devil," a trouble of the worst sort.

Though the child had a terrible sickness, the mother loved her daughter still. Afflictions do not dissolve affections. Rather, often affection grows when there is trouble.

In trouble the mother turned to Jesus. It is a blessed thirst that draws us to such a fountain. Our need, like the prodigal's, is often the means of bringing us to the Father's house. This mother turned to Jesus. It is always wise to turn to the Saviour in the hour of trouble.

The heart cry of this mother is given in verse 25, "Lord, help me." In her need she prayed to the point. She experienced no difficulty in expressing her need and heart's desire.

Dr. Joseph Parker once said, "The sense of need abbreviates our prayers and teaches us true eloquence. When the heart is in the grip of a deadly agony, it knows how to pray." Here is a good lesson for us. We need to be pointed and definite in our prayers, for we are a needy people.

Notice, also, that this mother's prayer was one of intercession. Though she said, "Have mercy on me. . ." and "Lord, help me," she was praying for another, and Jesus understood. She associated herself with her daughter's need so closely that she cried for herself; and if the daughter were healed, the blessing would be hers.

So it was that Moses prayed. If you read his prayers without understanding the story, you would think that he was praying only for himself. But in truth, he was asking nothing for himself but everything for Israel.

The Apostle Paul prayed in such a manner. He so closely identified himself with the interests of the Jewish people that he was able to say, "I could wish that myself were accursed from Christ for my brethren, my kinsmen according to the flesh."

Mothers' prayers are often heard because they pray as true intercessors, identifying themselves with their children.

And so we see a mother in serious trouble—her child was sick. It was wise for this mother to turn to Jesus.

II. A MOTHER'S TESTING

This mother had a great faith, but she faced great testing. She made her cry to Jesus, but the answer did not come at once. There were many things to test her faith.

1. *The Lord's silence.* She cried unto Him saying, "Have mercy on me, O Lord, thou Son of David; my daughter is grievously vexed with a devil."

The record says "he answered her not a word." His silence was not unconcern. He was testing her faith, as was sometimes our Lord's method. Remember how He put clay on the blind man's eyes and told him to go and wash in the pool of Siloam. Jesus could have healed with a word, but He believed in giving a test to the faith.

The Lord sometimes delays His answers to our prayers in order to test, then to establish our faith.

It was so with Mary and Martha when their brother Lazarus died. Jesus delayed, and they wondered at His absence and silence. But finally He appeared and brought a great blessing.

2. *Discourtesy of the disciples.* "And his disciples came and besought him, saying, Send her away; for she crieth after us."

Between the silence of Jesus and the surliness of His followers, her faith was severely tested.

The conduct of many of the Lord's disciples is more likely to drive away than to attract. Most of us are sad representatives of the gracious Saviour.

The disciples did not understand the Lord's silence, and they thought that He did not care. Though they had been with Him for three years, they still did not know much about Jesus.

3. *The Lord's apparent refusal was a testing of this mother's faith.* Jesus answered and said, "I am not sent but unto the lost sheep of the house of Israel." She did not belong to the house of Israel; therefore, as a heathen Gentile she had no claim on Him as the Son of David. Jesus answered her in the same manner as she had addressed Him. It seemed that His words formed a positive refusal.

4. *His rebuke.* As she continued to cry unto Him, He said, ". . .it is not meet to take the children's bread, and cast it to dogs." This seemed a very sharp thing to say, but this mother understood and accepted the place in which Jesus put her.

His refusal and rebuke were even better than His silence. As He talked with her, she knew she was in touch with Him; and there was a possibility of receiving a positive answer. Though her faith was tested, she did not give up. This brings us to our third part of the story.

III. A MOTHER'S TRIUMPH

Faith gives the victory. Nothing stopped this mother. She had faith in Christ and persistence to keep knocking at the door. She was not stopped by the silence of Christ, the discourtesy of the disciples, the refusal of the Lord or His rebuke.

When Christ said, "It is not meet to take the children's bread and to cast it to dogs," she snared Him with His own words: "Truth, Lord: yet the dogs eat of the crumbs which fall from their masters' table."

Martin Luther said, "This woman learned to wring a *Yea* from God's *Nay*; or rather to hear the *Yea* which many times works under His seeming *Nay*."

She said, "That's the truth, but as Lord, Thou canst give me also what I need." She took her place as a dog. She stated her need and pled her cause.

This woman possessed two wonderful characteristics: humility and faith. She was willing to take a humble place, and her faith was unwavering. "A broken and a contrite heart" He will not despise, and faith is the victory that overcometh the world. In the end she received more than she asked for. She was commended by the Lord for her faith: "O woman, great is thy faith: be it unto thee even as thou wilt. . . ." Her story of faith is written down for the whole world to read. Jesus did not commend her for her arguments, her patience nor her love, but for her faith.

Finally, she was rewarded by the healing of her daughter: "And her daughter was made whole from that very hour." Her prayer was answered, her faith rewarded.

We need more mothers who will bring Him their troubles and needs, then there would be more sons and daughters saved.

Here is real encouragement for mothers who have prayed long and earnestly for their children. Though the years have gone by, be not dismayed—silence is not unconcern. Jesus kept this mother waiting, but His grant was above her expectations. Faith was the key that unlocked the store of blessing which she needed.

Mother, continue to pray for that son and daughter who are still walking in the ways of sin. Be not weary in well doing, for in due season you will reap if you faint not.

Perhaps in this service there are some who had, or have now, praying mothers. Then make this the time when God will answer her prayers by your coming to the Lord.

A mother worthy of the name is anxious for one great thing— the salvation of her children. Deep concern should be in the heart of every mother until her children have come to Christ.

I think ofttimes as the night draws nigh
Of an old house on the hill
Where the children played at will;
And when the night at last came down,
  Hushing the merry din;
Mother would look around and ask,
  "Are all the children in?"

'Tis many and many a year since then,
  And the old house on the hill
No longer echoes to childish feet,
  And the yard is still, so still.
But I see it all as the shadows creep,
  And though many the years have been,
Since then, I can hear my mother ask,
  "Are all the children in?"

I wonder if when the shadows fall
  On the last short earthly day;
When we say goodby to the world outside,
  All tired with our childish play;
When we step out into that other land
  Where mother so long has been;
Will we hear her ask, just as of old,
  "Are all the children in?"

Faith to Fly: It is said that John Wesley and Charles Wesley were in a prayer service together. Charles Wesley said, "I feel so happy that if the Lord should tell me to fly, and I had wings, I would fly!" John Wesley replied, "If the Lord should tell me to fly, I would fly whether I had wings or not!"

"They that wait upon the Lord shall renew their strength; they shall mount up with wings as eagles; they shall run, and not be weary; and they shall walk, and not faint."

5. *Faith for a New Year*

*And the barrel of meal wasted not, neither did
the cruse of oil fail, according to the word of the
Lord, which he spake by Elijah.*
—I Kings 17:16.

We hear people wishing others a "Happy New Year." We
might well question: What are the possibilities for a happy 1951?
Surely there is nothing happy about the world situation. Sorrow
and heartaches are the sure prospects for the year ahead.

Our national situation is far from peaceful. Uncertainty
characterizes the whole world.

In the life of an individual, what is the prospect for a "Happy
New Year"? We feel the increase of living costs; crime is on the
rise, and we have rebellion against law and order.

If we look to our circumstances and surroundings, there is no
possibility for a "Happy New Year."

But there is the possibility for a happy new year in our God
and through faith in Him.

Let me give you a threefold foundation for faith for the new
year.

I. GOD'S PROMISES

If we are to advance this next year, it must be upon the
promises of God.

Elijah relied on His promises. After delivering his prophecy of
"no rain" to Ahab, the Lord sent him out by the brook Cherith,
telling him, "And it shall be, that thou shalt drink of the brook;
and I have commanded the ravens to feed thee there."

Elijah obeyed God and dwelt by the brook Cherith. Ravens

brought him bread and flesh in the morning and bread and flesh in the evening, and he drank from the brook. Elijah stayed there until God told him to move.

When the brook dried up because of the long drought, God sent His prophet to the house of a widow in Zarephath. He found there a woman in great destitution. Certainly she was in no condition to take care of another person. When Elijah asked for a morsel of bread, she said, "I have not a cake, but an handful of meal in a barrel, and a little oil in a cruse: and, behold, I am gathering two sticks, that I may go in and dress it for me and my son, that we may eat it, and die" (I Kings 17:12).

Elijah told her to go ahead and make the cakes, but to make him one first, then to make for herself and her son. Elijah said, "For thus saith the Lord God of Israel, The barrel of meal shall not waste, neither shall the cruse of oil fail, until the day that the Lord sendeth rain upon the earth" (vs. 14).

She did according to the word of Elijah, "And the barrel of meal wasted not, neither did the cruse of oil fail, according to the word of the Lord. . ." (vs. 14).

We have God's promise to provide all we need.

1. *Know the promises of God.* The great and mighty promises of our Father mean nothing to most people because they do not know what they are.

Of the 32,000 promises in the Bible, how many do you know? How can we have faith in His promise of peace, power, provisions, and all needful things unless we know His promises?

2. *Use the promises.* Too many people live poorly while wealth and abundance are stored nearby.

Mr. Spurgeon used to tell of the poor woman who framed a check for $12,000.00 which had been given to her by a dying friend. She had no idea of its worth and so retained it as a keepsake. Mr. Spurgeon turned it into cash for her so she could have a comfortable living.

We need to turn the promises of God into present possessions.

3. *Rely on His promises.* Some people know the promises, even try to use them; but they still are fearful and afraid. Why? Because they are not sure God is faithful to perform what He has

promised. In childlike faith believe what God has said and rest
your soul on His Word.

II. GOD'S PAST PERFORMANCE

Come with me to Mount Carmel. The stage is set for a tremendous event. Elijah has called the children of Israel, along with
the prophets of Baal, to the mount. See him as he stands before
the crowd and says, "How long halt ye between two opinions? If
the Lord be God, follow him: but if Baal, then follow him."

He instructs that two altars be built, one by the prophets of
Baal and one by himself. Sacrifices will be placed on the altars,
but no wood put under them. ". . .the God that answereth by
fire, let him be God."

Anyone can see that Elijah is in a tight place, but he is not
afraid. He is depending on God's promises and remembering
God's past performance.

The prophets of Baal pray and call upon their god, but nothing
happens. Elijah mocks them until they cut their bodies with
knives and lancets. This bloody and vain scene goes on until
evening time.

Finally Elijah calls the people to him. He repairs the altar of
the Lord that is broken down. He places a bullock upon the
wood. He commands that barrels of water be poured upon the
sacrifice and the wood and in the trench about it.

Can you not see Elijah standing nearby? The prophets of Baal
have failed. Their god did not answer by fire. It is about time for
Elijah to pray. Will his God answer his prayer?

I believe Elijah looked back and remembered God's past performances on his behalf. He remembered how he was fed by the
ravens at the brook Cherith. He remembered how the Lord had
supplied meal and oil in the widow's house. The Lord has not
failed His prophet—not once.

Now it is time for Elijah to pray. It is the time of the offering of
the evening sacrifice. The prophet comes near and prays:

"Lord God of Abraham, Isaac, and of Israel, let it be known

*this day that thou art God in Israel, and that I am thy servant,
and that I have done all these things at thy word.*

*"Hear me, O Lord, hear me, that this people may know that
thou art the Lord God, and that thou hast turned their heart
back again."*

As soon as the prayer is uttered, the fire of the Lord falls and
consumes the sacrifice—the wood, the stones, the dust, even the
water that is in the trench. God was faithful to answer prayer.

What has God done for you in the past? Has He failed you at
any time? You are forced to say that God has never failed in your
hour of need.

First, prayer has been answered again and again. This is the
testimony of people everywhere. Second, your needs have been
abundantly supplied. Sometimes you could not see how or see
your way out, but God sent His ravens (birds) to supply your
needs morning and evening. Third, God sustained you in your
hour of trial. When burdens came which you thought you could
not bear, God was faithful. He brought you through deep waters;
He gave you strength for the day. Fourth, comfort has been yours
in your hour of need. Has He ever failed? No, a thousand times,
no! We have failed, but God—never.

If God has been faithful in past days, then remember this: Our
God changes not. Hear His word in Malachi 3:6, "For I am the
Lord, I change not. . . ." Let us remember that "Every good gift
and every perfect gift is from above, and cometh down from the
Father of lights, with whom is no variableness, neither shadow of
turning." As God has graciously worked in your behalf in days
gone by, so will He do for you in the years ahead.

III. GOD'S PRESENT POWER AND WILLINGNESS

Notice two things: *God's present power.* He has the power to
do that which men say is impossible. Notice also, *God's present
willingness.* Some people have the power but not the willingness
to help. Others have the willingness but not the power. God has
both.

Have faith in God's power and willingness to help us in any

hour of need. Look not to yourself; depend not upon the flesh; rest not on the frail promises of men—but depend on God. My failures have been my failures, not God's. Then let us rely upon our supernatural and all-powerful God.

Someone has said: "Faith works better when there is no natural hope. If there be even a straw for sight to cling to, then faith finds difficulty."

George Mueller said, "Remember, it is the very time for faith to work when sight ceases; the greater the difficulty, the easier for faith. As long as there remain certain natural prospects, faith does not get on as easily as where natural prospects fail."

The greatest faith is born in the hour of despair. When we can see no hope and no way out, then faith rises and brings the victory.

J. Hudson Taylor's favorite verse was, "Have faith in God." As a man who lived by faith, he often said, "I have trembled and failed again and again, but God has never failed."

The barrel of meal and the cruse of oil will not fail if we step out upon the promises of God. Know that God is interested in you and desires to be your Helper. Remember that God is insulted and grieved when we look to ourselves, when we should be looking to Him.

Here is the basis of faith for the New Year: first, God's promises; second, God's past performance; third, God's present power and willingness.

Declare now that the coming year will be one of faith in God. When worries and cares beset you, turn at once to His promises; meet His conditions for their fulfillment, then leave it with Him.

Many of you cannot take the promises of God for peace and power and provision because you have not accepted His dear Son as your Saviour. You cannot pray, "Our Father," because you have rejected His Son. Your need is Christ. Your need is salvation.

Do not dare enter the portals of 1951 without settling this matter of your salvation. Right now, before this year dies and a new one begins, take Christ as your personal Saviour.

6. Faith and Five Stones

> Then said David to the Philistine, Thou com-
> est to me with a sword, and with a spear, and
> with a shield: but I come to thee in the name of
> the Lord of hosts, the God of the armies of Israel,
> whom thou hast defied.
>
> —1 Samuel 17:45.

Big, boasting Goliath represents an angry, raging world seeking to destroy all that is good and godly.

Fearful, trembling Israel represents a faithless people who
believe in God but, through weakness of faith, fail to conquer in
His name.

Strong, quiet David represents the Christian whose faith is in
God and whose dependence is in the power of God.

Every schoolboy knows the story of David and Goliath. The
Philistines were the old enemies of Israel. In the days of King
Saul they were forever fighting against God's chosen people.
Israel was often the victor in the conflicts, but then Goliath took
the lead of the Philistines. The situation became dark and
foreboding.

The Israelites had pitched their camp on one side of the mountain, and the Philistines on the other side. There was a valley
between.

From out of the army of the Philistines came a giant named
Goliath of Gath. He was a tremendous fellow. Some say that his
height ran to almost twelve feet.

For many days this giant stood and cried unto the armies of
Israel:

*"Why are ye come out to set your battle in array? am not I a
Philistine, and ye servants to Saul? choose you a man for you,
and let him come down to me. If he be able to fight with me, and
to kill me, then will we be your servants: but if I prevail against
him, and kill him, then shall ye be our servants, and serve us.
. . .I defy the armies of Israel this day; give me a man, that we
may fight together."*—II Samuel 17:8-10.

When Saul and the Israelites heard these words, they were dismayed and afraid.

But God always has a man for every situation. He may seem a
very unlikely person, but there is always someone to stand for
God's cause. In this instance it was David, a shepherd boy, sent
to carry food to his brothers in the army of Saul. As he talked
with them, the giant came forth and gave his challenge. David
heard these words. He saw the people were afraid. He asked why
they allowed this thing to go on. Finally, he turned to King Saul
and said, "Let no man's heart fail because of him; thy servant
will go and fight with this Philistine."

Saul weakly tried to dissuade him, but David gave his arguments and determined to go against Goliath. Saul's armor was
put on David, but the young shepherd lad refused it. His equipment, as he went against the giant, was his staff and five smooth
stones out of the brook and his sling.

The great giant came forth from his place. When he saw the
boy, he said, "Am I a dog, that thou comest to me with staves?"
It was an insult to send such a small youth out against him.

David's first words to the giant indicate his strength. "I come
to thee in the name of the Lord of hosts, the God of the armies of
Israel. . .for the battle is the Lord's, and he will give you into our
hands."

In dignified manner, the Philistine arose and came to meet
David. As David ran to meet him, he took a stone, put it in the
sling, and threw it at the Philistine. It struck him in the
forehead, and he fell upon his face to the earth. The victory was
won.

In this simple story we find a lesson on how to face our difficulties. The enemy is all about us. On every hand there are hindrances, obstacles and difficulties to be overcome. The success of your life depends on how you face your trials.

David had three things to help him as he faced the giant.

I. COURAGE

We admire courage anywhere we find it, whether it be on the battlefield, in the business office, in the school or in society. The need in every field today is for courageous men.

We need men of courage in the pulpits of our land. Men of stamina and courage are needed in politics. World leadership is suffering for the lack of men of courage.

It takes danger to bring forth courage. We often do not know of its presence in our life until the hour of danger.

There is an Oriental legend which tells of a barbarian chieftain who thought to honor Alexander the Great by giving him three noble dogs of matchless courage.

Shortly after the chieftain had gone, Alexander decided to test the dogs. He had a stag brought before them, but the dogs only yawned and went to sleep. Then he had a hind and an antelope put into the park with them. But the dogs were not interested.

Alexander, certain that the dogs were worthless, had them killed. A few days later, the chieftain returned to ask about his favorites. When he was told what had been done to them, he cried, "O Alexander, you are a great king, but you are a very foolish man. You showed them a stag and a hind and an antelope, and they paid no attention. But if you had turned a lion and a tiger loose on them, you would have seen what brave dogs I have given you." Yes, it is danger that brings forth courage.

It was danger of death that displayed the courage of the three Hebrew children. All threats and all danger could not make them bow down before an idol.

It was danger that showed the courage of Daniel. No power on earth could stop him from praying unto God.

It was danger that showed the courage of Paul, the missionary. He did not flinch from any adversary or any difficulty.

Danger reveals weakness. King Saul was a big, strong, husky specimen of mankind. He was head and shoulders above his fellow Israelites. He could brag and boast, but his life was not in danger. But in the face of Goliath he began to shake like a leaf in the wind.

Someone may be questioning, "Why this weakness on the part of King Saul?" The answer is not hard to find. His life was undermined by disobedience to God. Just a short time before the incident now before us, King Saul had been sent by the Lord to destroy King Ahab and the Amalekites. He disobeyed the order of the Lord and spared the king and much of the best of the sheep and oxen.

Through Samuel, God spoke a plain word on the subject of obedience. "Behold, to obey is better than sacrifice, and to hearken than the fat of rams. For rebellion is as the sin of witchcraft, and stubbornness is as iniquity and idolatry. Because thou hast rejected the word of the Lord, he hath also rejected thee from being king."

Lack of courage quite often is traceable to lack of obedience to God. The preacher or any Christian who lacks courage to stand for God will often be found as disobedient and unseparated from the world.

Danger showed Israel to be a cowardly people. They had not walked in the way which God desired of them. They had murmured against Him, begged for a king, and in many ways shown their dissatisfaction of God's dealing with them. In the hour of danger, they were unable to rest upon His promises and to face the army without fear.

Have courage as you face your difficulties. Let your courage stem from your assurance of God with you—and you with God.

II. MEMORY

As David went forth to face the giant, memory—the memory of God's working through him—went with him.

When Saul remonstrated with David about his desire to fight the Philistine, David said:

"... *Thy servant kept his father's sheep, and there came a lion, and a bear, and took a lamb out of the flock:*

"*And I went out after him, and smote him, and delivered it out of his mouth: and when he arose against me, I caught him by his beard, and smote him, and slew him.*

"*Thy servant slew both the lion and the bear: and this uncircumcised Philistine shall be as one of them, seeing he hath defied the armies of the living God.*

"*David said moreover, The Lord that delivered me out of the paw of the lion, and out of the paw of the bear, he will deliver me out of the hand of this Philistine.*"—I Sam. 17:34-37.

It is interesting to notice King Saul's response to this word of David: "Go, and the Lord be with thee." This was a very pious statement for a king, backed by his large army, to make as he sent forth the shepherd boy against a great giant.

David went forth with the memory of God's power and God's deliverance in former days.

It seems that Saul should have done some remembering also. He should have remembered the great heroes of the faith—Abraham, Moses, Gideon, Barak, Samson and others.

Saul should have remembered God's power and gone forth to fight the giant. His name might have been recorded with the great of the ages. But, no, he was a coward; and he sat down and permitted a boy to fight in his place.

The soldiers of Israel should have been remembering also. How strange that all the mighty events of history were forgotten! Think of the mighty march of God with His people from the land of Egypt to Palestine. Think of God's deliverance from a thousand enemies, His daily manifestations of power and providence.

But in this hour of calamity, Israel forgot, also, the work of God in their behalf.

Here is one of our serious mistakes as we face our daily trials, temptations and difficulties: we fail to remember all that God has done for us.

Christian, remember the salvation of the Lord. The same God who saved you from eternal doom can deliver you from every difficulty.

Remember God's provision and protection through the days of the past. His power has not changed. As He once delivered you, so will He now deliver you.

Let memory work for you as it did for David. Remember the power of God and His past performances in your behalf.

Remember your past failures because of dependence on self. The Lord who once helped you will help you again. This was the argument which David gave to Saul. Memory was walking with him.

III. FAITH

David had faith in God. Though skillful in the use of the sling and stone, it was not his skill that won the battle, but his faith. David believed that God was with him, so he could say, "If God be for me, then who can be against me?"

King Saul looked toward himself and his knees trembled.

Israel looked toward human leadership and it is written, ". . .they were dismayed, and greatly afraid."

Goliath, the giant, had faith in himself and soon died. What a monstrous man he was! His height was perhaps eleven feet and four inches. His armor was tremendously heavy. His spear was like a weaver's beam. He trusted in himself and his own power. He did not look to any god, even the false gods of his own nation. He rested in the arm of flesh and soon dropped in death.

David had faith in God. He used the means at hand—the stones and the sling. But it was his faith in the Almighty which delivered his people.

Think of faith for a moment.

Faith cheerfully faces hardships. It does not complain nor find fault.

Faith in God overcomes obstacles. David was just a youth, and the giant was a mature man of wide experience.

Faith looks beyond all difficulties to God who is greater than all.

Faith in God wins the victory every time. ". . .and this is the victory that overcometh the world, even our faith."

How do you face your difficulties? Whatever they may be—financial, domestic, personal, religious—this story will show us the way to victory.

Have courage—courage born out of faithfulness and of obedience unto God.

Remember God's past performances and the failures of the flesh. Remember the Bible stories of victory, and remember that God changes not.

Have faith in God. Don't look at the storms and the tempests about you, but look up unto God. It is He who gives the victory. David said, "I come to thee in the name of the Lord. . . ."

The victorious life is the goal of every child of God. This can be realized today.

The story before us is also a lesson to lost people. Goliath, though big and furious and boasting, was weak and ineffectual. Goliath illustrates the need of God in every life. Come to Christ. Receive Him today. Enter into peace and joy now.

Faith is the brightest star in the firmament of grace. It treads down seeming impossibilities, and it strides to victory over mountains of stupendous hindrances. It enthrones Jesus as King of the inner man. It kindles and fans the flame of love, and it opens the lips of praise and prayer. —Henry Law.

7. *Little Faith and Hasty Answers*

> *When Jesus then lifted up his eyes, and saw a great company come unto him, he saith unto Philip, Whence shall we buy bread, that these may eat?*
>
> *And this he said to prove him: for he himself knew what he would do.*
>
> —John 6:5,6.

The name of Philip appears a number of times in the New Testament. In Matthew and John it appears, referring to Philip the Apostle. The Philip in the book of the Acts refers to one of the first deacons. This message concerns itself with Philip the apostle. He is listed with the other apostles in Matthew 10:3.

In John 1:43, Philip was called to follow the Lord: "The day following Jesus would go forth into Galilee, and findeth Philip, and saith unto him, Follow me."

In John 1:45, Philip is portrayed as a soul winner: "Philip findeth Nathanael, and saith unto him, We have found him, of whom Moses in the law, and the prophets, did write, Jesus of Nazareth, the son of Joseph." Nathanael began an argument with Philip by saying, ". . .Can there any good thing come out of Nazareth?. . ." Philip's answer was, "Come and see." Nathanael came and saw the Lord and confessed Him as the Son of God.

Turn, please, to John 12. Here we find certain Greeks coming to Philip, desiring to see Jesus. Philip found Andrew and told him of the Greeks' request, and Andrew and Philip told Christ.

In these two narratives, we notice that Philip was very wise in pointing him to the Lord—first, with Nathanael when he said, "Come and see," and in dealing with the Greeks and bringing the problem to the Lord Jesus.

But in John 14, verse 8, Philip makes a strange and extraordinary request: "Lord, shew us the Father, and it sufficeth us." We are not sure what he was thinking about. Did he want the Lord Jesus to open up Heaven and let the invisible be made visible? Did he think that Christ could cause him and the others to fall into a trance and be transported to the third Heaven? It is an extraordinary idea that he presented to our Lord. But many people have wished to see God with their own eyes, to touch Him with their hands, and to hear His voice.

Christ made a very splendid answer to the request of Philip: "Have I been so long time with you, and yet hast thou not known me, Philip? he that hath seen me hath seen the Father; and how sayest thou then, Shew us the Father?"

For my part, I am glad that Philip made this request, for it gives us this plain word regarding the relationship of Christ to His Father.

We read now of the testing of Philip.

"After these things Jesus went over the sea of Galilee, which is the sea of Tiberias.

"And a great multitude followed him, because they saw his miracles which he did on them that were diseased.

"And Jesus went up into a mountain, and there he sat with his disciples.

"And the passover, a feast of the Jews, was nigh.

"When Jesus then lifted up his eyes, and saw a great company come unto him, he saith unto Philip, Whence shall we buy bread, that these may eat?

"And this he said to prove him: for he himself knew what he would do.

"Philip answered him, Two hundred pennyworth of bread is not sufficient for them, that every one of them may take a little."—John 6:1-7.

LITTLE FAITH AND HASTY ANSWERS   53

Christ was always concerned about others. The hungry multitudes stirred His compassion. At the same time, He was concerned to help one—Philip. Therefore, when Jesus lifted up His
eyes and saw the great company of people coming to Him, He
said to Philip, "Whence shall we buy bread, that these may
eat?" The next verse tells us why He said this—to prove or test
him.

Now, may we follow the story under three headings: first, the
test; second, the answer; third, the result.

I. THE TEST

Our Lord is always testing people, testing in order to help.
Philip needed his faith strengthened. Jesus knew that he was
prone to look too much upon the material and temporal;
therefore, He desired to prove him.

The Lord is also testing us. Sometimes it is by delays in
answering prayer. We have prayed earnestly and long; but still
the answer, the full answer, is withheld.

Sometimes we are tested by disappointments. Our minds have
been set upon certain things; then when the entire matter fails,
we are greatly disappointed. Disappointments test us.

We are often tested by the coming of death. When a loved one
is taken from our midst, it is a time to see if we will lean upon
Him.

Sudden emergencies come to test us. Sometimes it is an unusual financial situation; at other times, a problem tests our
faith.

But you say, "Why does the Lord test us?" I can suggest three
reasons.

1. *He tests us that we might know ourselves.* Simon Peter had
to be tested before he could be greatly used of God. He had to
discover his own weakness and learn to depend on the power of
God.

Young people have to be tested in order that they may know
themselves. I am constantly seeing young people announce their
intention to go into the Lord's work, then when the first difficulty

arises, see them fall away. God is testing to see if you mean business. Ofttimes I believe He is sifting out the weak and unworthy that His work might be done by those who mean business.

2. *He is testing to strengthen us.* If we pass the Lord's test, we are made ready for greater work. Philip was tested. He failed in his answer to the Lord; but after what happened, I am sure he must have been strengthened for greater work.

3. *The Lord tests us to destroy all self-sufficiency.* We are prone to look to ourselves and to our own resources instead of looking toward God.

May we learn to spread each difficulty before the Lord. May we remember that we are nothing, but He is everything; we are feeble, but He is strong; our resources are limited, but His are unlimited.

II. THE ANSWER

"Philip answered him, Two hundred pennyworth of bread is not sufficient for them, that every one of them may take a little."

This answer by Philip was given in spite of all the demonstration of power on the part of Jesus. If we turn through the gospel of John, we note His miracles before this happening. He turned the water into wine at the marriage of Cana of Galilee; He dealt with the woman of Samaria and turned her and many others to the Lord; He healed the son of a certain nobleman at Capernaum.

At Jerusalem He went down to the pool and found a great multitude of sick people waiting for the moving of the water. A certain man was there which had an infirmity thirty and eight years. Jesus said, "Wilt thou be made whole?" The man said, "Sir, I have no man, when the water is troubled, to put me into the pool: but while I am coming, another steppeth down before me." Jesus said unto him, "Rise, take up thy bed, and walk." The man was healed. He took up his bed and walked.

These and many other miracles were certainly performed before this testing of Philip; yet notice what he said, with the Son of God standing by his side: "Two hundred pennyworth of bread is not sufficient for them, that every one of them may take a little."

His answer was hasty. If he had taken more thought, he could have given a better answer.

His answer was self-sufficient. He was looking to his own resources and that of others around him.

His answer was faithless. No faith whatsoever was manifested in the all-powerful Son of God.

His answer was forgetful. He forgot what Christ had done in days gone by. He turned his eyes away from the Lord and began looking at the resources of men.

What is your answer in the hour of testing? Do you look to the Lord, or do you look to self? Do you look to Christ, or do you look to others?

In the hour of testing, it is a habit of most to look around for the assistance of others. Even before spending time in prayer, we search for the advice of man. Let us remind ourselves that our God can do miracles. He is not limited in resources. He can do the impossible.

George Mueller set out to build an orphange. He did not look to man but to God, and the need was supplied.

Dr. Barnardo, moved with compassion for the poor children of England, began building homes for them. Before he died at age sixty he had rescued, fed, clothed, housed, educated and established in life 60,000 once destitute children. Today his homes have done the same for 150,000, and have given temporary help to over half a million.

The budget today for the Barnardo Homes is three million dollars per year, and 8,500 children are cared for annually.

Are you faced with a great need? Then count on God. He may be testing your faith to see if you mean business. If he sees you are in dead earnest, He will supply that need.

Philip forgot Christ. This is the very heart of his failure. The Lord was by his side; but he thought, not of the Lord's past performances, but of His present power. He was simply counting on doing the work of feeding five thousand with the resources of man.

III. THE RESULT

Philip made a faithless answer; and in verse 9 we find Andrew, Simon Peter's brother, making a faithless answer. As he was faced with the task of feeding so many, he said, "There is a lad here, which hath five barley loaves, and two small fishes: but what are they among so many?"

Notice that Philip was disturbed that two hundred pennyworth of bread would only give a small portion to each one. Andrew was quite certain that five barley loaves and two small fishes would not go anywhere in feeding five thousand.

Unbelief is contagious. Andrew followed after Philip; likewise, both were blind to the glory of Christ. "What are they among so many?" is always the utterance of unbelief.

What matters the many when the Son of God is present? Andrew calculated without Christ. He saw only a hopeless situation. He could not see Christ because of the difficulty before him.

We must keep our eyes upon Him. When we do, the difficulty will not be seen. We are such frail, weak and unbelieving creatures in spite of all God has done. When the trial comes, we are doubtful and distrustful. Therefore, we must continually look to the Lord not to ourselves.

We must exercise care that our unbelief is not carried over to others. I have seen many churches be disrupted and hindered by unbelieving members. Even one faithless deacon can hinder the entire church. One penny-grabbing member, always looking at the pennies instead of looking at souls, can hinder the work of our Lord.

Let me repeat: unbelief is infectious. Don't let yourself be influenced by the faithless.

Now, with joy, we see what our Lord did. After the words of Philip and Andrew, Jesus said, "Make the men sit down." Christ always chooses us to be seated when He is going to feed us. The number of men in this company was about five thousand.

Jesus took the loaves, gave thanks, then distributed to the disciples, and the disciples to them that were seated. The bread and fish were given out. And when all were filled, He said unto His disciples, "Gather up the fragments that remain, that nothing be lost."

"When they were filled. . . ." The Lord fully satisfies the hungry. No halfway measures with Him. He gives the fullness of His blessing.

Philip is concerned that everyone take just a little. Christ is concerned that people be satisfied by His grace. ". . .he that cometh to me shall never hunger; and he that believeth on me shall never thirst."

Now it remains for us to see that our Lord is able to take just a little and make it into much. He did not scorn the loaves because they were few in number, nor the fish because they were small. Someone has given us this paragraph:

> He used the tear of a babe to move the heart of Pharaoh's daughter.
>
> He used the shepherd rod of Moses to work mighty miracles in Egypt.
>
> He used David's sling and stone to overthrow the Philistine giant.
>
> He used a little maid to bring the mighty Naaman to Elisha.
>
> He used the widow with a handful of meal to sustain His prophet.
>
> He used a little child to teach His disciples a much-needed lesson in humility.
>
> So here He used the five loaves and two fishes to feed this great multitude.

Dear friend, it may be that God wants to use you. You have given your excuses. You feel your limitations. You do not consider your talents to be many. But God wants you. He is asking that you place yourself in His hands, even as the loaves and fishes were given to His hands. Be not faithless, but believing. Place yourself in the hands of the Lord, and let Him use you.

Perhaps you have tried so long to accomplish something, but it has always been in your own strength. Failure has marked your pathway. It is time to turn from your self-sufficiency and turn it all over to the Lord.

Faithless, failing Christian, let God have His way with you.

Sinner, the Christ who fed five thousand with five loaves and two fishes, can save your soul and feed you with heavenly manna. Come to Him now.

Oh, for a Faith That Will Not Shrink

Oh, for a faith that will not shrink,
    Though pressed by ev'ry foe,
That will not tremble on the brink
    Of any earthly woe!

That will not murmur or complain
    Beneath the chastening rod,
But, in the hour of grief or pain,
    Will lean upon its God;

A faith that shines more bright and clear
    When tempests rage the while;
That seas of trouble cannot drown,
    Nor Satan's arts beguile;

Lord, give us such a faith as this,
    And then, whate'er may come,
We'll taste, e'en here, the hallowed bliss
    Of an eternal Home.

                —William H. Bathurst

8. The Dynamite of Faith

And Jesus answering saith unto them, Have faith in God.

—Mark 11:22.

Now faith is the substance of things hoped for, the evidence of things not seen.

—Hebrews 11:1.

It is my conviction that God has given directions for everything relating to the spiritual life. We have God's very simple plan for evangelism and missions. Those who are saved are to tell those who are lost. We are told of the blessings of following this plan, and we are warned of the drastic results if we do not.

Whether it be baptism, the Lord's supper, tithing, witnessing, or worshiping, God has a given plan. Follow His plan and have success; leave it and fail.

It is also my firm conviction that God has made available all that we need in this life, whether it be food, shelter, inward peace, power for service. It is not God's will for us to live poor, miserable, defeated lives. Such dishonors Him. He wants all to have peace and power.

How are these things obtained? In the simplest way—through faith in God.

Faith is looking to God for help. Faith is the hand that reaches out to take God's gifts and provisions. Faith is resting, relying on the Lord for the fulfillment of all His promises.

The tragedy is that we look to self and to the world instead of to God. This produces faithlessness or unbelief.

Unbelief damns the souls of men; therefore, shun unbelief as you would an awful contagious disease.

Unbelief hinders the Lord's working. When Jesus visited Nazareth, it is said that "he did not many mighty works there because of their unbelief."

Unbelief shuts out blessings. The vast host of Israel did not enter the Promised Land because of unbelief. For lack of faith, they saw giants and walled cities of Canaan, and declared, "We cannot take the land."

Unbelief keeps blessings from others. The disciples could not cast the demon out of the afflicted young man because of unbelief.

From this story we can see that want of faith hinders the effective working of God through us. But when we have faith, it brings blessings to others. This was true when the four men brought the paralytic to Jesus. He saw their faith and said to the sick of the palsy, "Son, thy sins be forgiven thee," and then "Arise, take up thy bed and walk." Faith brings blessings; unbelief hinders blessings.

One of the finest compliments that you can pay a man is to say, "He is a man of great faith."

Let us see what faith in God does. We shall see what Jesus meant when He emphasized, "Have faith in God."

I. FAITH SINGS

One without faith has no song. He is depressed, gloomy, despondent, blue. But one with faith can rejoice in the midst of every trial.

It is said that H. G. Spafford lost his entire family in a wreck at sea. In the midst of tragedy, this man wrote:

> When peace, like a river, attendeth my way,
>   When sorrows like sea billows roll;
> Whatever my lot, Thou hast taught me to say,
>   It is well, it is well with my soul.
>
> Though Satan should buffet, tho' trials should come,
>   Let this blest assurance control,
> That Christ has regarded my helpless estate,
>   And hath shed His own blood for my soul.

Out of his blindness, George Matheson could write:

> O Love that wilt not let me go,
>   I rest my weary soul in Thee;
> I give Thee back the life I owe,
> That in Thine ocean depths its flow
>   May richer, fuller be.
>
> O Light that foll'west all my way,
>   I yield my flick'ring torch to Thee;
> My heart restores its borrowed ray,
> That in Thy sunshine's glow its day
>   May brighter, fairer be.

Faith sings! Fannie Crosby fully illustrates this. As a baby of six weeks, hot cloths were placed upon her eyes, destroying her sight. She never saw the beauty of nature nor the faces of her friends, but she had faith in God, and a song was in her heart. Some of the most beautiful and beloved songs in our book were written by Frannie Crosby.

> Jesus, keep me near the cross,
>   There a precious fountain
> Free to all—a healing stream,
>   Flows from Calv'ry's mountain.

* * *

> I am Thine, O Lord, I have heard Thy voice,
>   And it told Thy love to me;
> But I long to rise in the arms of faith,
>   And be closer drawn to Thee.

* * *

> Safe in the arms of Jesus,
>   Safe on His gentle breast,
> There by His love o'ershaded,
>   Sweetly my soul shall rest.
> Hark! 'tis the voice of angels,
>   Borne in a song to me;
> Over the fields of glory,
>   Over the jasper sea.

* * *

> Take the world, but give me Jesus,
>   All its joys are but a name;
> But His love abideth ever,
>   Thro' eternal years the same.
>
> Oh, the height and depth of mercy!
>   Oh, the length and breadth of love!
> Oh, the fullness of redemption,
>   Pledge of endless life above!
>
> * * *
>
> Saviour, more than life to me,
> I am clinging, clinging close to Thee;
> Let Thy precious blood applied,
> Keep me ever, ever near Thy side.

On one occasion when Fannie Crosby was being questioned before a great audience of people, someone asked, "Out of all the songs you have written, which is your favorite?" Without hesitation, she replied,

> Blessed assurance, Jesus is mine!
> Oh, what a foretaste of glory divine!
> Heir of salvation, purchase of God,
> Born of His Spirit, washed in His blood.

Faith sings, for faith blasts away doubt and fear. Faith lets the light shine through the darkest clouds. Faith gives a lift to the heavy heart.

A few hours ago I talked with a young man who had no song in his heart because his faith was gone. He had been a missionary for a certain denomination but is today nervous and troubled, despondent and sick. He has no happy testimony but quickly tells everyone he has suffered a nervous breakdown.

To every despondent, troubled soul in this service, Jesus admonishes "Have faith in God." Faith will give a song and bring in the light of Heaven to cheer you.

II. FAITH SERVES

True faith always results in action.

By faith, Noah built the ark. It was by faith that he labored 120 years.

It was by faith that Moses served God and his people. He turned his back upon Egypt and chose to suffer affliction with the people of God.

By faith Joshua led Israel into the Promised Land. It was by faith that the walls of Jericho fell down after they were compassed about seven days.

By faith Gideon served God against impossible odds. He won a victory over the Midianites with only 300 men.

Faith does not ask for the easy way. Faith goes on despite the hardships and meager results. Faith serves, though the task seem impossible. F. B. Meyer said, "We never test the resources of God until we attempt the impossible."

Faith does not ask for present pay. If men do not applaud or appreciate, faith works on, willing to wait until the judgment seat.

III. FAITH SUPPLIES

Sinful man is by nature a worrier. He worries about everything—food, drink and clothing. He worries about tomorrow and its needs. He worries about things which have not happened and perhaps never will happen. It is only when man takes hold of the promises of God that worry slips away. Surely God delights in that man or woman who by simple faith achieves perfect peace and rest of heart.

God is glorified by that Christian who refuses to worry, knowing He will provide. But many good Christians refuse to believe the promises of God. They somehow do not believe that God will do what He says, and foolishly they seem to imagine that worry will help the situation.

Jesus gave these words to His disciples which we need to study carefully:

"Therefore I say unto you, Take no thought for your life, what ye shall eat, or what ye shall drink; nor yet for your body, what ye shall put on. Is not the life more than meat, and the body more than raiment?

"Behold the fowls of the air: for they sow not, neither do they reap, nor gather into barns; yet your heavenly Father feedeth them. Are ye not much better than they?"—Matt. 6:25,26.

In summary Jesus said, "Take no thought. . .What shall we eat? or, What shall we drink?. . . (For after all these things do the Gentiles seek:) for your heavenly Father knoweth that ye have need of all these things."

And now listen to this word of our Lord:

"But seek ye first the kingdom of God, and his righteousness; and all these things shall be added unto you.

"Take therefore no thought for the morrow: for the morrow shall take thought for the things of itself. Sufficient unto the day is the evil thereof."—Vss. 33,34.

Two things the Lord is commanding us to do: first, to have faith in God; second, to seek first the kingdom of God and His righteousness. Faith in God will keep us from worrying about tomorrow. Seeking first the kingdom of God will keep us in tune with our Heavenly Father.

Worry is sin. Paul recognized this and told the church in Philippi that he did not worry. Rather "I have learned, in whatsoever state I am, therewith to be content. I know both how to be abased, and I know how to abound: every where and in all things I am instructed both to be full and to be hungry, both to abound and to suffer need." Then to assure them of God's love and care, he said, "But my God shall supply all your need according to his riches in glory by Christ Jesus."

Look to the Lord for your daily needs.

IV. FAITH STANDS

In this day of hurry and rush, it is very difficult to have faith. But faith stands true to God when all the world turns against you.

Job lost all he had—his property, his family, his wife who told him to curse God and die. His body was afflicted with terrible sores. But he said, "Though he slay me, yet will I trust in him: but I will maintain mine own ways before him." (13:15). His faith did not falter when sorely tested.

When that noble man Joshua came to die, he delivered his message to the people. The text was, ". . .as for me and my house, we will serve the Lord." In plain words, he said, "You can turn to the worship of idols and other gods, but I am standing true to the Lord." Then the great general made a plea for the people to put away their strange gods and incline their hearts to the Lord God of Israel.

In a day of idol worship, Elijah believed in God. He stood before Ahab and said, ". . .As the Lord God of Israel liveth, before whom I stand, there shall not be dew nor rain these years, but according to my word." With a courageous heart he stood against the prophets of Baal and brought revival to Israel on Mount Carmel.

The Apostle Paul was hated and despised by his own people. They sought his life, but he stood true to God.

To all weak and vacillating souls, the Lord is saying, "Have faith in God." Faith will help you stand when the whole world is rushing pell mell into destruction. Faith will enable you to stand for your convictions, though family and friends despise you for it.

I am told that in the Yellowstone National Park you will find a tree called the lodge pole pine. Every year many of these trees fall to the ground. When a storm of some severity hits the area, the lodge pole pine topples over. Why? Because the roots spread out close to the surface and do not go down deep.

May I contrast the lodge pole pine with some of the sturdy trees of this area. The winds blow and the storms descend, but the trees stand. Why? The roots have gone down deep. The faith that stands is the faith that lays hold upon the promises of God. We must have a deep-rooted faith in order to stand when the storms of doubt, fear and persecution sweep over us.

V. FAITH SAVES

Faith saves Christians from mediocrity. The work of Christ suffers from too many ordinary Christians. The ordinary Christian worries, frets, vacillates. He looks and acts like the man of the world. But real faith makes men different.

There should be many illustrations of mighty faith, but we have so few.

It was not long before the end of George Mueller's wonderful life that a friend came to see him. This friend spoke of Mueller's great life work and of the marvelous faith he had in God. Mueller replied, "My friend, I have no monoply of God's grace. This same life is open to all."

How wonderfully true this is! The mighty faith exercised by men of days gone by can be our faith. Our God is the same yesterday, today and forever. He hears and answers prayer as He always has done.

To save Christians from the sin of mediocrity, let me suggest the following:

First, take God at His word. Believe the Bible. Rest on God's promises.

Second, remember that God has never failed. His past performances assure us of the present.

Third, God is concerned about you. He has always been concerned for others. He wants us to be mighty in faith. Our Heavenly Father cares for us, is "pulling" for us.

Fourth, be optimistic and cheerful no matter the problem. There is always a way out, and God will show it at the proper time. You may be confronted by a Red Sea problem, but nothing is impossible with God. He has a way out.

Fifth, launch out into the deep. Cease paddling around in shallow water. Believe that God is interested in your well being and your success as a Christian. Cast away from the shoreline. Launch out into the deep. Attempt the impossible.

It will only be as we follow these simple suggestions that we will cease to be ordinary, everyday, faithless individuals.

And last, faith saves sinners from Hell. Jesus said, "He that believeth on me hath everlasting life, and shall not come into condemnation. . . ." John said, "He that believeth on the Son hath everlasting life: and he that believeth not the Son shall not see life; but the wrath of God abideth on him."

Simple faith saved Simon Peter who was brought to Jesus by his brother Andrew. It was simple faith, not works. We know the Lord changes not. As men and women were saved in Bible days, so are they saved now. If you will come tonight in simple faith, believing in Jesus Christ as your Saviour, He will save you now. This is a part of saving faith.

The invitation is twofold. First, we invite Christians to come for dedication to a life of faith; second, we invite sinners to come to receive Christ Jesus as Saviour.

9. *The Victory of Faith*

For whatsoever is born of God overcometh the world: and this is the victory that overcometh the world, even our faith.

Who is he that overcometh the world, but he that believeth that Jesus is the Son of God?
—I John 5:4,5.

John plainly states that the believer overcomes the world.

This statement doesn't seem to harmonize with the defeated lives of many of God's children. All around us are those who declare positively that they believe in Christ the Saviour, yet admit they are living defeated lives.

WHAT IS A DEFEATED LIFE?

A life without fruit. We are commanded by the Lord to bear fruit. Jesus said, "Herein is my Father glorified, that ye bear much fruit; so shall ye be my disciples" (John 15:8).

A life without power. If the power were present, the life would not be defeated. Jesus said, "But ye shall receive power, after that the Holy Ghost is come upon you: and ye shall be witnesses unto me. . ." (Acts 1:8).

A life without a positive influence. The life of the victorious Christian points in one direction—toward the Lord. The defeated life has no positive influence.

A life dominated by the flesh. The Corinthians were defeated Christians. Paul called them "babes in Christ." They were carnal, not spiritual.

A life directed at times by Satan.

Are you saying that a Christian's life is never directed by the evil one? If so, you are speaking against the Word of God. Simon Peter said to Christians,

"Be sober, be vigilant; because your adversary the devil, as a roaring lion, walketh about, seeking whom he may devour:

"Whom resist stedfast in the faith, knowing that the same afflictions are accomplished in your brethren that are in the world."—I Peter 5:8,9.

James also said, "Submit yourselves therefore to God. Resist the devil, and he will flee from you" (James 4:7). These and many other Scriptures show that the Devil is constantly after us. Some Christians succumb to his enticing words, and they are directed for a while by Satan.

A life dictated by the world. John tells us, "Love not the world, neither the things that are in the world. If any man love the world, the love of the Father is not in him" (I John 2:15). The apostle indicates the danger of loving the world; therefore, he warns the children of God against this love.

In a much stronger way, James said, "Ye adulterers and adulteresses, know ye not that the friendship of the world is enmity with God? whosoever therefore will be a friend of the world is the enemy of God" (James 4:4).

The Apostle Paul, knowing the great danger of a Christian's life dictated by the world, said, "Be ye not unequally yoked together with unbelievers: for what fellowship hath righteousness with unrighteousness? and what communion hath light with darkness?" (II Cor. 6:14). And again, "Wherefore come out from among them, and be ye separate, saith the Lord, and touch not the unclean thing; and I will receive you" (vs. 17).

The defeated life is dominated by the world, the flesh and the Devil— three enemies who work for the constant defeat of a Christian.

God wants you to be victorious! Satan wants you to be defeated! Your soul is beyond his reach, but you can still be touched through the world and his subtle suggestions.

What a dead drag the defeated Christian is to himself and to all around him! What a hindrance to the cause of Christ! He does not glorify God, and he constantly sheds a negative influence of defeatism on others.

But listen to John: "For whatsoever is born of God overcometh the world: and this is the victory that overcometh the world, even our faith" (I John 5:4).

Who is born of God? Look at I John 5:1: "Whosoever believeth that Jesus is the Christ is born of God: and every one that loveth him that begat loveth him also that is begotten of him."

Who overcomes the world? The one who is born of God. When you become a child of God, the victory begins. You are saved, eternally saved. All of the essentials for victory are in your possession. Plainly John tells us that no one can overcome the world save he who is born of the Spirit.

Are you born of God? Then you are an overcomer. But how do we overcome? The answer—by faith. "This is the victory that overcometh the world, even our faith."

By the same faith through which you were saved, you overcome the world. This victory is not accomplished all at one stroke. It is a lifelong business. We are to be overcomers day by day as we exercise our faith.

Now here is a big verse that we need to remember—Romans 10:17, "So then faith cometh by hearing, and hearing by the word of God." This was so in salvation. We had to hear the Word of God; we were convicted by the Holy Spirit, and we received Christ as Saviour. It is so in the life of conquest. If there is to be overcoming faith, then we must turn to the infallible Word of God.

There are three things that I want to impress upon your minds tonight.

I. THE PROMISES OF GOD

As we turn to the Word of God to receive faith and to have the increase of our faith, then we are confronted at once by the promises of our eternal God. What about these promises?

1. *Made by One who cannot lie.*

"In hope of eternal life, which God, that cannot lie, promised before the world began."—Titus 1:2.

This needs to be established in our minds once and for all: what God says He means, and what God says is eternally true.

Our God is not like the man who called in a lawyer to make up his will. He told the lawyer to put down so many hundreds of dollars for this one, so many hundreds for another one.

Finally, the lawyer said, "But, sir, I don't believe you have all that money to leave."

The man replied, "Oh, I know that just as well as you, but I want to show them my good will."

God does not work on such a principle. What He says, He can fulfill. How foolish we are to doubt His word!

> It is strange we trust each other,
>   And only doubt our Lord;
> We take the word of mortals,
>   And yet distrust His Word.
> But, oh, what light and glory,
>   Would shine for all our days,
> If we always would remember,
>   God means just what He says.

2. *Change not.* Wars and conflicts, turmoil and strife do not change the promises of God. What He has said abides. The Father does not turn or change. With Him there is no shadow of turning.

The promises of men are so changeable! Here is a man who came to me and begged me to sign his note. He made a definite promise that he would stand back of his own signature and that I would not be involved in any way. He repeated his promises and reinforced them with many strong words. I believed him and signed the note.

The promise of the man was the promise of a weak person, for his promise was affected by working conditions, his own changeable mind, and the sin of his life. As a consequence, I had to pay the note of $119.00.

Ah, but God's promises change not! He is not affected by

world conditions or even the instability of His children. His promises change not!

3. *Cover every situation.* Yes, there is a promise for every need. Are you lonely? Then listen to the word of Jesus for He said, ". . .lo, I am with you alway, even unto the end of the world" (Matt. 28:20).

Are you sick? Then hear His word to the Apostle Paul, ". . .My grace is sufficient for thee. . ." (II Cor. 12:9).

Are you discouraged? Then listen to the psalmist, "God is our refuge and strength, a very present help in trouble" (46:1).

Do you feel a great weakness? Then listen to Isaiah, "But they that wait upon the Lord shall renew their strength; they shall mount up with wings as eagles; they shall run, and not be weary; and they shall walk, and not faint" (40:31).

Are you burdened with many cares? Then listen to I Peter 5:7, "Casting all your care upon him; for he careth for you." A promise for every situation!

II. THE PICTURES OF FAITH

In the Word of God we find a full gallery of the pictures of faith. On every side we see men and women who believed God, rested upon His promises, and found Him to be true. We cannot mention all, but we can think of a few.

Gaze for a moment upon Abraham, called "the friend of God." His faith led him to follow the Lord, though he knew not where he was going. "By faith Abraham, when he was called to go out into a place which he should after receive for an inheritance, obeyed; and he went out, not knowing whither he went" (Heb. 11:8). Abraham, the father of the faithful. See him as he offered up his son Isaac. What a test of faith, yet how true was this man of God.

Look upon the picture of Moses, a man of faith who turned his back upon the riches of Egypt and chose the afflictions of the people of God. By faith he led the children of Israel out of Egypt, crossing the Red Sea on dry land.

See the faith of Joshua who crossed the Jordan on dry land. He compassed the city of Jericho for seven days, and the walls fell down.

See the picture of Elijah, that noble man from Gilead. No one but God stood with him when he denounced the sin of the king. No one but God encouraged him on Mt. Carmel in the contest with the prophets of Baal. Elijah was subject to like passions as we are, but he had faith. He prayed, and the heavens were locked up. He prayed again, and the rain came.

Look for a moment upon the picture of Daniel whose faith failed not in a heathen land. He knew the purpose of God would not be turned aside by any earthly consideration. As a lad, his faith failed not when he was tempted to eat and drink of the dainties of Babylon. As a man, his faith failed not when he was commanded not to pray. As an old man, his faith failed not when he had to deliver the judgment message to the king. Here is a noble picture to behold.

Can you not see why the Word says, "So then faith cometh by hearing, and hearing by the Word of God." Everywhere you turn in the Bible, you see a picture of faith. In Old or New Testament, it is always the same. Look upon the portraits of such faithful men as the Apostle Peter, the Apostle Paul, the Apostle John. Yes, look upon the picture of John who penned the words of our text by the Spirit of God. He was an overcomer, despite all the enemy could do. He stood fast and lived out a long life without bowing his neck to the world.

Of course, there are other pictures of faith outside the Word of God—pictures made possible because men believed the Word.

J. Hudson Taylor, the missionary to China, was a man of faith. David Livingstone, who spent his life in Africa, was a man of faith. If you would have strong faith, allow these examples to speak to your heart.

III. THE PRACTICE OF FAITH

We can read the promises of God, study the pictures of faith; but nothing happens until we put into practice our faith. When the tempter comes, then we must take the shield of faith and quench the fiery darts of the wicked. When we are face to face with a great need, we must claim the promise of Matthew 17:20, "If ye have faith as a grain of mustard seed, ye shall say unto this mountain, Remove hence to yonder place; and it shall remove; and nothing shall be impossible unto you."

Constantly we look into the Word of God, then go out to walk the way of faith. We do not need to look to the morrow but receive the promises as manna for each day.

I believe the Word invites us to test the promises of God. I do not mean that we are to be presumptous and do foolish things, but we are to take the promises, believe them, put them to a test, and see that God means what He says.

I am reminded of the illustration of the preacher who visited an old man held fast to his chair by rheumatism. The man had his Bible open in front of him, and the preacher noticed that the word "proved" was written time and again in the margins. Turning over a few pages, he found by the side of "God is our refuge and strength, a very present help in trouble," the word "proved." So it went throughout the Book. The sick man had written his own experience on the margin beside every promise.

Remember—God gave the promises to YOU. We are so accustomed to thinking that what we read is for someone else that we fail to receive the blessing for ourself.

If you are saved today, it is because you believe God's Word regarding salvation. If you are to be victorious, then it must be because you believe the promises and overcome the world by your faith. One time D. L. Moody was to speak to several thousand prisoners in a certain state penitentiary. It had been announced that after Mr. Moody's address, a pardon would be presented by the governor to a certain prisoner who had made a good record. No one but the governor knew who the fortunate prisoner was.

There was high excitement. Finally the moment came. The governor stepped forward with a pardon in his hand. He read out a name. There was a wave of applause. He called out the name a second time. Still the prisoner did not move from his seat, held fast, doubtless, by his unbelief that he, a life termer, should be granted freedom. Finally, nearby companions pushed him from his seat, and the man came forward with tears streaming down his cheeks to take the pardon from the hand of the governor.

Then the warden commanded the great audience of prisoners to fall in and march back to their cells. When the cellmates came marching past him, the man, still holding the pardon, fell in and, taking up the locked step, started the long march back to his established place behind the bars. The attendants pulled him from the line saying, "Man, don't you know you are free!"

This story illustrates the manner in which many of you Christians fail to believe the promises of God. You harbor doubts about salvation because you will not take the assurance of the Word of God. You live poor, limping, halting lives because you will not believe the promise that God will supply every need, take care of every emergency.

Let us begin to practice our faith, believe the promises, be inspired by the pictures, and daily practice our faith in God.

When Cardinal Manning was experiencing great depression of soul and a darkening of his faith, he went into the shop of a well-known book concern. There he saw one of his own books entitled, *Faith in God*. As he waited for a copy of his book to be sent up from the storeroom, he heard a clerk calling up from the elevator shaft, "Manning's *Faith in God* is all gone!" He took the words to heart.—W. B. Knight

10. Faith Stabilizes

> *For he was a good man, and full of the Holy
> Ghost and of faith: and much people was added
> unto the Lord.*
>
> —Acts 11:24.

It was Luke the physician who wrote this brief but arresting description of Barnabas.

First, he paid him a compliment: "For he was a good man . . . ." This means Barnabas had some of the attributes of God.

He was not simply amiable, but he was possessed of an active and positive goodness. The characteristics of his goodness were generosity, sympathy, clear-sightedness, and self-forgetfulness.

Someone has said that the need of this hour is not for clever men, but for good men.

Second, Luke mentions the unique combination. He was "full of the Holy Ghost and of faith." The life of Barnabas issued from the Holy Spirit. He seemed just an ordinary man, but he was under the complete control of the Spirit. This came because of his surrender to the Lord.

Not only was he full of the Holy Spirit, but he was also full of faith. He believed in Jesus Christ as Saviour. He put his full dependence in God, and he gave his obedience to every command of the Lord.

Third, we see the consequence of being a good man and full of the Holy Ghost and of faith! He won souls. Barnabas engaged in the greatest of all works—soul winning.

But now I want us to give emphasis to the matter of faith.

We talk about faith, its power, its work in the lives of others.

We are impressed by the faith of preachers and missionaries and triumphant Christians.

Not only do we talk about faith, but we sing about faith. Many of our greatest songs are built upon the subject of faith: "My Faith Looks Up to Thee"; "Faith is the Victory"; "Faith of Our Fathers!" "My Hope Is Built on Nothing Less, Than Jesus' Blood and Righteousness," etc.

We desire faith. We know the way to get what we need is through faith. Therefore, it is essential that I tell you how to have faith.

Turn to Romans 10:17: "So then faith cometh by hearing, and hearing by the word of God." There is no other way for anyone to have faith except by reading and believing this Book and acting upon its promises.

Now with this as a background, I mention three things that faith does.

I. FAITH STABILIZES

We need that which stabilizes our lives. What I say will be an encouragement to some but a warning to others.

First, faith keeps us steady when adversity comes, when the going gets rough. Into each life there must come some sorrow, some reverses, some difficulties. But with faith in God, we can keep going when these times come.

There is much to encourage us in the darkest hour. Though all may be taken from us, we can still have our faith in God.

The story is told of a farmer who had worked hard gathering in the hay. After it was placed in the barn, a fire broke out in the middle of the night; and the hay was soon aflame.

The farmer was in despair; but when he stood watching the barn and hay burn up, he looked around and saw many swallows driven from their nests by the fire, flying frantically about, so close to the flames that their feathers were almost singed. They were flying back trying to save their homes and little ones.

As the farmer saw this, he was strangely stirred and exclaimed, "At least I have my home! My loved ones! My heavenly

Father! I can build another barn, and better days will come again."

We stop and number our blessings and see that "if God be for us, who can be against us?"

Disaster may come, but with God we can face that tragedy and move ahead.

Second, faith keeps us stable when success comes our way. Only a few people can live with success. I have known it to make haughty and proud even fine, humble Christians. Therefore, faith is essential if we have the good fortune to succeed.

Third, faith will keep us stable when evil words are spoken against us. Jesus never faltered when men spoke evil against Him. We are to follow His example.

When a British soldier was caught one night creeping through the woods, he was taken before his commanding officer and charged with holding communications with the enemy. The soldier's only defense, only plea was that he had gone into the woods to be alone so he could pray.

"Have you been in the habit of spending hours in private prayer?" the officer growled.

The soldier replied, "Yes, Sir."

"Then down on your knees and pray now," he roared. "You never needed it as much."

Expecting immediate death, the soldier knelt and poured out his soul in prayer. This kind of eloquence could only have been inspired by the power of the Holy Spirit.

When he finished, the officer said, "You may go. I believe your story. If you hadn't drilled often, you could not do so well at review."

Yes, keep praying when evil is spoken against you. God will give deliverance.

Fourth, faith will keep us steady when the work is hard. Some seem to think that work is an insult and a hard task something to be shirked. Not so! Work is a compliment to any man or woman. But there come a times when it takes faith to continue at a steady pace.

Do you have the faith that stabilizes your soul? The faith that keeps you moving straightforward in the midst of the darkest night?

In Luke 8:22-25 is the story of Jesus crossing the Sea of Galilee. The Master fell asleep. As He slept a storm arose and the ship was filled with water. The disciples ran to Him and said, "Master, Master, we perish." The Scripture says that He "arose, and rebuked the wind and the raging of the water: and they ceased, and there was a calm." After this was done, Jesus asked, "Where is your faith?"

Troubled soul, I ask you: where is your faith?

II. FAITH STERILIZES

Faith will cleanse us, will fix our eyes upon the Lord and separate us from the world. When we look full into His face, the things of earth will grow strangely dim.

Selfishness comes when we look wholly to self; but when we look to Him and keep our eyes fixed upon our eternal God, this selfishness is taken away.

Faith will lead us to depend upon God. Of a truth, faith is dependence on God. But faith will lead us to a greater dependence upon our heavenly Father.

Simon Peter knew what it was to have faith in God; but when the Lord spoke to him about going to the household of Cornelius, he thought it could not be done. However, when God showed him that it was to be done, his faith led him to depend on the Lord.

The Apostle Paul had faith in God, but step by step he was led to an even greater dependence as he gave Him his full obedience.

Faith in God will turn us away from sin. No man can look to God and sin at the same time. When we are looking to the Lord, sin has no part in our lives; when we look to sin, then faith in God fades away.

You cannot have evil and good thoughts at the same time; therefore, be sure that you have clean thoughts, thoughts which will stand in your darkest hours.

Does your life need cleansing? Then put your complete faith in God. Let all things of this world fade into insignificance and let faith reign supreme.

III. FAITH STIRS

What mighty wonders are wrought by faith!
First, prayers are answered when we pray in faith believing.

"If any of you lack wisdom, let him ask of God, that giveth to all men liberally, and upbraideth not; and it shall be given him.

"But let him ask in faith, nothing wavering. For he that wavereth is like a wave of the sea driven with the wind and tossed."—James 1:5,6.

All prayer is based upon faith in God. We are exhorted to ask, seek, knock—in faith, believing.

Second, faith will deliver us from the most frightening conditions. When young David gave his testimony to Saul, he said the following:

"The Lord that delivered me out of the paw of the lion, and out of the paw of the bear, he will deliver me out of the hand of this Philistine. And Saul said unto David, Go, and the Lord be with thee."—I Sam. 17:37.

Yes, faith will deliver us from all evils, even as it delivered David in his day.

Another striking illustration is given in Daniel 3:17. When the king ordered Shadrach, Meshach and Abednego to be cast into the burning fiery furnace, they made this answer:

"If it be so, our God whom we serve is able to deliver us from the burning fiery furnace, and he will deliver us out of thine hand, O King."—Dan. 3:17.

Yes, and God did exactly that. He delivered them out of the hand of Nebuchadnezzar. We can have faith to believe that God will deliver us from every stormy trial that may come our way.

Faith stirs—the indifferent has no faith.

Faith stirs—the sinful knows nothing of faith.

What does faith stir us to do?

First, faith stirs us to think of others. The Christlike concerns itself for those around us. The life of faith is the life of un-selfishness, which causes us to pray for others and be concerned for their salvation.

Second, faith in God leads us to live for others.

> Others, Lord, yes others,
> Let this my motto be;
> Help me to live for others,
> That I may live like Thee.

We can only follow in the steps of our Lord Jesus when we live for others.

Third, faith in God will lead us to witness. But our witnessing will achieve nothing when done in our strength. It must be by His power.

I trust that I have said enough in these brief words to stir your hearts and cause you to say, "I am determined I will look to the Lord completely and depend upon Him."

Read this Word! Believe this Word. Obey this Word. I repeat, "Faith cometh by hearing, and hearing by the Word of God."

To the unsaved, you can have no living faith until you have a saving faith in Jesus Christ. You must see yourself as a lost sinner and Jesus as the One who can save you.

A poet and an artist were once examining a painting which represented the healing of the two blind men of Jericho. The artist asked, "What seems to you the most remarkable thing in this painting?"

The poet replied, "Everything in the painting is excellently given—the form of Christ, the grouping of the individuals, the expression in the faces of the leading characters."

The artist seemed to find the most significant touch elsewhere. Pointing to the steps of a house in the corner of the picture, he asked, "Do you see that discarded cane lying there?"

"Yes, but what does that signify?"

"On those steps the blind man sat with a cane in his hand; but when he heard Christ coming, so sure was he that he would be healed, he let his cane lie there and hastened to the Lord—as if he could already see." Is not that a wonderful conception of the confidence of faith?

Yes, the artist was right. When Jesus comes, we must turn loose of everything. Too often we cling to our canes, crutches and other means of self-help instead of going to the Saviour, that divine One who can give us what we need.

Come to Christ, repent of your sins, believe in the Lord Jesus Christ and be saved. Salvation is yours at this moment, if you will receive the Saviour.

He Staggered Not

He staggered not; but marched right on,
That ancient hero, Abraham.
He trusted in the Eternal One
His heart had heard God say,
"I AM."

He staggered not: though unbelief
Sought everywhere to bar his way.
The promise gripped his eager soul,
And nothing could his progress stay.

He staggered not; but strong in faith.
Believing God with all his soul,
By faith o'ercame his every foe,
The promise led him to his goal.

He staggered not; but glory gave
To God, whose promise he believed,
Sure that in God's own good time
The promised heir should be received.

So let me live my life each day;
And stagger not, but still believe,
That in my Father's own good way,
All that is best I shall receive.

11. The March of Faith

> *And going on from thence, he saw other two brethren, James the son of Zebedee, and John his brother, in a ship with Zebedee their father, mending their nets; and he called them.*
>
> *And they immediately left the ship and their father, and followed him.*
>
> —Matthew 4:21,22.
>
> *The Revelation of Jesus Christ, which God gave unto him, to shew unto his servants things which must shortly come to pass; and he sent and signified it by his angel unto his servant John:*
>
> *I John, who also am your brother, and companion in tribulation, and in the kingdom and patience of Jesus Christ, was in the isle that is called Patmos, for the word of God, and for the testimony of Jesus Christ.*
>
> —Revelation 1:1,9.

There are helpful lessons to be learned from every Bible character. But it is interesting to note that all of the outstanding people in the Scripture rose to places of trustworthiness in the same way: they came out of nothing into the glorious liberty of the Son of God.

Check the life of Simon Peter and see if this be not so. Note how God brought Matthew from a despised position to a place of honor in the company of the apostles.

The same is true of Paul. A wicked persecutor of Christians

became the world leader of Christianity and the outstanding voice of our faith.

Now we consider John who became one of the greatest of all Christians. Before Christ saved him, he was an egotistical fisherman of Galilee: impetuous, vindictive, intolerant, and ambitious. But when Christ touched his life, the miraculous happened, as it does in any life. ". . .old things are passed away; behold, all things are become new."

Look at John, called the Son of Thunder. "And James the son of Zebedee, and John the brother of James; and he surnamed them Boanerges, which is, The sons of thunder" (Mark 3:17). This doubtless speaks of his energy and hot-headedness.

In Mark 9:38, we note that he was intolerant. "And John answered him, saying, Master, we saw one casting out devils in thy name, and he followeth not us: and we forbad him, because he followed not us." The Lord Jesus kindly corrected his servant, but in this act we see the intolerance of John.

In Luke 9:54, we read of his vindictiveness. When people refused to receive the Lord Jesus, it was John who said, "Lord, wilt thou that we command fire to come down from heaven, and consume them, even as Elias did?" Again Jesus corrected His servants and told them, ". . .the Son of man is not come to destroy men's lives, but to save them."

In Mark 10:35-37, we see that John was ambitious. The two brothers, James and John, came to Jesus and said, "Master, we would that thou shouldest do for us whatsoever we shall desire." Jesus said, "What would ye that I should do for you?" And they said, "Grant unto us that we may sit, one on thy right hand, and the other on thy left hand, in thy glory." We will not take time to see what our Master said to these ambitious followers, but we simply see an indication of what John had in mind as a young follower of Jesus Christ.

But wait! John, when touched by the Master's hand, became the apostle of love. In his epistle he refers to Christian love more than twenty-five times.

In his youth he was ambitious and self-centered. In middle age he grew in grace and in knowledge. In old age there was about him a sweetness and a compassion like unto the Lord Jesus Christ.

Now, in the life of John I see the "march of faith." First, I see his saving faith in Jesus Christ; second, I see his sustaining faith in Christ; third, I see his satisfying faith in the Son of God.

I. FAITH IN CHRIST BRINGS MAN INTO THE FAMILY OF GOD

"But as many as received him, to them gave he power to become the sons of God, even to them that believe on his name."—John 1:12.

"For this cause I bow my knees unto the Father of our Lord Jesus Christ,

"Of whom the whole family in heaven and earth is named."— Eph. 3:14,15.

It sounds like foolish presumption for a person to walk up to Heaven's door and say, "Father, open the door and let me in."

Ah, but the Christian can do exactly that! He belongs to God and God belongs to him. He is God's child through simple faith in Jesus Christ. Let me illustrate it by using my own experience.

1. *I am a child of God because of my faith in Jesus Christ.* I am not saved by works, church membership nor by baptism, but by simple faith in the Son of God.

There was a day when I came to recognize that I was lost and Hell-bound, and there was a day when I believed in Jesus Christ as my personal Saviour. From that day on I became and am a child of God through my faith in Jesus Christ. It was an act of simple faith, even as the Lord describes it in John 6:47: "Verily, verily, I say unto you, He that believeth on me hath everlasting life"—as simple as that.

2. *I can make my needs known to my Father.* He has promised to give me what is best for me. The way for me to receive daily from His hands is by prayer. I do not say that He will supply all my wants, but He will supply all my needs. He will not endorse any foolishness, but He will supply any need. So as one of God's

family, I make known to Him what I consider needful. "But my God shall supply all your NEED according to his riches in glory by Christ Jesus."

3. *I can walk and talk with God daily.* For successful living I must be constantly conscious of God's presence. I must judge my speech and my walk. I must not engage in things filthy and unchristian. I must avoid sinful and wicked company. I must walk and talk with my Lord.

Now what is it that brings me into the family of God? Faith in Jesus Christ. The way is open for each one who hears me now to come into God's family.

II. FAITH IN CHRIST OPENS OUR EYES

We are brought into the family of God through our faith in Jesus Christ; now we are to grow in grace and in the knowledge of our Lord and Saviour Jesus Christ. Therefore, we must have our eyes open to see what God wants us to see.

1. *Eyes need to be opened to see our mistakes and weaknesses.* As we study the life of John, we see first, that he was like a child. Selfishly he desired the best, but soon grew into an adult in Christ Jesus. Becoming aware of his mistakes, he turned from his intolerance and vindictiveness. He lost his sinful ambition. He now desired but one thing—to please the Lord.

Now simple faith in Christ will open the eyes. God grant that we shall see Him and grow out of the miserable things which surround us.

2. *Faith in Christ opens our eyes to the needs of others.* The Bible says a very serious thing about people: "For all seek their own, not the things which are Jesus Christ's."

Only Christ can make us aware of the needs of others.

Only our Saviour can keep us from being selfish.

Faith in Christ causes us to love others. Faith in Christ makes us turn from the evil that hate has caused.

I read some days ago this startling statement:

Within the time of authentic history, war has claimed the lives of 15 billion men. What a pyramid of skulls their fleshless heads would make—a thousand foot base on either side and an air-raised pinnacle 4,300 feet in height. What a deluge of gore their spilled blood constitutes—30,000 million gallons; a crimson sea 30 feet deep, 300 feet wide, 83 miles long—enough to float a fleet of battleships, 15,000 million. What an army! No mortal man can comprehend its numbers or can conceive its magnitude. It is a population of the world for 600 years—all the men, all the women, and all the children who have lived and breathed in the last six centuries.

Hate is back of every war. Hate is back of all bloodshed. Faith in Christ will cause us to love others.

Faith in Christ will open our eyes to God's almighty power. God grant that we shall be daily conscious of His power. May we see it in saving souls, in supplying our needs, His power in doing the impossible. Think, my friend, of the almighty power of God.

The Apostle John had revealed to him what would take place in this world. We are told of the coming of our Saviour, the tribulation upon the earth, the revelation of Christ, the establishment of the new heaven and the new earth. Read Revelation with open eyes and heart and God will give you His message.

III. FAITH IN CHRIST GIVES DYING GRACE

The Apostle John had the hand of God upon him to the end. It was Christ who gave him peace on the Isle of Patmos. What a revelation was made known to the apostle! How faithfully he recorded every word! The message of this Book is enough for all times. It will take us into eternity with God.

Christ gave hope to John. When the dark clouds gathered, the bright lights of Heaven shone around him.

What was the hope given to John? Jesus Christ. Any man can be victorious when he sees Christ. Only when our eyes get away from our loving Saviour do we have difficulties. Keep Christ before you now and forever.

There is a story told of an artist who was falsely accused and unjustly thrown into prison. He was allowed his brush and paints but he had no canvas. The man did not appear to be a criminal. His sensitive, delicate face spoke of higher things.

One day a student of human nature was passing through the prison and, seeing the man, said to him, "Friend, you do not have the look of a criminal. Why, may I ask, are you here?"

"I am here awaiting trial, but I have been unjustly accused."

"Is there any small service that I can do for you?" asked the stranger.

"Yes," said the prisoner. "I am an artist. I would to God I had a sheet of canvas."

The stranger looked about and could find nothing but an old soiled napkin. Pushing it through the bars he said, "This is the best I could do. See if you can paint a picture upon it."

The artist fastened the napkin to the wall of his cell and began to paint upon it the face of Jesus. He labored on it faithfully. Every day the touch of his brush brought out more wonderfully the radiant face of Christ. Later it became one of the world's famous paintings of the Master's face.

Keep your eyes upon Jesus. It matters not how difficult, how trying, how destitute, seems the way. Light will come when Christ looks down. Place your life in His hands and let Him bless you.

Christ gave John strength when his body weakened and when opposition gathered. John, though cast upon the Isle of Patmos, was not without God's presence.

God is everywhere. Christ is near you. He will give you the needful things of life. Lean heavily upon Him who never fails those who trust in Him.

What does Christ want? Men and women to stand with Him in spite of opposition, to stand when foes assemble against you.

The tragedy is, Christ is so often left alone. He wants to lead us, but too often we turn from Him and try to run our own lives.

People go back to Palestine and walk over the lands where Jesus walked, but they are no more walking with Him today than they did back when He was upon the earth. Christ is not popular today, not in this country nor in other countries. He is not popular in a nation that reeks with sin and vileness. He has been forsaken. He is calling for your help. Will you give it to Him? Will you follow Him?

When Jesus came to Golgotha,
They hanged Him on a tree;
They drove great nails thro' hands and feet
And made a Calvary.
They crowned Him with a crown of thorns,
Red were His wounds and deep;
For those were crude and cruel days,
And human flesh was cheap.

When Jesus came to our town,
They simply passed Him by;
They did not hurt a hair of Him;
They did not watch Him die.
For men had grown more tender;
They could not cast a stone;
They only passed Him on the street
And left Him there alone.

Still Jesus cried, Forgive them,
They know not what they do;
He prays that prayer for us tonight—
For you and you and you.
We pass Him by and leave Him there,
Without an eye to see;
And crucify our Lord afresh
As He prays on Calvary.

Christ is looking for men and women who will stand with Him. Thank God for the testimony of John! He stood with Christ, and Christ stood by him. He is the precious One. He is the One above all others. Don't pass Him by. Let Christ into your heart, then walk with Him.

We are told that a big lump of something lay for centuries in a shallow pool in North Carolina. People passing by saw just an ugly lump and passed on.

Passing by one day, a poor man saw the ugly lump. *A good thing to hold my door ajar*, he thought, and took it home. A geologist, who stopped by the poor man's door, saw a lump of gold, the biggest ever found east of the Rockies.

What do you see when you look at Jesus? Some looked upon Him and saw only a Galilean peasant and turned away. Some saw a prophet and stopped to listen. Some saw the Messiah and worshiped. Some saw the Lamb of God and looked to Him to save them from their sins.

There are people today who see in Jesus simply a perfect Man. They get nothing more from Him than the example of His perfect life. Others looking upon Him see the Son of God; but having no affinity for anything that is from heaven, they simply pass by on the other side. Others looking upon Him see the Lamb of God, the divinely chosen sacrifice and Saviour; and, realizing their greatest need is to be saved from their sins, they go to Him for salvation.

Will you come to the Lord Jesus now? Will you believe in Him and take everlasting life? He waits to save you now.

A traveler crossed a frozen stream
    In trembling fear one day;
Later a teamster drove across
    And whistled all the way.
Great faith and little faith alike
    Were granted safe convoy,
But one had pangs of needless fear,
    The other all the joy!

12. This is Faith

Now faith is the substance of things hoped for, the evidence of things not seen.

—Hebrews 11:1.

And the apostles said unto the Lord, Increase our faith.

—Luke 17:5.

The disciples often made very serious requests unto the Lord. On one occasion they said, "Lord, teach us to pray." In answer, the Lord gave the model prayer, a parable, and numerous encouragements to pray.

At another time the apostles said unto the Lord, "Increase our faith." In the face of the Lord's teachings, these humble men following Jesus felt their need for an increased faith. I can well appreciate their feeling; and I, too, would say with them, "Lord, increase my faith."

I. "LORD, INCREASE OUR FAITH TO WALK WHEN WE CANNOT SEE"

It is written of Enoch that he walked with God. The writer of Hebrews tells us that Enoch was a great man of faith. "By faith Enoch was translated that he should not see death; and was not found, because God had translated him: for before his translation he had this testimony, that he pleased God" (Heb. 11:5).

Therefore, we can understand that the walk of this godly man was by faith and not by sight. He did not ask to see the distant scene, but was content to take one step at a time.

This is certainly our need today. We need faith to walk with

God, not demanding to know all that is ahead of us but going forward by faith.

Abraham was another man who walked by faith. "By faith Abraham, when he was called to go out into a place which he should after receive for an inheritance, obeyed; and he went out, not knowing whither he went."

By modern-day standards Abraham was a foolish man. He left a comfortable living in Ur of the Chaldees and Haran, and traveled a day at a time as God led.

How different life would be if we had the faith of Abraham! Instead of living dry, ordinary lives, life would be full of adventure and thrills.

II. "LORD, INCREASE OUR FAITH TO WORSHIP AND TRUST GOD WHEN HARDSHIPS COME"

There are many things we cannot understand. The death of a beautiful child, the affliction of consecrated Christians, the Homegoing of Christians workers—these are just a few of the problems we face and the mysteries we cannot understand.

For example, I read last evening of the death of a missionary, his wife and one child in an airplane crash. The other child of eighteen months was not killed. When missionaries are so badly needed, it is hard to understand why this young couple should be taken so suddenly.

Let us pray for faith that we can worship and trust God when death comes. When loved ones are snatched away from us, when we cannot understand, then let us say, "Lord, Thy will be done."

Let us worship and trust God when illness and affliction come. Some people lose faith in God because they cannot understand the mystery of human suffering. But others have their faith in God increased, for they continue to worship and trust the Lord in the midst of suffering.

The saints of God who have blessed the world the most have been suffering saints. Great preachers and missionaries have come out of the school of affliction.

Let us pray, "Lord, increase our faith to worship and trust God when adversity comes." This world is not a friendly place. We cannot expect to have prosperity and ease at all times. Adversity is sure to come.

Reverse in business and in the home will often face us. The measure of what we are is found in our reaction to adversity. If our faith is strong, we will continue to trust God, no matter what happens. If our faith is weak, we may go to pieces, as many people do every day.

III. "LORD, INCREASE OUR FAITH TO WORK ON IN SPITE OF OPPOSITION AND RIDICULE"

It takes faith to work on when others are laughing at you.

The Wright Brothers had to have faith in themselves when they continued their experiments with the flying machine.

Henry Ford had to have faith in himself during those long years of tinkering about with a motor car.

Edison had to have faith to carry on his experiments with the talking machine and the incandescent lightbulb.

We who are Christians must have faith in God to carry on when there is opposition and ridicule. Noah had such faith, for he built an ark in the midst of a dry field. Here is how it is given to us in Hebrews 11:7 "By faith Noah, being warned of God of things not seen as yet, moved with fear, prepared an ark to the saving of his house; by the which he condemned the world, and became heir of the righteousness which is by faith."

Noah preached, and the people laughed at him. He continued his building operations, but even the carpenters working on the ark were not convinced of their need.

Nehemiah is another Bible character who had tremendous faith in God. He resolved to build the walls of Jerusalem. His enemies said it could not be done. They laughed at Nehemiah and said that a fox could tear the wall down, but Nehemiah continued in the face of their scoffing. When Sanballat and Geshem tried to pull Nehemiah away from his work, he said, "I am doing a great work, so I cannot come down." They sent messages four times and Nehemiah answered four times in the same manner. Finally, Sanballat sent a fifth letter, and this time he resorted to lying and gossip. "It is reported among the heathen, and Gashmu saith it, that thou and the Jews seek to rebel: for which cause thou buildest the wall, that thou mayest be their king, according to these words."

Sanballat concocted a plain lie against Nehemiah, thinking that it would stop him from working on the walls; but Nehemiah had faith in God, and he refused to be sidetracked.

It does take great faith to carry on a work for God in the face of opposition and ridicule. There are times when the enemies seem more than the friends. Perhaps this is because the enemies are so bold to express themselves, while friends so often fail to express their sympathy.

We have had a little opposition against the work of the Highland Park Baptist Church. One would think that the entire world would rejoice because of God's blessings upon us, but there are still some folk like Sanballat and Geshem who would delight to stop the work.

Some, like Sanballat, have tried to start their false rumors; and they have said, "Gashmu saith so and so." Our business is to carry on in spite of opposition. If our work is of God, then God will bless it and make it succeed. If it is of man, it will die of itself. We cannot but feel that God is with us, for His blessings have been upon our mission program, upon the building of Tennessee Temple University, upon our radio work, upon the distribution of our paper. His blessing has been upon us in the building of the new house of worship. But still we need to pray, "Lord, increase our faith, that we might work on."

What about your individual life? Have you ceased to work because someone laughed at you? Have you lessened your effort to win souls because of opposition at home? Have you absented yourself from the house of God because others disapproved? Have you ceased tithing because someone laughed and said you were a fool to give so much to the church? May God help us to have faith to carry on in spite of all opposition.

IV. "LORD, INCREASE OUR FAITH TO WATCH AND WAIT FOR YOUR COMING"

We are not obedient Christians unless we are watching for the coming Jesus. "Watch therefore; for ye know not what hour your Lord doth come."

We are exhorted also to wait for His coming. "And ye yourselves like unto men that wait for their lord, when he will return from the wedding; that when he cometh and knocketh, they may open unto him immediately" (Luke 12:36). Paul said, "And to wait for his Son from heaven, whom he raised from the dead, even Jesus, which delivered us from the wrath to come" (I Thess. 1:10).

Why do we not watch for His coming? There are many reasons. I will list three:

1. *The weakness of faith in His promise to return.* It goes without saying that many people do not believe Jesus will return. Yet He said, "I will come again." Therefore, we need to have our faith increased in the Bible and in the promise of His soon return.

2. *The Devil does not want us looking for His coming;* therefore, he works upon our minds and weakens our faith. The Devil knows that a Christian who is watching for the return of Christ is going to live right and do right. He will keep his house in order. He will seek the salvation of others.

3. *We do not watch for His coming as we should because of scoffers.* There are those who say, "Where is the promise of His coming? for since the fathers fell asleep, all things continue as they were from the beginning of the creation."

The postmillennialist is not looking for the return of Jesus. Why should he, since he believes that Christ is coming after the thousand years of the kingdom of God on earth? According to his definition, there is no reason to watch for the coming of the Lord. The modernist does not believe that Christ is coming. He says the Lord has already come one time—there is no other coming.

Hence we have today the confused state of affairs—worldly and weak churches, professing Christians who cannot be detected from the world, scoffers and skeptics who deny the plain teaching of the Bible. We need to pray, "Lord, increase our faith to watch and wait for the coming of the Lord."

13. *Arithmetic of Faith*

Jesus said unto him, If thou canst believe, all things are possible to him that believeth.
—Mark 9:23.

Our text comes from the story of Jesus healing the demoniac boy. The father brought his son to the disciples, but they were unable to heal him because they had no faith. When the matter was reported to Jesus, he said plaintively, "O faithless generation, how long shall I be with you? how long shall I suffer you? bring him unto me."

When the father had brought the boy in his pitiful condition before Jesus, Jesus asked, "How long has he been this way?"

The parent answered, "Since a child." He then made a passionate plea for Christ to help him, saying, ". . .if thou canst do any thing, have compassion on us, and help us."

Jesus answered, "If thou canst believe, all things are possible to him that believeth." Note the "if" of our Lord.

The father cried out with tears, "Lord, I believe; help thou mine unbelief."

Jesus healed the boy.

The arithmetic of man is two plus two equals four, three plus three equals six, etc. The arithmetic of faith brings in God; and with God present, we need nothing else. In the arithmetic of faith God is the only significant figure; and if you have Him, then you may add just as many zeros as you please. We may not see our way out of our difficulty, but with God we have the assurance of a way out. We may say, "How can this task be done? It is humanly impossible." But remember this: with God all things are possible.

When we think of the arithmetic of faith, we are reminded at once of the children of Israel wandering in the desert country on their way to the Promised Land.

God showed His mighty hand and delivered His people from Egyptian bondage. He opened the Red Sea for them to cross over. Now we find approximately three million men, women and children in the desert country without any visible source of supply. There are no clothing stores, no grocery stores, no supply lines, no water supply—just three million people in a desert country. How can such a great number exist? The answer is, God is in the midst of His people. He is there in fullness of grace and mercy. He is there to guide, provide and guard.

By day and by night the Heavenly Father was watching over His people. Manna fell from Heaven; water came from the rocks. They depended on God, and they lacked nothing. From man's standpoint, the whole story is impossible; but with God, all things are possible.

I turn your attention to this matter of faith in God, with a prayer that all of us will be strengthened and encouraged by these words.

I. THE NEED OF FAITH IN GOD

This is the age of grace, but it is no less the age of trouble, trials and tribulation. To be able to stand in the day of trouble, one must have faith in his Heavenly Father. I mention three things which make faith necessary.

1. *The presence of Satan.* No intelligent one will deny Satan's power in this world. Turn in any direction and you see the handiwork of the evil one. The Apostle Paul carefully pointed out to the Ephesians the fact that we are in constant battle against the wicked one: "For we wrestle not against flesh and blood, but against principalities, against powers, against the rulers of darkness of this world, against spiritual wickedness in high places." And again: "Put on the whole armour of God, that ye may be able to stand against the wiles of the devil." Still again he recommended: "Above all, taking the shield of faith, wherewith ye shall be able to quench all the fiery darts of the wicked."

No one can cope with Satan unless he has faith in God.

2. *The sinful fickleness of man demands faith.* If we had no one to trust in but man, we would all be sorely shaken; for it is increasingly difficult to place our trust in the word of any man.

Someone says that the middle verse of the Bible is Psalm 118:8, "It is better to trust in the Lord than to put confidence in man." The psalmist gives this advice because man fails, but God never fails. One is doomed to disappointment if he trusts in people. Only a strong faith in God will sustain in the hour that man disappoints.

3. *We need faith in God because of the hardness of the way.* There is no way to escape the troubles of this life. On every hand we see pain, sickness, affliction, sorrow and death. No home escapes very long. The hush of sickness and the shadow of death enter every abiding place sooner or later.

In the midst of these things we need faith in God. It is my privilege to observe our people in the days of sadness. My heart is often made glad when I see you sustained by faith in God.

This world is not a friendly place and will never be until Jesus comes and establishes His kingdom. Until that day disease will run rampant, tragedy will stalk the footsteps of man, adversity will crowd and press people to the breaking point. But, thanks be to God, even in this day, faith will help us to stand true and carry on. The way may seem hard; but remember the arithmetic of faith, ". . .all things are possible to him that believeth." When God is with you, you cannot fail.

II. THE WEAKNESS OF MAN'S FAITH

In this story of the demoniac boy the disciples failed. Why? Jesus said it was because they did not have faith.

From this account we can see that lack of faith dishonors Christ, whereas strong faith glorifies Him. Our Saviour did not do many miracles in Nazareth because of their lack of faith.

Lack of faith is a stumblingblock to others. When we are faithless, others are affected. For example, if a Christian behaves poorly in the hour of crisis, he is noticed by a lost world; and those people are caused to stumble. Faith in Christ does not free us from trouble, but it helps us to bear troubles as they come.

We all face weak faith. With the apostles of old we want to cry, "Lord, increase our faith."

Jesus did not say that our faith has to be of tremendous proportions; rather, He said, "If ye had faith as a grain of mustard seed, ye might say unto this sycamine tree, Be thou plucked up by the root, and be thou planted in the sea; and it should obey you" (Luke 17:6).

The father of the demoniac boy did not have a perfect faith, for he cried out with tears unto Jesus, "Lord, . . .help thou mine unbelief." Jesus heard his cry and healed his son.

The question comes, "How can my faith be increased?" The answer is twofold.

1. *By the Word of God.* "So then faith cometh by hearing, and hearing by the word of God" (Rom. 10:17). This Word of God is true, and every promise is to you. Therefore, faith will be increased as we read and hear God's holy Word.

A lot of you are worrying and fretting about small, insignificant things on which God has given His promise about in the Word. If you knew your Bible, you would not be faithless, but believing.

2. *Our faith is increased by using what we have.* This father of the sick boy did not wait for his faith to grow to a certain degree, but at once he cried unto the Lord, "I believe, help thou mine unbelief!" Use the faith that you have, and God will give more. Fail to use what you have, and it will soon diminish and vanish.

It needs to be said, also, that staying in the company of people of faith will help our faith to grow. If we travel with those who disbelieve the Word of God and trust only the visible, our faith will soon be weakened. My faith in God is always increased when I associate with men and women who have a strong faith in our Heavenly Father.

III. THE POWER OF FAITH IN GOD

I cannot think of any great blessing that comes from Heaven

which is not connected with faith. All great blessings come on the rails of faith.

Allow me to outline the things that faith brings unto men.

1. *Faith accomplishes great good in the world.* Mr. George Mueller of Bristol, England, began his orphanage by faith; and for more than fifty years fed two thousand orphans and provided for them entirely by faith. God honors the faith of those who seek to bring blessings to others. He honored Mueller's for many years, and today is still honoring his faith by sending in all that is necessary for the orphans.

Here in our own midst there are many illustrations of how faith accomplishes great good. Tennessee Temple University is a product of faith. The World-Wide Faith Mission Fund is another work of faith which God is honoring. Camp Joy is a work of faith. God is answering prayer and providing for the needs of this work. These are but a few of the many things that faith is accomplishing even before our eyes.

2. *Faith brings peace.* I wish that I had time to emphasize this properly, for today there are so many troubled hearts and all because of lack of faith. Faith in God brings peace. When we turn our lives over to our divine Father, peace floods our souls.

Paul had this in mind when he wrote to the Philippians: "Be careful [be anxious] for nothing; but in every thing by prayer and supplication with thanksgiving let your requests be made known unto God. And the peace of God, which passeth all understanding, shall keep your hearts and minds through Christ Jesus" (4:6,7).

The prophet Isaiah wrote regarding faith in God and peace as follows: "Thou wilt keep him in perfect peace, whose mind is stayed on thee: because he trusteth in thee" (26:3).

The song, "God Will Take Care of You," has a message that we need.

> **Be not dismayed whate'er betide,**
> **God will take care of you;**
> **Beneath His wings of love abide,**
> **God will take care of you.**

> **Through days of toil when heart doth fail,**
> **God will take care of you;**
> **When dangers fierce your path assail,**
> **God will take care of you.**
>
> **No matter what may be the test,**
> **God will take care of you;**
> **Lean, weary one upon His breast,**
> **God will take care of you.**

3. *Faith in God gives power to overcome temptation.* The reason we are so slow to win battles over selfishness, pride, jealousy, faultfinding, and worldly temptations, is that we trust too much in ourselves. We do not put our dependence in God, but try to win our victories alone. Faith will enable us to call upon God's resources and make them our own. With His power, we can overcome the tempter and win the victory.

Let the Apostle John speak to our hearts: "For whatsoever is born of God overcometh the world: and this is the victory that overcometh the world, even our faith" (I John 5:4).

The Apostle Paul points out, also, that using our faith, we will be able to quench the fiery darts of the wicked. To fight against and try to defeat the forces of evil in our own strength is folly and can only lead to defeat. But with God we can be victorious over temptation. Though it be strong drink, an evil mind, a slanderous tongue, a gambling nature—whatever it is, we can have victory through faith in God.

4. *Faith brings eternal life.* I have saved this for the last so that I might place it upon your hearts with great emphasis. There is no salvation, no everlasting life, without faith in Christ. We are saved by grace, yes; but it is faith that lays hold of the gift of God. Faith is the hand that reaches out to receive the precious gift.

"For by grace are ye saved through faith; and that not of yourselves; it is the gift of God: Not of works, lest any man should boast."—Eph. 2:8,9.

"For the wages of sin is death; but the gift of God is eternal life through Jesus Christ our Lord."—Rom. 6:23.

Let Simon Peter speak to you on this matter of faith:

"To him give all the prophets witness, that through his name whosoever believeth in him shall receive remission of sins."—Acts 10:43.

And finally, hear Jesus tell you that faith brings eternal life:

"For God so loved the world, that he gave his only begotten Son, that whosoever believeth in him should not perish, but have everlasting life."—John 3:16.

Turn to Christ now. Recognize your sinful, needy, helpless condition. Look to Christ and by faith receive Him as your Saviour. Faith in Christ brings salvation, peace and power. Without Him, we can do nothing. With Him, "all things are possible to him that believeth."

With Thee by faith I walk in crowds—alone,
Making to Thee my wants and wishes known:
Drawing from Thee my daily strength in prayer,
Finding Thine arm sustains me everywhere;
While, thro' the clouds of sin and woe, the light
Of coming glory shines more sweetly bright;
And this my daily boast—my aim—my end—
That my Redeemer is my God—my Friend!

—C. H. Ironside.

14. "O Woman, Great is Thy Faith

Then Jesus answered and said unto her, O woman, great is thy faith: be it unto thee even as thou wilt. And her daughter was made whole from that very hour.

—Matthew 15:28.

Jesus never indulged in loose flattery. Every word from His lips was true. When He declared that something was great, it was great.

While Jesus was ministering in the coasts of Tyre and Sidon, there came to Him a woman of Caanan who cried unto Him for help. She had a daughter who was grievously vexed with a demon. Jesus made no response to her first cry. The disciples were in favor of sending her away. Finally, Jesus said to the woman, "I am not sent but unto the lost sheep of the house of Israel. Then came she and worshipped him, saying, Lord, help me." Jesus gave a reply which was almost the nature of a rebuke: "It is not meet to take the children's bread, and cast it to dogs." In humility, the mother answered, "Truth, Lord: yet the dogs eat of the crumbs which fall from their masters' table." When Jesus saw the great faith of this mother, He said, "O woman, great is thy faith: be it unto thee even as thou wilt. And her daughter was made whole from that very hour."

Jesus did not hesitate to compliment the faith of this humble woman. Her faith was strong. She was not easily turned away when the Master delayed answering her request. Her faith was self-denying. She did not ask anything for self but for her daughter. Her faith was singular.

Since Jesus stood in the midst of a faithless people, the

woman's faith stood out as unusual and worthy of special commendation.

May the faith of this Syrophenician woman be passed on to the mothers of our day. May her worthy characteristics of persistence, prayer and faith be emulated by you mothers in this audience.

This hour calls for great faith, faith in the One who never falters, never fails. The blessings which come through faith in God are beyond number, but I would like to call your attention to just three of the major blessings which come through faith.

I. FAITH IN GOD GIVES PEACE OF HEART

Unbelief is the father of worry and unrest. Faith in God brings peace and rest.

1. *Gives peace about our needs.* We are all needy creatures. In our need, we can do one of two things: pray and trust God or worry and fret. Philippians 4:19 gives us the promise:

"But my God shall supply all your need according to his riches in glory by Christ Jesus."

Do you have material needs? Then pray and trust God. Do you have need of strength and courage? Then make your petitions to the Lord and have faith.

Here is a formula which is worth a million dollars if you will but follow it:

"Be careful for nothing; but in every thing by prayer and supplication with thanksgiving let your requests be made known unto God.

"And the peace of God, which passeth all understanding, shall keep your hearts and minds through Christ Jesus."—Phil. 4:6,7.

To worry about temporal and material things is to reveal your lack of faith. God has promised to watch over His own and to provide for every need. How foolish that we should worry.

2. *Gives peace about the future.* How many people are

troubled because of that which will come to pass tomorrow. The Word of God tells us what to do regarding this matter also:

"But seek ye first the kingdom of God, and his righteousness; and all these things shall be added unto you.

"Take therefore no thought for the morrow: for the morrow shall take thought for the things of itself. Sufficient unto the day is the evil thereof."—Matt. 6:33,34.

Jesus said that unbelievers are troubled about food, drink and clothing, but that believers are to trust in the heavenly Father, for, "your heavenly Father knoweth that ye have need of all these things."

3. *Gives peace in the hour of danger.* The three Hebrew children faced the fiery furnace with peace in their hearts, manifested by the inspired words of Daniel 3:17,18:

"If it be so, our God whom we serve is able to deliver us from the burning fiery furnace, and he will deliver us out of thine hand, O king.

"But if not, be it known unto thee, O king, that we will not serve thy gods, nor worship the golden image which thou hast set up."

Shadrach, Meshach, and Abednego knew that if God permitted them to be put into the fiery furnace, He would bring them out of it. Such marvelous faith cannot but give peace in the hour of danger.

Paul said, "If God be for us, who can be against us?" He went on to mention that in all things—tribulation, distress, persecution, famine, nakedness, peril or sword—we are safe because we are in God's hand and protected by His might. We are to keep our eyes upon the Lord and have faith in Him when danger surrounds us.

I read the story of the early days in the West when the circuit-riding preachers had to swim their horses across the rivers. They tell us that when crossing these swollen and overflowing rivers, if they fixed their gaze upon the swirling waters, they were likely to become dizzy, fall from the saddle and be swept away by the flood. But if they fixed their eyes upon the trunk of a great tree on the bank or upon some mighty rock or upon the summit of a hill or mountain, they rode through in safety.

In the storms of life, faith gives us balance and calm and safety, for we fix our eyes, not upon the shifting scene about us, but upon the eternal God.

4. *Gives peace regarding our salvation.* Many professing Christians are troubled day and night, not knowing whether they are saved or lost. This is lack of faith. If we have faith in God and His promise, we can have peace regarding our salvation. Here is what John has to say about it:

"He that believeth on the Son of God hath the witness in himself: he that believeth not God hath made him a liar; because he believeth not the record that God gave of his Son.

"And this is the record, that God hath given to us eternal life, and this life is in his Son.

"He that hath the Son hath life; and he that hath not the Son of God hath not life.

"These things have I written unto you that believe on the name of the Son of God; that ye may know that ye have eternal life, and that ye may believe on the name of the Son of God."
—I John 5:10-13.

Here is the record that all who believe in Jesus have everlasting life. We are to believe God's record, know that God is true and that He cannot lie. Then we can have peace regarding our salvation.

Yes, faith in God gives peace in the heart.

II. FAITH IN GOD GIVES PURPOSE TO LIFE

The man who believes in God knows where he is going. He does not waver, but moves straight forward according to God's plan.

Without faith, there is uncertainty. All of us have listened to the faithless person at some time. We heard him say, "I know I should do this or that, but I am afraid." Though God's purpose had been revealed, there was no faith to move forward. The Christian of faith says, "God has directed me to do this, so I fear not to go forward."

In Hebrews 11, we see how God's men moved forward without wavering when they had their orders.

Observe Noah:

"By faith Noah, being warned of God of things not seen as yet, moved with fear, prepared an ark to the saving of his house; by the which he condemned the world, and became heir of the righteousness which is by faith."—Vs. 7.

A hard task was given to Noah, a job that brought ridicule from scoffing unbelievers; but Noah had faith, so he did not waver.

Observe Abraham:

"By faith Abraham, when he was called to go out into a place which he should after receive for an inheritance, obeyed; and he went out, not knowing wither he went.

"By faith he sojourned in the land of promise, as in a strange country, dwelling in tabernacles with Isaac and Jacob, the heirs with him of the same promise:

"For he looked for a city which hath foundations, whose builder and maker is God."—Vss. 8-10.

Turn back to Genesis 12 and hear the command of God to Abraham: "Get thee out of thy country, and from thy kindred, and from thy father's house, unto a land that I will shew thee."

Abraham moved decisively and purposefully out of his own country and travelled by faith, not knowing whither he was going, but he knew God was directing him.

Observe Moses:

". . .when he was come to years, refused to be called the son of Pharaoh's daughter;

"Choosing rather to suffer affliction with the people of God, than to enjoy the pleasures of sin for a season;

"Esteeming the reproach of Christ greater riches than the treasures in Egypt: for he had respect unto the recompence of the reward.

"By faith he forsook Egypt, not fearing the wrath of the king: for he endured, as seeing him who is invisible."—Heb. 11:24-27.

God appointed Moses a task big enough to stagger a thousand men, but he moved forward with faith when God made clear His call.

Faith in God gives purpose to life. "A double-minded man is unstable in all his ways." The weak, vacillating, faithless one goes in a circle and wastes a God-given life.

Find what God wants you to do, then move forward with faith. Life is quickly going by. Let us not waste time in indecision. Let us not waste time in doubting and wondering. Let us find the will of God, have faith in Him who has called us, and go on.

III. FAITH IN GOD GIVES POWER

"Jesus said unto him, If thou canst believe, all things are possible to him that believeth."—Mark 9:23.

Unbelief and lack of faith cut off our power. You have never seen a great Christian who was always doubting God. The power of God is not poured out upon those who limit the Lord and doubt His power.

Faith in God gives power in prayer. When we waver in prayer, there is no answer. Listen to James 1:6,7:

"But let him ask in faith, nothing wavering. For he that wavereth is like a wave of the sea driven with the wind and tossed.

"For let not that man think that he shall receive any thing of the Lord."

We are wasting time in prayer when we fail to believe God.

Take the promises of God at face value. Believe that God means what He says, and make your petitions known unto Him.

The mother in our Scripture lesson today had faith in the Lord Jesus Christ and His power to heal her daughter. According to the testimony of Jesus, she did not doubt at all, but believed that if Christ would say the word, her daughter would be made well. Christ said, ". . .be it unto thee as thou wilt."

In the realm of prayer we have not touched the hem of the garment. Most of our praying is frivolous, foolish and faithless. We often pray when we do not mean it, and we often pray when we expect nothing to happen. This is an abomination in the sight of the Lord.

Faith in God gives power in living. The realization that God is with you means everything when you face a gainsaying and an evil world. Faith in God will bring a man through his temptations, trials and afflictions. Resting on the arm of flesh will bring failure every time.

The test of your faith is: Does it bring you through the temptations and trials of life?

Faith in God gives power to overcome the adverse things which come against us daily.

Today people laugh at faith. On every side we are urged to be practical-minded, to trust only in what we can see, touch and possess. This attitude accounts for the weakness of many people.

One minister, discussing this matter, illustrates it as follows:

> I can imagine a youth being conducted through the armory where he is to arm himself for the battle of life. When he is offered the sword of knowledge, he accepts it. When he is offered the sword of eloquence, he says, "I can use that; give it to me." When he is offered the sword of wit, he is glad to take it. When he is offered the sword of personality and charm, he eagerly lays hold on its hilt. But when he is offered the sword of faith, he turns away from it in disdain. "That weapon," he says, "was all right for my father and my grandfather and my great grandfather, but it is of no use to me. It is completely outmoded, a weapon that is all right for the museum, but not for the battle of life."

Friends, faith is not weakness. Faith is not foolishness. Faith is power. Faith in God is a sword that flashes and gleams like a meteor. It is the sword that brings victory when all others have been broken.

Faith in God gives power in witnessing. This is the power which we want and sorely need. When we try to win souls in our own strength, we fail miserably. We need supernatural power when it comes to giving forth the Gospel and calling men to salvation. To save the vilest men, we need faith in God, in God's Word, in God's Son.

May this prayer be offered today: "Lord, increase our faith." Let us not forget the word of the apostle, "So then faith cometh by hearing, and hearing by the word of God." May we fill our hearts and minds with the Word of God and believe what God says.

We now come to the invitation. Without question and without doubt, without quibbling and without wavering, we invite lost men and women to come to the Saviour. We know that He is able to save to the uttermost. We know that no one has ever come to Him in vain. He saves; He keeps; He satisfies. We invite the lost to come to Jesus.

We invite you poor, stumbling, wavering Christians to renew yours vows to God, to rededicate your lives and talents to the Saviour, to walk with God in the daily battle of life.

I do not know what may await, or what the morrow brings;
But with the glad salute of FAITH, I hail its opening wings;
For this I know, that in my LORD shall all my needs be met;
And I can trust the heart of HIM WHO HAS NEVER FAILED ME YET.

15. *Faith and Doubt*

So then faith cometh by hearing, and hearing by the word of God.

—Romans 10:17

Now faith is the substance of things hoped for, the evidence of things not seen.

But without faith it is impossible to please him: for he that cometh to God must believe that he is, and that he is a rewarder of them that diligently seek him.

—Hebrews 11:1,6.

Many Bible stories have mixtures of faith and doubt. This is true of the simple account given in Matthew 8:23-27. Jesus entered into a ship and His disciples followed Him. There came a great storm upon the sea. The boat was covered with the waves, and Jesus was asleep. His disciples came to Him and said, "Lord, save us, we perish." Jesus arose and rebuked them saying, "Why are ye fearful, O ye of little faith? Then he arose and rebuked the winds and the seas; and there was a great calm."

This story reveals both faith and doubt. The disciples had some faith, but they also had much doubt. So Jesus said, "Why are ye fearful, O ye of little faith?" Most of us, too, have both faith and doubt because we do not heed the Bible admonitions on how to have faith.

Strangely, we have faith in many ways. For example, we have faith in mailing a letter. We write it, sign it, seal it, stamp it, and put it in the box. We believe that the letter will be delivered.

We have faith in banking money. We go to one of our banks,

make out a deposit slip, hand it, with the money, to the teller and walk away with confidence.

We have faith in buying or eating our food. We buy with confidence, and we eat without fear.

We manifest faith when we go by plane to some distant place. We have confidence that the plane will hold us up and bring us safely to our destinations.

Even in the matter of drinking water, we are manifesting faith. We turn on the faucet, fill a glass and drink. The water could have poison in it, but we have faith to believe the statements of the city Board of Health that it is pure.

Even in starting our car we manifest faith. We get in the car, step on the starter; the battery turns over the motor, and the car starts.

I could go on mentioning other ways that we manifest faith: faith in doctors, in nurses, in medicines; faith in operations, in treatments—all manifestations of the faith we have in people.

But now, we are discussing faith and doubt, recognizing that the two are close together. I present the following outline:

I. A DISTURBED FAITH

In Matthew 11, we read that John the Baptist had been put into prison. From the prison cell he sent two of his disciples to Jesus to ask,

"Art thou he that should come, or do we look for another?

"Jesus answered and said unto them, Go and shew John again those things which ye do hear and see:

"The blind receive their sight, and the lame walk, the lepers are cleansed, and the deaf hear, the dead are raised up, and the poor have the gospel preached to them.

"And blessed is he, whosoever shall not be offended in me."— Matt. 11:3-6.

John the Baptist was a man of great faith, but for a time that faith was disturbed.

1. *Disturbed by conditions.* This was true of John the Baptist. The bleak walls of a prison were scarcely conducive to faith and happiness; therefore, John sent out word to inquire regarding the Lord Jesus. I believe in my heart that he knew, but his faith had been disturbed by the things which had happened.

The Lord Jesus, of course, knew of the greatness of John. He said these words:

"Verily, I say unto you, Among them that are born of women there hath not risen a greater than John the Baptist: notwithstanding he that is least in the kingdom of heaven is greater than he."—Vs. 11.

Conditions of life ofttimes bring disturbance. I read about a little girl who fell on the sidewalk and skinned her knee. She said to her mother, "Wouldn't it be wonderful if all the world were cushioned!" Ah, but the world is not cushioned; and in this life we will have some distressing circumstances, some unfortunate conditions to face.

Satan is going to see that your life is not easy. There is a primitive African tribe that believes that although God is good and wishes good for all, He has a half-witted brother who keeps getting in His way and mixing things up. This is pagan foolishness, but there is a Devil who is disturbing us all the time.

2. *Disturbed by delay.* Waiting is always hard: waiting for conditions to improve, for prayer to be answered, for a loved one to come to Christ. However, we must know that God sometimes delays His answers for a purpose. He is trying to increase our faith and dependence on Him.

But still we cannot understand how faith is disturbed by delay. For example, here is a wife who has prayed so hard for the salvation of her husband. She believes God. She has testified to her loved one. But there is no response, and she wonders why the delay.

3. *Disturbed by failure.* We have all had the experience of doing what we considered our best, then seeing plain, abject failure. I have known pastors to become bitter after their best work has come to naught.

Many of you have had the same experience. You have spent a lifetime trying to build up a business, then see it fail. Or perhaps you have spent years trying to acquire enough money to purchase a new home, then an illness comes; your money is spent; your dreams are blasted.

4. *Disturbed by criticism.* Criticism is certain to those active in the service of Christ. We do well to fortify ourselves for the assaults of the critics. Wherever you work, whatever you do, someone will criticize.

Now when disturbances come, we must run to the Lord Jesus Christ, even as John did. He sent two of his disciples to ask the Lord the question, "Art thou he that should come. . . ?"

The Saviour will tell us to fear not, but have faith in God.

II. A DOUBTING FAITH

These two thoughts are closely aligned, yet they are different. Faith may be disturbed but still be a strong faith. Sometimes doubts come, and we are rendered weak and incapable of strong work because of these doubts.

Doubts are usually symptoms of something underneath the surface.

1. *Sin brings doubts.* Sin breaks the chain of faith. Sin weakens your life. Sin blinds the eyes. Sin destroys your ability to lay hold on truth. Sin tries to put the blame on another. Whenever you allow sin to invade your life, be sure that you will soon begin to have doubts. The sin may be a sin of unfaithfulness, a sin of falsehoods, a sin of stealing or some other. Just remember that sin brings doubts.

2. *Idleness brings doubt.* I do not know why Thomas was absent on that first Sunday night when the Lord Jesus appeared to the disciples. The other disciples said to him, "We have seen the Lord." Thomas said, "Except I see in His hands the print of the nails, and put my finger into the print of the nails, and thrust my hand into His side, I will not believe."

Thomas was a doubter. He might have had a good reason for being absent that Sunday night, or he might have been absent because of his doubting heart. Whatever the reason, he expressed his doubts very plainly. The doubts were not erased until the Lord Jesus made an appearance before him and told him, "Reach hither thy finger, and behold my hands; and reach hither thy hand, and thrust it into my side: and be not faithless, but believing." The Bible tells us that Thomas answered and said unto Him, "My Lord and my God."

In John 20:29, He gives a word that should help us to overcome our doubts: "Thomas, because thou hast seen me, thou hast believed: blessed are they that have not seen, and yet have believed."

When you miss church, fail to read your Bible, fail to pray, fail to be active in soul winning, there is danger. Inactivity, idleness bring doubts.

3. *Refusing God's call brings doubts.* Many a man has lived a life of misery because he refused God's call to service. For a lifetime he was filled with uncertainty and doubts.

I cannot forget the man who whispered into my ear on the day that I answered God's call. W. A. Luckie said to me, "Son, if God has called you, never turn your back on His call. When I was a young man, God called me to preach; but I have never preached; hence, my entire life has been one of unhappiness. I have failed my God."

Some of you will recall the lady who came forward in our church and said that when God called her to be a missionary thirty-nine years ago, she refused His call. Sadly she said, "I have never prayed without being conscious of the fact that I turned my back upon God's definite call. Hence, my prayers have been ineffective, and my life has been unhappy."

4. *Doubts come by listening to wicked teachers.* When a youth sits under a teacher who is an infidel or an atheist, he will usually end up with some doubts.

Recently, a mother came to me quite distressed about her son. He had made a profession as a young man. He followed Christ in baptism, attended church faithfully; then when he went away to college, he sat under the wrong kind of teachers. Now the mother said, in tears, "His faith is gone."

5. *A doubting faith may be the result of the presence of trou-*

ble. Adversities will bring doubts. Too often our troubles raise a big question mark. The Devil takes the depressed mind and sows doubts.

III. A DYNAMIC FAITH

We have discussed thus far *a disturbed faith, a doubting faith*; now, allow me to emphasize *a dynamic faith.*

I believe the Bible tells us how we can build a strong and steadfast faith.

1. *There must be direction.* Faith will not come by looking to yourself. We must look toward Christ the Saviour. There must be a believing in the Son of God as your own personal Saviour, and there must be a resting upon Him.

I can see the importance more and more of having an eye single for the Lord. Looking at the world will never bring faith. Looking to self will only bring instability and weakness. But looking to Christ will bring faith.

2. *When we look toward Him, there will be assurance.* We have His promise, "I will never leave thee, nor forsake thee." He also gives His promise, "Lo, I am with you alway, even unto the end of the world."

David has assurance. This is expressed to us in Psalm 23: "The Lord is my shepherd; I shall not want."

3. *There must be purpose.* The purpose must not be selfish. Selfishness will always keep away a dynamic faith. Perhaps we can put the matter in a little different way. Why have a dynamic faith?

That He might be exalted. We should desire to honor Him always.

That His work might be done. We have a task, and we must do His bidding.

That others might be blessed. Faith is catching! My strong faith in God will help others. Yes, and my faith is increased by the faith of others. I have observed that when parents are of a doubting mind, the children usually have the same outlook toward life.

That souls might be won to Christ. We must have faith to press on in the winning of souls. Sometimes we are tempted to think that one cannot be saved, but this is not in our hands. Our part is to believe God, have faith to pray and work and witness until the lost soul comes to Christ.

"They that sow in tears shall reap in joy.

"He that goeth forth and weepeth, bearing precious seed, shall doubtless come again with rejoicing, bringing his sheaves with him."—Ps. 126:5,6.

God grant that we shall continue in faith to pray for others. Perhaps a thousand doubts have entered your mind. You have been tempted to give up your prayer life and your intercession for others. I lay upon your hearts—pray earnestly, fervently, believingly. Make sure that in all of your praying you are looking toward the Saviour and that your faith is firmly fixed in Him.

A few hours ago I was reading the story of Dr. John R. Gough. While a guest in a home, he was asked by a mother to talk with her boy. Upstairs in his room the great reformer found a miserable, degraded piece of humanity. "Edward," said he, "do you sometimes regret terribly the life you are leading?"

"Indeed I do, Mr. Gough."

"Then why do you not abandon it?"

"I cannot," came the answer. "I am bound hand and foot, and I will have to go on this way until I die."

"Edward, do you ever pray?"

"No, I do not believe in God. I do not believe in anything."

"Edward, do you believe in your mother?"

"Yes, Mr. Gough, she is the only thing in the world that I do believe in."

"Edward, do you think your mother loves you?"

"Oh, I am sure of it," said he.

Dr. Gough said, "Then you believe in love, don't you? You believe that there is at least one good thing in the world, and that is love, because your mother loves you?"

The poor, lost boy said, "Well, yes, I suppose I do believe in love."

Then Mr. Gough said, "Edward, when I have gone out, will you promise me that you will kneel down and offer a prayer to love, and ask love to help you?"

The boy hesitated, but promised. After Mr. Gough had gone, feeling as he said afterward, like a fool, he prayed, "O Love," and instantly there came a voice to his soul saying, "God is love." Then he cried, "O God!" There came back to him a verse which his mother had taught him, "For God so loved the world, that he gave his only begotten Son, that whosoever believeth in him should not perish, but have everlasting life."

Then the boy shouted, "O Lord Jesus Christ!" And the heavens opened, and into his life came a flood of forgiveness and joy. He received Christ as his Saviour at once and rushed down the stairs to tell his mother.

I beseech you to look to our Saviour, the One who gives life, peace and joy.

The world is full of doubts.

Satan will try to deceive you and filter every obnoxious thought that he can into your mind. But look to Christ! He will save. He will keep. He will satisfy.

God is looking, not for the man of ability but for the man of faith; the man who refuses to doubt; the man who believes that God is sufficient. He is looking for the man who believes not only God can, but is fully persuaded that God will.

—D. R. Shepson.

16. The Faith That Wins

*And he said unto them, Why are ye so fearful?
how is it that ye have not faith?*

—Mark 4:40.

*Jesus said unto him, If thou canst believe, all
things are possible to him that believeth.*

—Mark 9:23.

*And Jesus answering saith unto them, Have
faith in God.*

—Mark 11:22

Past eleven o'clock two telephone calls came to me from distant points—one from the North, the other from the South. Both were from fine young men, young preachers of the Gospel, but were having battles. They were not so much battles with self but a lack of faith in God. Certain problems had filled them with doubts regarding what they should do. I was happy to talk with them and urge them to look to the Lord for help.

That kind of advice sounds very general, but actually it is the best that we can give. Our victories all come from Him.

We live in a world full of trouble. And because of lack of faith, men worry. Worrying is sin. Worry has killed many a man, but it has never made a man great.

Regarding troubles, someone has given a good outline:

Your own troubles always seem the greatest. No tale of woe is quite as sad as yours. But trouble is not peculiar to any class, calling or profession. Plato said that if we could examine the heart of a king, we would find it full of scars and black wounds.

Many carry great burdens, yet keep cool. There is a world of meaning in Emerson's phrase, "Energy is repose." The Duke of Wellington, the military leader who defeated Napoleon, gave his commands in a tone which bordered on a whisper.

Eliminate those things which are useless to worry about. No man ever gave way beneath the burdens of today. There are two unlucky days—yesterday and tomorrow. Jesus said, "Sufficient unto the day is the evil thereof."

Your gravest trouble is always the present trouble, and your present trouble will remain until a new one arrives. Those big troubles today will be little troubles tomorrow.

There are first-class and second-class troubles. If you are going to have worries, let them be big, large, decent, respectable, aristocratic worries.

Now I am concerned to give a word about "The Faith That Wins." It is apparent from Scripture that faith is an important subject. Jesus honored faith and gave His blessing to those who had it.

I. THE DIRECTION OF FAITH

In Mark 9 is the story of the transfiguration scene. After the miraculous appearing of Elijah and Moses and their conversation with Jesus, Christ comes down off the mount with Peter, James and John. When He arrives in the valley, He sees a great multitude. One out of that multitude comes rushing up to the Lord saying, 'I brought my son, which has a dumb spirit, to Thee. First, I brought him to Your disciples that they should cast him out, and they could not.' Jesus answered him, "O faithless generation, how long shall I be with you? how long shall I suffer you? bring him unto me."

The poor boy with the dumb spirit was brought before Christ. This evil spirit caused him to behave in a lamentable fashion. He fell upon the ground and wallowed foaming. Jesus asked the father, "How long is it ago since this came unto him?" The father replied, "Of a child." Then he made his strong appeal to the Saviour: ". . .if thou canst do any thing, have compassion on us, and help us." Jesus said to him, "If thou canst believe, all things are possible to him that believeth." And straightway the father cried out, "Lord, I believe; help thou mine unbelief." Jesus then commanded the deaf and dumb spirit to come out of the boy. The lad was as one dead. But Jesus took him by the hand, lifted him up and restored him to his father.

Now please give attention to this point—the direction of faith. The disciples had failed. The man then came to Christ and the boy was healed. The lesson is this: It pays to look to the One with the power. We had as well save time and energy by first looking to that One.

This world is absolutely powerless. Men fail; circumstances change, yet God is ever the same. Therefore, let us put our faith in Him.

The world, the flesh and the Devil will try to turn you away from that simple faith; but don't be turned. Look to Christ.

There are many, many reasons why we should look to the Saviour; but I suggest three here.

1. *Have faith in One who never fails.* If I go to a person of the world with my problem, I am always conscious of his weakness. Not so when I come to Christ. He has all power to help me.

Yes, the world will try to destroy our faith. It is ever ready to laugh at those who exercise faith in God.

I was reading an interesting story about a knight who kindled a light at the holy sepulchre in Jerusalem and determined to carry it back home without ever allowing it to go out. The story points out the many experiences he had in trying to carry the sacred flame back with him. The entire story revolved around the fact that by so doing, the man was changed.

I believe there is something more to this story. Surely the knight must have found out how much wind there was in the world, all bent on blowing his flame out.

It is high time we recognize that the world will try to destroy our faith, try to cloud our minds, try to hinder our vision; but we must look upward toward our Saviour, remembering that He never fails.

2. *He knows your need.* The Bible tells us that the very hairs of our heads are all numbered. Our Saviour is keenly conscious of

our every need. In the Sermon on the Mount He tells us, "Take therefore no thought for the morrow: for the morrow shall take thought for the things of itself." He promises by His own word that He will supply our needs.

In the great portion on prayer found in Matthew 7:7-11 we find this thought carried out:

"Ask, and it shall be given you; seek, and ye shall find; knock, and it shall be opened unto you:

"For every one that asketh receiveth; and he that seeketh findeth; and to him that knocketh it shall be opened.

"Or what man is there of you, whom if his son ask bread, will he give him a stone?

"Or if he ask a fish, will he give him a serpent?

"If ye then, being evil, know how to give good gifts unto your children, how much more shall your Father which is in heaven give good things to them that ask him?"

He knows your needs, and He will supply as you make them known to Him. Therefore, direct your faith heavenward and pray in faith believing.

3. *He welcomes you.* We have already indicated this, but I emphasize it again. Some people have the attitude that we should not bother God about minor matters. Such people need to read their Bibles. All that concerns us, concerns His great, eternal heart. These words of our Saviour given in Matthew 11:28-30 are not empty words:

"Come unto me, all ye that labour and are heavy laden, and I will give you rest.

"Take my yoke upon you, and learn of me; for I am meek and lowly in heart: and ye shall find rest unto your souls.

"For my yoke is easy, and my burden is light."

II. THE DANGERS OF FAITH

Great faith brings great blessings. Little faith brings little blessings. Little faith closes the door to the blessings of God.

Most people confess their little faith; however, their confession is not as honest as the man in the Bible story before us. This poor man, desiring much for his son, cried out to Jesus. He had tears as he spoke. "Lord, I believe; help thou mine unbelief." There was no lightness in this man's cry. He was moved to the depth of his soul. In anguish of heart he cried out to the Saviour. This is the kind of faith that our Christ honors.

Three kinds of faith bring danger to us.

1. *Stunted faith.* Some people start out to grow in grace, obey the Lord, walk in His footsteps; then when some critic, some busybody, throws doubts into their minds; they cease to grow.

The person of stunted faith is ever miserable. He is a babe in Christ. He has not developed normally. He cannot take the meat of the Word but must feed on milk.

2. *Stymied faith.* A stymie on the golf course is when a ball is lying between your ball and the cup.

Sometimes faith gets stymied. Something gets between you and your accomplishment. You may begin your work with high and holy intention, then something gets between you and your objective.

Perhaps you started out to serve the Lord, then something came between you and the Saviour. His holy purpose for your life became hidden.

3. *Shattered faith.* Perhaps at one time your faith was wholesome, growing and increasing in power. Then came a happening that shattered that faith.

I have known people to have a shattered faith because of the death of a loved one. Thank God, it does not happen often. Usually people are strengthened in the going of a dear one. But occasionally I will find some man or woman who will express doubts in God simply because a dear one was taken by death.

Deception sometimes shatters faith. How often we are

deceived! How many times friendships are broken because of the deceptiveness of a friend.

Disappointments shatter faith. How careful we must be regarding the disappointments of life. Listen to this:

> **When faith in God goes,**
> **Man, the thinker, loses**
> **His greatest thought.**
>
> **When faith in God goes,**
> **Man, the worker, loses**
> **His greatest motive.**
>
> **When faith in God goes,**
> **Man, the sinner, loses**
> **His strongest help.**
>
> **When faith in God goes,**
> **Man, the sufferer, loses**
> **His securest refuge.**
>
> **When faith in God goes,**
> **Man, the lover, loses**
> **His fairest vision.**
>
> **When faith in God goes,**
> **Man, the mortal, loses**
> **His only hope.**

Whether your faith has been stunted, stymied or shattered, I lay upon your heart the great need of faith in God. Have a strong faith. Don't let your faith be like a tender plant easily bruised, but let it be like the mighty oak which stands in the midst of every storm.

> **Oh, for a faith that will not shrink**
> **though pressed by many a foe;**
> **That will not tremble on the brink**
> **of poverty or woe.**

"Have faith in God." Faith honors God, and God honors faith.

When we have a biblical faith, we can do all God would have us do. We can live for Christ. We can send the Gospel to the ends of the earth. We can accomplish mighty things for Him.

III. THE DYNAMIC OF FAITH

"Jesus said unto him, If thou canst believe, all things are possible to him that believeth."—Mark 9:23.

There are some things that we must keep before us.

1. *Faith is not always apparent.* A quiet person may not reveal his great faith, yet some crisis may bring out that hidden faith. We often find big people in hours of crises. And sometimes we find the so-called big people beside themselves when some trouble, some crisis, comes. It is not necessary to talk about our faith, but we need to live the life of faith.

2. *Faith comes from the upward look.* This means praying and seeking the face of God.

Daniel was a man of faith. There is something thrilling about seeing Daniel in his place of prayer. When his enemies were seeking to trap him, Daniel paid no attention to his opposition. Rather, he went home, opened the windows and prayed three times a day. There was nothing secretive about him. The enemies knew exactly where to find him.

This is surely an exciting scene. Here is a man who prayed. It was more than a religious habit—it was life itself. Daniel had to be true to God even if it meant death. So he prayed, faced the consequences, and trusted God.

That simple but beautiful story of Daniel illustrates one great thing to me: Take care of your faith and God will take care of you.

Again, Bible study, service, and especially worship are very important. An hour of worship will do more for the Christian than weeks of worry.

Alongside Daniel, I would ask you to think of Paul, that man of great faith. He was not afraid of man. He never lacked moral courage. Fearlessly, he testified before Felix. Courageously, he gave his testimony before the cynical King Agrippa. Paul feared not the crowds. Though they stoned him and left him unconscious, he went back into the city and continued his work. Where did Paul get this courage and strength? Here it is in Philippians

4:13 "I can do all things through Christ which strengtheneth me."

3. *Faith is always effective.* Faith will cheer you, and your faith will help others. Scores of fears can be vanquished by faith.

Many years ago the American philosopher, William James, said, "The sovereign remedy for fear is faith." This was given to us a long time ago in the Word of God.

The Christian does not have to look for some magic formula that will abolish fear. He simply need look to Christ. And believing Christ, he has the courage and power to move on without fear.

4. *Faith brings miracles.* Need I remind you again of the story given in Mark 9. The disciples failed. The father brought the son before Jesus. He exercised faith in the Son of God. It was not a complete faith, but he did the best he could. Jesus recognized this father's faith and healed his boy.

Faith will bring miracles to you, to others, and to the projects on your heart.

We need more people like the three Hebrew children who answered Nebuchadnezzar, "If it be so, our God whom we serve is able to deliver us from the burning fiery furnace, and he will deliver us out of thine hand, O king" (Dan. 3:17). They had no doubt about God's ability. They knew that He could deliver them from the burning fiery furnace; or if they were put into it, He could still deliver them, and did. We need that kind of faith that will keep us strong as we face any foes or problems.

The Latin American Mission has just released the story of the death of Ernest Fowler, age 58. Brother Fowler was a missionary under this mission. He was shot and killed on August 3 by a gang of seven bandits. Fowler was returning to his home when the heavily armed men intercepted him on the trail. They took away his rifle, then shot him twice through the head and once through the back after he had fallen.

Mr. Fowler was killed in the presence of his fourteen-year-old daughter. The bandits had stripped the house of all food and valuables and had locked up Mrs. Fowler and the children.

After the gunmen had left, the older boys recovered the

father's body from the trail and buried him thirty-six hours later in a shallow grave gouged out of the rocky surface of the mountainside. Then the boys hiked to the nearest neighbor, more than an hour away. Finally others came in to give help to the family. The Word says, ". . .be thou faithful unto death. . . ." This man was faithful. His family was faithful.

Now we close this message. If you are to have the faith that wins, you must repent of your sin of unbelief and believe in Christ and receive everlasting life. By your faith you must become a child of God so that you can bring Him your needs and exercise the faith that wins.

Leonard Ravenhill tells this story. For thirty years his father had spent every Sunday afternoon visiting in a hospital in Leeds, England. In the course of his hospital visitation, a sick man listened to his testimony, then jabbed back at him feelingly with, "I have prayed to God and He did not hear me. Why?"

Mr. Ravenhill answered him this way: "Suppose the king of our country came into this room right now, and I asked him for five pounds (about twenty dollars). Would the king give it to me? After all, I am a loyal subject of the crown."

The man thought for a moment, then replied, "I don't suppose he would."

"Well, then," Mr. Ravenhill continued, "suppose that after I had asked the king and had been refused, the Prince of Wales came into the room and asked him for a like amount. Would he get the money he asked for?"

"Oh, yes," answered the man. "But then he is the king's son."

"Exactly right," replied Mr. Ravenhill. "Relationship makes all the difference."

In order that you might have the faith that wins, you need to now exercise faith in Jesus Christ to save your eternal soul.

"He that believeth on the Son hath everlasting life: and he that believeth not the Son shall not see life; but the wrath of God abideth on him."—John 3:36.

17. How to Have Faith

(Fifth in the series on "How to Live")

So then faith cometh by hearing, and hearing by the word of God.

—Romans 10:17.

The Bible says there is only one way we can please God: "without faith it is impossible to please him: for he that cometh to God must believe that he is, and that he is a rewarder of them that diligently seek him" (Heb. 11:6).

No father would be pleased with a son who refused to trust and believe him. Just so with God.

To please God, we must have faith.

After being born again, we are to continue living by faith. The Apostle Paul said: "I am crucified with Christ: nevertheless I live; yet not I, but Christ liveth in me: and the life which I now live in the flesh I live by the faith of the Son of God, who loved me, and gave himself for me" (Gal. 2:20).

Our Christian walk is by faith. The apostle says, "For we walk by faith, not by sight." The battles of life are won by faith. In a word to young Timothy, Paul showed him how to ward off evil:

"But thou, O man of God, flee these things; and follow after righteousness, godliness, faith, love, patience, meekness.

"Fight the good fight of faith, lay hold on eternal life, whereunto thou art also called, and hast professed a good profession before many witnesses."—I Tim. 6:11,12.

The Christian overcomes the powers of the world and the Devil by faith in the Son of God. "For whatsoever is born of God overcometh the world: and this is the victory that overcometh the world, even our faith" (I John 5:4).

The Bible tells us that we will have battles to fight as we face the evils of the world. These can be overcome by faith.

Think of the many direct statements made regarding faith. We touch only a few of them.

"And Jesus answering saith unto them, Have faith in God."—Mark 11:22.

"And the apostles said unto the Lord, Increase our faith." —Luke 17:5.

"So then faith cometh by hearing, and hearing by the word of God." —Rom. 10:17.

"Now faith is the substance of things hoped for, the evidence of things not seen."—Heb. 11:1.

After this verse, we find an entire chapter devoted to one great subject—"faith."

We are dealing in this message with a very practical subject: "How to Have Faith."

I. BELIEVE GOD FOR FAITH

We have already read Paul's climactic statement, "So then faith cometh by hearing, and hearing by the word of God."

A brief study of the Gospels will reveal many things regarding faith. For example, faith can be seen. It was said of our Lord, "And when he saw their faith, he said unto him, Man, thy sins are forgiven thee" (Luke 5:20). Jesus was able to detect the faith of the men who brought the paralytic to him. In the same way, I believe our faith can be seen by others.

It is indicated in Luke 22:32 that faith can fail. Jesus said of Simon, "But I have prayed for thee, that thy faith fail not: and when thou art converted, strengthen thy brethren."

It is apparent that many have a misplaced faith. Some place

their faith in people. When people fail, their faith suffers. We may put our faith in the best of friends and be disappointed.

Others may put their faith in surroundings—beautiful home, good business, delightful social life. When these things are taken away, then their faith is gone.

Still others may trust in wealth. Theirs is the religion of the dollar sign. When all is well financially, they are happy. But when money fails, their faith is gone.

Now, the advice of the Bible is to rest upon the Word for faith. This Bible never changes. Here we have God's holy, infallible Word. And the Spirit tells us ". . .faith cometh by hearing, and hearing by the word of God."

It is faith that gives us freshness, vitality and vigor. Christians who go on vigorously serving God, vivaciously alive, have faith in God; and that faith comes by resting upon the Word.

Faith kills worry. No man can worry and trust God at the same time. If man had faith in God, he could put out of business the present-day doctors who deal with worry. There would be no patients for the hospitals, the mental institutions.

Faith claims the promises of God. This Bible becomes a new Book when read with the eyes of faith. There are 32,000 promises in the Bible, enough for you and me. In faith, read your Bible believingly and claim every promise.

Faith counts on the presence of God. Depend upon that promise. "I will never leave thee, nor forsake thee." You may leave Him, but He will not leave you. You may depart from the place of blessing, but God will be true to His promise.

BELIEVE GOD!

Believe the great prayer promises: "If ye abide in me, and my words abide in you, ye shall ask what ye will, and it shall be done unto you" (John 15:7).

Believe the promises that He will be with us when we launch out into His service: ". . .lo, I am with you alway, even unto the end of the world. Amen."

Believe that God will supply every need: "But my God shall supply all your need according to his riches in glory by Christ Jesus" (Phil. 4:19).

II. PRAY FOR FAITH

"And the apostles said unto the Lord, Increase our faith."—
Luke 17:5.

To these disciples the Lord said, "If ye had faith as a grain of mustard seed, ye might say unto this sycamine tree, Be thou plucked up by the root, and be thou planted in the sea; and it should obey you" (Luke 17:6).

James tells us, ". . .yet ye have not, because ye ask not," We recognize our need of faith; now let us come and pray with courage for what we need.

Prayer will increase our faith. Praying is an act of faith; and when we pray, God answers and gives the faith we need.

The Lord Jesus Christ had a perfect faith. He was the perfect man. His faith was entire and complete. He was God incarnate in human flesh.

Many Christians have baby faith. Such a faith was demonstrated by John Mark when he turned back from the missionary tour. The Bible simply says, ". . .and John departing from them returned to Jerusalem." However, at a later time, we find Paul and Barnabas in quite a discussion about John Mark. Disappointed that this man had such small faith, Paul did not want him to go with them. He had turned back on the first journey.

It is apparent that the Christians in Corinth had little faith. Paul called them, "babes in Christ." They were not exercising faith, not performing the duties given them. Hence, Paul classified them as babies.

We need mature faith—such a faith as the great servants in days gone by had. In Hebrews 11, we read of the faith of Abel, Enoch, Noah, Abraham, Isaac, Jacob, Joseph, Moses, and Joshua—early men of God who believed the Lord and had a mature faith.

The Apostle Paul also had a mature faith. His faith sustained him in dark hours, strengthened him in his weakness, stabilized him when others failed. That is the faith we need. Then we can stand alone, can fight our battles and win.

On the last page of a missionary magazine, I saw this word:

Was this world ever darker than today? The darkest days of sacred history had those who were all alone or shall we say, "only one." God has singularly used an only one through the ages.

Only one Noah—in a whole lost world.

Only one Abraham—ninety-nine years old when God "called alone."

Only one Moses—born in a heathen land.

Only one Joshua—his human leader dead.

Only one Naomi—a widow destitute.

Only one Ruth—a very young widow forsaking all the old life.

Only one Esther—alone, though encircled in wealth.

Only one Daniel—in a heathen court, but God honored his daring testimony.

Only one Elijah—swept into Heaven in a flaming chariot.

Only one widow—to be honored with the privilege of feeding Elijah.

Only one Stephen—to see Jesus standing at the right hand of the Father.

Only one Philip—to leave the big revival and go to the Ethiopian eunuch.

Ony one Paul—who fought a good fight—kept the faith—ready to be offered up.

Only one John—to witness and write of the revelation and to cry, "Even so, come, Lord Jesus."

Of everything that might be said about the names mentioned, they had one thing—faith in God.

III. USE YOUR FAITH

Jesus instructed His disciples, "Launch out into the deep, and let down your nets for a draught." Simon answered, saying, "Master, we have toiled all the night, and have taken nothing: nevertheless at thy word I will let down the net." Sense the very unbelief of Simon Peter. He felt they had done their best; now the Lord told them to go fishing again!

We need that word: "Launch out into the deep." We need the courage of a Joshua and a Caleb as they gave their report to the unbelieving Israelites. We need the courage to believe the Lord is with us and we need not fear.

To Joshua the Lord said, "Be strong and of a good courage; be not afraid, neither be thou dismayed: for the Lord thy God is with thee whithersoever thou goest" (1:9). I am glad for a verse like this. Since the Lord promised this to Joshua, He promises the same thing to us. "I am the Lord, I change not."

Use your faith or it disappears.

Use your faith for guidance in dark hours. Pray and believe. Ask for God's guidance and don't be afraid to follow when He points the way.

Use your faith for peace of heart. In troubled hours, rest upon God by faith. Peace will come. Believe Him.

It is faith that gives endurance! Many Christians would give it all up if it were not for the faith that keeps them enduring hardships.

I was reading the story of Josiah Elliott, the country preacher who continued to pray one prayer, "Lord, let me have one. Don't keep me a country preacher all of my life. Let me have one city church."

But God kept him in the country! One by one boys came out of his churches and went to college, to the seminary, and then out to preach the Gospel. One of the boys that he had led to Christ led George W. Truett to Christ!

I was reading about the family of Dr. John Scudder who was practicing medicine here in America. A child patient could not live through the night. The big-hearted doctor decided to stay with the family until the end came. Sitting beside the bed, he noticed on the wall of the room a large map of India, into which had been stuck white-headed pins indicating the location of every medical missionary. There was only one medical missionary for every 350,000 people.

In the days that followed, Dr. Scudder could not forget those white-headed pins. They even hindered his sleep. Finally, he and his wife went to India. Nine children were born. All became missionaries. So did their children. To date, the Scudder family has served more than one thousand missionary years. This is just another picture of faith giving endurance—believing God, trusting God, resting upon His promises.

Faith gives energy. The Lord will supply the energy we need for the work He wants us to do. Paul told the early Christians, "Be . . .fervent in spirit; serving the Lord." Fervency will surely come as we exercise our faith.

Faith gives vision—vision of a lost and dying world. Only by faith can we look at this dark and benighted world of today, with two-thirds still in Satan's power. The missionary work is decreasing, not increasing. If you get a vision of this lost world, God will send you out to do something. Put aside your personal feelings, forget your grudges, ignore the misunderstandings and launch out into the deep. Use your faith.

The work of our Saviour takes faith. It is this faith that God offers us. When we are saved by His grace, then we can reach out and lay hold upon faith. We are to read this Bible, believe and rest on its promises—and go forward.

I read the story of S. H. Hadley who was saved out of a life of drunkenness to become superintendent of the Water Street Mission of New York City. Hadley was a man of faith. At one o'clock on a certain morning, the last call came to his door. When Hadley opened the door, he saw before him an old man almost like a dwarf. His hair was matted. His beard was unkempt. His coat was fastened together at the top with a nail. He had no clothing under his coat. He had some old pieces of carpet wrapped around his feet. He leaned upon a mop stick. So wretched was that man that he could scarcely open his eyes.

He had been to the Water Street Mission three times before. Who was he? The law partner of one of the men who was in Abraham Lincoln's cabinet! Sin had brought him down.

Mr. Hadley looked at this poor wretch and said, "Colonel, you can't come in." The old colonel, leaning upon his mop stick, his poor old feet so sore that he could scarcely walk, went on down under the Brooklyn bridge.

Mr. Hadley went up to his bed but could not sleep. So at three o'clock in the morning, he went out after the man and found him lying huddled at the foot of one of the piers of the Brooklyn bridge.

Mr. Hadley was a lame man himself; but he stooped down, took the colonel in his arms, and fairly dragged him along the streets. He bathed him and put him into his own bed. The next morning he clothed him. When night came, with his arms around him, he led him to the altar. The old colonel dropped down on his knees and buried his face in his hands. He stained that famous altar with his tears as he cried, "God, be merciful to me, a sinner!"

Instantly as he rose up the chains were gone. He went back and was restored to his old position in his law practice.

One night he came into a meeting with his hair brushed from his brow, his eyes shining, his face bearing all the marks of refinement. What made the change? Jesus Christ. He had accepted the Son of God, and God remade his life.

He will do the same for you tonight, if you will simply by faith receive Jesus Christ as your own personal Saviour.

How are men saved? By faith. Jesus said, "He that believeth in me hath everlasting life."

A minister once dreamed that he had died and was standing before the judgment bar of God. He says that in his dream he heard God say to him, "Have you always been true?"

"No," he replied.

"Have you always been kind?"

"No."

"Have you always been just?"

"No."

And as he continued through the long list of questions, he had to answer, "No," to them all.

Then he said, "I thought the end had come and judgment was to be passed. I bowed my head and waited for a sentence. But I was conscious of a light before me. I looked up and saw a face, a face fairer than all the sons of men. I looked at the hands; and when I saw the marks, I knew who it was. Then I heard Him say,

'This man stood for me down in the world. I will stand for him here.' "

I am not trying to press every point of that simple story, but I am pressing this one: When you receive Jesus Christ as your Saviour, He will stand with you in this present life and throughout eternity. Come to Him now!

What is Faith?

Faith is the eye by which we look to Jesus. A dim-sighted eye is still an eye; a weeping eye is still an eye.

Faith is the hand with which we lay hold of Jesus. A trembling hand is still a hand. And he is a believer whose heart within him trembles when he touches the hem of the Saviour's garment, that he may be healed.

Faith is the tongue by which we taste how good the Lord is. A feverish tongue is, nevertheless, a tongue; and, even then, we may believe when we are without the smallest portion of comfort; for our faith is founded, not upon feeling, but upon the promises of God.

Faith is the foot by which we go to Jesus. A lame foot is still a foot. He who comes slowly, nevertheless comes.—George Mueller.

18. Faith on Their Faces

When Jesus saw their faith. . . .
—Mark 2:5.

Four men brought a paralyzed man to Jesus. The Saviour looked upon their faces and saw their faith. As far as the Gospel record tells us, they did not say a word. They did not present any letters of reference. They did not check with the housing authorities before tearing up the roof. They may have been ugly, dirty men. They may have been very poor men—poverty-stricken outcasts—I do not know. This one thing I do know—they had faith and Jesus saw it.

Four friends! Oh, the value of friends!

Someone has said:

> False friends are like vermin that abandon a sinking vessel or like swallows that depart at the approach of winter. True friends are like ivy that adheres to the tree in its decay. True friends are like the light of phosphorus: brightest in the dark.
>
> True friendship—gold cannot buy it. Poverty will not try it. Thrift may not cheapen it. Sorrow must deepen it. Joy cannot lose it. Malice cannot abuse it. Wit cannot choke it nor folly provoke it. Age can but strengthen it. Time only lengthens it. Death cannot sever friendship forever. Heaven is the true place of it. God is the grace of it.

Sam Davis, the Confederate spy, was executed at Pulaski, Tennessee. He was captured by the Union Army and found to possess some papers of great value to the Union. The officers knew it was impossible that he was responsible for his having those papers.

After he had been court-martialed, blindfolded and led before the firing squad, the officer in charge said, "If you will give us the name of the man who furnished you this information, you may go free." To this Sam Davis replied, "If I had a thousand lives, I would give them all before I would betray a friend."

The greatest of all friends is the Lord Jesus Christ. He is the Friend that sticketh closer than a brother.

It is said that when Count Zinzendorf was a boy, he would write little notes to the Saviour and throw them out of his window, hoping Christ would find them. Later in life, so strong was his faith in the friendship of Christ, that once when traveling he sent away his companion so he could converse more freely with the Lord with whom he spoke audibly.

How we need to cultivate the friendship of our Lord! We are to carry to Him every burden. We are to come before Him in confiding trustfulness.

> What a Friend we have in Jesus,
>   All our sins and griefs to bear!
> What a privilege to carry
>   Everything to God in prayer!
>
> Oh, what peace we often forfeit,
>   Oh, what needless pain we bear,
> All because we do not carry
>   Everything to God in prayer!

The paralytic had four friends. His condition was such that he needed four to carry him to Christ. He was helpless, but the four friends believed in the power of Jesus Christ.

Now look at these four. Please keep in mind this brief statement, "When Jesus saw their faith. . . ."

I. CONCERN FOR THE HELPLESS

These men were not content for their neighbor to lie sick and helpless when they knew that Christ could heal him. So they went after him!

I saw a beautiful picture of this recently in the action of one of our students of Tennessee Temple.

I was preaching in Williamson, West Virginia. Fred Merritt,

home visiting his father, brought him to the service. I felt impressed to speak to the father on Wednesday evening. He smiled and said, "I am not ready. When God is ready for me, I will go."

On Thursday night, he was back in the service. I could sense that God was speaking to him. During the invitation, I saw the son speak to his father. I felt impressed to go and say just a word.

Mr. Merritt, a man of sixty-two, came forward. He knelt at the front. His wife and son and daughter-in-law came and knelt also. I dealt with this man. The tears dropped from his eyes to the floor as he said, "Yes, I will now accept Jesus Christ as my Saviour."

After many had shaken hands with him, he came up on the platform with me and said, "I was so troubled after I left the service last night. This morning I rose early, went out to my garden, got on my knees and told the Lord I was ready."

He drove forty miles over mountains Thursday night and was wonderfully saved. I think what contributed most to his salvation was his son's concern.

We must have concern for the helpless. We must have the compassion of our Saviour. When He looked on the multitudes, He was "moved with compassion. . .because they fainted, and were scattered abroad, as sheep having no shepherd."

Christ's outstanding characteristic during His earthly ministry is encompassed in that word "compassion." Jesus cared for the crowds. He preached to them, fed them when they were hungry. He cared for the individual. What a mighty sermon He preached to Nicodemus! He cared for the sick and helpless, for the sorrowing. Even while on the cross, to a pleading soul He said, "To day shalt thou be with me in paradise."

This same concern and compassion should be ours. We must care.

II. UNITY OF PURPOSE

Imagine for a moment the four going to the home of the palsied man. Perhaps they were walking rapidly and saying among themselves, "Christ is nearby; we must get our friend to Him."

They arrive at the home of the sick man, their friend. They

begin talking all at once and with great enthusiasm. Standing around his bed, they are telling him about Jesus and what He can do. One gives one experience; another gives another. Their enthusiasm for Christ, their faith in Him convinces the palsied that he needs to be brought before Jesus.

The four gather around his bed, one on each corner, pick it up and start down the street. There is no argument about which way to go—they take the shortest route to Christ.

What mighty things can be done when God's people unite! The Great Commission can be obeyed at home and abroad when we join together. Singly we can do much, but together we can do more.

A united church can accomplish more for God's glory. Together we can win souls at home and abroad. We can erect buildings, reach the masses, challenge hearts of the multitudes. But, oh, the shame of a disorganized, disgruntled, critical church! I have talked to so many pastors who lament the fact that their churches are not united. They tell me of the many dull, dead services and how people find fault with all that is done. Thank God for a united church!

We need united homes, homes that stand together for God, homes united in their faith in Jesus and in their desire to serve the Master. How beautiful is a home where Christ is Master!

We need a united nation—I speak of our nation. Together we can do much; divided we fall. History records what happened to nations that were divided.

God is that one uniting force.

The *Wall Street Journal* had an interesting editorial telling about a recent graphics contest. The problem centered about typographic illustrations of "words we live with." The first prize went to a white rectangle with bold black letters stating: IN WE TRUST.

The point, explained by twenty-year-old Janet Horner, student at Pratt Institute of Art, is that people today put their trust in many things besides God. She said, "I felt my design would have greater impact with His name removed."

The downfall of our nation will come when we remove God

from our thinking. Our nation began with God and will continue just so long as we worship God and keep Him central in all we do.

A united person can do much. The Bible tells us, "A double minded man is unstable in all his ways" (James 1:8).

We must be united in our reception of Jesus Christ and in our acceptance of the Word of God. We can never achieve much unless there is a unity of heart and mind.

Now think again of these four men as they carried their sick friend unto Jesus Christ.

III. DETERMINATION

"And straightway many were gathered together, insomuch that there was no room to receive them, no, not so much as about the door: and he preached the word unto them."—Mark 2:2.

The four men came bearing their friend, but they could not get inside the house because of the crowd. But others seemed not to care. The four men looked at the crowds jamming the doors and windows—a hard situation, but they were not giving up.

Some people give up so easily. Some give up when the going gets hard. Others give up when the money runs out. Some give up when sickness comes. Many give up when family forsakes them.

But these four had determination. What did they do? Climbed up on the roof. The oriental houses were flat-roofed with outside stairways leading to the top. There the family could gather for a comfortable evening of rest in the cool breeze after the setting of the sun.

These men took the sick man to the roof, tore away a section and lowered him down into the very presence of our Lord.

How fortunate that the palsied man had such determined friends! How pathetic also would be our condition if we did not have determined ones about us—detemined regardless of difficulties.

One of God's great determined men was Paul who said, "I determined not to know anything among you, save Jesus Christ and him crucified." He also said, ". . .this one thing I do, forgetting those things which are behind, and reaching forth unto those things which are before, I press toward the mark for the prize of the high calling of God in Christ Jesus" (Phil. 3:13,14).

IV. FAITH IN CHRIST

As we look at these four, we see, first, a concern for the helpless; second, a unity of purpose; and third, determination. Then we see their faith in Christ. The Bible says, "When Jesus saw their faith. . . ." Jesus looked up and saw four heads through the hole from which the palsied had been lowered. They were looking straight into the face of Christ. Faith was written all over their faces. Trust was in their eyes. Every expression revealed confidence in Christ. Words were unnecessary. Faith spoke in eloquence.

Jesus knows every man's heart. He could see what was in their hearts, what they were saying: "Master, we know who you are. We believe in Your power, Your compassion, Your love. We know You can and believe You will heal this man."

Yes, Jesus saw their faith in their actions. They demonstrated their faith. They brought their friend to Christ.

Faith is not a strain. Faith is not wishful thinking. Faith is not laziness. Faith is believing God! Our God is ever touched by believing faith.

A man was giving testimony regarding his father who read the Bible morning and evening in family devotions. He said, "He started with Genesis and went through the Bible without a detour. Some pages presented words hard to read, but He read them just the same. To him, every word was inspired. Who was he to challenge God! So on he read!"

Thank God that we, too, can open the Bible, read, believe and live by the Book and be victorious through the Word of God!

Then the man said about his father: "I saw him in the presence of death. I heard him sing his favorite song:

> There's a land that is fairer than day,
> And by faith we can see it afar;
> For the Father waits over the way,
> To prepare us a dwelling place there.

"And during his last moments he could not speak but pointed to a motto on the wall that read, HE CARETH FOR YOU."

The four men brought a man to Christ. He was saved and he was healed. The sinner needs help. He does not come to Jesus by himself. Sinners do not accidentally run into Christ. It is the plan of God to use men to bring them to the Saviour.

I quote often the beautiful words about Andrew, written in John 1:42, "And he brought him to Jesus."

The sinner must be brought to Christ through love. There must be love for the worst of men. A picture of this is given in our Saviour's ministry. We must seek for the outcast, the drunkard, the thief—the vilest of man.

The self-righteous attitude is unChristlike.

I often think of the pastor who unburdened his heart to me about his church which had been so cold and unconcerned for sinners. Then on Sunday morning a lady came forward, knelt at the front and received Christ. When the pastor reported the good news to the audience, he noticed a coldness in their reception of this woman.

At the close of the service, one deacon came to him and said, "Pastor, that woman cannot belong to our church. She has a bad reputation. She is known throughout the city as a sinful person."

Despite the pastor's remarks and illustrations from the life of Christ, the deacon stuck to his conviction: the woman could not be baptized and become a member. Oh, such self-righteousness!

We must bring men to Christ through concern, through unity of purpose, determination and faith, not hindered by circumstances nor situations. We must rescue the perishing, care for the dying. We must go with hearts of love, find the sinner, arouse him, bring him in, overcome the obstacles, tear the roof off, and work with a holy recklessness. Men must be brought to the Saviour.

The four men brought their friend to Christ. They tore away the roof, lowered the man down before the Lord Jesus. "When Jesus saw their faith, he said unto the sick of the palsy, Son, thy sins be forgiven thee."

We bid you come to the Lord Jesus Christ today. He is ready now to save you. And we rejoice in this opportunity to present Him to your hearts.

Not Shortened!

The Lord's hand is not shortened, that it cannot save; neither his ear heavy, that it cannot hear.

—Isa. 59:1.

"Not shortened!" No! His hand is never shortened,—
  Although, at times, His coming shows delay;
Nor is His ear at any time e'er heavy,
  E'en if, to heed our cry, He strange doth stay.

"Not shortened!" No! His hand will ever save us;
  He nothing knows of problems or of task;
His powers remain forever all-availing
  To reach, and save, and lift,—when we may ask.

"Not shortened!" No! No! And so, if we are certain
  That naught on our part tends to keep Him back,—
That nothing grieves Him over which He waiteth,
  Then, sure indeed, we nothing good shall lack.

"Not shortened!" No! Yet—sometime He doth tarry;
  He sees, and knows,—and sure, His hand will save;
But He doth love our feeble faith to strengthen,—
  And we can honor Him by faith that's brave.

—J. Danson Smith

19. *Use Your Faith*

And Jesus said unto them, Because of your unbelief: for verily I say unto you, If ye have faith as a grain of mustard seed, ye shall say unto this mountain, Remove hence to yonder place; and it shall remove; and nothing shall be impossible unto you.

—Matthew 17:20.

And the apostles said unto the Lord, Increase our faith.

And the Lord said, If ye had faith as a grain of mustard seed, ye might say unto this sycamine tree, Be thou plucked up by the root, and be thou planted in the sea; and it should obey you.

—Luke 17:5,6.

He staggered not at the promise of God through unbelief; but was strong in faith, giving glory to God;

And being fully persuaded that, what he had promised, he was able also to perform.

—Romans 4:20,21.

Daily I see many examples of weak faith. Instead of singing, I hear complaining. Instead of praising God, many are blaming Him for their lot in life. Instead of fighting in faith, they are defeated in doubt.

Difficulties in faith are very common. They beset people at every age, in every circumstance of life. Some people live victoriously for a time, then fade away into a defeated life.

It is exceedingly hard to get people to see the simplicity of great Bible truths. For example, salvation is the gift of God. It comes to us when we simply believe in Jesus Christ. John tells us, "But as many as received him, to them gave he power to become the sons of God. . . ."

There are but two conditions to salvation. The one is repentance; the other is faith. They culminate in simple faith in Christ Jesus, and cannot be separated.

The Saviour said, "Verily, verily, I say unto you, He that believeth on me hath everlasting life."

It is also difficult to get people to see the simplicity of the Second Coming of Jesus Christ. It is the tendency of man to try to make everything hard. He is not satisfied to simply read the Bible and believe it! He wants to read into the plain statements of our Lord. Jesus said, "I will come again." And He tells us very plainly to "watch therefore: for ye know not what hour your Lord doth come."

It is also hard to get people to see the truth of separation as given in the Bible. Christians will say that they want to serve God, yet they do not want to separate from the world. Separation is a theme from the first chapter of Genesis to the last chapter of Revelation. God has ordained that we separate from the world. By separation from the world we are emptied of its evil and ready to receive the full power of God.

That, of course, brings us to consider the Spirit's filling. Here is a truth for everyone. We sometimes conduct ourselves as though the filling of the Holy Spirit is something that belongs to a select group of people, perhaps to missionaries or pastors or evangelists. But not so! Our Bible says very plainly that we all are to be "filled with the Spirit."

We read of what happened in the first century after Pentecost: ". . .and they were all filled with the Holy Ghost, and they spake the word of God with boldness" (Acts 4:31).

Now, I have given these illustrations of things that are hard to understand, that is, hard for the average Christian and hard for the man of the world. I give this to say that it is hard to get people to understand faith in God.

All people have some kind of faith, but too often it is weak faith, not working faith.

Consider the following:

I. PICTURES OF FAITH

Let us look back at one of the strongest, clearest pictures of faith ever given. My Bible is open to Hebrews 11. This is the chapter that repeats so many times the words, "By faith." God is calling the roll of his faithful people. He mentions in this chapter Abel, Enoch, Noah, Abraham, Isaac, Jacob, Joseph, Moses, and many others.

This is the Westminster Abbey of the Bible. Here we have the names of men and women strong in faith. The names are given not necessarily because they were prominent in the eyes of the world—some were very humble people—but because they were mighty in faith.

This picture gallery in Hebrews 11 is not restricted to a few, but is open to everyone who exercises faith in God.

The story of missions is a record of faith.

David Livingstone went to Africa because God called him. He went, not knowing whither he went, but leaving that entirely with God.

Adoniram Judson labored for years without a convert, but he did not lose faith in Him who could touch the hearts of men.

Robert Morrison was sustained by his faith. The captain of the *Trident,* the ship on which he sailed from New York City to China, knowing something of the impenetrable conservatism of the Chinese, said, "And so, Mr. Morrison, you really expect that you will make an impression upon the idolatry of the great Chinese empire?" "No, sir," returned Mr. Morrison severely, "I expect God will."

They tell us that Martin Luther, who built his work upon the statement, "The just shall live by faith," said this: "Faith is a living, busy, active, powerful thing. It is impossible for it not to do us good continually. It never asks whether good works are to be done, but has done them before it is time to ask the question; and it is always doing them."

As we view the lives of men and women of the past, we ask ourselves, *What kind of faith should we have?*

1. *We should have a strong faith.* On occasion, our Saviour had to say to His disciples, "O ye of little faith." He exhorted His followers to have a strong faith.

2. *We need a steady faith,* a faith that endures day by day, year by year, a faith that does not fail in trying situations of life, a faith that is not conquered by adversities, not spasmodic, but steady.

3. *We should have a singing faith.* When Cromwell lay dying and the good people who gathered about his bed felt or foresaw the troubles that lay in wait for them and for England, the great man lifted his powerful head and said, "Is there no one present who will praise the Lord?"

God grant that we might continue praising God day by day. Let your faith be a singing faith. Let the joy of the Lord fill your heart. You may be in the prison cell, as was the Apostle Paul, but you can still shout, "Rejoice in the Lord. . . ."

II. PROBLEMS OF FAITH

The disciples cried, "Lord, increase our faith."

The world says, "Faith is foolish." The world tells you to trust in only what you can see and believe in only what is evident. The world gives an approval to foolhardiness, but will laugh at faith.

The flesh says, "Faith is foolish." The flesh cries for food, shelter and plenty. The flesh is not concerned about promises. It wants realities.

The Devil says, "Faith is foolish." Satan would come to any one of you and chide, "What has your faith ever done for you?" The Devil emphasizes negative things, the tragic hours. He would try to make you see that your faith is a failure.

We need faith in God! As we have already said, Jesus reproved His disciples for their little faith. Perhaps some of us even now feel the correcting hand of our Lord as we think about our weak faith.

Yes, there are degrees of faith. There is one who has faith to believe in Jesus Christ to save his soul, but he has not learned to trust the Master in all other areas of life. He is satisfied to bear the name of Christ and to let it be known that he is a Christian, but he does not launch out into the deep, believing God.

Thank God, there is the faith of him who is always reaching out for more! He is ever longing for more light, more revelation, ever desiring to make more progress in his Christian life.

A little faith is better than none, but a growing faith is a necessity for the growing Christian.

When the disciples sought to heal the demoniac boy but could not for lack of faith, the Master looked lovingly and reprovingly upon them and exclaimed, "O faithless generation, how long shall I be with you?"

Christ was always pleased when He saw great faith and when He saw the desire for more faith. He was certainly gratified when the blind man cried, "Lord, I believe; help thou mine unbelief."

Now let us put down a few things about faith.

Unless your faith gives you courage in the dark hours, it needs revision. The dark hours will come to any one of us. Yea, dark hours will come to all of us sometime in life. But God has a purpose in these dark hours, and it is faith that gives us courage in such a time.

> God never would send you the darkness
> If He felt you could bear the light;
> But you would not cling to His guiding hand
> If the way were always bright;
> And you would not care to walk by faith
> Could you always walk by sight.

The darkness has a purpose. It makes us cling to the Lord. But I repeat, unless your faith gives you courage in the dark hours, it needs revision.

Unless your faith leads you to clean living, it needs revision. Faith in God should mean nearness, and nearness to God produces results.

Unless your faith leads you to happy giving, it is nothing. The longer I continue in the ministry, the more I am convinced that the manner in which a person gives to the work of the Saviour is an indication of the inner condition of his own heart.

Paul gave himself and all he had. He had this to say:

"But this I say, He which soweth sparingly shall reap also sparingly; and he which soweth bountifully shall reap also bountifully.

"Every man according as he purposeth in his heart, so let him give; not grudgingly, or of necessity: for God loveth a cheerful giver."—II Cor. 9:6,7.

Unless your faith leads to fruit bearing, it needs revision. Every child of God is to be a soul winner, and the faith that we have in Jesus Christ should send us out to win people to the Saviour.

III. POWER OF FAITH

Jesus said, ". . .have faith in God" (Mark 11:22). Faith in God makes victorious living a reality. "For whatsoever is born of God overcometh the world: and this is the victory that overcometh the world, even our faith" (I John 5:4).

Faith in God brings answers to prayer.

"Therefore I say unto you, What things soever ye desire, when ye pray, believe that ye receive them, and ye shall have them."— Mark 11:24.

"If ye abide in me, and my words abide in you, ye shall ask what ye will, and it shall be done unto you."—John 15:7.

Have faith in God to answer prayer. Meet the simple conditions as laid down in the Bible and rest upon His promises.

Since God is unchangeable, His promises are sure. None are outlawed by the lapse of time.

How often we look at one of God's promises doubtingly. We claim it very hesitantly. We get down on our knees half-believing the promise God has given. But God changes not, and He tells us that we are to pray about every need. Have faith in God to answer prayer.

Have faith in God to witness for Christ. Through faith in God, we witness for Him and not for ourselves. So often we tremble and fearfully give our witness when it should be given with courage.

We have touched upon three simple facts: First, pictures of faith; second, problems of faith; third, the power of faith. For our conclusion, let us consider what to do.

1. *Believe God, have faith in God.* J. Hudson Taylor paraphrased this divine command: "Reckon on God's faithfulness."

We need today as never before the shield of faith in order to quench all the fiery darts of the wicked.

Jesus said to Peter, "Satan hath desired to have you, that he may sift you as wheat: But I have prayed for thee, that thy faith fail not" (Luke 22:31,32). The Lord was primarily interested in maintaining Peter's faith. The Lord is looking for faith and praying that our faith shall not fail.

You remember the great story that I told you about Mr. Faraday who read a paper before one of the leading scientific societies of Great Britain. A vote of thanks was moved by the Prince of Wales; but when the chairman sought to deliver this vote of thanks, the scientist had slipped out to his prayer meeting.

A friend came to Mr. Faraday during his last illness and said, "What are your speculations now?" Faraday had a great answer. "Speculations?" he replied with a bit of holy swagger. "Speculations? I have no speculations. I have certainties. . . . 'I know whom I have believed, and am persuaded that he is able to keep that which I have committed unto him against that day.' "

This is the supreme knowledge. This is the best thing that we can have—faith in God.

2. *Give your faith a blood transfusion.* Bring it in touch with Him who died for you.

What I am trying to do in this simple message is to try to stir your faith and to get you to recognize the condition of your faith, and then to lay on your hearts the need to feed your faith. Read this Word and believe it, for "faith cometh by hearing, and hearing by the word of God."

There is an amazing little story given in *The Man Who Played*

God. A certain pianist, a deeply religious man, was touring Europe. One night he was invited to play before royalty; but enemies, in an effort to kill the king, threw a bomb into the room. Nobody was killed, but the explosion destroyed the hearing of the great musician. He became as deaf as the dead.

Broken in heart and hope, he had to give up his career. He came back to New York to take up his broken life, seemingly with nothing ahead but despair. But a friend came over one day and read from his Bible, "Are not five sparrows sold for two farthings, and not one of them is forgotten before God?"

"I do not believe that!" the pianist said bitterly. "I once did, but not anymore. How could a God of such tenderness take from me the one thing that I most loved?"

By and by this musician was induced to learn lip-reading. Soon he became very proficient. Little by little, he began amusing himself by standing at his window that overlooked Central Park and reading lips of those who passed by below.

One day he saw a frail, young chap come into the park with a beautiful young girl on his arm. It was evident that there was trouble. "We can never marry," he read from the lips of the young man. "The doctor tells me that I have tuberculosis. He says that I could be cured with the proper treatments and time. It would cost at least a thousand dollars, and that amount seems impossible for me." Then in desperation, the young man lifted his face toward Heaven and prayed.

The great musician's heart was touched. He went to his desk, wrote out a check for $1,000.00 and sent it down to the young couple with his congratulations. Their faces were so radiant that he felt some of their joy in his own heart. In fact, it brought such a thrill that he began lip-reading the prayers of desperate souls that came his way. More and more he forgot self. As he threw himself under others' burdens, his faith grew stronger and sweeter than ever before.

Use your faith. Get busy for God. This is the best exercise of faith one can have.

Oh, the tragedy of unused faith! Faith is the key to accomplishment. No one has ever done anything worthwhile without it.

Faith is the key to peace. "Peace I leave with you, my peace I give unto you," said Jesus. By faith we may receive it.

Faith is the key to inspiration. Faith inspires us to launch out and do greater things.

Very many years ago a man was sentenced to be hanged. On the scaffold he asked for a drink. The request was granted. His hands shook so violently that he could not bring the water to his lips. "Take time," said the king who sat by to see the end of the law. "You will not be hanged until you can drink it." Taking those words seriously, the doomed man dashed the cup, saying, "I will never drink! So by your word I can never hang." His life was spared.

I am saying to you—use your faith.

There may be some here whose faith is weak. You wonder what you can do to increase it. I have good news for you. Come to the Saviour! Take what He offers. With whatever faith you have, simply come to Him. Take His salvation. Take His presence for daily living. Take His power for accomplishing great things.

In a magazine I read a true story about a small girl who lived in the slums of London. One day, dressed in rags, the child wandered quite far from her home. She came to a splendid section of the great city. There she was intrigued by beautiful gardens surrounded by an iron fence. She looked lovingly at the profusion of blooms. Having saved a few pennies, she searched for a shop where she might purchase a few violets or a rose to give to her sick mother.

Presently she noticed a young lady moving about among the gorgeous flowers. In her innocency, the child asked the stranger if she might purchase a few. Untying a tattered corner of her ragged skirt, she drew out a few pennies.

"Come into my garden and we will talk it over," said the stately lady. The gate was unbarred, and the little one was shown through the lovely estate. "Choose the best you see for your mother," said the new-found friend. Soon the little urchin had a magnificent bouquet.

"Oh," said the child. "Would you be willing to give me all of these for just these few pennies?"

"No," the lady replied, "my father does not sell his flowers!"

"I'm sorry," said the child, disappointedly. "I thought you were going to let me buy them." The tears began to flow.

"But wait a minute, dear," said the gracious lady. "My father is a monarch of the realm. He does not sell his flowers; rather, he loves to give them away. Take these home to Mother and tell her they are a gift from the king!"

Wide-eyed with wonder, the child recognized that she had been walking in the royal gardens!

Jesus said, "And I give unto them eternal life; and they shall never perish, neither shall any man pluck them out of my hand" (John 10:28).

Triumph of Faith

During an earthquake that occurred a few years ago, the inhabitants of a small village were generally very much alarmed; but they were at the same time surprised at the calmness and apparent joy of an old lady whom they all knew. At length one of them, addressing the old lady, said: "Mother, are you not afraid?" "No," said the mother, "I rejoice to know that I have a God that can shake the world."—Charles Spurgeon.

20. *Fear and Faith*

And all the congregation lifted up their voice, and cried; and the people wept that night.

—Numbers 14:1.

And Jesus answering saith unto them, Have faith in God.

—Mark 11:22.

So then faith cometh by hearing, and hearing by the word of God.

—Romans 10:17.

Now faith is the substance of things hoped for, the evidence of things not seen.

—Hebrews 11:1.

For what is your life? It is even a vapour, that appeareth for a little time, and then vanisheth away.

—James 4:14.

Life is brief, uncertain. This we accept. But its acceptance must not dull our sensitiveness to the importance of living for the glory of God to the fullest.

Fear, the wrong kind of fear, renders us ineffective, weak and burdensome. Faith, the right kind of faith, gives us peace, purpose and power.

We have to face life. We cannot play "possum."

As a boy back in Kentucky we often would go hunting at night for possums. Sometimes when we would shake one out of a tree, he would wind himself into a ball, playing "possum." The dogs would bark; people would shout, and we would push him with our toe, but he still played "possum." But eventually he had to face life. So must we—courageously and forcefully.

In this message I will discuss fear and faith.

I. THE LIFE OF FEAR

The fear of God, the fear of doing wrong, has a controlling effect on us; and this is good. But I speak now of the wrong kind of fear.

Fear defeats. Fear brings illness, both mental and physical. The hospitals are crowded with the fearful. Doctors say that a high percentage of those patients hospitalized are there because of fear.

Fear destroys one's testimony. No man can speak winsomely of Christ when he is fearful. When he does not have faith in God, then his testimony is weak and meaningless.

Fear weakens the life. No man is at his best when fearful. Fear destroys happiness, shatters the nerves, weakens the mind. Fear defeats!

Fear dishonors God. Our God has promised to be with us always, every step we take, every breath we breathe. Listen to this wonderful promise given to Moses: "Be strong and of a good courage, fear not, nor be afraid of them: for the Lord thy God, he it is that doth go with thee; he will not fail thee, nor forsake thee" (Deut. 31:6).

Actually, fear is calling God a liar. Why? Because God promises to give us all things, to provide for our needs. This is written down in Philippians 4:19: "But my God shall supply all your need according to his riches in glory by Christ Jesus." He has promised to protect us. "I will never leave thee, nor forsake thee" (Heb. 13:5). We have the promise of His power. "But ye shall receive power, after that the Holy Ghost is come upon you: and ye shall be witnesses unto me. . . ."

Keep in mind that God cannot lie; therefore, when we fail to believe Him, we are dishonoring His name. Titus 1:2 says, "In hope of eternal life, which God, that cannot lie, promised before the world began."

Fear discourages others. I speak of your fear. Homes are discouraged by a fearful one. Businesses fail because one is afraid. Fear is contagious and quickly transmits itself from one to another.

Fear comes from looking in the wrong direction. Examine your fears. You will discover that they have arisen because of looking toward circumstances, not from looking to God. When your eyes are fixed upon Him, then you have courage. No wonder the Bible encourages us to look to God. This was a constant cry of David. This was also the word of the Apostle Paul. He emphasized looking toward God for everything. "Looking unto Jesus the author and finisher of our faith; who for the joy that was set before him endured the cross, despising the shame, and is set down at the right hand of the throne of God" (Heb. 12:2).

Fear comes from hearing the wrong things. The world uses evil and destructive words which never fail to do their destructive work. And if we listen to that which is evil, it is bound to affect our thinking. Soon we will find ourselves thinking and using their terminology.

Fear comes from doing the wrong things. When one engages in sin, the sinner knows the consequences of his wrongdoing; hence, fear comes. It shows in the face, in the eyes, in the actions, in the walk.

II. THE LIFE OF FEAR AND FAITH

We all admit that fear is wrong. We all confess that fear is a sin. Yet knowing this, we still live in fear—and in faith. One day we are believing and trusting; the next, doubting. One day we are looking to Him; the next, looking to man. One day we are rejoicing in His promises; the next, fearing that God has forsaken us. This type life is a mixture of success and failure. Because it is so common, we are tempted to feel it must be all right. But not so! Fear is wrong, and we must war against it.

The Israelites believed in God through all the turbulent days from Egypt to Canaan. They believed in God with a mixture of fear and faith. Their faith glorified Him; their fear shamed them.

Their faith made them victorious; their fears weakened them and made them cry-babies.

All of this is evidenced by Numbers 14. The spies brought back their report. Ten said, "We cannot take the land," but two, Joshua and Caleb, declared, "It can be done." These men had faith. They believed God. But the Israelites became so disturbed that they cried all night. They begged to be allowed to return to Egypt. Moses and Aaron fell on their faces before the assembly. Joshua and Caleb rent their clothes. But after all was said and done, because of fear the congregation wanted to stone Joshua and Caleb.

In their fear, the Israelites could not leave all in God's hands. Though He had been so good to them—providing all their needs, performing miracles in their behalf, giving them guidance by day and night—still they refused to believe in the power of God to work for them.

Oh, that we might look up and trust in God in our darkest hour!

There is a beautiful story told of an old man who passed a little fellow holding on for dear life to a ball of string stretching up into the air. When he asked, "My child, why are you still holding to that string? The kite is out of sight," the child answered, "I know it's there because I can feel the tug."

In the hour of doubt, in the moment of uncertainty, we can still know the presence of God for we can feel the tug of His hands of love upon our hearts.

III. THE LIFE OF FAITH

This is the life that God desires for you. This is the life that Jesus died on the cross to give you. This is the life that honors Him.

When Jesus walked among men, He looked for faith. We may look for prestige and power, for glamour and riches, but the Saviour looks for faith. I can prove this from the Word of God.

In Mark 2:1-12, four men brought a paralytic to Christ. They tore up the roof and lowered him down before Jesus. Jesus looked up into the faces of the four and "when Jesus saw their faith, he saith unto the sick of the palsy, Son, thy sins be forgiven thee."

In John 5, we have the story of the man at the pool of Bethesda who had an infirmity for thirty-eight years. No name is given him; but when Jesus spoke to him, He recognized that the man had faith and said, "Rise, take up thy bed, and walk."

In Luke 7:1-10, we have the healing of the centurion's servant. He was a man of faith and humility. Feeling unworthy for the Son of God to come beneath his roof, he sent messengers to ask Jesus to simply say the word and all would be well. Listen to verse 9: "When Jesus heard these things, he marvelled at him, and turned him about, and said unto the people that followed him, I say unto you, I have not found so great faith, no, not in Israel."

In Luke 8:43-48, we have the story of the healing of the woman who had been sick for twelve years. She came behind Jesus and touched the border of His garment. Jesus detected that somone had touched Him in faith. The woman came and fell down before Him. Then the Saviour said to her, "Daughter, be of good comfort: thy faith hath made thee whole; go in peace."

One of the most beautiful stories in the Bible is that given in Matthew 15:21-28. When the Syrophenician woman came before the Master and said, "My daughter is grievously vexed with a devil," Jesus gave no answer, and His disciples said, "Send her away. . ." But Jesus said, "I am not sent but unto the lost sheep of the house of Israel."

The woman came and worshiped him, saying, "Lord, help me." Jesus said, "'It is not meet to take the children's bread, and cast it to dogs." The woman answered, "Truth, Lord: yet the dogs eat of the crumbs which fall from their masters' table." After this Jesus stated, "O woman, great is thy faith: be it unto thee even as thou wilt."

Our Saviour searched, always, for faith; and when He found it, He honored the person who had that faith.

Believe God. Faith honors Him, and faith will bring to you that which is best.

Consider three things:

1. *Faith gives direction.* I mean day-by-day direction. There may be times when God will give His guidance for future days by revelation, but usually you will find direction for day-by-day living.

On the flyleaf of John Wesley's Bible were found these words: LIVE TODAY.

A good motto. Live each day under God's directive hand.

Faith gives direction—one day at a time and this is enough. In the old McGuffey's Reader is a story of the clock on the mantelpiece that had been running for a long time.

One day it began to think about how many times during the year ahead it would have to tick. It counted up the seconds— 31,536,000 seconds in a year. The old clock grew weary and said, "I can't do it," and stopped. When somebody came along and reminded the clock that it did not have to tick the 31,536,000 all at once but only one second at a time, it began to run again.

Think not of the future—believe God for today. Trust Him for the present.

2. *Faith makes for courage.* Our Heavenly Father wants His children to have courage. He commanded Joshua, "Be strong and of a good courage. . ."

Doubtless Joshua, like most of us, was trembling and afraid; but God said, "You can have courage! Move forward! Believe Me. I will see you through."

Courage does amazing things. I was reading this week about Glenn Cunningham. He was born on a Kansas farm and attended school in a one-room frame building. The building was heated by a big stove in the corner of the room, and Glenn and his brother were responsible for starting the fire each morning.

One morning they came early, as usual, to build the fire. This day they poured some kerosene in the stove to hurry the process. There were a few live embers from the day before, and an explosion occurred. Glenn turned and dashed for the door; but when he looked back, his brother was not with him.

They were both found at the door. Glenn had dragged his brother to that point before he had been overcome by smoke. His brother died a few days later, and Glenn's legs were badly burned. It was thought he would never walk again. Certainly no one dreamed he would grow up to be a record-breaking track star.

As little boys, Glenn and his brother had decided to break the world's record in running. Glenn's disappointment after the accident was tremendous. He stayed in bed for a long while, but eventually was able to lean on the plowshares and hobble across the fields following a mule.

At the age of eighteen he secured a position on the rear loading platform of a Kansas City packing house. He could not walk too well. He could run very little, but he could hobble in his own way at a very fast pace.

Glenn was still consumed with a passion and desire to be a great runner. He entered college in his early twenties. At twenty-five, though his legs were scarred from the accident years before and he could not walk too well, Glenn Cunningham broke the world's record for a mile run, with slightly over four minutes as his time. Two years later he broke his own record and established a new one. He had courage!

I say to you that faith makes for courage and enables us to move forward through the darkest hours.

3. *Faith changes lives.* A life of sin is changed by faith. What a wonderful story came to our ears at the Union Gospel Mission last Thursday evening. A fine young man and his wife came into the building. I met the man just before the service. He said, "Christmas night, 1961, I was saved in this Mission," pointing to the spot where he had accepted Jesus Christ.

During the service Brother Paul Rawdon asked for the men to give testimonies. This young man came to the front and stated, "I have never done this before, but I feel that I ought to tell what the Lord has done for me." That Christmas night, 1961, changed everything for him. When he received Christ as his Saviour his life was transformed.

I am speaking now of saving faith. I am speaking of that faith in Jesus Christ, the crucified Son of God. I am speaking of a personal faith in Christ who died for sinners. Do you have this faith? Are you resting in our Saviour?

Not only do we have salvation through faith in Christ, but we also have power for living. The course of life is changed when we exercise faith in God. Here is the way Isaiah says it: "But they that wait upon the Lord shall renew their strength; they shall mount up with wings as eagles; they shall run, and not be weary; and they shall walk, and not faint" (40:31).

This is the secret of victorious living from Isaiah. This is the secret repeated a thousand places in this blessed Book.

May I drive home to every lost sinner in this building: You need Jesus Christ! You need now to receive Him by simple faith. As a sinner, you are lost, undone; but Christ will receive you. Though your faith be small, even as a grain of mustard seed, look to Jesus. Receive Him as your Saviour.

Stumbling, faltering child of God, rest in Him. Wait upon the Lord. Fasten your eyes upon Him. Have faith in God!

The beginning of anxiety is the end of faith, and the beginning of true faith is the end of anxiety.—George Mueller.

21. A Picture of Faith

And Jesus answering saith unto them, Have faith in God.

—Mark 11:22.

And the apostles said unto the Lord, Increase our faith.

—Luke 17:5.

And the saying pleased the whole multitude: and they chose Stephen, a man full of faith and of the Holy Ghost. . . .

—Acts 6:5.

So then faith cometh by hearing, and hearing by the word of God.

—Romans 10:17.

Fight the good fight of faith. . . .

—I Timothy 6:12.

Flee also youthful lusts: but follow righteousness, faith, charity, peace, with them that call on the Lord out of a pure heart.

—II Timothy 2:22.

Now faith is the substance of things hoped for, the evidence of things not seen.

—Hebrews 11:1.

But without faith it is impossible to please him. . . .

—Hebrews 11:6.

. . .earnestly contend for the faith which was once delivered unto the saints.

—Jude 3.

It is good to be able to make a statement that no one can contest. Here is one: **All great Christians, both men and women, have great faith in God.** This can be proved true by the past; it can be proved true by the present.

The Bible gives us stories of men of faith, lengthy accounts of those whose faith in God wrought miracles. The record of the centuries since the first is star-studded with men of faith.

We talk of the faith of George Mueller, who fed thousands of children year after year, not making a single public appeal for money. David Livingstone, Charles Haddon Spurgeon, David Brainerd, and thousands of others further illumine the pages of history with their strong faith.

The same is true today. Nothing is done by doubters and unbelieving people, but much is done by men with faith in God.

The concordance says, **"Faith is a dependence on the veracity of another."** As we discuss the matter of faith, we are talking about having faith in God.

I. A PICTURE OF FAITH

Turn in your Bibles to Acts 6. Here is the record of the naming of the first deacons, and in the company was a man called Stephen. The Bible says he was "a man full of faith." Two chapters are devoted to his story.

1. *Stephen had faith in Christ for salvation.* There was a time—I do not know just when—when Stephen saw himself a sinner and Christ as his only hope. He turned and believed in the Lord and became a child of God.

The life of faith must ever begin at this point. There is no Bible faith aside from the Lord Jesus. We must know Him as Saviour. Then because of our relationship to the Lord, we have the right to exercise faith in God. Christ must be as real to you as a parent or as your child.

2. *Stephen had faith in God's leadership.* A quick reading of Acts 7 will certainly substantiate this statement. Stephen stood before the council and gave an address on the unbelief of Israel. Throughout this entire address he talked about God—what God had done and wanted to do for His people.

The chapter tells us of Stephen's faith in the Word of God. He knew the story of Israel and how God dealt with that nation. With faith he repeated the whole account. You have only to read through this chapter to see the many times Stephen mentioned God. He spoke of the voice of God, the words of God.

Stephen believed in the wisdom of God. There was no doubt in his mind regarding the work that God had done. Occasionally we hear people manifest doubt in God and His actions, express wonder that certain things have taken place. How foolish! We can have complete faith in the wisdom of God.

3. *Notice Stephen's faith in the will of God for his life.* The end of the story is not a very beautiful one, but it does show this young man's faith in God and his belief that all was well because God was with him.

4. *Notice his faith in a time of disappointment.* We all, sooner or later, experience times of great disappointment. It may be disappointment in the circumstances surrounding our life. At this time it is for us to exercise complete faith in God. Others may fail you, but God—never.

They tell us that in eastern Alberta, Canada, they at one time had a very hard year. The crops failed. The people were in a state of sore depression. On Thanksgiving Day, the pastor of one of the churches met with his people in the home of one of the tillers of the soil. They sang songs of praise and testimony.

Then one from the group stood up to give his testimony. He was no longer young. He had worked long on his farm. His face was weather-beaten and tanned. He was clad in overalls and a coat—all that remained of his Sunday best. He knew the meaning of poverty and of crop failure. This man said:

> Although the fig tree shall not blossom, neither shall fruit be in the vines; the labour of the olive shall fail, and the fields shall yield no meat; the flock shall be cut off from the fold, and there shall be no herd in the stalls: Yet will I rejoice in the Lord, I will joy in the God of my salvation.

He quoted Habakkuk 3, verses 17 and 18.

5. *Notice Stephen's faith in his last hours.* Dr. W. H. Griffith-Thomas said that four words summed up the final scene:

> *Madness.* Those who had heard the words of Stephen were angered: ". . .they were cut to the heart, and they gnashed on him with their teeth."
> *Manliness.* Through the fullness of the Holy Spirit, Stephen looked up into the presence of God.
> *Murder.* Nothing could stop the enemies, and they illegally put him to death by stoning. They accomplished their primary object in getting rid of Stephen, but they did not end the Christian religion as they hoped.
> *Martyrdom.* Confidently Stephen prayed to his Lord, and he fell asleep praying, "Lord, lay not this sin to their charge."

I have given you a picture of faith.

NOW, WHAT KIND OF FAITH DO I WANT? *I want a saving faith.* Thank God, this I have—faith in Jesus Christ to save, to keep, to satisfy.

I want a sustaining faith—a faith that believes God, a faith that does not doubt, a faith that keeps me strong when the world is against me.

Two parents lost a fine little boy by death. To their intimate friends, they sent a card printed in silver and containing these words:

> IN LOVING MEMORY OF LITTLE DONALD, LENT TO US FOR TWO YEARS, THE SUNSHINE OF OUR HOME; RECALLED BY THE FATHER AND NOW AT SCHOOL IN HEAVEN, WITH THE ANGELS AS HIS TEACHERS.

Such a hope is worth more than everything in the world.

I want a seeing faith, seeing the promises of God. I want to see the work of God. I want to see the truth of the coming of my blessed Lord.

Christ declared that He would come again, and this I believe. The angels confirmed that He would come again (Acts 1:9-11). The Gospel writers reaffirm His promised return. It is for me to look up and to wait His coming and be ready to be caught up into His presence.

II. A PATTERN OF FAITH

"Remember them which have the rule over you, who have spoken unto you the word of God: whose faith follow, considering the end of their conversation."—Heb. 13:7.

Let me emphasize that little part which says, ". . .whose faith follow. . . ."

Patterns of faith are given us in Hebrews 11. Here were men who enjoyed the presence of God. One man, Enoch, "walked with God." Do you feel at home in the presence of our Lord?

In Hebrews 11 we read of men who had the power of God. One such man was Moses. Through the power of God, he became the mighty leader of Israel. He turned away from the pleasures of sin to suffer affliction with the people of God. God worked through him.

This chapter talks of men who were used of God.

"And what shall I more say? for the time would fail me to tell of Gedeon, and of Barak, and of Samson, and of Jephthae; of David also, and Samuel, and of the prophets:

Who through faith subdued kingdoms, wrought righteousness, obtained promises, stopped the mouths of lions,

Quenched the violence of fire, escaped the edge of the sword, out of weakness were made strong, waxed valiant in fight, turned to flight the armies of the aliens."—Vss. 32-34.

Let me quote it again—". . .whose faith follow. . . ."

I want to follow the one who has succeeded in following his God. I want to follow the one who has proved that he is in touch with God, the one who has gained victories from God.

A few days ago a fellow took me aside to tell me how to do the work of Highland Park Baptist Church. I appreciate his interest, but I do not have much confidence in his recommendations!

Why? Because he himself is a failure. He has never accomplished a worthwhile thing for God.

But we can follow the faith of the men and women of old. The Bible gives their record. The God who blessed them will also bless us.

III. THE PRODUCTS OF FAITH

Jesus said, "Have faith in God." Let me ask of you a few questions.

1. *Does God answer prayer?* Jesus said, "If ye shall ask any thing in my name, I will do it." Yes, when I pray in faith believing, the answer comes. The failures are mine, not God's. Jesus said:

"For verily I say unto you, That whosoever shall say unto this mountain, Be thou removed, and be thou cast into the sea; and shall not doubt in his heart, but shall believe that those things which he saith shall come to pass; he shall have whatsoever he saith.

Therefore I say unto you, What things soever ye desire, when ye pray, believe that ye receive them, and ye shall have them."—Mark 11:23,24.

If I have a need and it is not supplied, it is my fault, not God's.

The story is told of the woman who was showing a massive piece of family silver. She apologized as she took it from the cabinet, saying, "It is dreadfully tarnished. I just cannot keep it bright unless I use it."

What is true of silver is true of faith. Faith must be used if it is to be bright. There must be daily exercise of faith to keep it shining.

2. *Does God give peace?* Yes, and we are exhorted to come and take it. Jesus said, "My peace I give unto you: not as the world giveth, give I unto you."

The Apostle Paul tells us that if we will pray regarding all of our needs, "the peace of God, which passeth all understanding, shall keep your hearts and minds through Christ Jesus."

This troubled world needs His peace. Daily we hear about the strife among the nations. Daily we read of the uprisings on the campuses of colleges and universities. Daily we hear about disturbances in churches and denominations. Man needs peace. This comes from repentance and belief in Jesus Christ.

3. *Does God give stability?* The answer is, "Yes!" We are exhorted to be steadfast. We are told how to live so as to produce a character that does not vary.

The writer of Hebrews gives us an admonition: "Looking unto Jesus the author and finisher of our faith." The secret for the steadfast life is looking to Christ. Steadfastness does not come by looking to the world, for the world is constantly changing. Steadfastness does not come from looking to organizations, for they live and die. But steadfastness will come by looking straight toward our Lord.

I remember so well my experience in learning to plow at the small farm near Louisville, Kentucky. I was instructed by my father to plow a certain field. He told me to start in the center and plow back and forth until the entire field had been broken up.

I found the center of the field quite easily, and I was sure there would be no problem in plowing a straight line from one side to the other. I began. As I plowed a few feet, I looked back to see what kind of a line I was making. It didn't take long to see I was plowing a crooked line.

My father showed me how to do it. He stepped off the center of the field, put the plow and horses at that side, walked to the other side of the field, stepped off the center, put up a tall pole, and put his red handkerchief on the top of it. He told me to plow the horses toward the pole and handkerchief.

I kept sight of that handkerchief, right between the two horses. When I arrived at the other side, I found the line was exactly straight.

The lesson is a very simple one: Keep your eyes upon the Lord Jesus; have faith in Him; go straight toward Him all of the time.

4. *Does God save souls?* Does God use us to win souls? If in faith I launch out into the deep to win people to Christ, He bless-

es. Every person, yes, every person, can win precious souls if he will give himself to the task.

Now, Christian friend, are you living like God expects you to live? Are you living a life of faith? Does your life present a picture of faith? Are you following a pattern of faith? Are you showing the products of faith?

God wants you to pray, to have peace of heart, to be stable in life, to win souls. This accomplishment will be reached when you fasten your attention on Him and go straight forward.

My lost friend, you need Jesus Christ! You cannot live a Christian life until you know Jesus. You need to be born again. You need to have a consciousness of a daily walk with Him.

Someone said:

> Faith is like the coupling which attaches the car to the engine. All the power and speed and momentum that belong to the locomotive now become transmitted to the car. The coupling is simply the medium of communicating to the car. The coupling is simply the medium of communicating that power. So faith joins the believer to Christ and makes him partaker of all that Christ has and is and does.

By faith lay hold on eternal life. By faith reach out and take Christ as your Saviour.

22. Faith—How to Get It

If ye have faith. . .nothing shall be impossible unto you.

—Matthew 17:20.

This message concerns everyone. Man fails without faith. Man stumbles without faith.

The aged need faith. A Christian man of years wrote me a beautiful note from a Chattanooga rest home. It was apparent that his hand was trembling. The words were shakily scrawled. This man, like all of us, needs faith.

In a few days Mrs. Talley will be one hundred years old! Mrs. Talley needs faith! It may not be the same kind of faith a girl of sixteen needs or a young mother of twenty-one needs, but it is faith nevertheless that is needed.

We are discussing Bible faith—a faith placed in the Lord God, a faith that does things!

I. HOW TO GET FAITH

There are no mysteries about this. The Word of God speaks very plainly on this matter: "So then faith cometh by hearing, and hearing by the word of God" (Rom. 10:17).

A few days ago I read a list of names given by an outstanding businessman. He stated, "These men strengthened my life." He told how he spent time thinking about these men, what they achieved, and what they meant to the world: Emerson, Paine, Edison, Darwin, Lincoln, Burbank, Napoleon, Ford and Carnegie.

This man stated that every night over a long period of years he held an imaginary council meeting with this group whom he called his "invisible counselors."

These men could not help me in my Christian life. I must have men who had faith in God.

Let us consider how to get faith.

1. *Read this Book*—the Bible, Perhaps I should say, "Hear this Book."

I will never forget when I spoke in Longview, Texas, and made some strong statements regarding Bible reading. I told the audience plainly that they would fail unless they practiced daily Bible reading.

After the message, a little lady came up to me. She was kindly in spirit. Her words were humble. She said, "Brother Roberson, I appreciate your sermon, but I cannot read. You stated that we *must* read the Bible. I wish I could, but I cannot."

I understood her problem. Remembering Romans 10:17, "So then faith cometh by hearing, and hearing by the word of God," I quickly said to this one, "Then you need to be in church every opportunity you have. You must listen carefully to every Sunday school teacher, to every preacher, to anyone who reads from the Word of God."

She said, "Oh, I do that. I never miss a service in the church. I love to come and hear the Word of God."

Yes, we must hear this Book! We must read and memorize the promises; we must live by them.

The world is filled with worried people. They are distressed about every minute problem, discouraged over their failures. Their lives are circumscribed by everyday affairs, not learning to have faith in God.

2. *Believe this Book.* Believe the verbally-inspired, God-given Bible from the first word of Genesis to the last word of Revelation. Paul wrote to young Timothy, "All Scripture is given by inspiration of God, and is profitable for doctrine, for reproof, for correction, for instruction in righteousness" (II Tim. 3:16).

Someone told of a professor who took the Bible, tore it into pieces, tossed it into a corner of the room and said to his class, "We are through with that!"

Oh, my dear professor, you are not through with it!
Man is never through with the Bible. This is God's Holy Word,
and you must face it one day. Jesus said, "Heaven and earth
shall pass away, but my words shall not pass away" (Matt.
24:35).

Dr. Len G. Broughton was at one time pastor of the Tabernacle Baptist Church in Atlanta, Georgia. He conducted a successful revival meeting in this church many years ago. Dr.
Broughton told the following story.

> When I was a medical student I could not accept the
> supernatural generation of Christ. I went to a doctor of
> divinity who reasoned with me and left me in greater
> perplexity than ever.
> My medical education finished, I went to the backwoods
> to begin my practice.
> One Sunday, a backwoods preacher of an old country
> meeting house knocked out more skepticism in one half-
> hour than I had got in three years.
> The preacher stated: "If there is anybody here troubled
> about the mystery of God becoming man, I want to take him
> back to the first chapter of Genesis and the first verse, 'In
> the beginning God'." He looked down into the audience very
> searchingly, and I felt he was looking directly at me.
> The preacher continued: "My brother, let me ask you
> this: Do you believe God was in the beginning—that is to
> say, before the beginning began, God was?"
> I said to myself, *Yes, I believe that.*
> Then he said, "If you believe that God was ahead of the
> beginning, you believe the only mysterious thing of this uni-
> verse."
> I said, *If I believe that, God knows I could believe
> anything else in the world.*
> I had gone to college and traveled through the mysteries
> of a theory of reproduction and the cell formation and had
> come to realize that I was just a common fool; that if God
> was in the beginning, that was the one supreme mystery of
> all mysteries of this mysterious universe of God.

3. *Use this Book against your doubts and fears.* Simply read
and believe it.

My heart goes out to the doubter. He places himself in a

foolish condition. His doubts do not indicate his wisdom but his foolishness.

This is God's Word. Let every word stand against your doubts and your fears.

Now, we briefly touched the first point of the message on how to get faith. First, read the Book; second, believe this Book; third, use this Book against your doubts and fears.

II. HOW TO DEVELOP OR HOW TO INCREASE FAITH

"And the apostles said unto the Lord, Increase our faith."—Luke 17:5.

He answered,

"If ye had faith as a grain of mustard seed, ye might say unto this sycamine tree, Be thou plucked up by the root, and be thou planted in the sea; and it should obey you."—Luke 17:6.

Now what was Jesus saying? Simply this: "Use your faith."

In Luke 5 we have the story of Jesus teaching the people from one of the ships at the side of the Sea of Galilee. The Scriptures tell us that when He left speaking, He said to Simon, "Launch out into the deep, and let down your nets for a draught."

You remember that Simon Peter told Him that they had been toiling all night and had taken nothing. But he said, "Lord, if you command us, we will let down the nets." They did so and enclosed such a great multitude of fishes that the net broke.

The part of the story that I want to emphasize is found in Luke 5:4 where Jesus said, "Launch out into the deep." Child of God, be wholehearted about what you are doing. Fear not to go all the way with Christ. Have implicit faith in His Book.

Let me point out how you can increase your faith.

1. *By obedience to His every command.* Does He command worship? Certainly. Then give your heart and life to worshiping God.

Does he command witnessing? Certainly. Jesus said, "Ye shall be witnesses unto me." Therefore, don't fail to witness.

Does He command tithing? Certainly. Then tithe faithfully, honestly.

Does He command the reading of the Word and prayer? Certainly. Then read the Bible and pray.

If there is the slightest doubt in your mind about what God will do, then simply try this and see. Worship faithfully. Tithe honestly. Witness daily. Faithfully read the Word of God. Fervently pray.

You may be saying there are times when you don't feel like doing these things. Then do them anyway! Obey His commands.

2. *By an appreciation of His love and presence.* The story is told about an atheist who was standing on the street corner blaspheming God. He finally cried out, "If there is a God in Heaven, I challenge Him to strike me dead in five minutes!" Breathless silence reigned as the seconds ticked off.

After the allotted time had gone by and nothing had happened, this sacrilegious scoffer cried out with a sneer, "You see, there is no God or by this time He would have struck me dead."

Just as he was about to leave, however, an elderly woman stepped up to him and asked, "Do you have any children?"

The man replied, "One son."

"If your son gave you a knife and said to kill him, would you do it?"

He quickly answered, "Of course not."

She said, "Well, why not?"

"Simply because I love him too much!"

Before she turned away the little lady exclaimed, "It's also because God loves you so much, even though you are an atheist, that He refuses to accept your foolish challenge. He wants to save you. He does not want you lost."

With these simple words, this dear woman gave utterance to one of the greatest truths found in the Bible—Romans 5:6-8:

"For when we were yet without strength, in due time Christ died for the ungodly.

"For scarcely for a righteous man will one die: yet peradventure for a good man some would even dare to die.

"But God commendeth his love toward us, in that, while we were yet sinners, Christ died for us."

I am saying to Christians: Come to a new appreciation of His love. Christ died for you that you might be saved. The Bible says, "For God so loved the world, that he gave his only begotten Son . . . . ." Let your faith increase as you meditate upon the love of God.

3. *By attempting the impossible.* Let me quickly give you a number of verses.

"But Jesus beheld them, and said unto them, With men this is impossible; but with God all things are possible."—Matt. 19:26.

"Jesus said unto him, If thou canst believe, all things are possible to him that believeth."—Mark 9:23.

"And he said, The things which are impossible with men are possible with God."—Luke 18:27.

Now think with me. What is the basis of faith? A right relationship to God. It means to know Christ as Saviour and to come before Him in humility for the blessings that you desire. Pride must be put away.

What is the instrument of faith? The Word of God with its untold wealth of precious and exceeding great promises.

What is the exercise of faith? Patience. A mark of a vital faith is that it endures.

We have seen some wonderful and mighty things accomplished here in our city. We have watched a small church grow into a large one.

By faith we established Tennessee Temple Schools. We have watched this school increase until it has become one of the greatest Christian schools in the world.

We saw the beginning of Camp Joy, beginning in such a meager way; but we have watched this work increase year by year. Why? Because of faith in God.

We could continue talking about the forty-three chapels, World Wide Faith Missions, Union Gospel Mission, and many other projects—all the result of faith.

In II Corinthians 5:7 we find a beautiful statement: "For we walk by faith, not by sight."

The Christian is to live by faith, but he is to walk by faith as well. Walking implies going forward, moving, making progress, going some place. It is my belief that your faith cannot be static; it must be moving and achieving. Therefore, we are not only to live by faith, but we are to walk by faith.

III. HOW TO USE YOUR FAITH

Allow me to give a simple answer to this third point.

1. *Use your faith to give you peace.* Peace is the promise of our Saviour, but peace will never be yours without the exercise of faith.

Years ago an old divine said:

> Faith may live in a storm, but it will not suffer a storm to live in it. As faith rises, so the blustering wind of discontented, troublesome thoughts goes down. In the same proportion that there is faith in the heart, there is peace also; they are joined together. ". . .In returning and rest shall ye be saved; in quietness and in confidence shall be your strength. . ." (Isa. 30:15).

A faith that does not doubt, a faith that believes, gives peace.

Many of us need to have the kind of faith the little girl had who became lost on a certain farm. The farmer who found her as she wandered in the fields said to her, "Do not cry. I will take you home."

The girl snuggled up to him and with a smile said, "I knew you would. I was waiting for you."

"Waiting for me? What made you think I was coming?" he asked.

"I was praying you would," she said.

"Praying? When I first heard you, you were saying, 'A, B, C, D, E, F, G.' What was that for?"

She looked up again and said, "Mister, I am just a little girl. I was praying all the letters of the alphabet and letting God put them together the way He wanted to. He knew I was lost. He knew how to put my prayer together so you would find me."

Sometimes we need such faith as that.

2. *Use your faith to help others.* They need faith in Jesus Christ for salvation. Let your faith send you out as a missionary, ambassador, soul winner, a witness to tell the story of Christ.

Witnessing requires faith! I do not need to say this to my people, for you have discovered this truth. No one will continue witnessing very long unless he has great faith in God. The discouragements, the rebuffs, the hard words—all will discourage a person unless he has faith.

Then use your strong faith to help other Christians. Many are saved but do not have faith enough in God to bring them to the place of victorious living.

What a beautiful story is told about a little eleven-year-old Indian girl by the name of Jenny Bitsy. Some years ago she was taken into the missionary hospital in New Mexico for treatment of rheumatic fever. This sweet child was very weak physically. A hymnbook and a Bible she cherished, and she carried these with her.

Jenny was a model patient. She was kind, obedient and almost too sweet for this evil world. Her health continued poor. It was noticed that her tremendously enlarged tonsils would have to be removed. Surgery in her case would be dangerous but absolutely necessary. Preparations were made.

Jenny said she was not at all afraid, for she loved the Lord Jesus and trusted Him.

A strange thing happened when she was on the operating table. Although she was under ether, she unexpectedly spoke just six words, **Dear Jesus, take care of me!**

The missionary pastor said, "Those were the last words ever spoken by Jenny. The operation was completed, but shortly afterward Jenny stopped breathing. Jesus took her Home."

The testimony of the little girl who said, *Dear Jesus, take care of me,* was used to strengthen other Christians.

Every child of God needs strong faith. The story given to us in Matthew 17 illustrates this. Jesus came down from the Mount of Transfiguration. A man brought to Him his son. He called upon Jesus to have mercy upon his boy. The man said, "I brought him to thy disciples, and they could not cure him." To the disciples Jesus said, "O faithless and perverse generation, how long shall I be with you?" Jesus rebuked the devil, and the child was cured from that very hour.

The disciples came to Jesus asking, "Why could we not cast him out?" And Jesus said unto them, "Because of your unbelief: for verily I say unto you, If ye have faith as a grain of mustard seed, ye shall say unto this mountain, Remove hence to yonder place; and it shall remove; and nothing shall be impossible unto you" (Matt. 17:20).

3. *Use your faith to glorify God.* We face the danger of the self life. It is easy to seek for faith, then dissipate that faith in a selfish way. Seek to glorify God in every act of your life. Work in faith. Pray in faith, giving God all the glory.

We have discussed how to get faith, how to develop faith, and how to use your faith. May God grant that each of you will live by faith, work by faith, walk by faith.

Perhaps some of you have not accepted Jesus Christ as Saviour. Your first step is to repent, believe and receive Him.

An evangelist was holding special meetings for boys and girls. A little girl named Helen accepted Jesus Christ as her Saviour. When the meeting was over, she rushed home and ran into her father's study, threw her arms around his neck and said, "Daddy, I am a Christian!"

The father said, "Helen, I am glad to hear that. When did you become a Christian?"

"This afternoon."

He asked her to tell what had happened.

"Daddy, the evangelist said that Jesus Christ was there in the room and that if we would receive Him, He would come in and live in our lives and make us His own."

The father said, "Well, go on. Tell me what else happened."

"Why," she said, "I received Him as my Saviour and Jesus took me in."

"Well, Helen," he said, "that is all very interesting; but how do you know that when you received Jesus as your Saviour, He took you in?"

The father said he would never forget the look on her face as she said, "Why, Daddy, because He said He would!"

Yes, we believe our Saviour. He died upon the cross that we might be saved, and this salvation is ours through simple faith in Him.

Faith is the grasping of Almighty power,
  The hand of man laid on the hand of God.
The grand and blessed hour
  In which the things impossible to me
Become the possible, O Lord, through Thee.

23. Living Out Your Faith on Your Job

When Peter, Andrew, James and John were saved, they were soon called to leave all and follow Christ. When Saul of Tarsus was saved, he, too, was called of God for full-time service. He left the old life and joined the cause of Christ and went on.

Please understand: Full-time service is not easy! Many discouragements and defeats await you. Satanic influences will work to nullify the ministry of the preacher or missionary.

But for this message I am not dealing with the full-time Christian worker. I am talking today about you Christians who go on with your work, whatever it may be, and live out your faith before others. The title tells the story: "Living Out Your Faith on the Job."

When many young people get saved, they must continue their work in school. They must live and walk with others. It is not easy—we confess this: the world is never friendly to the Christian.

When I got saved, I expected so many things. Salvation brought joy to my heart, and I expected others to share that joy. But I soon found that some ignored my salvation experience altogether. It seemed unworthy of notice or mention. This I found annoying for a while.

You young people in this service should bear in mind that

others may not rejoice in your salvation. You may get saved in the Highland Park Baptist Church and return home to find that your family may ignore your experience. Your friends may say nothing about it. Some made slighting and critical remarks about my stand for Christ. This will happen to many of you. People will ridicule and some will scoff. But some were happy when I got saved. How blessed that there are always some dear Christians who are glad when others come to the Saviour. That is the reason I make so much of the invitation and the moments following.

Now I want us to deal with this subject: "Living Out Your Faith on the Job." There are some suggestions I want to give you.

I. CLEARLY IDENTIFY YOURSELF

Make sure that you are fully aware of all that you have in Jesus Christ. Be able to say with the Apostle Paul, "For the which cause I also suffer these things: nevertheless I am not ashamed: for I know whom I have believed, and am persuaded that he is able to keep that which I have committed unto him against that day" (II Tim. 1:12).

Before you can identify yourself with others, you must first be identified in your own mind and heart. If you know that you are a child of God, then let others know that you have been saved, that you are now a member of God's family.

1. *Confess happily to your new life.* Regardless of what others may say or think, confess your faith. It is important to tell others of your salvation. Listen to these words coming from Matthew 10:32,33:

"Whosoever therefore shall confess me before men, him will I confess also before my Father which is in heaven.

"But whosoever shall deny me before men, him will I also deny before my Father which is in heaven."

Tell people that you are saved and be happy about it.

2. *Never make light of your conversion.* Others may laugh at your decision, but you will not join with them. That which has

happened is of primary importance. Bravely declare yourself on the side of Christ. Do not join with the scoffers. I have known some young people to get converted; and when someone laughed at their faith and said that because they were saved, they could not do certain things, the new convert made the cowardly statement: "Oh, I can go on doing just what I have always done."

The old story of Simon Peter comes to mind. When Jesus was taken from the Garden of Gethsemane, "Peter followed afar off." A little maid came up and said, "This man was also with him." But Peter denied it and said, "Woman, I know him not." A little later when another person came along and said also, "Thou art also one of them," Peter said, "Man, I am not." About an hour later, when a third person came and said, "Of a truth, this fellow also was with him; for he is a Galilean," Peter said, "Man, I know not what thou sayest." In Matthew's Gospel we find even stronger words: "Then began he to curse and to swear saying, I know not the man."

How shameful was this action of the apostle! We should be happy that the Bible gives a better record of this man after he came to himself and received forgiveness from God.

I beseech you in the name of the Lord Jesus Christ: always be happy and proud to be a Christian. Never make light of your conversion. Never follow others to make foolish, derogatory remarks about Christ and His work.

3. *Engage in things that identify people.* Attending church is a good identification. Determine to be faithful to the services of your church Sunday morning, Sunday evening, and Wednesday evening. Get a good Bible and read it. Talk about the Bible. Ask questions of others regarding the Word of God. Establish good prayer habits. Return thanks at the table. Do those things that would identify you as one who has been born again.

Let your appearance be that of a born-again person. Let not any dress or custom identify you in the slightest with the evil, gainsaying world.

Let your speech identify you! Let your work on the job, in the office, in the plant, on the streets—let all speak in such a way that people will know that you are a child of God. Avoid all words of profanity. Stay away from every evil thing that might cause someone to doubt your position in Christ.

I trust that I have made this first very clear. We are discussing living your faith on the job. To do this, one must identify himself clearly with the people of God, with the work of God.

II. COMPLETELY DEDICATE YOURSELF

"I beseech you therefore, brethren, by the mercies of God, that ye present your bodies a living sacrifice, holy, acceptable unto God, which is your reasonable service.

"And be not conformed to this world: but be ye transformed by the renewing of your mind, that ye may prove what is that good, and acceptable, and perfect, will of God."—Rom. 12:1,2.

From these verses we can see that dedication is both positive and negative.

On the negative side this means separation. "And be not conformed to this world. . . ."

I was just a new Christian back in Louisville, Kentucky, when I had to identify myself very plainly with the people of God. I had to make up my mind regarding doubtful and questionable things.

One evening I had been invited to a home—a Christian home. The people were active members of the local church. After awhile the lady of the house brought out some cards and said, "This is a game that we can all play. It is called Rook." I know nothing of the game and it looked harmless enough to me. But I saw the lady go to the front windows and pull down the shades. As a young high school boy, I asked her why she was doing that; and she said, "There may be some people passing by who will not understand what we are doing. They will think because we have cards in our hands that we are engaging in a game of gambling. I do not want them to have any wrong impressions."

I didn't know much about living for Christ; but when she said this, I at once replied, "I don't believe I will play. If there is some question about this matter and if it might be misunderstood, I would rather not engage in it."

I think this might be a rule for all of us to establish: If there is a doubt about a thing, then we had better turn from it. There may be a question mark; if so, it is usually wrong. Avoid the questionable. Separate yourself from the world.

Some years ago I was conducting a very fine revival campaign in another state. One evening a handsome man came down the aisle and accepted Christ as Saviour. I noticed that the people rejoiced in his salvation. I later learned that many had been praying for him for some time.

I greeted the man as I would greet any new convert. I, too, was happy that he was saved. A couple of nights after that, he came forward in the meeting again. This time he said, "I cannot continue in the business that I have had for many years." He had a very fine position in a brewery. He had spent a lifetime in this business making beer. He stated that when he got saved he thought he might continue in this work; but after praying about the matter, he knew that he had to change; and he did.

Now let us turn to the positive side. The Bible says "present your bodies a living sacrifice, holy, acceptable unto God." You are to be "transformed by the renewing of your minds." In other words, walk as a Christian. In business life, you are to walk as a child of God. It matters not what others may say or do. You are to be identified with those who know Christ, and you are to walk on the positive side of every issue.

To live out your faith on the job, you will need to dress decently and correctly and take a positive stand on correct attire. To everyone in the business field, it is your obligation to dedicate yourself to Christian standards. In political life you are to walk as a Christian. In home life you are to behave as a Christian. In school life you are to walk as a Christian. In every place you are to live as children of God and manifest an interest in those around you.

A tent meeting was in progress. A young man had been attending the meetings regularly but had not accepted the Lord Jesus Christ as his Saviour. The evangelist came after the service and said, "Your mother wants you to be a Christian. She is a Christian. Your father would be pleased because he is a Christian, an officer in the church." The lad was silent for a while before he thoughtfully said, "Perhaps you may not believe what I say, but neither my father nor my mother has ever asked me to be a Christian. I never expect to be one until they do."

The evangelist said, "What a shame that I should be obliged to waste one minute of my time or one ounce of my strength trying to persuade mothers and fathers to speak to their children about Christ."

Living out Christ on the job means that you manifest the Lord to others in action and speech.

III. ENTIRELY ACTIVATE YOURSELF

Oh, yes, there is something for you to do! God has a work for everyone! Every Christian is to be a witness! Note, I said "Every Christian!" No one must give you a job—you have one! Jesus said, "Ye shall be witnesses unto me. . . ."

1. *This calls for a clean life.* Keep out of your life anything that may be doubtful or that might hinder you from speaking to others. You can't win souls if the influence of your life is in question. "But if thy brother be grieved with thy meat, now walkest thou not charitably. Destroy not him with thy meat, for whom Christ died" (Rom. 14:15).

2. *This calls for a life of prayer.* Prayer is the power line.

In New York City some years ago there was a man named Jerry McAuley. He was saved out of a wretched life, became the head of a great mission and did a work that is still known to people the world over.

At Jerry McAuley's funeral, a shabby-looking, aged man appeared. He came to the men who stood at the front of the church, took off his tall, battered hat, and asked them if they would take the little bunch of white flowers which he had in his hand and have them placed on Jerry McAuley's coffin, adding, "And when you drop them with the rest, Jerry will understand. He was my friend. He will know that they came from Old Joe Chappy."

Mrs. McAuley got that little bunch of flowers and preserved them for a long time. Jerry McAuley had said, "When I die—and it may not be long—I want to die on my knees praying for a lost world. I would rather some poor soul that I was the means of leading to the Lord would put one little rose on my grave than to have the wealth of the millionaire." And it was so! Here came a man who had been led to Christ by Jerry McAuley; now he is giving a little bunch of white flowers to be put on the casket.

Activate yourself in the matter of prayer. Spend much time praying for others. Pray for your family, your friends, for missionaries, for the lost.

3. *This calls for a spoken witness.* The Bible exhorts us to speak out regarding the Lord Jesus Christ.

I had a call from Jack Wyrtzen, director of Word of Life in New York State. He was holding a meeting each week in one of the big auditoriums in Grand Rapids, Michigan. Thousands of young people were hearing the Gospel and hundreds were coming to know the Lord Jesus Christ as Saviour.

Jack was scheduled to give an address in a local high school. When he met the principal he was informed that he could speak, but he must not mention the name of Jesus. Jack asked if it would be all right to mention George Washington or Abraham Lincoln. The principal said, "Oh, yes, but you cannot talk about Christ. His name is controversial."

Then Jack said, "That is strange. When I came down the hallway, I heard the name of Jesus shouted out from the lips of quite a few young people. If they can use His name in that fashion in the hallways, why can't I speak His name from the platform?" When the principal stated again that he could not do so, then Jack Wrytzen did a very wonderful thing. He said, "If I cannot speak of the name of Jesus Christ to your young people, I shall not speak at all." With that he walked away and left the principal to explain the matter to his high school assembly.

Oh, yes, my friends, we must speak out for Jesus Christ.

During a season of revival, a friend was praying one evening for a certain unconverted neighbor in this manner: "O Lord, touch that man with Thy finger. Touch him with Thy finger, Lord." The petition was repeated with great earnestness. Then something said to him, *Thou art the finger of God! Hast thou ever touched this brother? Hast thou ever spoken a single word to him on the question of salvation? Go thou and touch that man, and thy prayer shall be answered.*

Yes, God is calling us to speak for Him. Jesus said, "As the Father hath sent me, even so send I you."

4. *This calls for concern.* There is no way for one to keep on going and endeavoring to win souls unless there is a definite concern for others. Our hearts must be broken. We must be filled with a compassion for the lost.

A young artist named Tucker painted the picture of a forlorn woman and a child out in a storm. This picture took such a hold on him that he laid aside his palette and brush saying, "I must go to the lost instead of painting them." He prepared for the ministry and for some time worked in the city slums. At length he resolved, "I must go to that part of the world where men seem to be most hopelessly lost." That young artist was none other than Bishop Tucker of Uganda, Africa.

One evening, past midnight, I was studying on this message. I picked up a book and read a story—a true story—that touched my heart. It was the story of a missionary, his wife Jane, and their three small children who had been serving for two years on one of the small islands in the Bahamas. Their living quarters was a boat because they could not find housing on the island. It was a hard life for a man and wife and three children. The weather was warm. There was no refrigeration, but the missionary was faithful because he felt that he was in the place where God had sent him.

Then one day the stove broke down, and they could not cook. Money was running low. They had been unable to buy any supplies. They wondered what to do next.

At about six o'clock that evening, the missionary decided to move the boat a little farther from the shore in an effort to get away from the tormenting insects. When he turned the ignition key to start the engine, he heard a peculiar sound. He said to his helper, "Something dreadful is about to happen." No sooner had he said this when there came an explosion. He was blown through the roof of the cabin. When he came to he saw that the top of the boat was blown off and the windows blasted out.

He ran to the back of the boat; the cargo hatches had been blown away. The interior of the boat was an inferno. He looked down into the flames and saw his three children lying there. He snatched three-year-old Donny. Then he caught seven-year-old Kathy. With his wife, he brought them all to the bow of the boat. Their clothing was burned off, and their flesh was blackened. The wife said, "All of us will die."

His helper, Carl Whitehouse, had been blown overboard. Somehow he got to land and came back in a small boat. He put the children into it and headed toward shore.

On the shore there was a long period of waiting. They radioed for an airplane from Nassau. The children and wife were burned. The missionary himself was severely burned in many places.

Finally the plane came and brought two nurses, but they had to be left behind. There was room for only the pilot and the burned family. When they got to Nassau, the jeep carried them to the Rassan Clinic. With all of them lying in the jeep, they called for the doctor. He came. When the doctor saw what had happened, he reached into the jeep and picked up Donna. Though dressed in a beautiful white suit, he pressed the body of the little girl against him and ran into the hospital. He treated Donna, then Kathy, then Donny, then at last he came to the parents.

The missionary said, "All that night I talked to God. I prayed. I called upon God for help." Soon after daylight Dr. Rassan said, "Your daughter Donna is dying."

The missionary said, "I could not believe it. Despite the nurses' protests, I got out of bed and went into Donna's room. He was right. She was dying." Donna said, "I feel like I am going away, but don't cry. Everything will be all right."

The missionary said, "I tried to hold her but my bandaged arms would not go around her. I laid my head on her little breast. When I looked up, I saw the nurses were weeping. I knew then that she was gone."

After many days, father and mother and the two children left were released from the hospital. There came the plane for their return back to the United States. The loss of their daughter was a great loss, but their hearts were filled with gratitude.

A few days later the missionary was to speak in his father's church in Jamestown, New York. He could not speak but stood and wept. God even used the weeping. The death of the child meant the salvation of many. They heard the story and accepted Him as Saviour.

That missionary is back on the field and is continuing with his work of winning souls. From his house he can look down into the harbor and see the shattered hulk of the "Bahama Star" which had blown up. He can walk a few feet and find the grave of his little daughter. Ah, but he is living out his faith on the job! He is witnessing. He is winning souls. He is doing the task that God has given to him.

FAITH IS NOT BELIEVING THAT GOD *CAN*, BUT THAT GOD *WILL*!

24. *Living the Life of Faith*

For we walk by faith, not by sight.
—II Corinthians 5:7.

Faith always delighted the Master. One illustration of this is in Matthew 8. The centurion came to the Lord Jesus and asked that He come and heal his servant. Jesus said, "I will come and heal him." The centurion answered, "Lord, I am not worthy that thou shouldest come under my roof: but speak the word only, and my servant shall be healed." Then this man of the world gave a word about himself and about the soldiers who served under him: "For I am a man under authority, having soldiers under me: and I say to this man, Go, and he goeth; and to another, Come, and he cometh; and to my servant, Do this, and he doeth it." Now I want you to see the delighted response of the Master in verse 10: "When Jesus heard it, he marvelled, and said to them that followed, Verily I say unto you, I have not found so great faith, no, not in Israel."

Notice carefully that lack of faith always distressed the Master. In Matthew 14:22-32, we find the story of the Lord Jesus walking on the sea. The disciples were fearful. He calmed their fears. Then Peter said, "Lord, if it be thou, bid me come unto thee on the water." Jesus invited him. Peter came down from the ship and walked on the water to go to Jesus. "But when he saw the wind boisterous, he was afraid; and beginning to sink, he cried, saying, Lord, save me." Now notice verse 31: "And immediately Jesus stretched forth his hand, and caught him, and said unto him, O thou of little faith, wherefore didst thou doubt?"

Jesus never reproved His disciples for lack of wealth or intelligence, but He did reprove them for lack of faith. He did not reprove them for lack of talents, but for lack of faith. The plain, positive exhortation of Scripture is: "Have faith in God" (Mark 11:22).

I suppose all of you are saying, "Yes, I do want faith. I want to live the life of faith."

BUT OUR FAITH IS OFTEN DISTURBED.

Disturbed by desire. When you desire sin, then your faith is disturbed. The sin may be pride—a desire for greatness or for the applause of the world or for the headlines. The carnal life is always a disturbed life.

Disturbed by drive. We talk about one having "great faith," by which we mean he has initiative and launches out into the deep. But sometimes drive is expressed in selfishness—personal drive. Sometimes your drive is just a desire to get ahead. The drive of some people wrecks their faith. Even preachers have been ruined by personal drive—wanting success so badly that they sacrificed even high principles.

Disturbed by doubts. Doubts are not a sign of intelligence, so put away your doubts.

The president of a great university was troubled by doubts for many years; but after his surrender to Christ as Saviour, he said, "Why did not someone tell me that I could become a Christian and settle my doubts afterwards?"

Thomas was often disturbed by doubts. The Saviour was kind and patient toward this doubter. Jesus—the risen Saviour—met with His disciples on that first Sunday evening. He came through the closed doors and stood in their midst. But Thomas was not present when the Lord came. When the disciples told him that Jesus had appeared to them, he said, "Except I shall see in his hands the print of the nails, and put my finger into the print of the nails, and thrust my hand into his side, I will not believe."

It was eight days later that Jesus met with the disciples, but this time Thomas was present, and suddenly the Lord Jesus came and stood in their midst and said, "Peace be unto you." Then to Thomas, the doubter, He said, "Reach hither thy finger, and behold my hands; and reach hither thy hand, and thrust it into my side: and be not faithless, but believing."

I do not know if Thomas did all Jesus told him to do, but I do know that he said, "My Lord and my God!"

Then the Saviour gave this word: "Thomas, because thou hast seen me, thou hast believed: blessed are they that have not seen, and yet have believed" (John 20:29).

We are endeavoring to build strong Christians. We believe that this is the answer to our problems.

At one time, the former President of the United States, Mr. Richard Nixon, and Mr. Art Linkletter met. The President made the statement that more people die in New York City from drugs than are killed weekly in Viet Nam. Let me quote from this paper:

> "The shocking drug abuse problem," Mr. Nixon said, "exists because of persons who do not think they are getting enough out of life.
>
> "That is really a reflection on them, not of life. This is a good life. This is a good country."
>
> Saying he has heard young people complain that these are difficult times to be alive, Mr. Nixon said, "My answer is not to sympathize on that and say, 'It is too bad. Please go off and we'll try to make it easier for you.' That is the worst thing you can do to young people—to make life easier for them. They need not be bored. They need a challenge. They need to be involved in something that is more exciting and important.
>
> "By retreating into drugs and these artificial things, I think all they do is to start down the dreary road which can only lead to destuction."

I have read these statements from the former President just to recognize the truth which is before us tonight. The way of excitement for young and old is to live the life of faith. When you live in this fashion, then you can be sure that there will be excitement and variety enough to keep life interesting.

I. THE LIFE OF FAITH IS BUILT
ON HIS PROMISES

We are told that there are 32,000 promises in the Bible. It is my business to receive God's promises and build upon them.

We read of Abraham, "He staggered not at the promise of God through unbelief; but was strong in faith, giving glory to God" (Rom. 4:20).

Let me illustrate this truth of faith in the promises of God by a simple story.

In China there was a young man, Mr. Marcus Cheng, a very fine Christian worker and beloved by many people. He told the story of his early Christian life. He said when he was a student in school all of his funds were exhausted. He was in great distress but was too proud to ask for help.

One night late he overcame his pride and went and knocked on the door of a missionary friend. His friend inquired, "What are you doing here this time of night? Is not this against the rules of the college?"

Marcus Cheng said, "I have no money."

Immediately sensing the situation, the friend opened the door wide and invited him in. Taking him into his study, he said, "All the money that I have is in this box. You may have anything you want. I do not have much, but it is for you." The missionary opened the box and said, "Take what you want."

Marcus Cheng said he trembled as he bent over and took the tiniest bit of silver he could see in that chest.

His missionary friend said, "Take more, take more; take all you need."

Marcus Cheng said he broke down and cried; first, because the missionary trusted him so much; second, because he had a glimpse of the infinite love of God. He could see that God had opened up the treasure chest and was saying, "Take all you need. Do not be content with the little. Take everything that you need."

Do you have needs? Then come and take of God. He invites

you to receive all He has for you. Believe His promises. Rest upon them. He will never fail.

Someone said, "Faith is a living power from Heaven that grasps the promise God has given."

He promises salvation. "Verily, verily. . .he that believeth on me hath everlasting life."

He promises His presence. ". . .lo, I am with you alway, even unto the end of the world. Amen."

He promises peace. ". . .not as the world giveth, give I unto you. . . ."

He promises to supply all of your needs. "But my God shall supply all your need according to his riches in glory by Christ Jesus."

He promises comfort. "Who comforteth us in all our tribulation, that we may be able to comfort them which are in any trouble, by the comfort wherewith we ourselves are comforted of God."

Men may make promises and never fulfill them. Sometimes promises are made and never intended to be kept. Sometimes promises are made and the one making them is unable to do what he promised to do.

To illustrate this: If I were to write out a check for a million dollars and give it to this church, it would not be worth anything because I do not have a million dollars. But let a multi-millionaire of this city write out a check for a million, it would be good anywhere.

Just so with our Lord. He has promised, and He is fully able to keep every promise He makes. The life of faith is built upon His promises.

II. THE LIFE OF FAITH IS SUSTAINED BY HIS POWER

I am referring to God's enabling grace, God's infinite power. There will come hours of weakness, hours when we must rest upon God and on His power. In Matthew 17:20 we find these words: "And Jesus said unto them, Because of your unbelief: for verily I say unto you, If ye have faith as a grain of mustard seed, ye shall say unto this mountain, Remove hence to yonder place; and it shall remove; and nothing shall be impossible unto you."

"If ye have faith as a grain of mustard seed. . . ." How tiny is a mustard seed! ". . .ye shall say unto this mountain. . . ." How big the mountain! Yes, Jesus, showing the power of faith, said a faith as a grain of mustard seed can move a mountain.

God has the power to bless us. He waits to bless us. He wants to bless us. Take the blessings from His hands. Remember, He said to Abram, ". . .thou shalt be a blessing." He is giving the same word to us and exhorting us to come and take from Him this blessing.

God has the power to answer our prayers. There is a little verse found in James 4 that often rebukes me—"Ye lust, and have not: ye kill, and desire to have, and cannot obtain: ye fight and war, yet ye have not, because ye ask not." Underscore that part of the verse—"ye have not, because ye ask not." What is God saying? He is telling us to pray and believe and know that He answers prayer.

God has the power to demonstrate His power through us. He wants to show the world what He can do and is waiting for someone through whom He can work.

Most of us confess that we are weak and finite beings. We do not seem to have much power. We have to rest upon the two little words—"but God." God can take us and use us. He is waiting to use you and me.

I suppose you have heard the story of the sculptor who commenced to carve the figure of a small cherub high up in the great cathedral. He gave so much time and skill to it that his fellow workmen began to laugh and say, "Why spend so much time and skill on something that will not be seen?" One workman said, "Why, only the sparrows will see it hidden in that little niche." Then the sculptor answered, "Only the sparrows—and God."

We confess our weakness, but God is waiting to work through us. His power is infinite!

III. THE LIFE OF FAITH IS EXPRESSED BY PERFORMANCE

We express our faith by obedience to the Word. What the Word of God says we must do. We must be submissive to His will. Hebrews 11 is a great illustration of this matter of faith. We have mentioned the names of many who lived by faith. The inspired writer began by giving a definition of faith, then went on to illustrate what he was talking about. He showed that faith is an audacious thing, that faith does the impossible, that faith surpasses all wonders of men.

Someone said in a very quaint way, "When God has a big job to do, it is always Faith that gets the contract."

One person made the statement that the story of George Mueller of Bristol, England, should be added to the account of Hebrews 11, written something like this:

> By faith George Mueller established five orphan homes, caring for thousands of fatherless children, helping multitudes of burdened and brokenhearted mothers, raising hundreds of thousands of pounds without appeal for money, seeing 30,000 people converted to God in answer to prayer, and demonstrating before an unbelieving world that Almighty God answers prayer and honors the faith of His children.

The life of faith was certainly expressed by his performance. There are three simple things that I want to say about faith.

1. *Faith is vicarious.* How beautifully this is illustrated in Mark 2. Jesus came to Capernaum. Crowds gathered around to hear Him. Then four men came bearing one sick of the palsy. They could not get him in the house by the doorway; so they climbed up on the roof, pulled away the rooftop and lowered the sick man down before Jesus. The Bible reads, "When Jesus saw their faith, he said unto the sick of the palsy, Son, thy sins be forgiven thee."

Jesus saw their faith! I am trying to illustrate the fact that faith is a vicarious matter. By our faith, great blessings can come to multitudes. By the faith of this church, thousands can be blessed. By the faith of our leaders, mighty things can be done. Oh, how tremendous the power of faith in God.

2. *Faith is venturesome.* Jesus said to His disciples, "Launch out into the deep, and let down your nets for a draught."

There are times when we must obey when all common sense would dictate otherwise. We must venture out into the deep. We must go forward in service for our Saviour. Do not let lack of faith detour you. Do not be defeated by a fluctuating faith—up one day and down the next.

3. *Faith is victorious.* "This is the victory that overcometh the world, even our faith."

> Encamped along the hills of light,
>   Ye Christian soldiers rise,
> And press the battle, ere the night
>   Shall veil the glowing skies.
>
> Against the foe in vales below,
>   Let all your strength be hurled;
> Faith is the victory we know
>   That overcomes the world.
>
> His banner over us is love,
>   Our sword the Word of God.
> We tread the roads the saints above
>   With shouts of triumph trod.
>
> By faith they like a whirlwind's breath
>   Swept on o'er every field.
> The faith by which they conquered death,
>   Is still our shining shield.

Jesus said, "Have faith in God." Faith is victorious.

We have often thought about the faith of J. Hudson Taylor, the missionary. There is an illustration of a happening in his early life that indicates that faith grows by exercise.

Hudson Taylor was an errand boy in the service of a doctor. One week the doctor forgot to pay him his wages. The money was much needed at home, but how was he to obtain it? Should he remind the doctor of the oversight or tell God about it? The boy chose to tell God. It was not long until the doctor remembered that he had failed to pay the boy. Faith grows by exercise.

A great faith is always simple. It is direct. It is utterly built upon the presence and the promises of God.

Later when Hudson Taylor was congratulated on his great faith, he remarked, "Oh, no! My faith is not great. It often trembles, is always weak, and just hangs upon God."

Believe God—live the life of faith!

If you have never accepted Jesus Christ as Saviour, then the first step is very clear. You must come to Him in repentance and faith and receive the salvation that He has for you.

Then, when Christ is your Saviour and God is your Father, you can begin to exercise faith in God. I remind you again that "this is the victory that overcometh the world, even our faith."

PSALM 17:11

I'm glad I cannot shape my way,
  I'd rather trust Thy skill;
I'm glad the ordering is not mine,
  I'd rather have Thy will.
I do not know the future,
  And I would not if I might;
For faith to me is better far
  Than faulty human sight.

—Anon.

25. *Faith in the Darkest Hour*

> *Notwithstanding the Lord stood with me, and strengthened me; that by me the preaching might be fully known, and that all the Gentiles might hear: and I was delivered out of the mouth of the lion.*
>
> —II Timothy 4:17

This was a dark hour for Paul. He was writing to Timothy from Rome. He had doubtless appeared before Nero, the vicious, bloodthirsty king of Rome. At this appearance, all of the Christans fled from his side. "At my first answer no man stood with me, but all men forsook me: I pray God that it may not be laid to their charge" (II Tim. 4:16).

Paul likened his trial before Nero as a little man before a fierce lion. The lion appeared and opened his mouth to devour him, but God intervened, and he was delivered. Paul praised God for his deliverance and said, ". . .the Lord shall deliver me from every evil work, and will preserve me unto his heavenly kingdom: to whom be glory for ever and ever. Amen."

As I read this final chapter from Paul, I am impressed by three things:

1. *By Paul's youthful attitude.* He was not young in years, but he was youthful in attitude and interest.

He addressed himself to young Timothy:

"Preach the word; be instant in season, out of season; reprove, rebuke, exhort with all longsuffering and doctrine.

"For the time will come when they will not endure sound

doctrine; but after their own lusts shall they heap to themselves teachers, having itching ears;

"And they shall turn away their ears from the truth, and shall be turned unto fables."—II Tim. 4:2-4.

Oh, yes, he said much about himself, but he also talked about others. At least sixteen persons are mentioned in these last verses. Sometimes older people face a danger of talking only about themselves. They talk about their ailments, their financial burdens, and their personal problems. But not Paul! He talked about others, too. Keep a vital interest in others. This will bring youthfulness. Do not lose your touch with people.

2. *By his helpful remarks.* He was concerned about Timothy so he said, "I charge thee therefore before God, and the Lord Jesus Christ, who shall judge the quick and the dead at his appearing and his kingdom."

In trying to help Timothy, he mentioned that Demas had forsaken him and turned back to the world. This was a kind way to relate a very painful matter. Paul was indicating that even the best of men fail.

He mentioned also Alexander—"Alexander the coppersmith did me much evil: the Lord reward him according to his works." And then he said to Timothy, "Of whom be thou ware also; for he hath greatly withstood our words." In other words, "Timothy, watch out for this man. He will cause you trouble." Paul was warning a youth. He was concerned about others.

3. *By his hopeful remarks.* Others had failed, but the Lord stood by him. He was not troubled at all about the Lord! He knew that God would never fail. He was ready for death or for the appearing of Christ. "Henceforth there is laid up for me a crown of righteousness, which the Lord, the righteous judge, shall give me at that day: and not to me only, but unto all them also that love his appearing" (II Tim. 4:8).

Paul was looking ahead. This is good for young and old. Paul had endured much suffering, but he made little mention of it. His attitude was hopeful. He was like the man who addressed his aging body thus:

When you can go no further, I shall leave you and be free. When we separate, I shall continue to exist. A power greater than you and I started us on our journey. Your journey is approaching its end, and you are aware of it. My journey has merely begun, and I know it because I have never been more alive. Our separation is therefore not one of sadness but of joy. You are weary and want to stop, and I am longing to alight from this slow vehicle and go on without you.

This seems to be somewhat the thinking of Paul as he looked toward the end of life and thought of coming into the presence of the Lord. Paul enjoyed life. The wholesomeness of his words indicates this, but he was ready for the time when he could come into the presence of God.

Paul was positive—not negative.

I was reading about the mother who was quite negative in her thinking. Riding on the train with her four children, she did not try to interest the little ones, only sought to restrain them. Her conversation was a mere series of ejaculations: "No!" "Stop!" "Don't do that!" One little fellow ran to the other end of the car beyond the mother's range of vision. She sent his older sister with the injunction, "Go see what Willie is doing, and tell him to stop it."

This is not the attitude of the apostle. There was a hopefulness as he looked to the future.

Another outline forced itself on me as I read the chapter:

Paul's personal dilemma. Some of his friends had turned away from his side. He felt a bit lonely.

Paul's personal danger. He had been delivered from Nero, but still he faced death.

Paul's personal deliverance.

". . .the Lord stood with me. . . ."

". . .the Lord. . .strengthened me. . . ."

". . .I was delivered out of the mouth of the lion."

". . .the Lord shall deliver me. . . ."

". . .the Lord. . .will preserve me. . . ."

You can't stop a man like that! His faith was supreme! Now as we consider the subject, "Faith in the darkest hour," let us look at the apostle again and think of this outline.

I. THE FOUNDATION FOR HIS FAITH

Go back to the Damascus Road. His faith in the living Christ actually began on the day he watched the stoning of Stephen. No, he was not saved on that day, but it was then that he saw the power of the living Son of God. But on the Damascus Road, Christ Jesus met him face to face. There came a light from Heaven and a voice saying, "Saul, Saul, why persecutest thou me?" As a result of that encounter, Paul said, "Lord, what wilt thou have me to do?"

Go back to the Arabian years. He was saved, then he took the time to orient himself to his new position in life. I think that this indicates that we might be better off were we to stop once in a while and adjust our own hearts and thoughts to the situations surrounding us. Often God has something He wants us to know; but because we are so busy, we do not take time to listen to His voice. Paul went up to Arabia, then returned again to Damascus. Take time to get aside and hear Him speak to you words that may change your whole life.

Then as we think about the foundation for his faith, we go back over the years of Paul's preaching and witnessing. Had God ever failed him? No. Suffering? Yes. Privations? Yes. But God was always there. He never once failed of all His promises to Paul.

Now in order to have faith in the darkest hour, one must get established.

Be sure Christ is the foundation. Paul said in writing to the Corinthian church, "For other foundation can no man lay than that is laid, which is Jesus Christ" (I Cor. 3:11). No one will ever get far without knowing Christ as Saviour and resting in Him.

Be established by the Word. Paul had no doubt about God's Word—none. He wrote, "All scripture is given by inspiration of God, and is profitable for doctrine, for reproof, for correction, for instruction in righteousness."

Be established in His work. God has a task for every child of His. He has called each to that task. Let us be sure we do it and do it efficiently.

II. THE FORCE OF HIS FAITH

". . .I was delivered out of the mouth of the lion."

Who delivered Paul? Paul knew God had delivered him, and he said, "The Lord shall deliver me from every evil work. . . ." Faith brought results to the Apostle Paul.

His faith saved him. Simple faith in the crucified, risen Son of God saved the Apostle Paul. The same faith in Christ will save you, my lost friend. Jesus said, "Verily, verily, I say unto you, He that believeth in me hath everlasting life."

His faith sent him. God called him; he answered and then moved out by faith. He was sent out on his missionary tours by the Holy Spirit who said, "Separate me Barnabas and Saul for the work whereunto I have called them."

A few hours ago I talked to a poor man—I said poor man, but he lives in a $40,000.00 home, has a wonderful job, and a nice family. This is what he said: "God has called me into full-time service. I am forty-one years of age. I need to get started at the work God wants me to do, but my wife refuses to leave home. She will not agree to follow me if I answer God's call and go out in service." This man testified to his salvation, and he knew God had given him a call, but he is standing still. Not so with the Apostle Paul! His faith sent him.

His faith sustained him. In the miserable, lonely hours, his faith sustained him. In the prison cells, his faith kept him strong. When he was beaten with rods, stoned and left for dead, his faith sustained him. In weariness and painfulness, in hunger and thirst, in cold and nakedness, his faith sustained him.

The force of his faith! Faith has power!

Jesus said, "Have faith in God"—such faith in God that you will obey His command. Have faith in God to fight sin. Have faith in God to lift up Christ. Have faith in God to obey Him.

III. THE FULFILLMENT OF HIS FAITH

"And the Lord shall deliver me from every evil work, and will preserve me unto his heavenly kingdom: to whom be glory for ever and ever. Amen." —II Tim. 4:18.

Paul's faith did not fail. The Lord cannot fail. Our faith and God's faithfulness make an unbeatable combination.

Paul's faith has been pictured for us to let us see the value of strong faith.

O for a faith that will not shrink
Though pressed by every foe
That will not tremble on the brink
Of any earthly woe.

That will not murmur nor complain
Beneath the chastening rod
But in the hour of grief or pain
Will lean upon its God.

A faith that shines more bright and clear
When tempests rage without
That when in danger knows no fear
In darkness feels no doubt.

Lord, give us such a faith as this
And then, whate'er may come
We'll taste e'en here the hallowed bliss
Of an eternal home.

The French sculptor Rodin was accustomed to carrying about with him a tiny but exquisite piece of sculpture, frequently taking it from his pocket to study intently its beauty. He declared he found encouragement for his work by constantly keeping before him this example of the best work produced in an earlier age.

I confess to you that I like to keep before me a picture of Paul and his faithfulness. He strengthens me and sends me on.

In Paul we see the value of a strong faith.

His faith brought him into the presence of God. When the time of his Homegoing came, he was "absent from the body. . .present with the Lord."

Nero had everything of the world but nothing of God. The porticoes of Nero's palace were a mile long. The walls were so arranged as to shower lovely perfumes upon his guests. Nero's crown was worth $500,000.00. His mules were shod with silver. Nero fished with hooks of gold. When Nero traveled, a thousand carriages accompanied him to carry his wardrobe. It is said of Nero that he never wore a gament the second time.

Nero had nothing! He knew not the Saviour. He had no faith in God. His arm had conquered, but his heart was unsatisfied.

But Paul had faith in Jesus Christ. He had peace. He had salvation. He had the hope of Heaven.

LET ME ADMONISH YOU TO DO THREE THINGS:

Fasten your faith in Him. Do not look to man but look to God. Do not trust in the circumstances of life. Trust in Christ. Have faith in a person, not in a principle.

Build your faith by the Word of God. ". . .faith cometh by hearing, and hearing by the word of God." Therefore, read the Book. Listen to the Book. Saturate your life in the Holy Word.

Use your faith to help others. Paul did, and we must do likewise.

Dr. James Stewart tells the remarkable story of twenty Christians who gathered again and again for Bible study in a foreign land. Some people had suggested that they close the doors of the little church and give up. But a few held on. They kept praying, kept on studying the Bible. Their faith was mighty.

They were poor, but they brought their tithes into the church and laid them upon the altar. They kept on seeking the face of God. The biggest thing in their lives was their faith. It was the one thing that crowded their horizons. It was the theme of their talk.

Then Dr. Stewart said that he went to hold a meeting in that strange and spiritually desolate place. In the course of the meetings, hundreds were saved. The building seated 800 people, and it was packed for every service. The people had no pastor, but they established twenty mission stations in the area around them. Though they had nothing from the human standpoint, they went on to work mightily.

Let us use our faith! Let us go on to accomplish our work for God.

Let me remind you that faith does not hide the difficulties or belittle them. If you are to have faith, then you must look beyond all of your difficulties and dark places. Satan will war against you. Problems that seem like giants will come against you. In it all, look up. Have faith in God!

Remember that we have no more faith at any time than we have in the hour of trial.—Spurgeon.

26. *The Faith That Moves Mountains*

And Jesus said unto them. . .If ye have faith as a grain of mustard seed, ye shall say unto this mountain, Remove hence to yonder place; and it shall remove; and nothing shall be impossible unto you.

Howbeit this kind goeth not out but by prayer and fasting.

—Matthew 17:20,21.

The ordinary interpretation of this passage is that a little faith can do mighty things—and this is true! The mustard seed—a tiny seed—is used to illustrate the smallness of faith.

But there is another way to look at this scriptural portion. The mustard seed is alive. A mustard seed dropped into the crevice of a rock can split the solid mass and heave it from its bed. How? By simple growth.

Faith is mighty—faith is alive!

The mountain is a mass of dead, inert matter. It cannot move itself. Not so with the mustard seed. In it is life; and the life brings growth, motion and reproduction.

The mountain is a picture of a huge obstacle. It is something in the way of spiritual progress.

Jesus said, "If ye have faith. . . ."

In the Scripture before us, it is illustrated that our failures are the result of our faithlessness. When Jesus and Peter, James and John came down from the Mount of Transfiguration, there came a multitude unto Him. Out of the multitude a man said,

"Lord, have mercy on my son: for he is a lunatick, and sore

vexed: for ofttimes he falleth into the fire, and oft into the water.

"And I brought him to thy disciples, and they could not cure him.

"Then Jesus answered and said, O faithless and perverse generation, how long shall I be with you? how long shall I suffer you? bring him hither to me."

When they brought the child, "Jesus rebuked the Devil, and he departed out of him: and the child was cured from that very hour."

The disciples came to Jesus and asked, "Why could not we cast him out?"

Jesus made answer, in the text which I read to you a moment ago:

You failed "because of your unbelief: for verily I say unto you, If ye have faith as a grain of mustard seed, ye shall say unto this mountain, Remove hence to yonder place; and it shall remove; and nothing shall be impossible unto you."

It is faith that brings us blessings.

It is faith that glorifies God.

It is faith that marches on despite all odds.

Now, let me quickly lay before you the verse given by Paul, "So then faith cometh by hearing, and hearing by the word of God" (Rom. 10:17). We use this verse much in dealing with the unsaved. We endeavor to show a man the power of the Word of God; but I want us to use this also to show that faith comes to the Christian by hearing, believing and resting upon this Word of God.

Now, permit me to identify from the Bible the kind of faith that God wants us to have.

I. AN ESTABLISHED FAITH

Yes, established on the Word of the eternal God. In Titus 1:2 we read: "In hope of eternal life, which God, that cannot lie, promised before the world began." God has given His promises to us, and God cannot lie.

Every promise He has given is true, every promise is dependable. We are to establish our faith from these promises.

1. *Don't try to establish faith in man.* Man is guilty of falsehood, and man is prone to fail. The promises of man are as nothing.

A very fine minister of the Gospel called me one day. He told me of a very sore condition in which he finds himself. And apparently from the conversaton that we had, his condition was brought about by the failure of a friend of his.

He had put his faith in a friend. The friend had lied to him, and the pastor found himself in a very dejected condition. He acknowledged on the phone that his failure was due to his faith in man.

Don't try to establish your faith in man. Man is human and fallible. Man is weak and easily deceived.

2. *Don't try to establish faith on circumstances.*

There was a man I used to know in the early part of my Christian life. He was a gracious man. He had a fine appearance, a good voice, and a rather eloquent vocabulary. But he was always a failure. He was forever telling his friends, "I am sure conditions will change." I can almost hear him say, "Yes, I know circumstances will be quite different for me in the spring. And if you will wait, I know that I can take care of my obligation to you."

He was forever depending upon circumstances. He always believed that a brighter day was ahead. He was relying on conditions.

3. *Don't try to establish faith on your own fluctuating feelings.* You may feel victorious today but defeated tomorrow. Most of us have discovered that we change from day to day.

It is only by the grace of God and by our continual looking to the Bible that we have an established faith.

Jesus often reproved His disciples for their little faith. He would say to them, "O ye of little faith!" What was wrong? They were depending upon themselves and they failed.

In Matthew 8. we have a five-verse story given of Jesus asleep in a ship. The storm arose, and the ship was covered with the waves. The disciples awakened Him saying, "Lord, save us: we perish."

Jesus arose and said, "Why are ye fearful, O ye of little faith? Then He arose and rebuked the winds and the sea; and there was a great calm."

What was wrong? They were not trusting the Saviour. He was with them, but they failed to recognize His presence.

To establish your faith, do the following:

Read the Word of God. This is God's eternal Word. George Mueller, the mighty man of prayer, read his Bible for lengthy periods before he prayed. This established his faith in the Word of God.

Believe the Word. I know some folks who read the Bible but do not believe what they read. Put your finger on it and say, *This I do believe!* And if you can't do any better then cry out like the father of the child whose story is given to us in Mark 9, "Lord, I believe; help thou mine unbelief."

Act on the Word. Move forward. Obey Him.

Let your faith be established on the Word of God.

II. A WORKING FAITH

True faith is never static! Even the faith of a Christian shut-in can be active and working.

1. *A working faith leads us to pray "in faith believing."* We are told to pray about everything, and this is exactly what we will do when our faith is fixed in the Lord.

"Be careful for nothing; but in every thing by prayer and supplication with thanksgiving let your requests be made known unto God."—Phil. 4:6.

2. *A working faith leads us to give.* Have faith to believe the promise of God as given in Malachi 3:10:

"Bring ye all the tithes into the storehouse, that there may be meat in mine house, and prove me now herewith, saith the Lord of hosts, if I will not open you the windows of heaven, and pour

you out a blessing, that there shall not be room enough to receive it. "

Tithing is relying on His promise to care for every need. He told Israel,

> "I will rebuke the devourer for your sakes, and he shall not destroy the fruits of your ground; neither shall your vine cast her fruit before the time in the field, saith the Lord of hosts" Mal. 3:11.

Every child of God should know there is great joy in giving. Even the smallest child should be taught the blessing of giving to God's work.

Someone told about the little girl who went out into the yard and picked a few weeds and put them together. She thought they were beautiful flowers. She carried them in and gave them to her mother. The mother understood and was happy that her daughter had thought to give her a "gift."

Though our gifts seem so very small, let's be sure we give them in the Spirit of Christ and for His glory.

3. *A working faith enables us to witness.* We are commanded to go into all the world and preach the Gospel. Jesus said, "Ye shall be witnesses unto me. . . ." This means that in season and out of season we sow by all waters. We keep on witnessing for Christ. If your faith is not a working faith, it may be a false faith.

III. A HAPPY FAITH

The Apostle Paul had a happy faith. I have only to turn to the book of Philippians to prove this. He said, "Finally, my brethren, rejoice in the Lord. . . ." Again Paul said, "Rejoice in the Lord alway: and again I say, Rejoice." The joy of the Lord was his stay, and Paul never failed to give forth a strong testimony to those about him.

As an old man, John had a happy faith. The key verse of I John is chapter 1, verse 4: "And these things write we unto you, that your joy may be full." It is evident that John believed that the Christian should have a happy faith.

I do not say that life is easy. I do not say that you will live your days without problems, but I do say that faith in God will give you peace of mind in the midst of any and all adversity.

A letter came to me one day from a lady in another state. She spoke of her great trials and heartaches. She stated that she knew the Saviour, but somehow she was so discouraged and depressed. She stated that I had prayed with her at the altar of her church some twenty-four years ago. Because of this slight touch upon her life, she was writing me twenty-four years later, asking that I pray for her.

To that friend I could simply state that God has not changed, that He is the same yesterday, today, and for ever. He wants you to have a happy faith.

A vigorous, happy faith makes happy people. When Cromwell lay dying and the good people around his bed foresaw the troubles that lay in wait for them and for England, the great man lifted his powerful head and said, "Is there no one present who will praise the Lord?"

I think we see a bit of Paul's happiness in II Timothy 4:6-8:

"For I am now ready to be offered, and the time of my departure is at hand.

"I have fought a good fight, I have finished my course, I have kept the faith:

"Henceforth there is laid up for me a crown of righteousness, which the Lord, the righteous judge, shall give me at that day: and not to me only, but unto all them also that love his appearing."

Paul and his happiness at the close of life remind me of the story of the wise old man who had lived buoyantly through fourscore years. Someone asked him, "What is the happiest season of life?"

He replied, thoughtfully, "Spring," and then stated:

When spring comes and in the soft air the buds are breaking on the trees, and they are covered with blossoms, I think how beautiful is spring!

And when the summer comes and covers the trees and branches with heavy foliage and singing birds, mingled with the branches, I think how beautiful is summer!

When autumn loads them with golden fruit and their leaves bear the gorgeous tint of frost, I think how beautiful is autumn!

And when it is sore winter, and there is neither foliage nor fruit, then when I look up to the leafless branches and see as I can see in no other season the shining stars of Heaven, I think how beautiful is the winter of life!

When Paul approached the close of his days, nothing was in the way. He could see straight into the presence of God, and he rejoiced.

Psalm 23 is a beautiful expression of faith. There David said, "The Lord is my shepherd; I shall not want."

Psalm 121 is an expression of happy faith. There the psalmist said, "I will lift up mine eyes unto the hills, from whence cometh my help. My help cometh from the Lord, which made heaven and earth."

FOR YOURS TO BE A HAPPY FAITH, DO THE FOLLOW-ING:

Depend on God to provide. In Philippians 4:19, we are told, "But my God shall supply all your need according to his riches in glory by Christ Jesus."

Thinking of God's wise provision, I saw this story the other day. A lady was entertaining her friend's small son. "Are you sure you can cut your meat?" she asked, after watching him struggle.

"Oh, yes. We often have it as tough as this at home," he replied.

I repeat: depend on God to provide every need.

Depend on God to stand with you. Since we have His promise that He will never leave nor forsake us, then we can rest upon the strong arm of our Lord. David said, "I will say of the Lord, He is my refuge and my fortress: my God; in him will I trust" (Ps. 91:2).

Depend on God to strengthen you. The hours of weakness will come to one and all. Times of depression will touch every life. It is then that we must rush to our Lord and lay before Him our needy souls. Here is the promise given to us:

"But they that wait upon the Lord shall renew their strength; they shall mount up with wings as eagles; they shall run, and not be weary; and they shall walk, and not faint."—Isa. 40:31.

IV. A REWARDING FAITH

We have discussed thus far the importance of having, first, an established faith; second, a working faith; third, a happy faith; now fourth, we talk of a rewarding faith.

The judgment seat is just ahead. At that day when we stand before our Lord, our works will be tested. How blessed if we can hear Him say, "Well done, thou good and faithful servant!"

But we must not forget that faith rewards us here and now. Even today we can see some of the special blessings of God.

A visitor in our city had been walking around the buildings of our church and of Tennessee Temple Schools. When he saw the services, the young people of the schools, the extent of the work as represented here in this local spot, he said, "I am interested in what you are doing. How did all of this get started?"

In just a few moments I told him of our beginning back in 1942, the starting of the great work of our church, the expansion of our work to reach out into many fields. I spoke of the beginning of Tennessee Temple Schools in 1946. Then I added, "Sir, this is a faith work."

There are three special joys that I would like to mention.

1. *The joy of seeing His work progress.* We must move forward "by faith." Hebrews 11 will strengthen your faith and stir you to greater works.

2. *The joy of seeing precious souls saved*—the greatest joy of all! Almost every week I meet someone I had the joy of leading to the Saviour years ago. People tell me of being converted in revival meetings that I conducted; or of being saved in churches where I pastored. I do not know any greater joy.

They say that Phillips Brooks once received a letter which read:

"I am a tailor in a little shop near your church. When I can, I attend. When I hear you preach, I forget you, for you make me think of God."

Our work is to try to make people everywhere think of God.

3. *The joy of knowing that one day we shall stand before Him.* This verse may awaken some of your hearts.

"And now, little children, abide in him; that, when he shall appear, we may have confidence, and not be ashamed before him at his coming."—I John 2:28.

Will you be ashamed at His coming? Are you ready to face the Lord Jesus? Or have you become so occupied with things below that you have had little time to think about the One who is coming to receive us, and before whom we must stand?

Dr. William Ward Ayer tells about how an out-of-town visitor to New York City got out of the subway train at Times Square and asked the subway guard, "When I reach the surface, I want to find such-and-such a street. Can you tell me where it is?"

The subway employee, with typical indifference, answered "Don't ask me anything about 'up there,' Mister. All I know anything about is down here."

I am afraid that too many Christians are like that. They know only about what's going on around them, not much about up there.

Oh, the joy of one day standing before Him! Have faith in God; have faith in the promises of God; expect the return of our Saviour at any moment.

For many years I have been signing beside my name in Bibles Romans 8:28: "And we know that all things work together for good to them that love God, to them who are the called according to his purpose."

I recently signed my name and that verse in one of the books at a funeral home. "Lee Roberson, Romans 8:28." Later on I received an envelope addressed to Reverend Lee Roberson, Room 828, Highland Park Baptist Church, Chattanooga, Tennessee!

May I say that there is where I want to live—in Room 828. I want to live in the place of faith—faith in God for today and for tomorrow.

Not long ago the wife of the late Dr. R. G. Lee passed away. Dr. Lee was one of the world's most famous preachers. He was a friend of this work and spoke here on numerous occasions. He and his wife had served together through so many years. When she passed away he sent me a telegram: "LADY LEE HAS GONE HOME TO BE WITH GOD." The man who conducted her funeral told me how Dr. Lee stood at the head of the casket and shook hands with literally hundreds and called the names of almost all of them.

Dr. Lee was demonstrating the faith that God can give to a man—the faith that enables one to stand true in every trial. This is the faith that moves mountains!

If you have never accepted Jesus Christ as your Saviour, then I beseech you now to repent of your sin and believe in Him.

If Christ is your Saviour, then let me exhort you to begin today to live the life of faith. Walk in the steps of the Master. Love Him and serve Him.

27. *Fanaticism or Faith?*

We are fools for Christ's sake, but ye are wise in Christ; we are weak, but ye are strong; ye are honourable, but we are despised.
—I Corinthians 4:10.

For we walk by faith, not by sight.
—II Corinthians 5:7.

But without faith it is impossible to please him: for he that cometh to God must believe that he is, and that he is a rewarder of them that diligently seek him.
—Hebrews 11:6.

Faith in God often brings trouble. It did for Shadrach, Meshach and Abed-nego. Nebuchadnezzar gave orders that everyone should bow down to the image he had made. But when the three Hebrew children refused to do so, they were cast into a fiery furnace. Deliverance came to them through the Son of God. This amazing record is given to us in Daniel 3:25: "He answered and said, Lo, I see four men loose, walking in the midst of the fire, and they have no hurt; and the form of the fourth is like the Son of God."

I repeat, your faith in God may bring you trouble. Others may not share your beliefs and so seek to hinder you. But keep in mind that God is with you! "If God be for us, who can be against us?"

Faith in God will often bring strange decisions. Philip was conducting a sweeping revival in Samaria; but God led him to leave it all, go into a desert country, and witness to just one man. The account of this performance is found in Acts 8:26-40.

Faith in God often brings suffering. Paul suffered much. "Of the Jews five times received I forty stripes save one. Thrice was I beaten with rods, once was I stoned, thrice I suffered shipwreck, a night and a day I have been in the deep" (II Cor. 11:24,25).

When we think of the Apostle Paul, we think of a mighty man of God—yet, what suffering! In all of this, he was sustained by the grace of God.

Faith in God will bring strange accusations. Your family, your friends and your associates may tell you that you are beside yourself. They may say that your religion has made you mad.

I recently met a quiet little man who told me that he worked as a mail carrier for the United States Government. He said, "When I got saved seven years ago, God laid it on my heart to witness to university students. Now I spend all my spare time on the campus of the state university handing out tracts, gospels of John, and New Testaments. I witness to every student I meet." Of course, many think him foolish. Some would say he is a fanatic. Some would quickly say he is not trained for that kind of work. He is not even a college graduate. A dedicated Christian will sometimes be called a fanatic. He may provoke the laughter of some, and he may be ostracized by others. Remember what the Apostle Paul said, "We are fools for Christ's sake." It will do us good to remember that faith will have some disturbances. But we must face life's problems and do that which will establish our faith.

Establish your faith by the Word of God. Paul said, ". . .faith cometh by hearing, and hearing by the word of God." Know where you stand by the Word. Don't feed on the world, but on the Word. In Isaiah 44:20 we read: "He feedeth on ashes. . ." Anyone can see that ashes would make a mighty poor diet. The world is a mighty poor diet for the child of God. Establish your faith by a study of the Word of God.

Establish your faith by the conscious indwelling Holy Spirit. When we accept Jesus Christ as Saviour, the Holy Spirit comes in. Jesus said, "And I will pray the Father, and he shall give you another Comforter, that he may abide with you for ever" (John 14:16). These assuring verses come to us in Romans 8:14-16:

"For as many as are led by the Spirit of God, they are the sons of God.

"For ye have not received the spirit of bondage again to fear; but ye have received the Spirit of adoption, whereby we cry, Abba, Father.

"The Spirit itself beareth witness with our spirit, that we are the children of God. . . ."

Establish your faith by the recognition of world needs. Those near to the Saviour know that men without Christ are lost. Christians must have concern over the lost.

Again, men will think you fanatical because of your faith. They thought our Lord a very strange person because of His actions and words.

Establish your faith on the basis of world needs. This world needs Christians with strong, overcoming faith.

Now, let me put it down a little closer to where we live. What should people of faith manifest? What should we show to the world?

I. MANIFEST THE JOY OF THE LORD

In a world troubled by every imaginable kind of sin and dissension, we need to reflect the Lord Jesus. He was the Saviour of joy. He exhorted men by saying, "Be of good cheer; I have overcome the world." Joy should be on our faces.

In the writings of a literary genius, there is the story of a storm at sea—one of those terrific storms which make men panicky and fearful. The passengers were huddled together, terror-stricken, in the center of the ship. Doors leading out onto the deck were tightly shut. Men dared not go out for fear of being washed overboard by the mighty waves.

Finally one man, braver than the rest, ventured on deck, clinging with all his might to ropes and posts. He slowly made his way to the pilothouse. Reaching it, he looked up at the pilot as he grasped the wheel with all his strength.

The pilot turned and looked at the white-faced man and smiled as he looked. That smile did something; and making his way back to the passengers, he exclaimed as he joined them, "I saw the pilot's face, and he smiled! All is well!"

In the midst of the shattering, boisterous sea of life, steal away and look into the face of the One who is fearless and unafraid.

But I must remind you that sin takes away joy. When King David fell into sin, the joy of the Lord was taken away. In Psalm 51:12 he pleads, "Restore unto me the joy of thy salvation; and uphold me with thy free spirit." David had not lost his salvation but the joy of it. He got right with God by confessing and forsaking his sin.

The testimony of many Christians is impaired by sin. Consequently, they are melancholy and discouraged. They worry, complain and find fault. This comes because the heart is not right with God.

Notice how much Jesus had to say about rejoicing and living without worry. In the Sermon on the Mount:

"Wherefore, if God so clothe the grass of the field, which to day is, and to morrow is cast into the oven, shall he not much more clothe you, O ye of little faith?

"Therefore take no thought, saying, What shall we eat? or, What shall we drink? or, Wherewithal shall we be clothed?

"(For after all these things do the Gentiles seek:) for your heavenly Father knoweth that ye have need of all these things." —Matt. 6:30-32.

The Apostle Paul expressed himself on worry in these words in Philippians 4:6,7:

"Be careful for nothing; but in every thing by prayer and supplication with thanksgiving let your requests be made known unto God.

"And the peace of God, which passeth all understanding, shall keep your hearts and minds through Christ Jesus."

The Apostle John had some words to say about joy also: "And

these things write we unto you, that your joy may be full" (I John 1:4). This is the key verse of I John.

Now please notice that I said we must manifest "the joy of the Lord." The world's joy does not last, but the joy of the Lord will abide in every storm.

The story comes out of London about a poor, nervous wreck of a man who called upon one of the leading physicians. Said the doctor, "You need to laugh. Go down to the theater and hear Grimaldi, the famous clown; all London is holding its sides at him." But the visitor straightened himself up and said, "Doctor, I am Grimaldi."

Grimaldi was like a lot of people today. He made a good appearance when he stood before the audience, but he was a poor specimen of peace and joy when he stood alone.

II. MANIFEST A CONSTANT GROWTH IN GRACE

"But grow in grace, and in the knowledge of our Lord and Saviour Jesus Christ. To him be glory both now and for ever. Amen."—II Pet. 3:18.

Some Christians do not grow! They remain as baby Christians. A description of them is given in I Corinthians 3. They are the troublemakers in God's work. They are the ones who cry and complain.

Some years ago I saw a most interesting and pathetic illustration of this truth.

I was having dinner in a fine Christian home when the husband and wife informed me about their son. He was 27 years of age but had never talked nor walked. He was just a little larger now than when he was born.

After they had informed me regarding the boy, they took me in to see him. I do not wonder that the mother stood there and wept!

Too many Christians are like that poor lad. You have never grown. You are in the world, but you have never developed.

Some Christians grow for awhile, then stop. In the years of my ministry, I have seen this happen again and again. I watched a man work for ten solid years. Then he quit coming to church. He quit reading his Bible. He quit praying. Of course, many thoughts raced through my mind: *Perhaps he had never been saved. If he was saved, how long would it take him to come back?*

Shame on the Christians who drop out of the light to walk in the shadows! This dishonors our Saviour and damages His work.

We are to be ever growing! Set maturity as your spiritual growth. Do that which produces growth. The writer of Hebrews said, "Therefore leaving the principles of the doctrine of Christ, let us go on unto perfection; not laying again the foundation of repentance from dead works, and of faith toward God" (6:1).

Do that which brings increased faith. Read and believe the Bible. Test the promises of God. Avoid all things that would prove detrimental to your growth—worldly amusements, doubtful companions, evil books, indifference toward service.

III. MANIFEST OBEDIENCE TO THE LORD'S LEADING

He has promised to guide us. He will guide us. It is ours to obey Him.

Love should prompt our obedience. Jesus said, "If ye love me, keep my commandments."

Good common sense will prompt obedience. God's way is ever the best.

Obedience to the Lord's leading is an expression of faith.

Elisha was expressing faith when he left the plow to become a prophet of God.

Abraham was expressing faith when he left Ur of Chaldees to follow God, not knowing where he was going.

Paul was expressing faith when he allowed the Lord to guide him day by day.

Yes, we walk by faith!

Faith in a person—Christ. This means that I can walk without the slightest fear. When He is with me, all is well. I agree with David Livingstone that one of the sweetest verses in the Bible is, ". . .lo, I am with you alway, even unto the end of the world."

Faith in His power. He said, "All power is given unto me in heaven and in earth. Go ye therefore. . . ."

He leadeth me! O blessed thought!
O words with heav'nly comfort fraught!
Whate'er I do, where'er I be,
Still 'tis God's hand that leadeth me.

Sometimes 'mid scenes of deepest gloom;
Sometimes where Eden's bowers bloom;
By waters still, o'er troubled sea,
Still 'tis His hand that leadeth me!

Lord, I would clasp Thy hand in mine,
Nor ever murmur nor repine;
Content, whatever lot I see,
Since 'tis my God that leadeth me!

IV. PEOPLE OF FAITH SHOULD MANIFEST A CONCERN FOR OTHERS

1. *I must have a concern for God's people.* I must not live selfishly, but I must seek to be a help to all I meet. I can and must pray for others, for Samuel said, "God forbid that I should sin against the Lord in ceasing to pray for you" (I Sam. 12:23).

I can set a right example for others. It is important that when people look at my life, they can know I am following my Lord. That is what the apostle meant when he said, "Follow me, as I follow Christ."

I can give direct help to others when God leads. I must not close my eyes to the needs of others.

2. *I must have a concern for the lost,* a loving compassion for poor, lost sinners.

During the days of Charles Finney's great revivals, there was a farmer who knew how to wait upon God. When he learned of a forthcoming meeting for Finney in the city, he left his farm and all his interest and went into town and engaged a hotel room. He gave instruction to the clerk to send a jug of water and a loaf of bread and leave it outside the door, and under no circumstances was he to be disturbed.

Often the farmer had finished praying and had left before Finney arrived, but upon his arrival Finney would inquire about this friend. When he learned that the farmer had been there, he would say, "My praying friend has already been here, and he has gotten the victory. We shall have a great revival."

We must have the concern Jeremiah had, who said, "Oh that my head were waters, and mine eyes a fountain of tears, that I might weep day and night for the slain of the daughter of my people!" (9:1).

Let me repeat this last point: We of faith should manifest a concern for others.

I told the students of Tennessee Temple how I had led two young ladies to the Lord on Monday evening. We had had a gracious service with a good response. The audience had been dismissed. A young lady came to the platform, put out her hand and said, "I enjoyed the service." I felt impressed to ask her if she was a Christian. She replied, "No."

Standing at the pulpit, I opened my Bible and read to her verses on salvation. I asked if she believed the Bible. She did. I asked her to put her fingers upon the promises of God, then I prayed that she would accept Jesus Christ as Saviour.

When I finished praying, she said, "Oh, yes, I want to trust Him now as my Saviour." I told her to tell the pastor, Rev. Ed Johnson, what she had done. She did so. It was her first time to be in the house of God. Later, I told her to read John, chapter 3. She informed me that she did not own a Bible. The pastor secured one for her.

Then two others came up to the platform. I shook hands with each of them, then turned to a young lady and asked, "Are you a Christian?"

"Well, I am not quite sure."

"Have you been born again?"

"Oh," she said, "I suppose I have always been a Christian."

Again, I opened my Bible on the pulpit and showed her verses on salvation. The girl who had brought her to the platform began tugging at my coat, and she said, "You don't quite understand. That girl is studying to be a nun."

I said, "Oh, that's wonderful! Nuns need to be saved, too."

After reading a few verses of Scripture and having a prayer, this young lady accepted Jesus Christ also. I sent her from the platform to the pastor to tell him that she had been saved. She did so, then came back to the platform again.

Is salvation so simple? Of course it is. God made it that way so poor lost sinners can be saved.

I believe the two young ladies were saved while standing at the pulpit in that church. The first one did not even own a Bible, though she lived in the city of almost a million people. The second one saved owned a Bible but knew nothing about it.

Let me urge the lost people in this audience to look up to Jesus and be saved.

You recall the story of Charles Haddon Spurgeon, the great English preacher. He was converted when he heard a lay preacher in a Methodist church speak on the text, "Look unto me, and be ye saved, all the ends of the earth: for I am God, and there is none else." The lay preacher fixed his eyes upon young Spurgeon and said, "Young man, you are in trouble. You will never get out of it unless you look to Christ." That day Spurgeon was saved.

That reminds me of the little girl passing through a graveyard with her parents. They came to a beautiful figure of Christ leaning upon a massive marble cross. Upon His face was a look of suffering, love and pity. As they paused to look, she said in a low voice, "I can hardly lift up my eyes to look on Him—I have done so many wrong things."

We can appreciate the humility of the child.

My friends, it is because we are sinners that He invites us to look to Him. Our sinfulness is the reason for looking, not an excuse for turning away. I beseech you to look unto Jesus and be saved.

Now, let me quickly review what I have tried to give you. What should people of faith manifest? What should we show the world?

First, we should manifest the joy of the Lord; second, we should manifest a constant growth in grace; third, we should manifest obedience to the Lord's leading; fourth, we should manifest a concern for others.

We beseech you to look up and behold the Lord who died upon the cross for you. Receive Him now as your Saviour.

28. *The Finest Confession of Faith in the New Testament*

> *And Thomas answered and said unto him, My Lord and my God.*
>
> —John 20:28.

Where was Thomas on that first Sunday night? This thrilling scene is given to us in John 20:19-23. The disciples were assembled in a room with the doors shut "for fear of the Jews."

It was then that Jesus came and stood in their midst and said unto them, "Peace be unto you." The Saviour showed His hands and side to the disciples.

The disciples were made happy when they saw the Lord. To them Jesus gave His Commission. He said: "Peace be unto you: as my Father hath sent me, even so send I you."

Ah, but Thomas, one of the twelve, was not with them on that first Sunday evening!

The first picture of Thomas: Much of the story of Thomas is given in four portions of the Word. In John 11 Jesus and His disciples had gone away into a secret place. His enemies were seeking His life. In the midst of this there came a message from near Jerusalem, from the home of Mary and Martha in Bethany, an urgent message to say that their brother Lazarus was dying.

Jesus told His disciples that He must go at once to awaken Lazarus out of his sleep. The disciples were apparently upset by this news. It was then that Thomas, who is called Didymus, said, "Let us also go, that we may die with him." Thomas felt that going back to Jerusalem meant sudden death; but he was loyal and courageous, even putting to shame Peter and John. He was ready to go even if it meant dying for Christ.

The second picture of Thomas is in John 14. Jesus had been talking to the disciples about Heaven. He had pointed out the many mansions and also mentioned His coming again, then said,

"And whither I go ye know, and the way ye know." It was then that Thomas said, "Lord, we know not whither thou goest; and how can we know the way?" The messages of Jesus about Heaven and the Second Coming were excellent, but Thomas was disturbed. He wanted to know the way to Heaven. Then Jesus said, "I am the way, the truth, and the life: no man cometh unto the Father, but by me."

The third picture we have of Thomas is in John 20. We have just given a brief summary of that Sunday evening when Jesus appeared before the disciples, but Thomas, one of the twelve, was not with them. Neither was Judas, for he had already committed suicide. But where was Thomas? He might have been at home brooding about happenings on Calvary's hill. Or he may have been walking about the streets of Jerusalem. It has been suggested that perchance he went out to Golgotha to see the three crosses, gaunt and empty.

But being absent on that first Sunday night, Thomas missed the joy which came to the other disciples.

The fourth picture of Thomas is also found in John 20. The disciples told Thomas what they had seen. And he said, "Except I shall see in his hands the print of the nails, . . . and thrust my hand into his side, I will not believe." This is why he is called "Doubting Thomas." Perhaps the title is not kind.

But eight days after the first scene, the disciples were together again, "then came Jesus, the doors being shut, and stood in the midst, and said, Peace be unto you." On that occasion the Lord turned to Thomas and said, "Reach hither thy finger, and behold my hands; and reach hither thy hand, and thrust it into my side: and be not faithless, but believing." Then we read, "And Thomas answered and said unto him, My Lord and my God."

This is surely one of the finest confessions of faith in the entire New Testament.

NOW, WHAT DO WE FIND IN THIS ENTIRE SCENE?

The loving concern of Christ. You cannot avoid seeing the emphasis Jesus placed upon the individual.

Thomas is not the greatest of the names given to us in the New Testament. But here on this Sunday evening it was to Thomas that Jesus said, "Reach hither thy finger, and behold my hands; and reach hither thy hand, and thrust it into my side. . . ." It was to Thomas that Jesus said," . . .be not faithless, but believing."

Here is shown the compassion of Christ. Never let your mind get far from the glorious scenes of compassion: His compassion for the poor, the sorrowing, the confused, the sick, the wicked, the backslider, the doubting one. You recall the story of Evangelist Henry Varley. Mr. Varley was dealing with a backslider who had been out of fellowship for many years. The man testified that he had been saved but was away from God. He told Mr. Varley that he would do anything to come back to the place of victory. Varley said, "Would you like to be restored at this moment?"

Amazed, he answered, "I suppose so."

Varley said, "Suppose your daughter had sinned against you, causing you and your wife great sorrow. Then one night she came and threw her arms around her mother's neck, saying, 'O Mother, I am so ashamed of myself for having given you and Father such anxiety and sorrow! Will you please forgive me?' I ask you, can your daughter restore herself, or must her restoration be your act?"

The backslider said, "It must be mine."

And Varley said, "How soon would you restore her? In twelve years? in twelve months? in twelve hours?"

The man said, "I would restore her at once."

Then Mr. Varley said, "I bid you to see that you are God's child, and the heavenly Father is ready now to receive you upon your confession. Confess your sin. Ask for His forgiveness. He will restore you."

What must the backslider do? Be ready to confess and forsake his sin, and to seek again fellowship with God. "If we confess our sins, he is faithful and just to forgive us our sins, and to cleanse us from all unrighteousness" (I John 1:9).

The open wounds of Christ. Jesus said to Thomas, 'Stretch out your hands, touch me, be not faithless, but believing.' Jesus was saying, "Thomas, I am the One who died for you upon the cross. I took your place upon the tree. I bore your sins in My body. Now I am standing here before you. Be not faithless, but believing."

We need to emphasize again the substitutionary death of the Saviour, that "Christ died for our sins according to the scriptures." Paul said, "Christ also hath loved us, and hath given himself for us."

Some years ago one of the White House guards lost his life while defending the President of the United States. Public sentiment rallied to the support of his widow, and a collection was made for his orphaned children. One newspaper reporter wrote in his column: "This is a very worthy project, but the part that really attracted my attention was a paragraph in which the President is quoted as saying, 'You can't imagine just how it feels when someone else dies for you!' "

Our hearts should be deeply stirred when we think about our dear Saviour dying for us.

There is an old story about a Roman servant who knew that his master was in danger of being put to death. He clothed himself in the royal man's garments that he might be mistaken for him. When the enemy came through the gates, the disguised servant was immediately slain.

In memory of his deed, his master had a statue of him fashioned in brass and erected as a monument to his self-sacrificing love.

We see the finest confession of faith in the New Testament. Thomas said, "My Lord, and my God." In a single statement Thomas was wrapping up his faith in the eternal God, and in Christ, the Son of God. He expressed his belief in the Messiah who died upon the cross for him. He confessed the Lordship of Christ. His testimony was simple but profound.

Now permit me to give three very practical suggestions, as based upon this story.

I. THE SIMPLICITY OF A SINCERE TESTIMONY

There is no question that the testimony of Thomas was sincere. Yes, and simple. We do not argue about the fact that Thomas missed something when he was absent on that first Sunday evening. We can suppose that he had a week of misery as he waited for the next Sunday. Missing church is always costly. But when he came face to face with the Lord Jesus Christ, he gave this testimony: "My Lord, and my God."

Don't seek for the world's wisdom as you speak of the Lord Jesus. Don't argue about secondary matters. Let your testimony be positive and ringing, simple and sincere.

Are you a Christian? This is the question that demands a "Yes" or "No" answer—there is no middle ground.

I ask many people, "Are you a Christian?" Sometimes they say, "Well, I think I am a Christian." Other times I might hear them say, "I am as good as anyone else." Occasionally a man will say to me, "I am not sure just what you mean." These are all evasions of the question regarding Christ.

1. *You can know you are saved.* This Book answers the question in a number of verses. For example in I John 5:12: "He that hath the Son hath life; and he that hath not the Son of God hath not life." The answer is given to us in John 1:12: "But as many as received him, to them gave he power to become the sons of God, even to them that believe on his name."

All of Christendom is hurt by uncertain testimonies. Let yours be positive and sure.

2. *Live so that you can speak without fear.* The tragedy of this hour is that so many who profess to be saved cannot speak of the Lord Jesus Christ because their lives do not bear the marks of the Saviour. Many Christians compromise with the world. Many Christians engage in the affairs of the world. They profess to know Christ, but they do not live so that they can testify of Him.

3. *Be simple and direct in your answer.* Don't limp about from side to side. Let people know where you stand. Your positive answer will help them.

II. THE SINFULNESS OF A LYING TESTIMONY

Listen to these words found in Matthew 7:21-23:

"Not every one that saith unto me, Lord, Lord, shall enter into

the kingdom of heaven; but he that doeth the will of my Father which is in heaven.

"Many will say to me in that day, Lord, Lord, have we not prophesied in thy name? and in thy name have cast out devils? and in thy name done many wonderful works?

"And then will I profess unto them, I never knew you: depart from me, ye that work iniquity."

There is grave danger in profession without possession. This present world is filled with those who profess to be saved, but are they? They go through the rituals; they answer correctly the questions of the churches, but do they know Christ?

Judas was a professor but not a possessor. Being in the company of the twelve disciples did not make him a saved man.

Some people join the church and try to make themselves believe that they are all right. They lie to themselves and to others.

Don't deceive yourself about this all-important matter. Face your need! Recognize your sinfulness. Come before the Lord in all humility and claim His salvation.

Don't deceive others. If you are a professor of religion, not a possessor of faith in Christ, then someone else may be deceived by your life. Be careful that you are not leading someone else astray.

Don't dishonor Him. You certainly recognize that Jesus died for sinners. What if you refuse to receive Him? Then you are dishonoring Christ.

You can know that you are a child of God. Romans 8:16 says, "The Spirit itself beareth witness with our spirit, that we are the children of God."

I read about a gentleman who once entered a store that sold fine glass and Chinaware. Approaching the proprietor he said, "I would like to buy all of the glasses that are pitched in the key of A."

The owner of the store, looking amused, said, "Well, friend we don't buy glasses for their musical qualities, so I cannot tell you which ones have the proper key!"

The inquirer then took a tuning fork from his pocket and struck it on the counter. Immediately every glass pitched in the key of A on the shelf responded.

When the soul is saved, we respond to the voice of God. We delight in His teachings. We are in tune with His commands.

III. THE SUCCESS OF A POSITIVE TESTIMONY

Christ demands and deserves a positive testimony. We are commanded to go into all the world and preach the Gospel to every creature. Why? Because He died for us. This lost and undone world needs a positive testimony.

A positive testimony brings the blessing of God. Perhaps you have been missing some spiritual blessings because your testimony has not been positive and plain.

A positive testimony strengthens others, while a weak testimony hurts both family and friends.

A positive testimony points men to Christ. It is our desire here to make this an unusual year in witnessing. We would like for every child of God who holds membership in Highland Park Baptist Church to speak of the Saviour daily.

What if a thousand of us would endeavor to win one soul to Christ *per month!* This would be 12,000 per year. In ten years—120,000—more people than live in Chattanooga! Think of that! This with only a thousand of us! Only one soul per month!

If a thousand of us could win one soul *per week,* this would be 4,000 per month and 52,000 in a single year.

Let's give ourselves to winning people!

NOW WHAT DOES GOD EXPECT OF HIS OWN?

1. *He expects consecration.* This is essential for the fulness of the Spirit. The fact that the twelve disciples were subject to the frailties and weaknesses of fallen humanity is revealed in the gospel story. But when they were filled with the Holy Spirit, they had the power which enabled them to witness and to win souls.

Satan will put forth every effort to keep you from living the consecrated life. He will try to make you compromise in some way, even in the smallest way.

Most people are not guilty of great sins against society. But our danger is the temptations to small sins. (I am not trying to classify sins as large or small. In the sight of God, sin is sin. But I am sure you recognize that there are some sins that do not seem as important or as detrimental as others.)

A famous explorer in South America was once driven back and forced to abandon his journey by an almost invisible foe. He was equipped for leopards, serpents and crocodiles, but these proved no threat. He had failed to reckon with the little fellows—the billions of "chiggers," so tiny they could not be seen. Someone composed a little ditty about the "chiggers."

> Here's to the chigger,
> The bug that's no bigger
>   Than the end of a very small pin;
> But the itch that he raises,
> Simply amazes,
>   And that's where the rub comes in!

It is tiny things which spoil our testimony. We have to be on guard against "the little foxes," the hasty word, outburst of temper, snap judgment. Yes, God expects a life of consecration.

2. *God expects faithfulness.* The Bible says, ". . .be thou faithful unto death, and I will give thee a crown of life."

The early disciples were faithful to the end. Here is an article that appeared in THE EVANGEL, dealing with the various ways in which the apostles and leaders of the early church were put to death:

> Matthew is supposed to have suffered martyrdom by being slain with the sword at a city of Ethiopia.
> Mark was dragged through the streets of Alexandria in Egypt, until he expired.
> Luke was hanged on an olive tree in Greece.
> John was put into a cauldron of boiling oil at Rome, but escaped death. He afterwards died a natural death at Ephesus.
> James the Great was beheaded at Jerusalem.
> James the Less was thrown from a pinnacle or wing of the Temple, and then beaten to death with a club.

Philip was hanged up against a pillar at Hierapolis, a city of Phrygia.

Bartholomew was flayed alive at the command of a barbarous king.

Andrew was bound to a cross, from whence he preached to the people until he expired.

Thomas' body was run through with a lance at Caromandel in the East Indies.

Jude was shot to death with arrows.

Simon Zelotes was crucified in Persia.

Matthias was first stoned, then beheaded.

These men set us an example of faithfulness.

3. *God expects of His own a constant testimony daily.* How often that word "daily" is found in the opening chapters of the book of Acts. "And daily in the temple, and in every house, they ceased not to teach and preach Jesus Christ" (5:42). God is expecting of us that we daily follow Him.

Daily we give our testimony of faith in Him. Daily we tell of His mercy and grace. Daily we point out that His blood cleanses from all sin.

An unknown author put down some things which he called:

THE GREATEST OF ALL

My greatest loss—to lose my soul.

My greatest gain—Christ as my Saviour.

My greatest object—to glorify God.

My greatest work—to win souls for Christ Jesus.

My greatest joy—the joy of God's salvation.

My greatest inheritance—Heaven and its glories.

My greatest neglect—the neglect of so great a salvation.

My greatest crime—to reject Christ, the only Saviour.

My greatest profit—to live godly in this present world.

My greatest rest—". . .the peace. . .which passeth all understanding."

My greatest knowledge—to know God and Jesus Christ, whom He has sent.

How many of you can say that Christ is your Lord, your God, your Saviour? Is He the Lord of your life?

We give an opportunity now for many to come to testify of their faith in Christ.

Many of you Christians may desire to come for rededication of life or the fullness of the Spirit or for dedication to soul winning. Some of you may want to straighten out some of the weaknesses of your lives by seeking God's forgiveness. Many in this building should come by profession of faith. Come repenting of the sin of unbelief. Come believing, receiving Christ as Saviour.

For This Crisis

We must have Faith, for darkness is about us;
    There's light beyond, though we have lost our way.
Oh, falter not! We'll find again the home path,
    And see the sunlight of a brighter day.

We must have Hope, for we are near despairing,
    And Hope will be an anchor to the soul;
Though stormy winds may roar their weird enchantment,
    Hope, radiant Hope, will help us find the goal.

We must have Love, and Love will lighten burdens;
    And Love will bring us cheer and banish care.
The greatest blessing life can ever bring us
    Is Love, which gives us strength to do and dare.

We must have God! Without Him we are helpless!
    We've failed because we've tried to go alone—
And now in sorrow, care and tribulation,
    Come, seek the Lord, and bow before His throne.

The Light will come! It never, never fails us!
    God ever lives—His promises are sure;
He holds the waves—the winds are in His fingers,
    In His blest care our future is secure!

—Annie Agnes Smith

29. *Faith for This Strenuous Day*

And Jesus said unto them. . .if ye have faith as a grain of mustard seed, ye shall say unto this mountain, Remove hence to yonder place; and it shall remove; and nothing shall be impossible unto you.

—Matthew 17:20.

And Jesus answering saith unto them, Have faith in God.

—Mark 11:22.

Now faith is the substance of things hoped for, the evidence of things not seen.

—Hebrews 11:1.

So then faith cometh by hearing, and hearing by the word of God.

—Romans 10:17.

I am discussing having simple faith, but actually all faith is simple. Coming from a humble, ordinary human being up to an eternal God, faith has to be simple.

Let's consider how one gets faith.

1. *One must come to Jesus Christ.* No one can know faith unless he first comes as a sinner repenting, believing and receiving Christ as his Saviour. Without Him there can be no faith. If tonight you have never been saved, then you must repent, believe and receive Christ in order to have faith in your heart.

2. *One must believe His Word.* "So then faith cometh by hearing, and hearing by the word of God" (Rom. 10:17). Feed your faith on the Bible. If you are a child of God, feed your faith daily.

Daily seek to learn from the Bible new thoughts to thrill, to stir, to inspire you.

Someone has said, "Feed your faith and your doubts will starve to death."

3. *One must use his faith.* When we do not use the faith God has given, it is lost.

Notice: it takes faith to pray. If I try to pray without believing that God is hearing and answering, I soon grow weary. But if I pray in faith believing, then I can pray with joy and rejoicing, knowing God is hearing and will bless.

It takes faith to be a soul winner. We can't save a soul; we can't give a person everlasting life, but we can give the Word of God, and the Spirit of God will use the Bible to bring a soul to salvation.

It takes faith to read the Bible. "All scripture is given by inspiration of God, and is profitable for doctrine, for reproof, for correction. . . ." We must believe that this is the eternal Word of God. God is everywhere, but our faith must be in God and in His Word.

It takes faith to look to the future. We've been singing tonight about the coming of our Lord. We have to believe that by faith. We look with anticipation, with joy, for His second coming.

I had you sing awhile ago a song we use quite often—"He Keeps Me Singing."

Luther Bridgers was a great Methodist preacher. He and his wife had two lovely daughters. They lived in a town in Kentucky.

Mr. Bridgers was preaching somewhere in Georgia, a short distance from us. In the midst of his revival campaign, a message came that his home had burned to the ground and his wife and two daughters had lost their lives in the fire.

This Methodist evangelist was brokenhearted by this awful news. And for a time it was thought that perhaps he would not preach again because of his despondency.

But Luther Bridgers came out of that and wrote the song that you sang a moment ago:

There's within my heart a melody,
Jesus whispers sweet and low;
Fear not, I am with thee; peace, be still,
In all of life's ebb and flow.

Though sometimes He leads through waters deep,
Trials fall across the way,
Though sometimes the path seems rough and steep,
See His footprints all the way.

Jesus, Jesus, Jesus—
Sweetest name I know,
Fills my every longing,
Keeps me singing as I go.

We sing it in a rather lilting, happy mood. I'm not against that. But this song was born out of much heartache.

With Heaven upon his heart and mind, one finds peace for everyday living.

Why do Christians fail? Because they turn from the Bible. Oh, get back into your Bible!

Christians also fail because they do not exercise faith in God. No matter how dark it may be, exercise your faith.

We fail also because we close our eyes to God's promises. He has promised to be with us. He has promised to answer prayer. He has promised us a home in Heaven. We fail when we do not rest upon these promises.

Now to my subject: "The Power of a Simple Faith."

I. SIMPLE FAITH FOR THIS STRENUOUS DAY

This is a day of violence. We can expect it in the newspaper today—bombings, murder, kidnapping or some other tragedy. This is a time of murder, rape, robberies. Yes, this is a strenuous day, a day which calls for simple faith, a plain faith that lays hold of God's promises.

This is a day of corruption, of sin, dishonesty, lying, even in our highest offices of government. This day cries for honest men—honest in business, honest in politics, honest in church involvement.

I read a story about Abraham Lincoln last week which thrilled me.

Back in Cincinnati in 1850 two companies were about to go to trial. One was the McCormack Reader Company, the other, Manning Corporation. They were planning on a big crowd. Lawyers were coming from several places.

The Manning Corporation wanted to get the best lawyer it could find, so they chose Abraham Lincoln. When he arrived, he walked in with an umbrella in his hand, tied with a blue bow.

Lincoln was big and gawky, with long arms—ugly in many ways. He was just a plain, simple man.

When they saw him, Stanton of Manning Corporation looked at him one time and said, "I won't have him! I don't want that big ape around! Take him away!" He said it so loud that Lincoln heard him. This was in 1850.

But a strange thing happened. On April 14, 1865, just 15 years after that, at 7:22 in the morning, Stanton was standing by the bedside of Abraham Lincoln, who had been shot.

(Lincoln had gone through crucial years in his administration in those Civil War days.)

Now Stanton was standing nearby. In his hand was his silk hat. Here is the doctor, also one of the surgeon generals. Others were around the bed.

After awhile, when Lincoln stopped breathing, Stanton put his hat on as if to leave, then pulled it off and said, "Dr. Greeley (pastor of N.Y. Presbyterian Church in Washington, D.C.), lead us in prayer." Dr. Greeley did. When he had finished, the surgeon general walked over and pulled down the shades. At 7:22 a.m. the sun was bright in the room. Again Stanton pulled his hat from his head, this man who, in 1850 had said, "I won't have him! I don't want that big ape around!" Now 15 famous years in the life of Abraham Lincoln have gone by, the last five extra famous years. As the shades were pulled, Stanton stood with tears coursing down his cheeks looking upon the dead body of Lincoln. He gave tribute to one of the greatest men this nation has ever had in these words: "Now he belongs to the ages."

Lincoln, a simple man, but one who had faith.

In a day of corruption like ours, this story came back to me.

Oh, how we need more men like Abraham Lincoln, men who stand true!

This is a day of pressure on people everywhere. What should we do in a day like this?

Get back to the Word of God. Let me ask you to do something this week. Read through the book of Philippians. Will you? Let God speak to your heart through it. Get back to the Bible. Read the Psalms. Read John's gospel. Read Romans. Read the Bible. Let God speak to you.

Get back to prayer. Have you knelt in prayer today? Have you been down before God asking His help for yourself, for your family?

Get back to trusting God—not self, but God; not your ingenuity, your plans, your ideas, but God's.

Happiness comes when we exercise faith. Don't give way to doubts. Be positive in your testimony.

Our need is simple faith in a strenuous day.

II. SIMPLE FAITH FOR THIS SORROWFUL DAY

". . .man is born unto trouble, as the sparks fly upward," says Job 5:7.

There is no home without a hush. All need simple faith for this sorrowful day. We know not what a day may bring forth.

How do people stand their sorrows without faith in God? What can a person do without faith in the eternal God?

I have a friend out in Texas, a great Southern Baptist, who has written many, many books—all on comfort. He autographs them and sends me all his new ones.

A loss of a little daughter just a few years of age broke his heart. So he began writing books to comfort others. They are fine books.

My friend, today our need is simple faith in God. In days filled with sorrow and sadness, we must depend on His promises for comfort.

This afternoon as we had the Scripture reading by the graveside, I said to the Wilson family, "This is not the hardest hour; it will be tomorrow and the next day and the next. There will be many sorrow-filled times when tears will fall, when questions will arise. But you dear ones will simply trust in God."

I say that to all: we must have simple faith for this hour and for all of the hours ahead.

1. *We must have faith in times of shadows.* Shadows are on every hand, but these can help us. Shadows can help this dear family. Shadows drive us up to the side of our Lord, the Light of the world. When shadows come—as they will—we can feel His presence. Sickness, death and accidents draw us to His side.

2. *We must have faith in times of temptation.* He understands. When Satan comes to tempt and pull us away, we can be strong in our Lord. He will never fail. He will be with us in our hour of temptation.

3. *We must have faith for our material needs.* You have needs. I have needs. For home, for loved ones, we need certain things. God, who promised to supply, never fails.

4. *We must have faith in times of failure.* Help others even when you yourself fail to trust in God, to rest in Him. Help them by your faith. To exercise faith in God helps others.

God help us to have simple faith in times of sorrow.

The story is told of one family who lost a little girl, young in years, sweet in life, strong in faith—a Christian child who helped her companions and friends.

After the funeral, a group of children came by the house. With tears, they said to the parents of the little one who had departed, "We would like to put a little piece of cardboard on her grave with a message." Of course the parents consented.

The children, young in years but old enough to know what they were doing, went out to the grave, put down a little marker with a message, then left.

The next day the parents went out to the cemetery. The card, written with a crayon, said:

IT WAS EASIER FOR US TO DO GOOD AND BE GOOD
WHEN SHE WAS WITH US.

This is part of our gift to life. We are here to help. I have my heartaches; you have yours—but let's help others. In this sorrowful, sin-sick day, may we aid, assist and comfort those in need.

III. SIMPLE FAITH FOR A SINFUL DAY

Face it! This is a day of lowering standards. This is a day of profane speech. This is a day of vulgarity, loose standards in dress and increased immorality. Twenty-three percent of all babies born here at Erlanger Hospital are illegitimate! This ought to shock us. This is a day of open sin.

Some 600,000 young people of New York state had one of their rock concerts. When they left the grounds, authorities said that the rubbish—whiskey bottles and beer cans—was a foot deep on the 90-acre farm—600,000 long-bearded, dirty, unkempt people. Perhaps you saw the report, with pictures, on televison.

This is a day of open sin, drunkenness, dope, immorality, looseness. This day calls for people with faith in God, calls for people with convictions. Everything is shaky. People have lost all their standards, their convictions. They have turned away from things meaningful to follow after the flesh. Men with convictions, folks who will stand against open sin, is our need.

We need folk like the little mother in Atlanta who called her pastor and said something like this:

> Pastor, I want to confess something which has bothered me for forty years. When I was young, I worked in a big store here in Atlanta. Thinking no one would miss it, I took some money from the cash register one day. Then the next day I took a little more.
>
> For a number of months I took a little money daily—just small amounts. No one said a word. No one suspected anything. The more I took, the less troubled I became. My conscience was becoming hardened. I thought, *This big store—it will not lose anything. They've got money; why should I worry about this!*
>
> In recent years, this theft keeps coming back to mind. I'm a professing Christian; I believe I know Christ; yet I cannot pray. I'm troubled, distressed. Preacher, can you tell me what I can do about this?

Without hesitation the good pastor told her, "Take the money back and confess your wrong."

She had no other choice if she wanted God's ear. I'm sure the company would be lenient in her case. After forty years I'm quite sure the present management would forgive.

She kept thinking, *I've got to get this matter attended to*, yet she kept putting it off. Year after year she failed to right the wrong. Year after year she stayed troubled, knowing God would not hear her when she prayed.

In this evil day, stand for your convictions! Be honest! Be upright! Don't allow the crowd to sway you—in business, in the store, in the office, nor in the home.

THE TEARS OF AFFLICTION ARE OFTEN NEEDED TO KEEP THE EYE OF FAITH BRIGHT.—Spurgeon.

30. *Unlimited Faith*

And, behold, I send the promise of my Father upon you: but tarry ye in the city of Jerusalem, until ye be endued with power from on high.

And he led them out as far as to Bethany, and he lifted up his hands, and blessed them.

And it came to pass, while he blessed them, he was parted from them, and carried up into heaven.

And they worshipped him, and returned to Jerusalem with great joy:

And were continually in the temple, praising and blessing God. Amen.

—Luke 24:49-53.

And, being assembled together with them, commanded them that they should not depart from Jerusalem, but wait for the promise of the Father, which, saith he, ye have heard of me.

—Acts 1:4.

On this last Monday I paid a visit to an elderly lady in one of the hospitals. When I stepped up to the bedside, she said to me, "Brother Roberson, I want you to pray for me. Pray that I might have faith in God." I said, "We'll pray right now." So I bowed my head and prayed that she would have faith in God.

The request of that lady is not unusual. It is not always stated as abruptly and pointedly, but with all of us there is a cry that we might have more faith in God.

We begin this message with this illustration as given in the Word.

Jesus led His disciples out to a certain place and told them what to do. "Go back to Jerusalem and wait until you be endued with power from on high." His command was that they should go. This is given again in Acts 1.

With implicit faith these disciples went back to Jerusalem. They didn't try to escape, but went right to where He had sent them. He had given them a promise, and they knew He could not lie. They waited patiently, knowing not what would happen. The Bible says they waited joyfully; they "were continually in the temple, praising and blessing God." They waited for the fulfillment of that which had been promised. In their thinking, the Saviour could do nothing but good for His own. They had a conviction about this. So with eager anticipation they waited in faith.

How blessed is faith, when you simply take God at His Word!

Lack of faith brings fear. How often Jesus rebuked His disciples because of their little faith. He was asleep in the boat. A storm came up. They awakened Him because they were frightened. "Master, Master, we perish!" He arose and rebuked them because of their lack of faith.

Lack of faith brings impatience. We are to wait as did Joshua and the children of Israel when they marched around the city of Jericho. We are to wait for the fullness of the Spirit as did the disciples on the day of Pentecost. Lack of faith will bring impatience and a trust in the flesh.

Lack of faith brings doubts. John the Baptist had some doubts about Jesus, so sent some men to Him to question, "Are You the one?" We, too, doubt many times. Why do these doubts come? Because of lack of faith.

Lack of faith brings failure. The powerless disciples in Luke 9:37-43 could not cast out the demon. Jesus came and walked in their midst, and the man came to the Son and said, "Your disciples couldn't do it." They failed, and the Lord Jesus rebuked them because of their lack of faith.

Lack of faith brings weakness. If there is no faith in God, there is no power in the Holy Spirit. Notice, your faith must be in God. It must be a faith that begins with God the Father, Christ the Son, and is continued by the Father and the Son throughout all of life. It must start there, end there, and must continue day by day. In every way, your faith must be in the blessed Lord Jesus Christ. Jesus said, "Have faith in God."

Sometimes we get away from these things. We fail. We are not as trusting as we should be, not as simple in our faith, in resting upon the promises of God for all the needs of our lives. He is with us. He is ready to guide us. He is always our helper and guide.

A beautiful and humorous story was given in a convention held in Philadelphia some years ago and led by the late Dr. W. B. Riley, a famous Baptist preacher. On the platform was Dr. William Evans whose books on soul winning are used here in some of our studies in the school. Dr. Evans was preaching in one of these big auditoriums with two balconies. On the top balcony in the front row sat a scrubwoman named Sophie, quite famous for her faith in God. (Maybe you have read about her.) Dr. Evans was quite dramatic in what he was saying. He was preaching to these thousands of people on Revelation 1:8, "I am Alpha and Omega, the beginning and the ending. . . ." As he was waxing eloquent, he stood back and dramatically shouted, "I AM ALPHA AND OMEGA, THE BEGINNING AND THE ENDING." He just stood there for a moment, saying nothing.

Right in the stillness of that dramatic moment, Sophie shouted out: "YES—AND HE IS ALSO THE SAVIOUR, NOT ONLY AT THE BEGINNING, BUT ALL THE WAY THROUGH TO THE END!"

The crowd began to laugh, making it hard for Evans to get their attention again.

How true! He is with us at all hours, and until the end!

I. THERE MUST BE UNLIMITED FAITH IN GOD IN EVERY PLACE

Whether in Chattanooga, New York City, Chicago, San Francisco, Dallas, or elsewhere, there must be faith in God. Faith at home or on the foreign field works everywhere the same.

Faith in God produces a godly life. Samuel illustrates this. It will produce gratitude of heart.

The ten lepers came, were healed, and went away. Only one came back to give thanks. Faith had produced a gratitude in his heart.

Faith in God will produce results. Whether in building a church or a school or running a mission program—whatever it may be—faith will produce results. In the business world, it works the same. If God is guiding, unlimited faith in Him produces results wherever it is, whatever it may be.

Faith in God will bring us out of tight places. You will find or have found yourself in some difficult places, even as did the children of Israel when they came to the Red Sea. Moses said, ". . .stand still, and see the salvation of the Lord." He gave his cry. They stood still and obeyed, and God opened up the way for them to go through in safety. But sometimes the tight places may be of our making—by some failure, by some sin, by debts unpaid. But God will guide and help if you are repentant and will right the wrong.

No matter where we are, nor where we may be led in our ministries, we must always have unlimited faith.

II. UNLIMITED FAITH FOR EVERY CRISIS

Unlimited faith for the crucial hours. Times of poverty and need will be the lot of all of us. It is then when we must have faith in God. Young and old, let all things press you up to the side of your Saviour. Some of your richest blessings will not come out of days of affluence but out of days of poverty; some of your sweetest touches with God will not come out of times when you have all you need but when you are praying for God to supply your need and waiting upon Him.

Unlimited faith for the time of illness. Sickness comes to these bodies. But think of Job's faith. Think of Hezekiah's faith when he was sick and asked God for an extension of time. Think of Paul's faith with his thorn in the flesh and God saying, "My grace is sufficient."

A man called me last night from Birmingham, wanting me to

pray for him. "I have about two months in the hospital awaiting me now, so the doctors say. I must undergo a serious operation." He went on to tell me: "I am not worried, for I am trusting God, convinced that He will bring me through."

Unlimited faith in seasons of persecution. Persecutions will come; you can count on that. In Acts 12 we find Peter asleep but trusting God. In Acts 15 Paul is rejoicing from jail. On the Isle of Patmos, John, a prisoner, is waiting and writing the Revelation.

We need faith in our moments of failure. When everything seemingly has failed, when you feel you cannot possibly go on, when your life has been frustrated, then is the time to rest upon God, to trust in Him. Having faith in God will see you through.

Unlimited faith in times of chastening. The chastening hand of God may be placed upon you in love. "For whom the Lord loveth he chasteneth, and scourgeth every son whom he receiveth." He does chasten us in love, but we need faith when chastening comes. When the tears flow and you feel that you cannot take any more, have faith in God.

I've been touched by all these things I have mentioned—and more: poverty, illness, persecution, failure, and others. But faith in God brought me through and gave me peace of heart and His guidance. He has made provision for our every need. Please remember that.

What is it tonight? What is troubling you? What is this thing that is upon you? Place it all in His hands.

III. UNLIMITED FAITH FOR EVERY AGE

In youth, in middle age, in old age.

The faith of Caleb at eighty-five. Caleb and Joshua, two of the twelve sent to spy out the land, came back and reported, "We can take it," while the others said, "We can't do it," and turned back. Caleb's faith did not waver. Joshua's faith did not waver. When the land was conquered, Caleb went to his friend Joshua and said, "Give me this mountain." At eighty-five asking for a mountain, a rough place encircled by hard people to conquer! He was believing God and asking for a place of service.

The faith of young David facing Goliath. We read in I Samuel

17 that the others had turned away and said, "It can't be done," but here is the faith of a young man who said, "It can be done." While men were trembling before a giant, David was saying, "Let no man's heart fail because of him; thy servant will go and fight with this Philistine." As a young man, David did conquer because he said, "I can do it."

The faith of Stephen. I am trying to pick out different years of life when men conquered. Here is Stephen, a man full of faith— "full of faith and power," the Bible says of him. He was abused by the Jews and caused to suffer because of his faith. He defended himself in Acts 7, but they stoned him. In his dying hour he gave his testimony for Christ.

We are considering unlimited faith in every place, in every crisis, for every age. Jesus said, "Have faith in God." This faith is illustrated when the disciples saw the Son of God ascend into Glory. When He instructed them, "Wait in Jerusalem," they waited; they obeyed, believing and trusting.

THREE QUICK SUGGESTIONS:

Use your faith. Let faith erase your worries. Use what faith you have to walk out and trust the Saviour every step you take, every move you make.

Reveal your faith. Some say they have faith in God, but do nothing about it. Spurgeon did. Moody did. Mueller did. Wesley did. I like to talk about my faith and tell what God has done for me, how He answered my prayer.

A young man came back to see me last Sunday who had been to see me before. We had prayed together about a financial need. Now he came to tell me, "I had sent to me a check for $175.00, which more than covered my needs. Praise God!" He was revealing his faith.

Give your faith to others. Faith of the parents can be imparted to their children. Friends can impart their faith to their friends. If we have faith in God, if we believe the promises of God, then we should share with those around us, giving our faith to them.

In thinking of an illustration of this point, I thought of the strangest times surrounding my father. He is a quiet man. He has never done anything publicly in church. He has not even taught Sunday school. Being a deacon is the extent of his work because of his quiet nature. But my father is a man of faith.

Before his salvation, he cursed and was very profane. Many times he had been arrested and jailed in Louisville. Then when God saved him, there was a revolutionary change in him. I watched his faith. I saw heartaches come. I saw him when he was beaten down to the ground, when everything was gone. I saw him live for years in an old chicken house. I am not exaggerating—an old chicken house, with a floor but no windows. He covered the openings with canvas. I've stayed in this place with him. My father suffered. BUT NEVER ONCE DID I HEAR HIM COMPLAIN. My family has never heard him complain. When all these heartaches and tragedies came upon him, his faith in God stayed strong. All this time he went on to church carrying his Bible. He went on to prayer meeting. These tragedies changed not one thing about him. He varied not an inch.

Somehow his faith was imparted to me—that simple faith in God. I saw that God is ever faithful. I, too, have tried to share my faith. I don't intend to complain. I don't intend to find fault with God. I don't intend to blame Him for my heartaches. I know that God has led me this far, and I know He will lead me on.

Use your faith. Reveal your faith. Give your faith. Have a faith that can be shared with those hungry hearts around you.

WHENCE COMES THIS UNLIMITED FAITH?

Through an experience with Christ, knowing Him as your Saviour. That happy, exultant feeling you had when you first got saved is for all your life! When you walked down the aisle and accepted Christ, or knelt in your home, or however or wherever it may have happened—when you got saved, there was a feeling of a load lifted.

God wants you to have that same feeling all your life! If you lose it, it will not be God's fault. If you depart from it or grow cold in spirit, don't blame God. He wants you to keep that same feeling all the time, that feeling of rejoicing. Faith comes through an experience with the Lord. There is no doubt of what He can do for you. You have the assurance of His presence with you. He is ready to help you in everything, at any time. So rest upon Him constantly, rejoice in Him continually.

Whence comes this unlimited faith?

Through reading and believing the Book. Read your Bible—I don't care where you read. Take the Psalms; the Sermon on the Mount; the Epistles of Paul; the writings of John—anywhere you read you will find something to bless your heart. When you read, believe and rest on these promises. Your faith will expand and reach out.

Whence comes this unlimited faith?

Through a daily walk by faith. One step at a time, moving forward by faith. Trust God, then step ahead. Don't worry. Don't fret. Simply trust, knowing that He will bring you through.

Whence comes this unlimited faith?

Through honest dedication to God. Place it all down before God— your life, your talents, your abilities—whether large or small. Tell Him, "Lord, I give myself to Thee. Give me that which I must have; make me what you want me to be, that I might shed abroad your message."

There must be an honest dedication. This will bring separation from the world. It will mean a filling of the Holy Spirit, a resting upon God's eternal power for your life.

Isn't it a shame that God wants you to have so much and most have so little! Isn't it pathetic that although God wants us to have a heart of rejoicing, most are fretting, worried, frowning, unhappy and miserable!

Here are the riches of God opened up to us. How do we get them? By faith. How are these things imparted to us? By faith. The joy of the Lord will be our stead. We can rest on Him. He will fulfill His promises. He will give what we have need of.

The world offers some things, but those things pass away. They are only fleeting and without foundation. We Christians have to rest upon God's promises. And He has promised to comfort and to guide. Unlimited faith stands. It cannot be shaken. It is a faith that enables us to walk steady, stand tall, speak courageously, witness without fear, and live so others can see and know that we belong to our blessed Saviour.

I know how many times I fail, but this is what I want—all I want. When I walk among people, talk to people, I want them to know that I have something that will stand throughout all time. I want my faith in God to be seen, to be felt.

I thought of this strange illustration. A man living in Chattanooga acquired a lot of money. When he died, he left his fortune—500 million dollars. When the will was read, it stated he was giving this 500 million dollars to 500 people. None were aware of the gift. The Will went on to read that the names of the 500 people "will be given on this coming Friday at 6 o'clock on the courthouse steps in Dalton, Georgia." Five hundred Chattanooga people will be getting 500 million dollars! I would be willing to say that the highways between here and Dalton will be crowded. Don't you think so? I, too, would be there if I thought there was a chance I might be named among the 500, becoming a millionaire in just a few moments of time. The people will fill all of Dalton. They will listen to the man on the platform read names as they listen and wonder, *Is my name going to be read?*

(Later: My name was not among those read!)

Dearly beloved, you are an heir with God and a joint heir with Jesus. You don't have to go to Dalton or anywhere else. Stay where you are. God has promised you everything. Every need has been supplied, if you will simply trust in Him.

We need unlimited faith—faith in God who cannot fail, faith in God who cannot lie, faith in God to cheer in the darkest hour.

Rest upon God's promises in unlimited faith.

31. The Power of Faith

Finally, my brethren, be strong in the Lord, and in the power of his might.

Put on the whole armour of God, that ye may be able to stand against the wiles of the devil.

For we wrestle not against flesh and blood, but against principalities, against powers, against the rulers of the darkness of this world, against spiritual wickedness in high places.

Wherefore take unto you the whole armour of God, that ye may be able to withstand in the evil day, and having done all, to stand.

Stand therefore, having your loins girt about with truth, and having on the breastplate of righteousness;

And your feet shod with the preparation of the gospel of peace;

Above all, taking the shield of faith, wherewith ye shall be able to quench all the fiery darts of the wicked.

And take the helmet of salvation, and the sword of the Spirit, which is the word of God:

Praying always with all prayer and supplication in the Spirit, and watching thereunto with all perseverance and supplication for all saints.

—Ephesians 6:10-18.

Now, come back to verse 16, please:

"Above all, taking the shield of faith, wherewith ye shall be able to quench all the fiery darts of the wicked."

The Heavenly Father has given us enough to make every day both happy and successful. Life will have its heartaches, its sorrows, its perplexing problems; but God has given us an antidote for all these things. He has given us a way, yes, a recipe on how to be peaceful and useful. That day and that way are the way of faith, as given here in verse 16, "Above all, taking the shield of faith. . . ."

The Apostle Paul, one who knew the secret of victory and purpose for living, wrote this text to the church at Ephesus. Paul had his heartaches, his disappointments, but he could still exhort us, "Rejoice in the Lord!" He could still sing at midnight in spite of a bleeding back and stocks on feet and hands.

Paul's friends may have failed him, but he could still praise God. Ephesians 6 is a well-known chapter, about as well known as Psalm 23, John 14 or John 3.

But here is a portion I want you to see this morning. Sometimes we miss what is right in the very center of it. Underscore verse 16, *"Above all, taking the shield of faith. . . ."* Then the rest of the verse says: ". . .wherewith ye shall be able to quench all the fiery darts of the wicked." Concentrate upon that thought—the shield of faith.

In verse 14 is the armor for the Christian: ". . .your loins girt about with truth, and having on the breastplate of righteousness; And your feet shod with the preparation of the gospel of peace. . . the shield of faith. . . .the helmet of salvation, and the sword of the Spirit, which is the word of God." All these things are given to us.

Now in Ephesians 6:10-17 we have the source of power: ". . .be strong in the Lord, and in the power of his might." We have provision for power: "Put on the whole armour of God, that ye may be able to stand against the wiles of the devil." We have the employment of power, because we use this power against Satan. He said, "Put on the whole armour of God. . . ."

Think on this single verse: "Above all, taking the shield of faith. . . ."

Faith comes by the living Word, by Jesus Christ. We are saved by faith in the Son of God, our blessed Saviour.

Faith comes by the written Word, by the Bible. "So then faith cometh by hearing, and hearing by the word of God." So by the Living Word and by the written Word we come to this matter of faith.

Now it is faith in God that achieves miracles. The shield of faith protects our life. The shield of faith produces courage. The shield of faith produces peace of heart, for Jesus said, "Let not your heart be troubled: ye believe in God, believe also in me."

The disciples requested of the Lord, "Increase our faith." Jesus said, "Have faith in God."

Now four simple things this morning:

I. FAITH FOR SALVATION

Jesus said, "Verily, verily, I say unto you, He that believeth on me hath everlasting life."

Now, what is saving faith? How are we saved? The Bible answers the question very clearly. It is faith in the crucified, buried and risen Saviour. By this faith the soul is saved from eternal destruction. The Apostle Paul said, "Christ died for our sins according to the scriptures." By our simple faith in the Lord Jesus Christ, we have life everlasting.

When our Saviour walked upon the earth, men turned away from Him because He declared Himself the Saviour. "I am the way, the truth, and the life: no man cometh unto the Father, but by me." He declared Himself as the only way.

Not being able to take that, they turned against Him, saying, "We cannot receive this man." Why? "Because he sets Himself up as the Saviour." But Jesus said, "I am the Saviour; I am the way. He that believeth in me hath everlasting life."

In this day we have the same battle. Today people are divided on how one is saved. One says by joining the church; one says by keeping an ordinance; one says by the observing of certain good works; one says by baptism. All of these things bring salvation, they say. Not so!

The way of salvation is clearly defined for us: by faith in Jesus

Christ. "For by grace are ye saved through faith; and that not of yourselves: it is the gift of God: Not of works, lest any man should boast."

Now, we find this interesting: Paul was saved on the road to Damascus. A light came down, and a voice spoke to him. Magnificent, wonderful things happened; and Saul of Tarsus accepted Christ as his Saviour and became the Apostle Paul, a great and mighty preacher.

Again, we have an illustration given of the jailer saved in Philippi. God sent an earthquake to shake the prison. Paul and Silas' bonds were loosed; they stood up, and they were free. The jailer as well as his family was saved.

But Paul is not saying that to be saved you have to have certain things happen, like an earthquake. He didn't say you have to have a light shine from Heaven. He simply said that for one to be saved, he needs only a faith in Jesus Christ, the blessed Son of God. Life is for all who look to Him.

Look to the Lord Jesus Christ this morning. If you have never accepted Him, then today repent, believe and receive Christ as Saviour.

Some people think life is all play. They emphasize recreation—playing through life. Others say that life is all pain and suffering and anguish. But the Bible says that life is Christ, and life is in Christ.

Now salvation is yours through faith in Jesus Christ, the Son of God.

II. FAITH FOR SUCCESS IN LIFE

I am using the word "success," even though it has been tossed about by people and used in rather strange ways in this present age.

Look at your Bible again: "Above all, taking the shield of faith, wherewith ye shall be able to quench all the fiery darts of the wicked." To be successful, you must quench the fiery darts of the wicked. How? By the shield of faith. "Above all, taking the

shield of faith, wherewith ye shall be able to quench all the fiery
darts of the wicked"—these fiery darts of Satan that come
against us.

1. *The fiery dart of doubt.* I meet with people almost every day
who have their doubts. They doubt the Bible. They doubt the
way of salvation. They doubt the efficacy of the blood of Jesus
Christ. They doubt the Second Coming. These are all fiery darts
of doubt.

Now, to doubt the presence of God, the peace of God, and the
power of God will bring heartache. Doubting the love of God will
cause anguish of heart. Of course this is what Satan wants. He is
trying to drive a dart into the heart of believers, trying to make
them wonder, *Is it all right?* He causes you to wonder about your
salvation, wonder about the future; he causes you to doubt other
things. Don't listen to him! Put your rest in the Lord. God is
love, and God loves you. God cares for you.

Someone tells about the preacher going to see a lady who was
having much trouble. Her husband, though sick, was still trying
to work. With a child in the hospital, a sick baby at home, she
was much troubled. She said to the pastor, "I don't know how I
can make it. Why doesn't God let me get out of this some way?
Here is a sick baby in my arms; my husband is sick and trying to
work, and my other child is in the hospital." She was in anguish.
She was doubting the love of God.

The pastor answered her in a strange way: "Ma'am, why don't
you just take your baby in arms and throw him out the door?
Why not get rid of the baby?"

"Why, Pastor, how could you say a thing like that! I love my
baby! I wouldn't dare think of doing a thing like that!"

"Would you do more for your baby than God does for you?
Does God love you less than you love your baby?" he asked.

"I never thought of that. I know God loves me, and I love Him.
Through these discouragements, I see how He loves and cares for
me."

The Devil uses sickness, adversity and problems to cast
doubts.

2. *The fiery dart of temptation*—and this comes to many of us.

He tempts us to follow the world. He tempts us to follow the things of the flesh. He tempts the lad to cheat on his examination. He tempts the man to lie on his income tax report. The Devil is always tempting us. But again only by using the shield of faith can one overcome the fiery dart of temptation.

3. *The fiery dart of laziness.* The Apostle Paul rebuked some in the church in Thessalonica: "Why are you not working? If you don't work, you can't eat. It's necessary to work, to apply yourself to the task given you."

4. *The fiery dart of criticism.* How skillfully Satan uses this! I've known Sunday school teachers to stop teaching, after years of experience and years of active service for Christ, because someone criticized them. Choir members have quit because someone criticized them. Ushers have quit because of criticism. Deacons, even pastors, have turned aside because someone criticized them.

Now, here is the Devil's weapon. You must use your shield of faith against him. Guard yourself against this dart of criticism. God will see you through.

5. *The fiery dart of procrastination*—just putting it off. You are saying, "After a while; some other time," when God is saying, "Now."

A man in North Carolina came to me and said, "Brother Roberson, God called me to preach years ago, but I never preached. I'm going to some day. I plan to a little later."

I said, "How old are you, sir?"

"Sixty-five."

"When do you plan to start?"

"When I retire, I plan then to start preaching."

I said to him, "Sir, you have already gone too far. I doubt if God can use you at all after these years of disobedience, these years of reluctancy in doing His will. I doubt if you can succeed in serving God."

Wait a minute! The Devil had him putting it off, delaying. A fiery dart!

O my dear friends, how important that we answer the Devil and the fiery darts hurled against us. I have indicated just a few of them; there are many others. What is the answer? The shield of faith. "Above all, taking the shield of faith," holding it up and saying, "O God, I care not what it cost, I'm moving on! forward! I am determined to go on serving my God!"

III. THERE MUST BE FAITH FOR SUPPLICATION

To pray effectively, we must have faith in God. Prayer is dead, meaningless, unless we believe in God.

1. *Effective praying depends on childlike faith,* just simple faith. It's not being intricately involved; it's not lengthy words and beautiful expressions; it's coming before God, asking, seeking and knocking, like a little child asking a gift of his father and receiving it. Effective praying depends on childlike faith.

In my contact with pastors and evangelists through many years, I have watched so many great men of God. Some of the greatest men I have ever known have had childlike faith.

Let's take Dr. Ernest Reveal, who was a mighty man of prayer. He prayed like a child, yet God gave mighty answers to his prayers.

Take the famous medical doctor, Dr. M. R. DeHaan, now with the Lord. I listened to him pray. I observed his life. There was a simplicity and a childlike faith about him when coming before God.

There must be faith for supplication.

2. *Effective praying depends on submission to His will.* "Father, thy will be done. Not my will; thy will be done." Rebellion causes us to be a failure in prayer.

3. *Effective praying depends on preparation,* getting your heart right with God. "If I regard iniquity in my heart, the Lord will not hear me." If you are holding on to sin or countenancing sin, then you will fail. The life, the heart, must be right in order to get through to God.

Faith for supplication—believing God, have faith in God. "Above all, taking the shield of faith. . . ." Without faith in God, the whole thing fails. Your Christian life is miserable, meaningless, unless you exercise faith. The shield of faith has to be held up against all the onslaughts of the Devil. The darts of the Evil One will try to turn you aside.

Somebody wrote a poem, just a simple little thing about a humble Christian named Jim. It reads:

For years each day he would rise to pray;
And when in church he would bow his knee and meekly say, "Dear God, it's Jim."
And when he would leave, we all could see God's holy presence walk with him.

As Jim grew old the chastening rod of years left him ill and drawn;
His path to church is now untrod,
But in his heart each day at dawn he hears the words, "Dear Jim, it's God."

Effective praying depends on preparation, having faith, believing God and resting in Him, knowing that He never fails.

It takes effort to pray well. It takes preparation to pray meaningfully. It takes diligence to pray faithfully. But prayer is our business as Christians.

Faith and supplication, believing God, praying in faith believing, is the call given us by God.

IV. THERE MUST BE FAITH FOR SOUL WINNING

We have been discussing briefly faith for salvation, faith for success in service, faith for supplication. Now, think of faith for soul winning.

Here is where you have to war a good warfare. Here is where the Devil fights. Here is where every Christian has to do battle. Here is the one place where Satan will try to stop you. Here is where you have to hold up the shield of faith and say, "O God, since I've been redeemed, I must be faithful!"

You see, the Devil wants to stop your witnessing, and he succeeds with most Christians. Ninety-five percent never try to witness at all.

This morning let God speak to you. Have faith for soul winning. Not trusting yourself, nor your own power, but trusting Him and asking God to help you witness and be a winner of souls.

Witnessing is God's command. He said, "Go ye. . . ." He said, "Ye shall be witnesses unto me. . . ." The Great Commission, given to us all, commands, "Go ye into all the world, and preach the gospel to every creature." If you are not obeying that command, you are disobeying God. You are failing your God because of your lack of willingness to do what He says.

Witnessing is for all Christians. Young and old, rich or poor, high or low—no matter who you are—you are to witness at all times.

An unsaved lady came through an operation in a fine way. The doctor came in to see her each day, checking on her progress.

One day when he walked in, she said, "Sir, I wonder if you would do me a favor? I want you to sign my album, if you will please. Then I can have this remembrance of you and your help to me, which has meant so much."

He said, "I'll be glad to do that. Now do you mind if I put a prescription in here with my name?"

"Write what you want to," she replied.

He signed his name, then wrote, "O taste and see that the Lord is good: blessed is the man that trusteth in him."—Psalm 34.8. Then he put it by her bedside.

As a result of that simple testimony of a surgeon, that woman got saved. She said, "When I left the hospital and gained my strength, I went to church for the first time, heard the message of Jesus Christ and accepted Christ as my Saviour."

The quiet witness day by day of the businessman, the doctor, the housewife, the high school student—of anyone, wherever we may be, always witnessing, always telling the story.

Faith for soul winning! Don't rest upon your words—rest upon His Words. Don't rest upon your power—rest upon His power.

Witnessing is always blessed of God. "He that winneth souls is wise." You may not always see it, may not always understand what is happening; but if you are faithful, then God will be faithful in blessing you because of it. The important matter is faith for soul winning and faith in God.

The power of faith. "Above all, taking the shield of faith,

wherewith ye shall be able to quench all the fiery darts of the wicked."

Do you ever wonder why you don't witness? I can tell you why. You are a victim of Satan's darts. He scares you! You say, "I can't do it. I'm afraid to speak to people. I don't like to embarrass anyone." That's not your difficulty. You fail to witness because you are afraid. You are not holding the shield of faith. The Devil is throwing the darts at you; and you are getting them into your mind, into your heart, and you refuse to do what God says.

Witnessing is always blessed of God. Faith for witnessing, faith for salvation, faith for success, faith for supplication are all blessed of God.

In soul winning we have to forget self. Self is a great enemy.

In soul winning we must depend upon the enduement of the Spirit of God, that we might speak His words with effectiveness to hearts everywhere.

In soul winning we must stir ourselves to remember the lost estate of man. Man without Christ is lost and Hell-bound! It may be your dearest friend, it may be your sweetest child who, without Jesus, will burn forever in Hell.

I listened a few moments this morning to a black preacher on television. I guess he was of our city. Brother, he was pouring it out on the matter of salvation through faith in Jesus Christ and the awful results of one who turns his back on Him.

We have to stir ourselves to remember the lost condition of man and urgently go with the shield of faith before us, trusting God, resting upon God's power, and knowing that God never fails.

Rowland Hill, the great English preacher, was once speaking in a large auditorium. In the middle of his sermon Lady Anne Erskine, who did not often attend church but who was much in evidence at every prominent concert or ball, made an ostentatious entrance.

She had been heard previously to say that she would like sometime to hear Hill preach, just "to please herself." Of course, when she entered and the audience turned to see her in all her finery, the preacher recognized who she was.

All at once he stopped abruptly. "My friends," he shouted, "I have something here for sale." Everyone was startled. "I am going to auction something worth more than all the crowns of Europe—the soul of Lady Anne Erskine.

"Will anyone bid for her soul? Hark! I think I hear a bid! Who bids? The world!"

The lady's surprise was indescribable, as all eyes were now focused upon her.

"World, what will you give for her soul?"

"I will give pleasures, honor, and riches, a life of luxury and good times."

"Nothing more? Then your price is too small for us. For what would it profit the lady if she gained the whole world and lost her own soul? Hark! I hear another bid. Who bids? Satan!"

"I will give her the lust of the eyes, the lust of the flesh, and the pride of life. She can satisfy all her cravings with me."

"And what do you demand in return?"

"Her soul! She passes once for all into my power."

"Your price is too high, Satan. You are a murderer from the beginning, a liar, and the father of lies. I can hear another bid. It is the Lord Jesus Christ."

"I have already given my life for the lady. I have poured out my heart's blood for her when upon the cross I paid the ransom for the whole world. I will bring peace into her soul. I will clothe her with the garment of righteousness, and adorn her with the gold of faith. I will keep her and take her to be with myself in Glory, for where I am, there shall my servant be also."

"And what dost Thou ask in return, Lord Jesus?"

"Her sin, her evil conscience, all that torments her."

"Lord Jesus, Thou shalt have her." And then, turning to the lady, he asked, "Lady Erskine, are you satisfied?"

"Yes," she answered with a loud, firm voice, while deep emotion passed through the whole meeting. And Lady Erskine kept her word. From that hour her life was changed. She also became a friend and mother to the poor and sick, the miserable and distressed. No one made so many sacrifices as she for the cause of Jesus Christ. Throughout the remainder of her life she thanked God for the impulse which took her to hear Rowland Hill and for the love that snatched her from the clutches of a deceiving world.

My friend, this morning the Devil is pleading and begging for everyone in this audience. The Devil is after every sinner. He is trying to turn you away from salvation. Oh, I beg you to be wise and say, "Lord Jesus, I come now."

The Devil is after every Christian. He is trying to destroy your life. He is shooting his darts at you. You have to take the shield of faith and rest upon that.

FAITH IS TO BELIEVE WHAT WE DO NOT SEE, AND THE REWARD OF THE FAITH IS TO SEE WHAT WE BELIEVE.—St. Augustine

32. *A Living Faith*

And when they were come to the multitude, there came to him a certain man, kneeling down to him, and saying,

Lord, have mercy on my son: for he is lunatick, and sore vexed: for ofttimes he falleth into the fire, and oft into the water.

And I brought him to thy disciples, and they could not cure him.

Then Jesus answered and said, O faithless and perverse generation, how long shall I be with you? how long shall I suffer you? bring him hither to me.

And Jesus rebuked the devil; and he departed out of him: and the child was cured from that very hour.

Then came the disciples to Jesus apart, and said, Why could not we cast him out?

And Jesus said unto them, Because of your unbelief: for verily I say unto you, If ye have faith as a grain of mustard seed, ye shall say unto this mountain, Remove hence to yonder place; and it shall remove; and nothing shall be impossible unto you.

Howbeit this kind goeth not out but by prayer and fasting.

—Matthew 17:14-21.

All of you will discover that I deal with certain subjects in different ways over and over again.

I like to talk about the worth of the Word of God, the infallible, inerrant Bible. This is the Book that I preach from and we believe in this place—in the school, in the church, every portion of it, from the first word in Genesis to the last word in Revelation.

I speak on the importance of prayer quite often. I talk about salvation by grace. You hear me speaking about dying to self, and the fullness of the Holy Spirit. I speak often on the second coming of Jesus Christ.

This morning, I am touching on what I think is a very important theme—a vital, living faith.

What are the most astounding illustrations of faith in the Bible?

Perhaps you would say Noah and the building of the ark.

Perhaps you would say Abraham walking by faith. Remember he was seventy-five years old when he left Ur of the Chaldees and went out.

Maybe you would talk about Moses and the Red Sea and the people of Israel, when he said, "Stand still, and see the salvation of the Lord."

Maybe you would talk about Joshua crossing the Jordan with the people of Israel and Judah, coming around Jericho, the taking of the city and starting to conquer the land.

Maybe you would talk about Elijah on Mount Carmel praying down fire and then rain, in answer to prayer.

There are many other illustrations, all illustrations of faith in God.

Come to the New Testament. For example, Acts 7 records the death of Stephen. I think that is a marvelous display of faith.

In Acts 9:32-35, there is the healing of Aeneas by Simon Peter.

In Acts 9:36-43, Peter prayed and Tabitha was raised from the dead.

In Acts 16, we see displayed the faith of Paul and Silas.

In Acts 19, there are the miracles wrought by the hands of Paul.

Now, there are many, many others all the way through the entire Word of God. Some people might be saying that the day of miracles is past, but not so! God still answers prayer.

God still heals the sick. I constantly say to men that I meet, "It is good when God can use us, but He does all the healing. Man can operate, but God must heal."

Again, God still uses people in the preaching of the Word of God. God still saves souls the same way that He saved souls back in the days of Nicodemus, the woman of Samaria, Zacchaeus, the thief on the cross, and Saul of Tarsus.

Now, here are some exhortations that I want you to have.

1. *Establish your faith*—establish it upon the Word of God, not upon man nor on man's promises.

Jesus said, "Have faith in God," but establish that faith upon the Book. What God says is true. When you pick up your Bible and read it, you say, "This is what God has promised me; I can rest upon the inerrant Word of God and the promises of God." Establish your faith.

2. *Use your faith.* If God touches your heart, blesses you and gives you the knowledge of His presence and power, then use that faith to do things for Him.

I have been reading this week about J. Hudson Taylor, long head of China Inland Mission. He went to China and built missions all around the seacoasts of China. Then he said, "I must have more."

He began praying. He talked to some people about it. "I want to send them to the interior of the country." Before the death of J. Hudson Taylor, he had sent 1,000 missionaries into the interior—by faith.

3. *Watch your faith.* If God has blessed and by faith you have accomplished much, then be careful.

Beware of laziness. This is such a dangerous thing, relaxing upon your accomplishments. I am aware of the fact that God has blessed us here in a mighty way at Highland Park and Tennessee Temple Schools, but I am not relaxing, not in the slightest. I still have visions of things that God wants us to do. God is still exciting my mind and heart. Up until the last day of my life I want it to be this way.

Beware of laziness. You may say, "Well, I have accomplished something; now I'll sit down and let up." Not so!

Beware of presumption. "God used me, and I am sure He will do it again." He may not. The Bible records that some men were greatly used of God; then because of presumption, laziness and getting away from God, God did not use them the second time. God may not use you the second time, either. So beware of presumption.

Beware of self-confidence. There is a danger there. We are strong just as long as we maintain our contact with God, but we are weak when we lose that contact with Him.

Joshua and Israel at Jericho marched around and conquered the city, then sent up a few men to take the little town of Ai. It should have been done, but they didn't take it. Men died because of their foolishness, their self-confidence. Watch yourself on this. Our strength lies in a self-distrust rather than in a self-confidence.

Now, these are some warnings for all of us.

4. *Witness to your faith.* Tell others what Christ means to you. Tell of your salvation. Tell of answers to prayer. If God has blessed you, then tell it.

We did something in our Men's Class this morning that I felt impressed to do. This week when I sent a letter out to all the men I included a little prayer card and asked the men to write down their prayer requests. Many did. I gave out cards in the class this morning. At a certain time, I asked them to come forward.

Those 238 men present this morning walked up to the front with little 3 x 5 cards which contained prayer requests. They put them on the table down at the front; then we had prayer for these requests.

These men were moving out. This is a matter of faith in God, witnessing to your faith and believing God hears and answers prayer.

Has He ever answered a prayer for you? Yes! Then He will answer yet another one, and another one, and will keep on answering as long as you come to Him with your needs.

God is gracious and good, but "ye have not, because ye ask not."

Now, I want to give you three very simple points:

I. I NEED FAITH IN GOD TO FACE THE UNCERTAINTIES OF LIFE

1. *Faith to face failure.* Accept it and come out of it. I have failed. You have failed. Some people fail and stop. They get down in the slough of failure or the slough of despondency and stay there. Accept the failure and confess it. Have faith to face and acknowledge failure, then rise and move on, trusting God.

2. *Faith to face the breakdown of the body.* The young, the old, the busy, the retired, all people must face sickness some time.

Some of the finest people in our church, active men and women who have been so full of vim and vigor, have done so much for this great church in all of these years, have today been put on the sidelines. They cannot be up and going like they once were.

Some have been put aside completely because of illness and a breakdown of the body. But we must have faith to face sickness, infirmity, old age. We can still rest in God and keep looking up. To the last day of your life, whether well or sick, you can still serve God. If you cannot move, you can pray. Some of the finest warriors are prayer warriors. Though they can do nothing else, they can still get hold of God.

3. *Faith to face the multitude of life's problems.* I've got to have faith for the problems that come every day.

We have had a great beginning for Tennessee Temple Schools, the best we have ever had. Never have I had so much fine cooperation from my leaders, my deans and my teachers. The students are wonderful, and I thank God for you.

But as I arose Saturday morning (we have a staff meeting every Saturday) I went to prayer about the work of Saturday, about the school; then I thanked the Lord for such a great opening, such a wonderful week. I thought of Dr. Fred Brown's preaching, the souls that were saved, the many hearts touched. I thought, *Surely there will be something disturbing today.* There was—and there always will be. We have to face life's problems. Whether they be financial or some other adversity, I have to face them with faith in God, knowing He understands and will give victory as I trust Him.

4. *Faith to face death if Christ tarries.* If He tarries His coming, then death is sure to come, either to you or to a loved one. You can face this with faith in God.

Let your faith ever turn you toward Jesus. Keep looking, not toward self nor towards others, but toward Christ.

Let your faith ever rest upon His promises. God will fulfill every promise He has made. If He said, "Lo, I am with you alway," then depend on it. When you obey Him He is with you every step you take.

Let your faith ever stir you to greater endeavors. By faith in God move on, not stopping, not slowing down, not giving up, but moving on to do what He wants you to do.

Hold to this first thought if you will. I need faith for the uncertainties of life. I do not, you do not know what tomorrow will bring. But I know that God never changes. I know that we are standing upon a solid foundation—the Lord Jesus, who cannot change. I know I am a child of God. I know I can pray for my needs. I know I can face life's uncertainties by faith, knowing all is well.

We must have a vital faith.

II. I NEED FAITH TO CLAIM HIS PROMISES

He wants me, invites me to come to the Word of God, to claim His promises. He is saying, "This is for you; now come and take it."

For example. . . .

He promises peace. "Peace I leave with you," He says. Many of you here today are troubled, distressed, with no peace of heart. This is wrong. Peace is promised you by the Lord. "My peace I give unto you." And here is what Paul said: "And the peace of God, which passeth all understanding, shall keep your hearts and minds through Christ Jesus." Now claim the promise of the peace of God.

He promises courage. He commands us to be strong and of a good courage (Josh. 1:9). "Wait on the Lord: be of good courage, and he shall strengthen thine heart" (Ps. 27:14). Look at the courage of the Hebrew children, the courage of Daniel and others.

Do you sometimes wonder how people can stand it? Do you sometimes wonder how they can keep going, keep on facing what they must face? God gives them courage.

1. *He promises to answer prayer.* He said, "If ye shall ask any thing in my name, I will do it" (John 14:14). Have faith in God. How much? "If ye have faith as a grain of mustard seed," you can remove a mountain. A little faith will go a long, long way.

2. *He promises to supply every need.* My friend, rest on that. Depend on that. Depend on the power of God to supply the needs of your life.

I know things distress some of you. They distress me every once in awhile. This is a strange and awful day. No one knows where we are going. It is not being remedied at all through Washington, D.C. or any other place.

There are many problems, many difficulties; but He will supply every need you may have! We can depend upon Him.

I like the little story that came out in the *Associated Press* about the crow feeding the dog. Did you read that? It said that a little family lived with a construction gang. They had a tamed crow and a dog. The dog disappeared. They noticed every day when they fed the crow he would take that food, fly away and not come back for awhile.

They kept on watching. After some days they decided to follow the crow. When they did, the crow led them to where the dog had been caught in an animal trap. He had been there for six days, and for six days that crow had been feeding the dog.

The man who wrote the article for the *Associated Press* said he had read a story somewhere about Elijah being fed by the ravens.

God will feed you, too. He will supply every need you may have!

3. *Again, He promises direction.* ". . .I will guide thee with mine eye" (Ps. 32:8). God knows what He wants you to do. Now wait upon Him, and He will guide you step by step, day by day. Don't run ahead. Don't stop. Don't back up, but follow His direction for your life.

4. *He promises power for every task.* "All power is given unto me in heaven and in earth. Go ye therefore. . . ." He promises Holy Spirit power.

If there is one thing we need in this day, it is for Christian people to be filled with the Spirit so God can use you as a mighty vessel for His glory. He promises power, and He will give you that power.

God wants to use you. He is just waiting—waiting for your submission, waiting for your willingness.

Now let your faith be active, vital and powerful. A dead faith brings worries, frets, doubts and failures.

Rest upon God's eternal promises. God never fails! He will supply, so just rest upon Him.

III. I NEED FAITH IN GOD TO WAIT PATIENTLY FOR HIS COMING

". . .the patient waiting for Christ" (II Thess. 3:5). Dr. Brown spoke last evening on the second coming of our Saviour. He has promised to come. He has promised to receive us unto Himself. He has promised a joyous eternity with Him.

Now, the Thessalonians were disturbed, upset. When death came to some of their loved ones, they couldn't understand it. Paul had to write them a letter, inspired by the Spirit of God, to explain and to correct their thinking, to make them look up and believe the Lord is coming.

He urges us to be patient and working. He asks us to "be not weary in well doing" (II Thess. 3:13). And Christ said, "Occupy [be busy] till I come." We are to win souls and do all we can for our blessed Saviour before He returns.

Now, I need faith to wait patiently for His coming.

I started preaching on the second coming of Christ up in Greenbrier, Tennessee, a long time ago.

Back when I started preaching on the second coming of Christ, you never saw such interest. I held a meeting in the First Baptist Church in Monterey, Tennessee, a little mountain town, and preached twice a day on the second coming of Jesus Christ. They were simple messages. The building was packed and jammed. Many, many were saved!

Dr. Brown is right when he said folks don't jump, don't get enthused, very much today except in strong fundamental churches like ours when you talk about the second coming. Most people say, "Well, so what?"

Child of God, listen! He said, "I will come again." Here is the promise of a gentleman, a gentleman of the highest integrity, a promise that cannot fail.

Now, what's my business? To wait patiently for His coming. I don't know when it is going to be, but I can wait patiently, as commanded.

Let this comfort your heart: He is coming again; the dead in Christ shall be raised, the living changed and caught up to meet Him in the air.

Let this establish you. Don't turn aside to the varied religions of this day, all of the "isms," the cults that are popping up everywhere. They are on radio and television. Everywhere you turn, you will find these various cults coming at you. Now, you stay steady. Let His coming establish you in the things of God. Don't be in and out, on and off, but stay steady, going right down the line! I can't think of a word more needed in this church than **steady**, just being steady.

Christians come and join our church and stay with us for a while, then they jump around. "Well, I want something else." Looking for some other kind of show. Looking for some other display of man's wisdom and of man's organization.

Let your heart be established in the truth that He is coming again. Don't turn aside to the cults and various concepts of man that are being pushed in books, pamphlets, and circulars. Be established by the second coming of Christ.

Then let this truth send you out to tell the story of Jesus. Witness every day.

Are you saved this morning? Do you have a vital, living faith? Is there a faith in your heart that stands in the darkest hour? Hold to it. Put your faith not in man but in God, in His Word, in His promises; not upon what man says, not upon what man thinks, but upon the eternal Word of God.

Have a living, acting faith, a vital faith that cannot be stopped by any adversary that may come against you.

Christian friend, stand steady, stand tall, stand true. Be so that others can tell what you are and who you are. Be so that they can know you as a child of God, faithful in the service of the blessed Saviour.

I am glad I am saved. I have something that stands with me. I have already tested this whole thing. I have tried it like many of you have.

I have tried the poverty line. But God has never failed. I have tried the sickness line. I have tried the cancer line. I have had it all given to me, first and last; and I have found that God gives peace of heart and leads through every single difficulty, if one has a living, active faith.

Have faith in God. ". . .faith cometh by hearing, and hearing by the word of God." "If ye have faith as a grain of mustard seed, ye shall say unto this mountain, Remove hence to yonder place; and it shall remove." I am not going to explain it away but take what the Bible says. Nothing shall be impossible to the one who has faith in God.

I know some folks will say we are foolish. Occasionally somebody will come to me and say about students when they exercise such faith in God, "They are just not very sensible in what they are doing." I am not so sure about that. I am not going to stop them. I want them to exercise more faith.

This is for all our church—our deacons, our ushers, our Sunday school, our Baptist Training Union, the missionary societies. I want you all to recognize this and put yourselves upon His promises and depend upon God to help us.

A graduate of our school sent me a little folder this week. It was a dandy. I put it on my desk. I thought it was a marvelous thing.

It told about mountain climbers going up a high mountain. This group was climbing up, pushing upward, pulling themselves on the rocks by the ropes, protecting and guiding one another until they got to the top.

At the very top they could look out and see the sky of clouds beneath them, and then the portions of the terrain around them. They rejoiced and said, "This is it!"—happy in what they had accomplished.

The story went on to tell about Columbus and his three boats crossing the ocean, trying to discover America; Columbus with his boats and half-starved men worried to death because of their failure to see anything for so long. When they finally saw land, they shouted, "This is it! We have found it!"

It went on to tell about a poor man who had been out searching for gold for a long lifetime. He had gone everywhere; now he was an old man. He had been prospecting in every hill, every valley, every mountain side.

Finally, coming toward the end of life, he discovered a beautiful, big nugget of gold that made him a wealthy man. He cried, "This is it! I have got it! This is it!"

The story went on to tell about a man standing before the warden of a state penitentiary. He had been in jail for more than twenty-five years. The warden with a pardon in his hand was smiling. He said to the man before him, "This is for you. You are pardoned. Go your way."

The man standing there had been behind the bars so long that he was somewhat in a daze by what had happened. He took the pardon in his hand, looked at it, and knew he was a free man, knew he could walk out of there without any constraint; so he shouted, "This is it! This is it!"

Here were the pictures of all these people who had said, "This is it!"

But how long did it last? The mountain climbers came down from the mountain and back to the valley. For a few days people applauded them.

Here is the old man who got a nugget out of the hillside, making him a rich man. Then he begins to say, *What have I done? I have lost what I used to have. Lost the place where I used to live. Lost everything. Now I am most unhappy.*

Here is the picture of Columbus and his men discovering America. They sailed back to Spain after a long, arduous trip. For a while they were acclaimed, of course; but then the journey was over, and the excitement waned.

Here is a prisoner, free; and with his pardon in hand, he goes outside. But no one wants him. They turn away from him. They say, "We have no place for you." Now he wonders, *I thought this was it, but it is not.*

My dear friends, we have all had many things that we thought were "*it.*" We thought we had "*it.*" But how long did "*it*" last?

I look forward to vacations, when I can be with my family. It is not being away from the church; I would rather be here than any other place in the world. But I look forward to being with them, of traveling and preaching while on vacation. I think when I get near, "This is it!" But *it* is just about like it always was. I preach, and I move on to the next town.

Here is a man who has a big business. He makes money; he accomplishes a whole lot, and he feels, *If I could just get so much, this would be it!* But when he gets that much money, he is still unhappy, dissatisfied.

Here is a family. They begin praying, planning and working on building a home. Finding a location, they build a beautiful home. Everything is just as they want it. "This is it! This is it!" They have it for awhile, then see something else they like better, buy it; and this dream house is sold and forgotten.

Again, here is someone who makes a fortune. He puts it away and says, "This is it!" But it is all gone in a short time.

Wait a minute! These things are not the answer. My friend, the only answer is in Jesus Christ. This is *it*! He is the One. If you don't have Him, you have nothing. But if you have Jesus, you have everything.

This morning we invite you to come and receive Jesus Christ as your Saviour.

33. Faith Can Change Any Situation

And in the morning, as they passed by, they saw the fig tree dried up from the roots.

And Peter calling to remembrance saith unto him, Master, behold, the fig tree which thou cursedst is withered away.

And Jesus answering saith unto them, Have faith in God.

For verily I say unto you, That whosoever shall say unto this mountain, Be thou removed, and be thou cast into the sea; and shall not doubt in his heart, but shall believe that those things which he saith shall come to pass; he shall have whatsoever he saith.

Therefore I say unto you, What things soever ye desire, when ye pray, believe that ye receive them, and ye shall have them.

—Mark 11:20-24.

If any of you lack wisdom, let him ask of God, that giveth to all men liberally, and upbraideth not; and it shall be given him.

But let him ask in faith, nothing wavering: for he that wavereth is like a wave of the sea driven with the wind and tossed.

—James 1:5,6.

When Jesus saw their faith. . .

—Mark 2:5.

. . .how is it that ye have no faith?

—Mark 4:40.

: . .thy faith hath made thee whole. . .

—Mark 5:34.

My friends, true success cannot be achieved without faith in God. You may rejoice in your salvation; but without faith in God, you lack success in your Christian life.

It may be you are happy that the Holy Spirit dwells within; but without faith, without resting on God's promises, you fail. You may be a preacher, a teacher, a missionary, or in some other field of service; but without faith in God, you fail. We cannot have true success without faith in God.

Books on faith are sent to me from all over the world. I have one now on my desk which talks about developing faith in yourself. That is not the faith I am talking about. We have too much of that. I am talking about faith IN GOD, resting on His promises.

Without faith in God, "it is impossible to please him" (Heb. 11:6).

Without faith in God, our accomplishments are negligible.

Without faith in God, our homes are not happy. Faith changes homes, businesses and, most of all, us.

Faith in God honors Him. It gets answers to our prayers.

Some things ought to be established when we talk about faith in God.

Is your faith fixed in Christ the Saviour? You must have this. Can you with assurance say, "I know Jesus Christ as my personal Saviour"? Do you know Him? Have you accepted Him? Do you belong to the family of God?

Is your faith resting upon God's infallible Word? Not upon what man says nor upon certain circumstances nor conditions nor on situations, but upon God's infallible Word?

Again we say, "Faith cometh by hearing, and hearing by the word of God" (Rom. 10:17).

I. ADVENTURE OF THE LIFE OF FAITH IN GOD

Life is an adventure of faith. We must know we are walking by faith. Every day has its uncertainties. We do not know what a day will bring forth, what tomorrow holds for us.

I visited in a hospital some time ago a famous athlete, paralyzed from his neck down. This handsome fellow was lying flat on his back, unable to move. He could look only straight up. I had to walk to the head of the bed and look over into his face. Paralyzed, yet big of body—a great athlete who had lost the use of his body in a single afternoon of play.

Uncertainty is all around us.

Put down these few things about faith.

1. *Faith in God gives joy.* The Apostle Paul illustrates this when he admonishes us, "Rejoice in the Lord." The key word in Philippians is "rejoice" or "joy."

2. *Faith in God gives assurance of His presence.* Moses had to know that God was with him before undertaking the leading of the Israelites out of Egypt and across the Red Sea.

By faith in God we have assurance that He is walking with us; we have the promise of His presence, for Jesus said, "Lo, I am with you alway, even unto the end of the world."

3. *Faith in God gives health.* "That's a strange thing to say, Brother Roberson." Not strange at all. Dr. Walter Alvarez, formerly of Mayo Clinic, now retired, put out a book, *Live at Peace With Your Nerves.* It is quite interesting. He says in it that a lot of the aches and pains and other assorted miseries which beset most of us tell us how many of our difficulties can be dissipated by faith.

Many people are suffering, and some greatly, but suffering without really a reason. What they need is faith.

Dr. Alvarez just talks about faith, while I am talking about faith IN GOD.

4. *Faith in God gives peace.* The Lord said, "My peace I give unto you." Take, by faith, the peace of God that passes all understanding. Reach out, troubled friend. Faith gives that peace of heart.

5. *Faith in God gives direction.* Obey and follow Him. He will guide you. Abraham found it so when God brought him out of Ur of the Chaldees. Nehemiah found it so when God led him out of

Babylonian captivity back to his country to rebuild the wall. Joshua found it so. We find all through the Bible faith in God giving direction.

6. *Faith in God supplies all our needs.* I am not bringing a profound message, but what I am saying is needed. The Bible promises, "But my God shall supply all your need according to his riches in glory by Christ Jesus." Have faith in God and believe.

I was reading this week about a young couple who had come before a preacher to be married. The pastor's wife stood up as one of the witnesses. The couple exchanged vows. It was a happy ceremony.

As they started to leave, the young man handed the minister an envelope. Inside was a crumpled dollar bill with this note:

Dear Sir:

I wish I could give you more for marrying us, but I only have two dollars. This will leave us one dollar to get started on.

A lot of you had about that much when you started a home. I had five, given by my wife's father as a wedding present. That went a long way in Depression days. In and through it all, one must have faith in God.

It is faith in God that supplies our needs. It is resting on His promises.

I repeat: life is an exciting adventure for those who put their faith in God.

7. *Faith accelerates the joy of living.* With faith in God one can overlook a lot of difficulties. He can say, "Lord, You are with me; I know I can trust You." It accelerates the joy of living.

8. *Faith aggravates an unbelieving world.* I like to do that— aggravate folk who don't believe in God or the Bible or in holy things. I enjoy saying, "I believe God supplies my every need."

9. *Faith always anticipates future blessings*—blessings today and tomorrow. Faith anticipates the second coming and all that we will have when He comes.

II. ADVERSARIES TO LIFE OF FAITH IN GOD

The adventure. I would urge everyone here tonight to get hold of faith in God. I'm preaching faith, not foolishness. Believe God will see you through and direct you in life's every activity.

The adversaries. The Devil will fight you. If you determine to exercise faith, you may be sure he will throw something in your way to hinder. So will the world. It will call you a fool and tell you that you can't do this or that. Then your flesh will say it can't be done. Listening to the Devil, the world, the flesh, you are likely to say, "I just can't do this. I can't do that. I don't have faith."

I have a great time with our young people here in school. I hope I am kind to all who come to see me about their problems. But sometimes I may not be so, or may not seem to be so, when you come with all your worries and your need for money.

I met a lad the other day who was so troubled about so many things; troubled about what he would do, how to get his bill paid, and so on. The same day I got a check in the mail for $150.00 for him. He doesn't know it yet, and he is sitting in this auditorium right now. He knows who I am talking about, how worried he was. The Devil wants you to doubt. But you can rest on your faith in God.

I don't mean you are to be lazy. That's the flesh. God is not saying, "Just have faith. No need to work. No need to worry. No need to do anything. Just sit down and have faith." When the Bible says, "Have faith in God," it doesn't endorse laziness, giving up and doing nothing. The child of God is to be busy, active while he is *trusting God.*

My life's text is Romans 8:28, "And we know that all things work together for good to them that love God, to them who are the called according to his purpose"—now and in the future.

"All things" work together for good—not just a few, not just a part, but *all things.* Like the notes of a beautiful composition of music, all fit together. One may be a high note, one a low note. One may be loud; one may be soft. It matters not—all things work together for good.

The evil trinity—the world, the flesh, the Devil—will seek to turn you from your faith and cause you to worry.

I received yesterday a letter from a fine, noble missionary, one of our own who is coming home after only a few months on the field. I don't know the problem, the trouble, the situation. I'm not blaming him. I could, like some people, blame him and say he is a sissy, a quitter. I don't think that. He is coming home because something has gone wrong. Listen! Satan is always working. The missionary told me in his letter some of the things that had been working against his ministry, keeping him from doing what he felt God wanted him to do. So he felt there was nothing left but to come back home. Satan works everywhere.

Again, Satan works on all people—the rich and the poor, the high and the low, the educated and the uneducated, the young and the old. We have absolute assurance that the Devil will be working against us. He will try to turn us aside, discourage us, cause us to doubt God and His providence and plans for us.

I will never forget talking with Brother Dodson in Greenbrier, Tennessee, who belonged to the church. I remember asking this man nearing eighty, "Brother Dodson, does the Devil bother you very much?" He gave his answer: "Yes, Son, I suppose more now than ever before."

Dr. R. G. Lee is coming here in February. At age eighty-seven he is still strong, vigorous and victorious in his preaching. If you were to ask Dr. Lee, "Does the Devil ever bother you?" he would say, "Why, of course. I have to battle him all the time. We never get through." The Devil is always fighting Christians.

Again, Satan works to lessen our faith in God. Wife, children, husband, young and old—whoever you may be—if you lack faith, then know the Devil is working. God is trying to help while Satan is trying to hinder that faith. Jesus would say, "O ye of little faith! What's wrong with you? Why not trust Me? Why not have faith in Me?"

What a statement by Jesus! How we need to rest upon His promises. "O ye of little faith!" He also said, "If you have faith as a grain of mustard seed," you could remove mountains. Your faith may be small, but it can accomplish great things.

III. ACCOMPLISHMENTS OF THE LIFE OF FAITH

The adventure, the adversaries, the accomplishments of a life of faith.

Someone has said, "Nothing ventured, nothing gained." How true!

In Hebrews 11 is a background for any discussion on faith. "By faith Abel offered unto God"; "By faith Enoch was translated"; "By faith Noah. . .prepared an ark"; "By faith Abraham. . . obeyed"; "By faith Moses. . .refused to be called the son of Pharaoh's daughter". It goes on listing names in this Westminster Abbey of Faith, telling what was accomplished by faith.

All worthwhile things come through faith. Everything is a matter of faith in God, of resting on God's promises, of doing what He says.

Write down these few things.

1. *Faith changes defeat into victory.* I think of Mr. R. G. LeTourneau, that multimillionaire earthmover who lost everything in the Depression, by the workings of society, etc. But he came back. From defeat, his faith brought him back to victory.

There was Colonel Sanders. At age sixty-five he had nothing except his Social Security. Then he was led out into a business—Kentucky Fried Chicken—and he testified that Jesus Christ was his Saviour, that he was trusting and believing in Him. When he was here with us for a meeting, he stated to me in the dining hall that he had faith in Jesus and was resting upon His promises.

I am trying to show that faith can change defeat into victory. You may feel defeated, feel you are a complete failure, that everything has gone wrong in your life; but I urge you to have faith in God.

2. *Faith changes depression into joy.* Some people get so depressed, so sad, so melancholy when they fail to look to God, when they fail to have faith in God. They act as if God is dead. These folk are resting upon what they can do, not upon what God can do. He can change depression into joy if you will let Him.

I will never forget a night when two dear people came to our home in Fairfield, Alabama, where I was then pastor. They knocked. I went to the door. There stood two Germans. I invited them in. I never saw people so sad. The man had worked in the steel mills all his life. He was then up in years. They told me they had lost everything, that they now had nothing to live for. "We may as well commit suicide."

I asked them, "Have you been saved?"

They told me they were Lutherans and knew nothing about being saved.

I took my Bible and pointed both to the Lord Jesus. On their knees, both accepted Jesus Christ as Saviour. From that sad depression came bubbling joy. After I had baptized them, they were bubbling over with happiness. As long as I knew those people, they stayed joyful.

Faith in God will change depression into joy.

3. *Faith changes danger to safety.* When He surrounds us, then we have nothing to fear. It matters not whether he be a successful businessman in Chattanooga or a missionary in the heart of Africa, man has nothing to fear if he has faith in God, for faith changes danger into safety. Faith in God, resting upon His promises, will change any situation, in any place around the world.

Things fail when we are quivering, shaking, sad, melancholy, blue, despondent. Without faith in God, not resting upon His promises, everything goes wrong—people, food, bed, car— everything. But faith causes us to walk triumphantly forward, looking for and trusting in Him. Then God blesses, brings us out and gives us joy and peace.

Faith can change any situation, no matter where or what it is. He will supply. Faith brings peace.

Lou Little was coach of the football team at Columbia University years ago. One day as he walked across campus, the Chancellor stopped him and said, "Lou, the father of one of your players has died. Someone called to tell us. I'm asking you to break the news to the young man."

Lou Little went to him and said, "Son, your father has just passed away. They want you home at once."

He said he would go immediately.

But before he left, the coach told him, "Take all the time you want and need, even two weeks if necessary. If you need time to get the family affairs straightened out before you come back, we will understand."

He left on Wednesday. On Friday of that same week, when he looked out on the practice field, the coach saw this young man practicing. Calling him, he said, "Son, why are you back so soon?"

He answered, "We had the funeral yesterday. My mother, my other brothers and sisters are there to take care of the details; so I came back. I have a reason for returning today. Coach, I've got to play in that game tomorrow."

Coach Lou Little looked straight at him and said, "But, Son, you are not a starter in a game. We have never started you. You are put in occasionally, but you are not a regular."

"Coach, I know that. But I've got to start tomorrow. Please."

The coach said, "Son, I just don't think that is possible."

After much persuasion, the coach finally said, "All right. We toss to find who kicks off and who receives. If we are receiving, I'll put you in the back to catch the first ball. You can have the first play, but I can't promise anything beyond that."

This young man seemed happy. They won the toss, and the ball was kicked off to Columbia. As it soared through the air, it landed in the hands of the boy whose father had just died and was buried on Thursday. He took the ball, raced down the field and almost made a touchdown, running right through the midst of their opposition.

From there on out, they watched that boy, who had always been in the background and, most of the time, sitting on the bench. But the coach left him in this time. He played with a power, an enthusiasm, some inner drive that he had not seen before. Whatever he did, whether it was tackling or carrying or catching the ball, it was the same way. He stayed in the whole game. His team won by three touchdowns, all made by this young fellow.

After one of their greatest games, they filed into the locker room. The crowd was standing around talking. The coach walked over and said, "Son, I don't know what happened to make you play the way you did. I'm glad I let you stay in. That's the best football playing I've ever seen. How did you do what you did?"

The boy came back with calm, sweet answer: "Coach, you never met my dad, did you?"

"No, Son, I never did. I once saw you and him walk down the field arm in arm like you were real buddies."

"We were real buddies. Coach, for most of my father's life, he was blind. He never saw me play a game in high school or here in the University—never saw me play until today. Coach, that's the reason I played as I did. My dad is in Heaven, for he had trusted Christ. Today I played for my father. I wanted to play in the first game so my dad could see."

Are you listening? That is beautiful faith—faith in the Word of God, faith in Jesus Christ, faith in the promises of God, faith in the eternal, faith in all of those who are now with our Saviour.

The adventure of the life of faith, the adversaries of the life of faith, the accomplishments of the life of faith.

Little faith will bring your soul to Heaven; great faith will bring Heaven to your soul.—Spurgeon.

34. *The Product of a Great Faith*

> *Therefore they that were scattered abroad went every where preaching the word.*
>
> *Then Philip went down to the city of Samaria, and preached Christ unto them.*
>
> *And the people with one accord gave heed unto those things which Philip spake, hearing and seeing the miracles which he did.*
>
> *For unclean spirits, crying with loud voice, came out of many that were possessed with them: and many taken with palsies, and that were lame, were healed.*
>
> *And there was great joy in that city.*
>
> *And the angel of the Lord spake unto Philip, saying, Arise, and go toward the south unto the way that goeth down from Jerusalem unto Gaza, which is desert.*
> —Acts 8:4-8,26.

Tonight I want you to see just one name, one single name—Philip. Notice in verse 5: "Then Philip went down to the city of Samaria. . . ." Philip, the deacon—not an ordained preacher but a deacon, a humble evangelist and layman, the father of four daughters (Acts 21:9,10). His story is given primarily in Acts 8. Here we see this deacon-evangelist out preaching and winning souls. He brought revival wherever he went. In verses 26 to 40 we find him preaching to just one man and leading him to the Lord, an Ethiopian but a high official in the government.

I. THE POWER OF ONE LIFE

Philip, a layman, a deacon, an evangelist, a father. This is the man God used.

1. *He was saved.* In chapter 6 he was made a deacon of the church. Philip was a saved man, converted just as you and I were converted—by faith in Jesus Christ.

God uses saved people. He used Philip. He can also use the unsaved. He can use a strange nation, a heathen nation, if He wishes to. But primarily God uses saved people. ". . .ye are not your own? For ye are bought with a price: therefore glorify God in your body, and in your spirit, which are God's."

2. *He was filled with the Holy Spirit,* "a man full of faith," says Acts 6:5. These early deacons including Stephen, and Philip, and Prochorus, were all men of faith and of the Holy Ghost. Philip was a deacon because he was saved and manifested the Spirit and power of God.

Now the fullness of the Spirit means full surrender. This was Philip—fully surrendered to the Lord. The fullness of the Spirit means separation from the world. This was Philip—separated from the world. Every deacon should be empty of self and filled with divine power. It is no little thing for a man to be chosen and ordained a deacon. If God in mercy and love has chosen you, if the hands of many have been laid upon your head, you have one of the highest positions one can have. It is up to you to so live that others can see Christ in you. No compromising! No messing with the world! No doubtful things in your life.

Deacon, are you like this man Philip? You should be.

"Do you know that you are saved?"

"Are you living a separated life?"

"Will you be faithful to the services of the church Sunday morning, Sunday night, and Wednesday night?" (If a deacon is not faithful, I have no part with him at all.)

"Will you be loyal to the church?" (I have no part with a deacon who is not loyal to his church.)

Philip was filled with the Holy Spirit and was led of the Lord. Look in chapter 8 again. The disciples were scattered—

". . .they that were scattered abroad went every where preaching the word" (vs. 4). This included Philip. He went down to Samaria (Gentile country) "and preached Christ unto them." He was still right with the Lord after some experiences given here with Simon, down to verse 26, when he left one part of the country and went to the desert country. There God sent him to speak to one lone man, to witness to that man about the Saviour.

Now I am getting to the power of one life. Your life, dear friend, must have divine power. My life must have it. Unless you and I have it, we will fail.

Your talents are nothing unless dedicated to God.

Your money is nothing unless dedicated to God.

Your ability is nothing unless dedicated to God.

When there is divine power, the life can be mightily used of God. Come, let Him have His way with you. You deacons, as well as every member, live for God. But pastors and deacons should do so in a very special way because God has called us and we are to be faithful examples.

I read a strange story the other day. A man, a preacher, said he wished his church walls were made of glass. "I wish so much that people driving by could look inside and see us singing and worshipping God." I wish for that here sometimes. When you sing happily, I would like the outside world to see what God is doing in one single church.

But it is not so essential that we have glass windows to let people look inside. They are looking at us anyway, watching us every day. Where? In the business world. Businessmen, they are watching you. Young people, they watch you in high school, in elementary school, in college. They watch your social life. Children of God are forever before the gaze of people. NOW—are you living so they can see Christ in you? Oh, the power of a single life—one life!

Don't come back at me with, "Well, Brother Roberson, I don't have much of an education." I care nothing about that. Let your light shine for Christ. Live, walk, talk so when people see you, they know you are a man or woman of God, living the power of one life. Let that one life of yours ring out in the home, in your business, in your social affairs, in your educational pursuits. Let that one life always radiate for Christ.

A man stopped me the other day and asked, "Sir, aren't you a preacher?"

"Yes, Sir, I am."

"I thought so. I never saw you before, but I just thought you were a preacher."

I had an opportunity to witness to him very strongly and, I trust, helpfully.

II. THE PREACHING OF ONE MAN

In verse 5 of chapter 8 Philip preached Christ. In verse 4 he preached the Word. Here is Philip preaching in a clear, positive way.

To preach Christ means you preach His virgin birth. It means you preach His sinless life. It means you preach His atoning death. It means you preach His bodily resurrection. It means you preach His glorious ascension back to Glory. It means you preach His present position at God's right hand, interceding for us. It means you preach His personal return, His coming back to this earth to reign. When you preach Christ, these seven things must be included.

Now the modernist cannot preach that. Nor can the liberal. Both cannot preach on the very first point—the virgin birth. The modernist says, "I don't believe that." Then when he comes to the resurrection—"I am not sure about the resurrection," and he turns away from that. About the second coming—"I am not sure about the second coming." He has no assurance that Christ is coming again because he does not receive the infallible, inerrant Word of God.

Here is the preaching that tells of Christ the Saviour, the only Saviour, the only Christ, the winning Christ. Here is the message that the world needs, a world full of crime, drugs, self, sex. We live in a day of rebellion and lawlessness, a time of industrial and political unrest, a time of uncertainty, of filth, of corruption. We have a Saviour who can save, keep, satisfy whosoever will, in any age, anywhere.

1. *Preaching like Philip did in the first century is the preaching of the twentieth century.* There is no difference: "Jesus Christ the same yesterday, and to day, and for ever." The same offer of salvation: ". . .whosoever will, let him take the water of life freely." Philip went down to Samaria and preached Christ to the people. We, too, are to preach Christ in the same manner.

2. *Preaching like Philip's will work miracles today as then.* I believe in miracles, not from the standpoint of man but from the standpoint of God. He can do anything.

You approach me and ask if I believe in divine healing. I will answer, "Yes, I do. I can't do it, but God can."

There were some miracles performed back there. ". . .unclean spirits, crying with loud voice, came out of many" (Acts 8:7). That was in the first century, before the Bible was in the hands of men, before the full Word of God, the inspired Word, had come to its completion. These were things that established people and awakened sleeping hearts and made people aware of their need of Christ.

Here is the preaching of this man Philip: the miracle of redeemed souls, the miracle of changed homes, the miracle of revived churches.

A little mother called me just before I came down to church. She said, "My boy died this morning at 4:30."

I said, "How old was your boy?"

"Thirty-one years old."

"Was your boy saved?"

"Yes, Brother Roberson. Roy Richardson led my boy to the Lord. He had testified to his salvation, and we will have the funeral service on Tuesday at 2:00. I am grieving in his going, but I know that he was saved."

Oh, listen to me! There is nothing like the miracle of a saved soul! Here is how God used one man.

3. *Preaching like Philip's will bring conviction and salvation.* He "went down. . .and preached Christ unto them." The people listened; many were saved, and there was great joy in the city. Things happened because of preaching Christ.

What shall we do? Just keep on preaching, winter and summer.

I want you to hear my message next Sunday morning on "Forty-Seven Years on a One-Way Street." I am not dissatisfied, not unhappy. I haven't longed for anything else.

Preaching like Philip's will bring conviction and salvation. Those who are lost in sin will hear the message, will repent, believe and be saved.

Some of you saw the write-up the other day in our papers. It was entitled, "Where Do Sermons Go?" It told the story of a preacher who had died. He had tied his messages up with a ribbon and left them, I suppose, on his desk. On top he had written: *"Where has the influence gone of all these sermons? Where has it gone?"* Then he had put under that question on top of the stack one word—OVER. Turning it over they found written:

> Where are last year's sun rays? They have gone into fruits, vegetables and grain. Where are last year's raindrops? They too have gone the same way—into fruit, grain and vegetables for people. In all of this, where are they gone? My sermons may seem to have disappeared, but they can still bring forth fruit.

They do, though we may not always see it. Faithful preaching stirs hearts and doesn't die. And this is what counts.

Some of you have heard me mention the great Dr. George W. Truett who preached just what I preach on the Lord Jesus Christ and His power. This Southern Baptist preacher and I differed in just one strong way—on the second coming. I am premillennial; he was not. He has been some time now with the Lord and has changed his mind about that! But he was a mighty preacher.

I have read his story. It told how he, before he died, would go to the window and stand there and preach to his people. He was mighty sick. His mind was not as strong as it had been. Things were confused. But his family said he would stand there at the window and preach some of his mighty sermons he had given to his people for forty-six years at First Baptist in Dallas.

After his death, the family began to search through all his belongings. Truett would study at 2:00 or 3:00 a.m., then turn off the telephone and go to bed. He had a button that turned the phone off, and he would leave it off until he wanted to get up. That was Dr. Truett. That was his way of doing things. He would write on a little piece of paper, or maybe a little scrap from an envelope, his sermon notes. He had a magnificent speaking voice.

When he died, his loved ones looked for his notes. They found some up in the attic in gunny sacks, sacks full of these pieces of paper—his sermon notes.

You say, "Is that all he had?" Oh, no! His sermons are still walking up and down the streets of Dallas in saved souls, in transformed lives. That is what counts most. That is the thing we are after. The influence of a sermon lives on and on.

That is what we find here in the story of Philip and his preaching. He gave the message; God began to move, and the man from Ethiopia got saved. Then the leading official of his country goes back as an ambassador for our Lord.

Where are my sermons? Typed out by my secretaries— hundreds and hundreds of them—and stored away. In recent years I have been writing them out on pieces of paper and sticking them in my Bible and carrying them with me. For a long time I dictated them ahead of time. I have them by the hundreds.

But my sermons are not actually in typewritten manuscript or in books. Where are they? Out among people. With these fine young people of Camp Joy. With the 292 missionaries whom we are helping support on the foreign field. With all the work of our church and schools. It is not just putting them into some manuscript form, in some book, but it is there in the preaching— the preaching that brings conviction to souls, and souls to the Saviour.

III. THE PRODUCT OF A GREAT FAITH

First, the power of one life; then the preaching of one man; now the product of a great faith.

This man was full of faith, as was Stephen also.

Philip's faith made him daring. He dared to go into Samaria. Then he dared to go out in the desert and preach to just one man.

His faith made him obedient. He went in the desert country and found a man riding in a chariot. Here was a man with a book in his hand. He was reading from Isaiah 53:7 and 8. Here was a man with an emptiness in his heart. All hearts are empty without Jesus Christ. Here was a man with an open mind to receive the message. "Then Philip opened his mouth, and began at the same scripture, and preached unto him Jesus" (Acts 8:35). He heard the preaching, and his faith made him obedient.

Then, his faith made him happy. He led the man to Christ. He baptized him. The Spirit of the Lord caught him away. Great faith always gives great happiness. We can rejoice in the Lord when we know Him. The product of a great faith can be summed up in three words—joy, guidance and results.

Paul's joy was rejoicing in our Lord. Read Philippians carefully.

You have often heard that the shortest verse in the Bible is "Jesus wept." No, the shortest verse is, "Rejoice evermore." It is important that a child of God rejoice in the things of God.

Then when we are living a life of faith, we are guided by the Holy Spirit. He directs in the way He wants us to go, and we are flexible in the power of the Spirit.

Then something will happen when we have faith in God. Something is going to happen in your life, in your home, in your business, and in your church. Faith in God brings results.

A man gave his testimony some years ago from this platform in a missionary conference. Do you know what that poor fellow said? "I have been a missionary in India for ten years. I suppose some would think it strange, but I haven't led a soul to Christ, not one. I haven't seen a single convert in ten years." He stood here and somewhat boasted about the fruitlessness of his life.

As I listened, I thought, *I know there have been missionaries who have gone five or six years, like Judson, without winning souls. I know that; but I can't understand a missionary in this day standing up and bragging about not seeing any results in ten years!*

My dear friend, I could find a little boy or a little girl somewhere and lead him or her to Jesus. I could find some poor, old, helpless paralytic who is wanting the love and concern of somebody. I could do **something**. But this man said, "I have gone ten years without leading a single soul to Christ!"

Wait a minute! My friend, if you have faith in God and His power, there will be results. God will give you victory. Things will happen. God honors faith.

Faith brings results on the mission field.

Faith brings results in the pastorate.

Faith brings results in the business world.

Faith brings results in the home, everywhere you go.

Faith in God and rest in Him mean results.

That is my message. I want you to think about it. What about your life? Can you say, "I know these things that are manifested here in the life of this simple man"?

There doesn't seem to be anything profound about Philip. He seems just ordinary. If you are just an ordinary Christian, this can fit your life. Here is a man, the power of one life. O God, take my one life and use it for Thy glory.

Here is the preaching of one man, not a preacher but a layman, a deacon. Here is the product of a great faith as he believed God and rested upon His promises and gave the message.

Tonight, you should be saying, "O God, I want this for my life. I want my life to be like the life of this man Philip. I want you to take and use me."

35. *Faith—Mighty Faith*

The Lord is my light and my salvation; whom shall I fear? the Lord is the strength of my life; of whom shall I be afraid?

When the wicked, even mine enemies and my foes, came upon me to eat up my flesh, they stumbled and fell.

Though a host should encamp against me, my heart shall not fear: though war should rise against me, in this will I be confident.

One thing have I desired of the Lord, that will I seek after; that I may dwell in the house of the Lord all the days of my life, to behold the beauty of the Lord, and to inquire in his temple.

Hear, O Lord, when I cry with my voice: have mercy also upon me, and answer me.

—Psalm 27:1-4,7.

When my father and my mother forsake me, then the Lord will take me up.

Teach me thy way, O Lord, and lead me in a plain path, because of mine enemies.

Deliver me not over unto the will of mine enemies: for false witnesses are risen up against me, and such as breathe out cruelty.

I had fainted, unless I had believed to see the goodness of the Lord in the land of the living.

Wait on the Lord: be of good courage, and he shall strengthen thine heart: wait, I say, on the Lord.

—Vss. 10-14.

Is any thing too hard for the Lord?

—Genesis 18:14.

Jesus said unto him, If thou canst believe, all things are possible to him that believeth.

—Mark 9:23.

And he said, The things which are impossible with men are possible with God.

—Luke 18:27.

I can do all things through Christ which strengtheneth me.

—Philippians 4:13.

By faith Abraham, when he was tried, offered up Isaac. . . .

—Hebrews 11:17.

Today my subject is, "Faith—Mighty Faith."

This week a call came from a young preacher boy who said, "Brother Roberson, praise God! We had sixty-two in Sunday school yesterday—one of our finest days!" He had been there three Sundays, I think. Now isn't that wonderful? Then he said, "I believe in a short time we can have one hundred. I'm rejoicing in the Lord!"

This young preacher was exercising faith. He was believing God would help him build a church.

When one has faith in God, then he can rejoice. When one looks to the Saviour, he can rejoice. When one is trusting God, he can rejoice. And this preacher was doing just that—rejoicing in the Lord.

Dr. George W. Truett died after pastoring First Baptist Church in Dallas for forty-five years.

When the church called Dr. W. A. Criswell, then a young man about thirty-two, as the pastor, he said something like this: "I feel led of God to accept your call. I believe we can build a great work there. In spite of the fact that you had one of the greatest preachers in the world as your pastor for all these years, yet God can still do mighty things at and for the church."

The interesting thing was that Dr. Truett was a postmillennialist and Dr. Criswell a strong premillennialist.

God has worked mightily under Dr. Criswell's leadership. He has been as long in that church as I have been in this one.

Years ago, in a little country town in Kentucky, there lived a fellow by the name of Russ Hill, brother to Dr. John L. Hill of the Southern Baptist Convention and Sunday School Board. Russ was a humble businessman. I was with him a number of times in meetings. This tall, handsome-looking man had great faith in God.

Mr. Hill was elected head of the Sunday school and was asked to teach a class in the First Baptist Church in his town. He told the little group of maybe ten or fifteen students, "I believe we can make this the largest class in the world."

The people laughed. "Why, that's foolish talk!"

But he believed God and did it! He taught what became the largest class in the world for a number of years. It averaged, the last year he was there, 1,100 per Sunday. On one special occasion more than 3,300 came from all parts of the United States. This is a country town in Kentucky! Russ Hill, the inventor, the multi-millionaire, had faith in God.

I am saying that we are to exercise our faith; we are to believe it can be done. Have mighty faith that God can work through you.

Businessmen, preachers, teachers, Sunday school workers, in order to please God, we all must have faith that God can do anything.

A good friend of mine died recently. Dr. Beauchamp Vick never finished college, was never ordained, yet he pastored the large Temple Baptist Church in Detroit for more than thirty years. The last year he lived, he preached only five times in twelve months. His custom was to bring in special speakers Sunday after Sunday.

But Dr. Vick had faith in God. He believed and built an auditorium seating 4,500 and costing more than 3 million dollars. The building is paid for. The church has given multiplied thousands and thousands to missions. He died at age 73.

Somebody exercised faith in God and believed it could be done.

Those who walk by faith are counted dreamers, impractical, fanatics, even foolish.

I love to preach on certain things. I love to preach on salvation and the cross. I love to talk about the second coming. I believe in and love to talk about being separated from the world. I love to preach on faith, mighty faith, the faith that can remove mountains.

Many times we have heard Dr. J. R. Faulkner quote these words: "Faith, mighty faith, the promise sees and looks to God alone; laughs at impossibilities, and cries, 'It shall be done.'"

I. ESTABLISH YOUR FAITH

A right beginning is obligatory. You must have faith.

1. *Fix your faith in God.* Know that you are in Him and only in Him. Christ only can save. There can be no Bible faith without salvation. Establish your faith, not in any denomination; not in a local church, for churches may fail; not in an ordained minister, for they often fail; not in the promises of man, for man fails. But establish your faith in God who never fails.

2. *Fix your faith on the promises of the Bible.* This is the infallible, inerrant Word of God, given to us all for our reading, for our edification, for our daily guidance.

Fix your faith on God and His Word. Rest upon these promises, "If thou canst believe, all things are possible to him that believeth." True faith is always based upon some Bible promise.

3. *Fix your faith by remembering God's faithfulness.* God has never yet failed in all the ages past. Read how He stood by His people, how He fulfilled His Word, both in the Old and New

Testaments. Fix your faith by always remembering that God cannot, will not EVER fail.

We could spend much time talking about establishing our faith, but I am trusting God to make it so real to you until you will say, "I want my faith in Jesus as Saviour. I want to depend upon His Word. I want my faith established so that it cannot be shaken, no matter what may come or what may take place."

II. STAND BY YOUR FAITH

Never be ashamed of your faith. Never be timid in talking about it to others, telling them what faith in God will do for them.

1. *Feed your faith on the Bible.* ". . .faith cometh by hearing, and hearing by the word of God" (Rom. 10:17). To have strong faith, one must come back to the Book and get hold of God's promises. ". . .all things are possible to him that believeth."

Jesus said, "Have faith in God." Fix your faith, then feed it on the Bible. Feeding on the Bible will drive away foolish fears.

Life is full of fears. Many know paralyzing fear. The answer is faith in the Word of God and God's promises. "What time I am afraid, I will trust in thee" (Ps. 56:3). Also, Isaiah 26:3 promises, "Thou wilt keep him in perfect peace, whose mind is stayed on thee."

Feed your faith on this holy Book. Rest upon the promises of the eternal God.

Simon Peter and the other disciples looked and saw Jesus walking on the water. Peter said, "Lord, I would like to walk on water, too. Bid me come to thee." Jesus bade him.

Peter crawled out of the boat, got on the water and began walking. But seeing the wind and boisterous waves upset him. When he looked down and saw the danger, the Bible says, ". . .beginning to sink, he cried, saying, Lord, save me." Jesus stretched out His hand and brought him up to safety.

I am saying that one has to train himself to look to the Lord. When we look at things around us, we have trouble; we become distressed. Not so if we keep our eyes fixed on the Lord. Feed your faith on His Word, keep looking to Jesus, have confidence in Him, knowing He cannot fail.

2. *Live the life of faith.* This will free you from worry and strain. Think on this, then tell the Lord, "I am going to live my life by exercising faith in You, living by faith."

Worry is unbelief in disguise. Many people worry. One outstanding doctor said many of those in hospitals could get up and walk out. He said that forty percent of his patients worry over things that have already taken place, and they can't do one thing about it. He also said that twelve percent worry about their physical health, when perhaps nothing is wrong with them.

The doctor was saying that people worry and fret about unimportant, non-existent things.

It is for you and me to live by faith. We are not to worry about tomorrow; we are to trust God for today—just one day at a time.

Some of us think about and worry over what may happen a year from now or five years from now or ten years from now—way down the road. When I do, I pull myself back.

I think about our church, about my ministry, about what we are doing. I begin to look ahead and think, *What about five years, ten years from now?* What I need to do is, do my best today and God will take care of the tomorrows, the years ahead.

I want to be adventuresome, to have the eyes of faith but at the same time, to depend on God. What I think may take place may never come to pass.

I read about a bassoon player in the orchestra conducted by Toscanini. He came to the great conductor and said, "Mr. Toscanini, I have trouble. My bassoon will not play the high E flat."

Toscanini had memorized every score; so he said to the young man, "Don't worry about that. There is no E flat in the music anyway. So you won't have to play an E flat tonight. Forget it."

Sometimes what we worry about never happens.

Faith is opposed to sight. To walk by sight means to have visible means of support. The walk by faith is a moment-by-moment reliance on God.

The flesh shrinks from complete dependence on God. It looks for a cushion against possible losses. But we are to rest on God, to live by faith.

On Psalm 27, Dr. H. A. Ironside said something that I liked very much. Verse 1 says, "The Lord is my light and my salvation; whom shall I fear?" David here is not afraid of anything.

Then skip to verse 7 and read, "Hear, O Lord, when I cry with my voice." We detect a little element of fear here. The psalmist shows his weakness.

Dr. Ironside said it was mighty strange that David would have such great peace in the first part, down to verse 7, and from verse 7 through the rest of the chapter experience such difficulty. But this is common to all men. First is his established faith, then everything changes when he says in verse 7, "Hear, O Lord, when I cry with my voice." In other words, "Hear me in my troubles."

Then in verse 14 David says, "Wait on the Lord: be of good courage, and he shall strengthen thine heart: wait, I say, on the Lord."

Rest on God, depend on God, knowing He never fails.

A little lady was giving her testimony. The husband was taking their daughter to school on his way to work. She had told them both good-by as they got in the car and drove off. In just a short time the message came that their car was involved in a crash and both were killed.

The woman, left alone now, said in her testimony, "Without my faith in God, I could not have stood it."

Then there was the Christian millionaire who had his office in a large building in the city. He had planned to give as much away as he could. This was back in the Depression era.

He went to bed one night; and when he awoke the next morning, all was gone. The stock market had crashed, leaving him penniless.

Here is his testimony: "Had it not been for my faith in God, I would have ridden the elevator to the 28th floor and jumped off. But faith in God kept me steady."

I went to Birmingham, Alabama, in 1935. I began hearing strange things. This country boy had never had any money, so money didn't bother me one bit. Those were the Depression days. Neither was I worried about the Depression. If offerings back then averaged ten cents per person coming to the meeting, that was a pretty good offering. I was hearing things.

When the Depression hit Birmingham, I saw the steel businesses going to pieces. Things were happening. Banks were closing. Somebody announced that the president of a certain bank had committed suicide. Why? Because he couldn't face the losses they were having.

Wait! Live a life of faith! Whatever comes or goes, keep on trusting God.

And may I say this: Prepare yourself for testing. Anyone who determines to walk by faith will be tested. When he comes to the end of his human resources, he will be tempted to turn from God to follow man.

> **Doubt sees the obstacles; Faith sees the way;**
> **Doubt sees the darkest night; Faith sees the day;**
> **Doubt dreads to take a step; Faith soars on high;**
> **Doubt questions, "Who believes?" Faith answers, "I!"**

Share your faith. Establish your faith. Feed your faith. Live on the Word of God. Live by the promises of God. Then share your faith in God.

It is blessed to have faith in God, blessed to have peace and power of God in the heart, blessed to know God is with us. But it is selfish when we cuddle that faith and say, *This is mine; I will not share it with a soul.*

You are sharing faith by being here this morning.

I went down the street to have a picture made. The newspaper wanted it. I met some people leaving church. When I asked, "Are you going to church?" I got this answer: "No, we are going home this morning."

"Are you going to church?" I asked another. I got the same answer: "We have been to Sunday school; now we are on our way home."

To one fellow who frankly told me, "I love Sunday school but don't like church at all," I said, "You are dead wrong. If you are saved, worship is always first."

These are not sharing their faith. They were walking away from the house of God! They are not sharing in what we are trying to do here! They are not sharing in the mission program. They are not sharing in the winning of souls. They are missing it all.

Share your faith. Share your salvation experience. If you are saved, tell others about this wonderful salvation. That great mission's man, Dr. Ernest Reveal, did it all the time. Pat Withrow told people night and day. If you are saved, tell about it!

Second, share your prayer experiences. Has God answered your prayer? Done something special for you? When God answers prayer, He deserves a telling to others about it.

Praise God for the $75,000.00 check for Tennessee Temple Schools which came this week! God answered prayer.

Third, share your experience of God's help in times of weakness. He strengthens. Certainly Paul found that to be true. That thorn in the flesh—what was it? It might have been the same thing that I have in mine. I'm glad I don't know what he had. I know one thing: he went to God about it, praying three times. But God said, "You just keep it, Paul. Keep that thorn in the flesh. My grace is sufficient. I will be with you in times of weakness."

I have found that God never fails. Day by day walk with Him. Share your faith with others.

Faith stabilizes. Faith strengthens when we face temptation. Faith gives light in darkness. Faith gives companionship when lonely.

Hebrews 11 is a beautiful portion, telling about the men of faith in days gone by. This week I had to read it again. I wanted to hear it once more. How amazing, how wonderful the faith of these men—and women, too! Some most unlikely characters had faith in God.

Oh, yes—I read about them all: Abel, Enoch, Noah, Abraham, Jacob, Joseph, Moses, Rahab and others—read of their faith in God.

Which had the greatest faith? I don't know; I believe it could have been Abraham. I know about Moses; about Joseph and Jacob; I know what Noah did about the ark; about Enoch walking with God; but when I read about Abraham offering up his son, I said, *That's it! His was the greater faith!*

Abraham is a type of Christ. God also gave His Son. Jesus came down and died that we might have everlasting life, that we might have faith to live as we walk down this pathway of troubles and trials.

I have two more things to say. First, to the lost. If you have never been saved, you need Jesus. You have nothing without Him—nothing. You may have money, position, prestige, fame—everything; but without Him you have nothing.

Today you can walk the aisle and tell Jesus you want Him as your Saviour. Tell Him you want to walk with Him, want to exercise faith, mighty faith.

And to you worrying Christians, you discontented Christians, you unhappy Christians, I say, get hold of faith, rest upon that faith, knowing that God never fails.

O lost one, come to Christ!

I read the story of an Oriental prince who had a little son. He wanted to teach him not to trust anybody. So he put his son up on a ledge and said, "Jump!" The little fellow jumped and his father caught him.

The next day he put him up there again and said, "Son, jump!" Again the boy jumped and his father caught him, as any father would.

The next day he said, "Get up on the ledge." The boy did as he was told. "Now, Son, jump!" Again the little tyke jumped, but this time his father stepped back and saw his boy fall to the floor, injuring himself. His body was bruised when he hit the floor with great force. He began to cry. His father picked him up and said, "Son, let that be a lesson to you. Never trust anyone, not even your own father."

You say, "Brother Roberson, you don't like that story, do you?"

No, but I know one I can always trust—the Lord Jesus. He will never step back, never fail those who trust Him.

FAITH IS DEAD TO DOUBT, DUMB TO DISCOURAGE-MENT, BLIND TO IMPOSSIBILITIES, AND KNOWS NOTHING BUT SUCCESS IN GOD.

36. The Dynamics of a Daring Faith

And Moses said unto the people, Fear ye not, stand still, and see the salvation of the Lord, which he will shew to you to day: for the Egyptians whom ye have seen to day, ye shall see them again no more for ever.

The Lord shall fight for you, and ye shall hold your peace.

—Exodus 14:13,14.

And it came to pass at the time of the offering of the evening sacrifice, that Elijah the prophet came near, and said, Lord God of Abraham, Isaac, and of Israel, let it be known this day that thou art God in Israel, and that I am thy servant, and that I have done all these things at thy word.

Hear me, O Lord, hear me, that this people may know that thou art the Lord God, and that thou hast turned their heart back again.

Then the fire of the Lord fell, and consumed the burnt sacrifice and the wood, and the stones, and the dust, and licked up the water that was in the trench.

And when all the people saw it, they fell on their faces: and they said, The Lord, he is the God; the Lord, he is the God.

—I Kings 18:36-39.

. . .Lord, I believe. And he worshipped him.

—John 9:38.

So then faith cometh by hearing, and hearing by the word of God.

—Romans 10:17.

Someone said, "God works as long as His people live daringly; He ceases when they no longer need His aid."

Most have faith of some kind, but it is often misplaced. Many have "faith," but it lacks a solid foundation. The faith that stands is the faith fixed in Jesus Christ and growing as we feed upon the Word of God.

There is such a need for daring, dynamic Christians—those who believe the Word of God, those who stand for it, those who profess their faith in Christ, those who are moving out and on for God.

Too many are at ease in Zion. Nothing moves them; nothing shocks them; nothing amazes them. No service does anything for them. They are not looking for something from God. There is a need for daring, dynamic Christians.

There is a crying need for daring, dynamic churches—churches that are pressing forward to obey the Great Commission. Such churches give their youth and their money.

We need churches wholly committed to God's great plan for His church, churches established on the Word of God, churches unafraid of a wicked, gainsaying world.

There is a need for daring, dynamic crusades—crusades to awaken the sleeping. Listen to what I am saying. We need revival meetings to awaken the sleeping.

We are planning a crusade in our city, a crusade that can touch fifty thousand homes, if our church stands back of the movement. We are working out the details now. There is a need for daring, dynamic crusades doing the job.

I. CONSIDER THE MEMORY OF A DARING, DYNAMIC FAITH

The things that are best remembered are the daring things. Not foolish, but daring. Not for men's applause, but for God's approval. Not for spite, not to exceed another, but to do God's will.

In this year we are celebrating the 200th Anniversary of the founding of this great nation. Books are being written and many have already been written about it. Plays are presenting this two hundred years of the history of America. Songs are being revived. New ones are being written about America. All is good, but what do they write about? Commonplace events? No! About some painless topic? No! They write about the daring things performed in this nation by such men as Washington, Lincoln, Lee, Roosevelt and others. The dull, the painless, the drab things are forgotten.

The daring things stand out in your life. Yet so many of you live drab, commonplace lives, never achieving anything. Life to you means nothing. You just exist.

In the story of Dr. Gartenhaus, did you notice what stood out in his memory? Did you notice what we portrayed on the platform tonight? Not little commonplace events, but events that shake, stir and move people. That is what you recall.

Looking back over my boyhood, I find I did not do very much; but once in a while I took a little chance. I only had one bike in my life, and I played the fool with it. A few times I rode up one of these rampways where you jump about ten or fifteen feet and land on the other side. The bicycle came apart, just split in two. That ended my bicycle riding.

One day some crazy boy dared me to jump off a fence. "Did you ever dive off a fence right into a field?" he asked.

I said, "No. I wouldn't do that. That's silly."

"That's not foolish. Anybody can do it. Just get on the fence, put your arms out like this and dive."

"All right," I said, "If that's the way you do it, I'll do it." I got on the fence, stood up, put my hands together and dove off into the ground. I hit—and broke—my arm under the old board fence. I never did that stunt again.

The daring things, the foolish things of life stand out.

I was brought up in poverty. Wanting to make money after I finished high school and before I started to college, I said to a young man, "Let's make some *good* money."

We left in an old T-Model Ford car. In the first twenty-five miles we had five blow-outs! It took us one whole day to make twenty five miles because we had to repair tires!

In Topeka, Kansas, we got a job pitching wheat. My, what

money we made! Three dollars a day! That was gone before we turned around. Then, after that job, we could not find another. I spent the rest of the summer eating peanut butter and crackers.

The unusual things of life, the dynamic things, the daring things, are what we remember.

I lived in the back of a church for three years in Greenbrier, Tennessee. No restrooms, no bathing facilities—nothing but a little light hanging in the middle of the room. Nothing wrong with this at all. But in comparison with today, when people have to have so much, it was quite a strange and interesting three years.

Deuteronomy is a sacred book of memory. Moses is recounting the deliverance of the people from Egypt. He said, "Beware lest you forget the Lord which brought thee forth out of the land of Egypt." He talked about what was coming and how they should prepare for it.

You might say about the book of Job, "Well, the book is about so and so." No. Job is a book of extraordinary interest, an account of a man's faith in God and what God did with this man. Faith is always exciting. Job, the rich man, lost everything.

He lost his property. The trial of one's pocketbook is often the test of one's faith.

He lost his ten children, but kept his faith! ". . .the Lord gave, and the Lord hath taken away, blessed be the name of the Lord."

He lost his health. Satan touched Job with the finger of disease. A tortured body is a test of faith.

He lost his friends. Even the friends who stood by for a while criticized him; they condemned him.

He lost his wife. She turned from him and said, "Curse God, and die." But Job's faith did not falter. He had absolute confidence in God. He loved God better than wealth or family or health or friends or wife.

Here is the picture, here is the memory of what faith has done in days gone by. So many people live dull, uneventful lives. They refuse the challenge. They close the doors to opportunity. I challenge you to put God first.

Put Him first in church attendance. Some of you could alter

your whole life if you would determine from this night on to never miss another service Sunday morning, Sunday night or Wednesday night, unless too sick to get out of bed.

Challenge yourself about giving. Let this coming year be the best in your giving for our God, in living for Christ, in witnessing. Make whatever you do the unusual.

II. THE BUILDING OF A DARING, DYNAMIC FAITH

1. *By the Word.* This Bible says, "Faith cometh by hearing, and hearing by the word of God." We build dynamic faith from the Bible, the Word of God.

I want to challenge you to something. We are now studying the book of Revelation in our Sunday school. Will you read Revelation through this coming week? It won't take very long. Study it as much as you will, but read it through first.

If you want to establish and build your faith, then read the Word of God. Faith comes from the Book.

2. *By worship.* Make it meaningful. Revamp your whole life regarding going to church. Make this a dynamic, daring thing of trusting God, having faith in God, and honoring God as you faithfully come to His house. Enjoy the singing, the announcements, the message—all of it.

Some people never get that. A lot of churches are built on entertainment. I love singing, but you don't go to church just for that. Some go to hear certain well-known quartets who travel from place to place. That's not why you should attend the house of God.

A lot of folks go to the services of the so-called "faith healers." Now faith healing is the only kind there is, and I believe in that. But some go just for the show. That isn't why we should attend church.

Build a daring, dynamic faith by singing, praying, and worshiping in the house of God.

3. *By courageous actions.* Do what God commands no matter what others may think. I mentioned Dr. Ernest Wadsworth in a recent message. He spoke here once. Dr. Wadsworth is head of the Great Commission Prayer League.

I visited his office in the old Moody Building in Chicago, a little room they had provided for him. He lived in that room almost sixty years.

One day Dr. Wadsworth prayed something like this: "Dear Lord, help me. I have occupied this room all these years and have never paid any rent for it. Please give me something to give to Moody Bible Institute, something I can hand to them."

After praying that way, in a few days, Dr. Wadsworth received a fifty thousand dollar check in the mail. He endorsed it, then thanked the Lord for that answer. Then walking down to the office of the Moody Bible Institute he gave them the check and told them, "I prayed that I could do something for you after all these years of kindness. God answered by sending this fifty thousand dollars."

Some people said, "Dr. Wadsworth, why didn't you just give them ten thousand and keep the other forty thousand? Or give them half and keep the other half for yourself? You need it. Remember, you are not young."

He said, "No, no! I promised God that if He would give it, I would give it."

Now that dear man, though up in years, was daring in his faith. The check was made out to him, belonged to him; but he wanted Moody Bible Institute to use it for its needs.

Build your faith—your faith in God.

Put up three big signposts: First, have a daring faith this coming year. Believe God, trust God, have faith in God's Word: Second, rest upon the power of God in your life for all the coming days; Third, do what God says. You can pray; you can witness; you can be a soul winner.

Build your faith in God. Then when things are shaky and you feel you can't make it, go back to the Book again and see what God has promised and believe His promise.

A young lady said to me the other day, "Dr. Roberson, I will have to quit school for lack of money. I owe $550.00 and I just don't have it."

I said, "We will pray about it. Come back to see me later and let's see what can be done."

She prayed and I prayed. The very next day she came to say, "You know, a wonderful thing happened. God answered our prayer yesterday!"

From back home, a friend had sent a check for $550.00. This student said, "I never thought I would receive it, so I was thinking I would have to drop out of school." God did answer.

It is not always that easy. It may be He wants you to dig down and work hard. He may give you a job; and if He asks you to do certain things, go ahead and do them. Trust God and have faith in Him. Apply yourself to a God-given task. Build your faith, exercise your faith in God.

In Georgia a man, after graduation from one of our big state universities, got a job with the Coca Cola Company. He became one of the top men. He married and had two little girls. They were very, very happy. He was successful in his business in Georgia.

Then the company decided that they would like to send him to a European country. He was to establish there the Coca Cola Company.

He left his wife and girls in the United States and flew overseas, saying, "When I get everything set, I'll send for you." He bought a home, furnished it, then sent notice to his wife, "Come now and bring the children."

They got on the plane in Atlanta, Georgia; but the plane crashed into a mountain, killing his wife and daughters.

The man came back to America with the bodies of his loved ones. At the funeral services as he sat and listened to the preacher, he rededicated his life. Though tears were falling, he said, "I will trust God every step of the way."

He resumed his work in this country. To his church, he said, "I want to do all I can. Would you allow me to furnish one of the departments in the Sunday school?"

In one department he put in all new furniture, put in an organ, put up pictures in memory of his wife and two daughters.

My friend, we don't know what is coming next. I wish I could shake up some of you.

I preached a funeral yesterday at one o'clock. The family had lost their seventeen-year-old son. I poured out my heart.

Oh, that something might awaken people to get right with God and serve Him and live by faith, doing what God wants them to do.

III. THE ACHIEVEMENTS OF A DYNAMIC, DARING FAITH

In Genesis, chapter 12, is the story of Abraham. He was seventy-five years of age when God called him to leave his loved ones. "I will make of thee a great nation, and I will bless thee, and make thy name great; and thou shalt be a blessing." Genesis gives the record of Abraham's faith.

Hebrews 11 confirms the faith of Abraham and his achievements for God.

The achievements of faith! What faith can do in your life and mine. How God wants to work through us and make us what He wants us to be. I hope we never get away from this. Know what faith can do when you believe God.

I can't explain everything. My good friend Charlie Thompson came by and picked me up one day. He said, "I want you to see something." I didn't have much time, but I went with him. After driving a long while, finally we came to a place out on Bonnie Oaks Drive. He said, "That's it right there. That's where I am going to build a church."

I said, "Charlie, do you own the land?"

"No, but I will own it, because I feel that's where it ought to be."

I said, "If that is where God wants you, He will provide. Take it by faith." We had prayer together.

Charlie Thompson bought that piece of land. There stands today Trinity Baptist Church, with its school.

Say what you will about Charlie Thompson, but he started by a simple faith in God. From an empty lot that he did not even own, he said, "I plan to start a church here." And that is where he has been for a number of years.

Have faith in God. I know that there are times when it may seem foolish.

I was almost twenty-two when I went to my first church in Germantown, Tennessee. I wanted to do something. I looked at other churches and said, "If others can have Sunday schools, we can, too."

This church had been built back before the Civil War days. It was beautiful, old-fashioned, and not one Sunday school room. I said, "Let's build some back there."

I got on the phone and called a brick man and said, "Would you ship a few thousand bricks out here? I want to build a building."

He didn't ask any questions. I didn't tell him that I was only twenty-two. I hoped that I sounded older. He said, "We'll ship them out."

I will never forget. The man shipped the bricks out of Memphis by train. I had to pick them up with a wheelbarrow and haul them down to the location—about a block away! I had no money, but I got a couple of men and said, "I want you to build me a building back here."

I knew nothing about drawing plans, but I drew them anyway—on the ground—and said, "All right, make it like this."

The men built the building. We then had only thirty-two members. I had been there only a few weeks.

You say, "Brother Roberson, that was foolish." I don't know if it was or not. Some people did say that; but when the building was finished, it was paid for! That's more than you can say about a lot of things that you have built!

We filled the Sunday school building on Sundays. The old church, which had stood there since about 1860, began to revive and move forward. It had been only a half-time church in all its history. I turned it into a full-time church.

Faith in God sometimes seems so foolish to some people.

In a previous article I told you about the time I went to Birmingham, Alabama, as an evangelist with the Birmingham Baptist Association. I bought brand-new, beautiful tents in my own name from the old Nashville Tent and Awning Company in Nashville, Tennessee.

One beautiful tent I had put up in Hueytown next to the Pleasant Ridge Baptist Church. I had paid only a part payment on it because I didn't have any money.

I got experts to put it up. They staked it down and got it ready. We put the benches in. Everything was ready for the meeting. That evening a storm came and tore the brand-new tent to pieces, rumpling it on the ground like a piece of paper.

Some of the women of the church took thread and needles and began to sew that tent together.

We got it back up and had one of the most successful meetings that Hueytown has ever had. The tent was paid for in just a short time. The big rips didn't seem to hurt. We went ahead trusting the Lord.

I'm saying that often one has to do some things by faith.

You would be amazed to know how many folks said, "You're a fool," when I moved from Fairfield up here. We had averaged every Sunday for one year in Fairfield, Alabama, 852 in Sunday school.

When I came to Highland Park, the Sunday school was running 200, 250 or 300. (I don't recall the exact number.) Some Fairfield people said, "It's foolish for you to go there and leave here where God is prospering."

Wait a minute! I was answering the call of God. And you have to answer His call, too, to be in His will. God knew what He was doing. I didn't see it then; I didn't understand it at all then.

When I got here to Chattanooga, I thought, *This is not for me. I don't want to stay too long.* I told my wife not to unpack everything. "We will leave in a little while," I said. But we stayed. Now I have about decided to make it a life's work!

Faith in God, resting upon God, depending upon Him—this is what I am trying to emphasize. If God directs, if you know God is in a thing, though it may be a tremendous step of faith, you move out.

When we had the official vote to start Tennessee Temple Schools on July 3, 1946, we did not fully understand all we were doing. I simply said, "All in favor of having a school—Tennessee Temple—(I gave a few particulars) please stand." All stood.

God knew what He was doing. I had said this to many of you

people but I have said it away from here a few times. I prayed for fifty students the first year. The first day we had 109! That so shocked me that I went home and told my wife, "We're going to close this thing down before it starts. I have too many students."

God knew what He was doing.

The buying of Camp Joy was done on faith. I had no money. My associate didn't have any either. We went to a big sale on the Tennessee Valley land. I only had a few pennies in my pocket. They outlined the T.V.A. property—what was on the right and left, north, south, east and west—almost one hundred acres. The man said the lowest bid they would take was $3,000. "We will take the bids and go on from there."

I said, "I'll bid $3,000." Nobody else bid, so I bought it.

I walked up to the man and said, "Sir, when do I have to pay it?"

He said, "All within thirty days. If you don't have it paid by then, it will have to be auctioned off again."

I said, "It will be paid for," and walked out. I had only a few pennies and nothing else. No bank account for Camp Joy.

One of the greatest projects this world has ever had has been the work of Camp Joy. Last year hundreds were saved at the Camp. Every year since its beginning in 1946, God has been blessing the work.

What I am saying is that you have to find a place God wants you to take, then do the job God has for you to do. Have a daring faith and a dynamic faith in God.

If man is not careful, he will look for the safe place in bank accounts, insurance policies, and other places of safety. We are tempted to live by sight and not by faith. We fail to experience the excitement of saying, "O God, we trust thee!"

Perhaps you are asking tonight, "Brother Roberson, what is the purpose?"

First, I would like to get people to Jesus Christ. I want you saved. After you get saved, I challenge you to have faith in God, a dynamic and daring faith that reaches out to do things for God.

Miracles still take place. They still happen in this church. There are more things to come. We are looking for new attitudes, new channels whereby we can do a better job for God and Chattanooga, and around the world.

The Christian will find excitement in walking by faith.Get a vision, and follow through. God knows what He wants you to do right now. Ask Him what it is. He will show you. Get everything out of the way so He can speak to you.

Second, seek new ways to glorify Him. Use what God has said, then ask for some new ways whereby you can glorify His name.

Accept new challenges. If God opens up a challenge, take the challenge, then launch out into the deep. Have faith in God. This matter of a daring, miraculous faith can be yours when you simply trust God.

Christians, tonight have faith in God. Don't be ordinary, commonplace Christians. Folks may laugh at you once in a while, but go ahead and trust God, have faith in God. If they say, "You are a fool," still keep that faith in God.

God may want you to do something unusual. I could stand here tonight and talk about orphanages, about schools and about various other things.

I could tell you about Jack Hyles. I was in his church on the day he made one of his greatest decisions. The whole church membership was divided. At one time, 286 people walked out. Then others left, of course. I was sitting in his office talking to him when two women came by. I have never seen women so mad. I can take a mad man, but a mad woman bothers me. These two were really mad. They walked in the office and said, "We want to talk to you."

Jack looked at me and said, "Brother Roberson, you'd better leave and let me talk to them."

I walked out in the hall. They lowered the boom on him. They told him what they thought of him. When they had finished, I saw them prance down the hallway, still as mad as they could be.

When I walked back in the office, he said, "Well, they told me what they thought of me and my ministry."

I said, "What are you going to do?"

"I don't know. What do you think I should do?"

I said, "I think you ought to stick by the guns and keep going."

We had prayer together and he said, "I think God wants me to stay here."

God has kept him there, and he has done one of the most miraculous works of the entire world.

What am I saying? That faith does the job. There may be some problems, opposition, some heartaches, but trust God, Christian friend. Have faith in God. Don't stop, but do what God says.

God help you who have never been saved to come to Christ now and be saved.

Someone has said that Columbus practically found America before he left Spain. And far from being surprised when he saw the Western continent, he would have been surprised if he had not seen it. The expectancy of faith is a large element in success.—G. H. Hallock.

37. *A Faith for This Breathtaking Age*

And when Jesus departed thence, two blind men followed him, crying, and saying, Thou son of David, have mercy on us.

And when he was come into the house, the blind men came to him: and Jesus saith unto them, Believe ye that I am able to do this? They said unto him, Yea, Lord.

Then touched he their eyes, saying, According to your faith be it unto you.

And their eyes were opened; and Jesus straitly charged them, saying, See that no man know it.

But they, when they were departed, spread abroad his fame in all that country.

—Matthew 9:27-31.

And the apostles said unto the Lord, Increase our faith.

And the Lord said, If ye had faith as a grain of mustard seed, ye might say unto this sycamine tree, Be thou plucked up by the root, and be thou planted in the sea; and it should obey you.

—Luke 17:5,6.

Every age, every person has distinct problems and needs. God has exactly what we need, the very thing that we desire.

The disciples cried, "Lord, increase our faith."

Jesus said to these two men, "According to your faith be it unto you."

God has provided everything that we have need of.

This is a breathtaking age. Sin comes at us at such awful force that we are shocked almost beyond words. The strange, erratic religious movements of today are shocking, weird. Pressures placed upon us are both shocking and breathtaking. They are almost too much for us to handle. The most severe things are moving us, speaking to us. The one single antidote for all this is faith in God.

Feeling inadequate to cope with their problems, people are searching for strengthening faith.

That accounts in part for a man like Bill Gothard. I'm not giving criticism, just reporting. I'm sure those who hear him go because they are burdened and concerned and needing more faith. I am told that he speaks in a very beautiful way, saying what ought to be said, pointing out to people certain ideals he feels will help them cope with today's pressures. There is no choir, no special music, no gimmicks. People hear him because they are searching, hungry, needing help.

So many are pulled aside from the Word of God, even from churches, by listening to someone who may turn them aside to some other thought, to some other idea. Every good thing we have comes from above. No matter where else you may look, our needs are all met in the Bible.

Viciousness of this day calls for faith. This is a tough, bloody day. Read your paper. Listen to your newscast. Murder, rape, deception, drunkenness abound. Where can we turn but to the Word of God!

Blindness calls for faith. Men do not see the course they are taking. With eyes closed, they plunge ahead. Some are afraid of the present scene; others are afraid to look to the future.

Unconcern calls for faith. People seem to care so little, are so unconcerned about others' troubles.

Instability of many Christians calls for faith. Folk are in and out, up and down, on and off, "wishy-washy." It is hard to find those who are standing steady and true. Young people, beware! Determine at the beginning of this school year to be established, stable, faithful in all God's work.

Gullibility calls for faith. Many are taken in by every wind of doctrine.

Unfaithfulness of many reveals the need of faith. They come for awhile, then quit. They have nothing; they get nothing. There is a spiritual weakness which shows a need. Strength comes when we have faith in the Almighty God.

Two Scriptures, used at the beginning of this message, come to mind:

"Then touched he their eyes, saying, According to your faith be it unto you."

"Increase our faith."

Now I give you four simple thoughts.

I. USE THE FAITH YOU HAVE

If I were to ask you, "Do you believe the Word of God?" ninety-nine percent of you would raise your hand indicating you do believe the Bible. Then use it. Again, if I were to ask, "Do you believe God answers prayer?" you would reply that you do. All right, use that! Use the faith that you now have.

Do you believe God can do all things, has all power? Then use the faith you have. Don't set it up on a shelf and forget it.

Faith is indefinable, but faith is useable. Jesus said, "Have faith in God" (Mark 11:22). Though it be small, like a grain of mustard seed, use it; for it is dynamite!

Use your faith, you who are weak and needy. Joshua had to have the strength of his faith when he took over leadership of Israel. The Apostle Paul suffered in body, and God had to tell him, "My grace is sufficient for thee" (II Cor. 12:9).

Others need to see your faith. Mother, Dad, your children need to see your faith in God. Young people, your friends need to see it. Stand true. Don't waver. Let your faith be seen.

I want others to know I have faith in God. Don't you?

I get a weekly church bulletin from a pastor in another state who loves the Lord. But he does something I wish he would stop doing. He writes a whole page in that bulletin almost every week complaining. I never saw a fellow with so many troubles, and he just openly puts them all down on paper. He talks about how he feels; he talks about the financial problems; he talks about the unfaithfulness of some of his people. By the time you have finished reading what he has written, your faith is gone for sure. He doesn't uplift, inspire nor encourage.

Friend, use your faith to strengthen others. Around you may be a weak person whom you can help to serve God. I want others to know I have a personal faith in God, that God answers prayer, that I am resting on Him.

II. PRAY, "LORD, INCREASE MY FAITH"

". . .faith cometh by hearing, and hearing by the word of God," says Romans 10:17.

Every day brings new emergencies—sickness, accidents, the death of a loved one, financial reverses. So every day we need to know how to get that increase in faith.

Who knows what tomorrow may bring? Our great friend Bill Rice is sitting at the dinner table, eating his meal and talking to his "Princess" and family. All of a sudden a stroke hits. He is rushed to the hospital helpless, unable to walk and talk. Suddenly it happened. (Dr. Bill is now with the Lord.)

Here is our good friend, Lester Roloff. In a personal letter he wrote, "September 13 is the deadline. If we don't make it that day, we are closed; we are through." This letter went out to thousands. (Dr. Roloff is now with the Lord.)

No one is exempt from trouble, from death, from sorrow, from sickness, from reverses; so daily we must pray for an increase of faith. Only God knows what the future holds, what is going to happen.

How is faith increased?

1. *By study.* Suppose you received a death message this afternoon that a loved one had gone. Would you turn to the Word of God for comfort? Would you lay hold on some of those precious Bible promises? Would it be Isaiah 26? Would it be Psalm 91? Psalm 23? Psalm 120? Would it be Romans 8? or Revelation 21?

If some reverse came, what would you do? Study your Bible? Let God speak to you?

2. *By use.* Every achievement of faith leads to greater faith.

3. *By faith.* Does that seem like a strange statement? We are tempted to put our trust in material things instead of having faith in faith.

Listen to this: "Faith is the key that unlocks the past. It is the formula for the problems of the present. It is the magic wand that opens the sealed future." Our finite minds can only understand a part of life, then faith comes in to help us understand that which is lacking.

How can one grow great faith, stalwart faith? By the Bible. Read what God has done for others. He says, "Prove me, try me; challenge me. Launch out into the deep."

Notice that I said, "by faith," not by foolishness.

A young man came to see me last night. He has a wife and two children. He said he is coming here to school. He came to town looking for a job. I helped them find a place to stay last night. He doesn't have any money, so I shall pay for it. Now some would say he is foolish. But if he is trusting God, believing God, then God will supply a job, a place to live, and money for his schooling. I pray that he has faith.

III. USE THE FAITH OF OTHERS

Here is a type of plagiarism that God approves. If a preacher preaches another's sermon, we say he is guilty of plagiarism, which means stealing. We don't approve of that. But we know it is done and sometimes done without guilt.

I write books. I tell preachers they can quote from my sermons if they wish. But when they copy it into a written sermon, that is plagiarism, with some problems involved.

In Cincinnati some years ago, I went to a beautiful church to speak on Monday and Tuesday nights. The pastor came to me and asked, "Do you plan to preach any of your sermons from your book, *Five Ancient Sins*?" I said, "Sir, I don't know yet. But is there some reason why I shouldn't?" He answered me with:

"Yes, sir. I preached the last of the five last night. For five Sunday nights I have preached on those five ancient sins!"

It didn't bother me so much about his preaching the sermons, but it did bother me that he didn't want me to sell my book!

Yes, plagiarism of a certain kind is frowned upon. But if it's using the faith of others and taking what others have, then that plagiarism is good.

1. *Use the faith of Old Testament men.*
The faith of Moses—the Red Sea.
The faith of Joshua—conquering Canaan.
The faith of Gideon—the Midianites.
The faith of Elijah—the prophets of Baal.
The faith of Daniel—in a heathen land.
The Bible tells us about them so we can use the faith they had.

2. *Use the faith of men in this age of grace.* I speak of men like the Apostle Peter who said, "We ought to obey God rather than man." I speak of the faith of Paul who said, "I believe God." The faith of John who said, ". . .this is the victory that overcometh the world, even our faith." The faith of missionaries—Adoniram Judson, C. T. Studd, David Livingstone, J. Hudson Taylor, and David Brainerd, to name a few. We can and should use their faith.

3. *Use the faith of living men.* Look around you: see the faith of the living, and let that encourage you. If God was with them, He will be with you. God is no respector of persons. If He will bless one man, use one man, He will use you, too. God is not prejudiced against you. If you want to be used, if you want God to put His hand upon you, then what God has done for others, He will do for you. Have faith, trust God to do what He wants to do through you. Use the faith of others.

IV. LET FAITH ADD TO YOUR LIFE

So many people, even Christians, complain of emptiness of their lives.

Faith in God adds peace to one's heart. Worry, fret is no honor to God. Listen to these words:

"Be careful [anxious] *for nothing; but in every thing by prayer and supplication with thanksgiving let your requests be made known unto God.*

"And the peace of God, which passeth all understanding, shall keep your hearts and minds through Christ Jesus."—Phil. 4:6,7.

1. *Faith adds peace,* the very thing that all of us want, the very thing that we need in this troubled day. Faith for a day when you can't tell what is going to happen tomorrow; faith when everything seems in an uproar and confusion.

2. *Faith adds courage.* If God be for us, who can be against us? "Be strong and of a good courage," God told Joshua. We, too, need his courage. We, too, need his faith in God. Faith gives one courage to move on.

3. *Faith in God adds adventure.* It takes away the drabness of life. I've been testing this a long time, and I know it is true. The excitement of following and of doing what God says adds adventure to life. Let God take care of the uncertainties of tomorrow while you rest in and trust Him.

Tennessee Temple began in 1946. My ministry here started in 1942. No one ever thought we would do what we are now doing. I thought that first year we would have perhaps 50 students. On the first day we registered 109! I went back to my house thinking, *That's too many for me—109 students!*

It went from that to thousands who come here now each year. We turn down many for lack of room. I wish for a larger auditorium; and we are working at it, one that will bring us together in one building. (The new auditorium is completed and seats over 6,000.) We need more dormitories. But all this takes faith.

Faith in God gives adventure to life. Older people, don't lose it. Young people, don't lose it. You don't know what is going to happen, but you can trust God for the future.

I went away for the first time to old Bethel College in Russellville, Kentucky, a small two-year Southern Baptist college, with not a thing in the world, not even a timepiece! I had one suit and some homemade shirts, but not a penny of money. So I had to find a job. I tried to find one in town but couldn't. I washed dishes in the dining hall at the college. I didn't like it, and I don't like it now, but I did the only job I could find.

You know what my pay was back then? Twenty-five cents an hour! Top wages! The first day I washed dishes for 130 students. We had no modern machinery, so with my hands I washed them; and with my hands I dried every dish, every glass, every cup, every saucer, every piece of silverware.

One day I stacked carefully washed glasses on a big tray, then took a drying cloth and began taking them off and drying them from one side. It never occurred to me that I was doing something wrong. As I took them off, the other side kept getting heavier. Soon the tray toppled over and down onto the floor, breaking twenty-five glasses. I had to work a week to pay back my breakage! That was my humble beginning!

Worse things happened after that, but I trusted God and went ahead. Faith in God adds adventure.

I know what it is to go to school without money. No guesswork about that. I had to work, whether at mowing grass or washing dishes or whatever.

I was the only boy in a little country home, and I usually got my way. And when I got to school, things were different. I was put in a room with a big fellow. I weighed 175-180 pounds, but he was bigger. In this four-story dormitory, we were on the top floor. I walked in the room and said, "This is strange. Where's the bed?" (There were a couple of old chairs and an old desk.) This big fellow said, "It's a Murphy-in-the-door bed." I had never heard of such a thing. He explained that you open the door and pull down the bed.

After the bed was pulled down, I was told, "This is for both of you to sleep in."

The first night we crawled in. I slept on top of him part of the night; he was on top of me the rest of the night. I never had such a night! That little Murphy-in-the-door bed—in the daytime you made it up and pushed it back in and closed the door to have more room.

The next day I found a big, long two-by-four and put it in the bed. I couldn't put it under the mattress because it made the mattress too small, so I put it in the center of the bed and tied it on both ends. I said to my roommate, "You sleep on that side of the two-by-four, and I'll sleep on this side."

Faith in God adds adventure! Trust Him every step. Depend on Him to bring you out of every difficulty.

Let yours be a Bible faith. Let your heart and life vibrate with the reality of trust in God.

Hear the men as they cry, "I know whom I have believed. . . ."

Hear them as they say, "The Lord is my Shepherd."

Hear them as they assure us that "all things work together for good."

Hear these comforting words, "God is our refuge and strength."

Base your faith on the Word of God.

Let yours be a redeeming faith. Make sure your faith is fixed in Jesus Christ. "Believe on the Lord Jesus Christ, and thou shalt be saved" (Acts 16:31).

Let yours be a rejoicing faith. Faith in Christ will give a song. Other faiths are in the minor key, but ours is in the major key. We have Christ as our Saviour and Heaven as our Home.

Our faith is expressed in the songs: "My hope is built on nothing less than Jesus' blood and righteousness"; "Blessed Assurance, Jesus Is Mine"; "I am Thine, O Lord," and "How Great Thou Art!" which we sang a bit ago.

Yours can be a rejoicing faith.

Let yours be a dogmatic faith. Nothing is certain or settled, but we can stand on the solid Rock, Christ Jesus.

Turn away from humanism, naturalism, communism and atheism to Christ, the one and only Saviour. He has the answer for all things in His Word.

Establish your faith, examine your faith, exercise your faith, and let God lead you.

38. *Three Dimensional Faith*

And again he entered into Capernaum after some days; and it was noised that he was in the house.

And straightway many were gathered together, insomuch that there was no room to receive them, no, not so much as about the door: and he preached the word unto them.

And they come unto him, bringing one sick of the palsy, which was borne of four.

And when they could not come nigh unto him for the press, they uncovered the roof where he was: and when they had broken it up, they let down the bed wherein the sick of the palsy lay.

When Jesus saw their faith, he said unto the sick of the palsy, Son, thy sins be forgiven thee.

But there were certain of the scribes sitting there, and reasoning in their hearts,

Why doth this man thus speak blasphemies? who can forgive sins but God only?

And immediately when Jesus perceived in his spirit that they so reasoned within themselves, he said unto them, Why reason ye these things in your hearts?

Whether is it easier to say to the sick of the palsy, Thy sins be forgiven thee; or to say, Arise, and take up thy bed, and walk?

But that ye may know that the Son of man hath power on earth to forgive sins, (he saith to the sick of the palsy,)

I say unto thee, Arise, and take up thy bed, and go thy way into thine house.

And immediately he arose, took up the bed, and went forth before them all; insomuch that they were all amazed, and glorified God, saying, We never saw it on this fashion.

—Mark 2:1-12.

Let me begin by calling your attention to I John 5:4.

"For whatsoever is born of God overcometh the world: and this is the victory that overcometh the world, even our faith."

A remarkably simple but beautiful story is given in Mark 2. It tells about Jesus in Capernaum and about the people who had gathered.

"Straightway"—happening at once—is the key word for this Gospel. The people gathered around Jesus, and He "preached the word unto them." Then four men came bearing one sick of the palsy. But because of the crowd, they could not get near Jesus; so these four carried him up on the roof, tore away a portion and let him down where Jesus was.

Notice the words, "When Jesus saw their faith. . . ." That is what I want you to see—"When Jesus saw their faith, he said unto the sick of the palsy, Son, thy sins be forgiven thee."

Then the Pharisees, Sadducees and Scribes objected. They didn't like this one pretending to be God. ". . .who can forgive sins but God only?" They did not know that Jesus was God incarnate in human flesh. Then the Lord answered by healing the man of his disease. The people were amazed: "We never saw it on this fashion."

Now focus on those words in verse 5: "When Jesus saw their faith. . . ."

I. VISIBLE FAITH

Jesus looked at them and saw their faith. Isn't that

something—the Son of God reading the hearts and minds of people! He saw the faith of these four men. What faith the man sick of palsy had is not mentioned; Jesus saw what faith these four had. He could read their innermost thoughts. He could also read the thoughts of the Pharisees, Scribes and others, and did so here in verses 6 and 7.

Now what were these four doing with their faith?

1. *Expressing sympathy,* showing that they cared for this paralyzed man, showing their concern. They put the man on a bed; the four picked him up and carried him to see Jesus.

What does that say? Let your own heart be moved by faith, then let your faith reach out to move others.

They cared. We too have to care for those about us—the rich and the poor, the high and the low—all.

They expressed sympathy by giving of themselves, as we express sympathy in giving of ourselves and means to carry on the Gospel.

2. *Joining in Unity.* Here were four carrying the man to Christ. It took all four. There could have been trouble had two backed out about halfway and announced, "We don't want to do this; this is just too much. The sun is too hot; the day too disagreeable. We are going back home. You fellows can take him on by yourselves if you wish."

No—all four brought him up to Jesus. They tore away the roof and lowered him down before the Saviour. Blessed unity!

Unity is so important in a church the size of ours. We may not agree on everything. Perhaps neither did these four. But they kept to their job and were unified in what they were doing.

What is true for a church is also true in a revival campaign. This coming revival is sure to fail unless we unite together, stand together, work together.

I was asked to preach in a tent revival in Tarrant, Alabama. Six or seven churches joined in the meeting. There were great crowds. We began on a Monday night. People were saved the first night, the second night, the third night. We were having blessings right along.

Then I noticed that about half the preachers had disappeared.

I had no better sense than to ask why. "Gentlemen, you are not now in the meeting. Is there some reason why?"

One spokesman said, "Something is wrong. Your preaching is good. We like the singer and the singing. You are not doing anything wrong as far as we can tell. But since one preacher in this crowd is stealing the converts, we refuse to support him.

"Every night we watched. He went down to the front when people got saved and talked to them. We know he's trying to get them to join his church. We will not back such a man."

Wait a minute! We still had a great revival. We still had a packed tent night after night, and many souls were saved. But people asked questions about the absence of these pastors from the platform. They were not joining with us, and that was tragic.

We must have unity in revival efforts.

These four men brought the man in the right direction—toward Jesus. Their faith gave them the right direction. They had the right purpose and were going in the right direction. They came to the Son of God, to the One who could heal this man of palsy.

A letter came this week from a friend up North who was writing about his son. It said something like this:

> My son was away in the service of his country for some years. We are Baptists. We have been faithful to our church. We love the Lord. So did my son before he left. But when our son came back home, he turned against both his family and his church. He had paid a man $500.00 to get into a certain organization. He called it a 'religion'; but it wasn't Christian, wasn't biblical, wasn't anything that we would believe in.

Now what was this man he paid the money to doing? Directing this young man in the wrong direction, away from God.

These four had a visible faith. Jesus saw their faith, rejoiced in their faith, honored their faith.

LET OTHERS SEE YOUR FAITH:

By your attitude. For example, by your attitude toward adversity. Troubles come to us all. Heartaches are the lot of everyone.

Then is the time to rise and say, "I want others to see and know that I have faith in God."

I mentioned in another chapter about the wealthy businessman who lost everything when the crash, the Depression, came and how he felt like walking to the window of his office on the 26th floor and jumping out, but how faith kept him strong in his adversity.

Your faith can keep you strong. Let others see your faith by your attitude.

Let them see your faith by your attitude toward tragedy. It may come on suddenly. Things happen in a moment's time—on the highways, in cars, on planes, or other ways.

Let others see your faith by your attitude toward opposition. Don't become bitter. Be Christlike.

The four men could have said, "The crowd is too large." They could have said, "We are not going up on top of that house and tear away the roof to let a man down!" Instead, they revealed their faith by their attitude. They got to Jesus despite opposition of roof and men.

I am sometimes disappointed in people's attitudes. We hear of some folks who come to church, even members, who say, "We can't find a place to sit," or, "We can't find a place to park; so we are planning to join another church where there is plenty of room."

My dear friend! That is not the attitude of faith. Nor is that attitude one of good will toward the service of Christ. Nor is that the attitude one should have toward fundamentalism, toward the Bible as we hold to it here—when you would sacrifice any blessing just for the sake of having a better seat in a church!

I wonder how some feel who go to some churches where they have twenty feet of space to sit in if they want that much room, or a whole bench if need be, but few blessings! When they leave and go back home, their hearts are cold. They have had no blessing, felt no call of God in their hearts, sensed no reality of Christ. They are suffering spiritually, and they will keep on suffering.

I am trying to lay upon your hearts your attitude of faith. Let faith be seen by your standing fast under any circumstances, under any inconvenience, under any hardship.

By your obedience. Show your faith by obedience: in worship, in ·devotions, in giving, in witnessing.

By your persistence—your importunity, your pressing on. Refuse to quit. How many do quit! How many do turn aside! This reveals lack of faith. Keep praying! Keep on working!

Yes, these four had a visible faith. "When Jesus saw their faith. . . ."

II. VICARIOUS FAITH

Vicarious means a substitute, acting on behalf of another, representing another, taking the place of another, as Jesus took our place on the cross.

These four had faith, and Jesus saw their faith. Did the sick man have faith? Maybe so. The Bible doesn't say. But we know the four men did. They brought the man to Jesus. This man was willing to be borne of the four, who had vicarious faith.

Mothers need vicarious faith, praying for the children, for the husband, for the home, never giving up. By your persistence in prayer, by your importunity, you reach God and things happen. Don't be discouraged. Just keep on praying even when you feel like giving up. Keep on witnessing when the going gets hard. Keep on trying when it seems of no use. God will bless.

Sunday school teachers need vicarious faith. You may want to say, "It's too hard work. They are not responsive. Things are not going as planned." Keep on. Faith will win out in the end. God has that blessing in store for those with faith in Him.

Pastors need vicarious faith. Pastors here this morning, you who are in the ministry, must believe God. You must believe for yourself and also for others.

No one can stop. This vicarious faith reaches out to others, stirring them, compelling them to move out for God.

NOW WHAT IS THE PRACTICAL TEACHING HERE? IT IS:

Your faith helps others. Strong and steadfast faith will help others.

I mentioned being in a church in Montgomery, Alabama. Two young men are pastors of one church and both are doing a marvelous job. I believe they will have 425 in Sunday school today. With bad weather, there were 376 present last Sunday.

When these young men moved into town, not one person did they know. They were from Texas and Mississippi. Both graduated from Asbury College in Kentucky, a Methodist school. They left the Methodist church and became Baptists. Both felt led to come to Montgomery, the capital of Alabama, to build a church that would glorify God.

They started with nothing, not a soul! Then God began to send people in. They borrowed $110,000.00 and built a beautiful building. When I asked how they got the money, they said, "We just went to the bank and borrowed it. We signed a note, got the money, and built this building."

Now they have moved on to other things—a Christian school, for instance.

Your faith helps others. Mother, you have faith! Father, you have faith! Young people, you have faith! Preacher, your faith in God will help someone else.

Your life helps others. How do you live? Do others see Christ in you?

Your fervency of spirit will help someone else. ". . .fervent in spirit; serving the Lord" (Rom. 12:11) and trusting God.

It is important that we have vicarious faith in order to serve our Lord.

III. VICTORIOUS FAITH

First, it was a visible faith that Jesus saw; second, the men had vicarious faith—they came and brought another: God using them to bring someone else was certainly vicarious faith. ". . .this is the victory that overcometh the world, even our faith" (I John 5:4).

The four men kept on. They persevered. The crowd was great and the people not cooperative. None backed away to give room and say, "Bring him on in." So the four men had to crawl up on the top of the roof and tear it away. There were no committees to guide them. They didn't have time for a Finance Committee nor Deacon's meeting. They just got up on top, wrecked what was necessary and lowered the palsied man down. Here is victorious faith.

1. *A victorious faith must be placed in the Lord.* In Luke 8:22-25 we find a storm brewing on the Sea of Galilee. The disciples are afraid. Jesus is awakened. When He has calmed the storm, He turns to them and asks, "Where is your faith?" (Luke 8:25).

I ask you:

Where is your faith in the time of death?

Where is your faith when finances are low, or completely gone?

Where is your faith when your friends forsake you?

Where is your faith when sickness touches your body? or that of a loved one?

Don't put your faith in appearances, nor in the promises of man. Put it in God.

2. *A victorious faith must be placed in the promises of God's Word.* The Bible says, ". . .faith cometh by hearing, and hearing by the word of God" (Rom. 10:17). When you rest upon the Bible, then you can keep on pleading and laying hold of every promise.

3. *Your faith must be placed in prayer to God.* "If ye shall ask any thing in my name, I will do it" (John 14:14). Prayer and faith cannot be separated. You cannot have the one without the other. You are not really sold out to God until you learn the secret of prayer, prayer with faith, believing.

You have faith. It must be placed in prayer to God. A victorious faith! A faith that rests upon God and His promises.

In order to have conquering faith, one must be constant in prayer. To have a strong faith, one prays for it. The all-powerful God wants you to have strong faith, victorious faith. It is God's will that we have a faith that will endure every persecution, a faith that will stand when hardships roll heavy upon us, a faith that is ours when family life is disrupted by sin of some worldly member.

WHAT DOES THIS VICTORIOUS FAITH DO?

It overcomes barriers and handicaps. First, we see the

paralyzed one, the palsied and helpless one; second, we see the
helpers, the four who surround him; third, we see the hinderers
in the crowd who wouldn't cooperate by letting them in; fourth,
we see the healer, Jesus.

In every work of God there are hindrances. Every time
something begins to happen in church, in Sunday school, in
youth work, you find the Devil working.

A young man called me the other day. I never heard a fellow so
excited! I let him talk on, occasionally interrupting with: "Praise
God!" "This is wonderful!" "You're right on top!" He said ex-
citedly, "I sure am! This is the greatest thing I've ever had happen to me!"

After he got through, I said, "Son, I believe I would make
myself ready; tomorrow the Devil is going to walk in."

Later he told me that my prediction came true. "In spite of all
the souls saved and other happenings, with God mightily moving, one of the deacons came in to criticize everything I was doing. He announced he was leaving the church. 'And we will work
to get you to resign. We don't think your method is right.' "

Overcome your barriers, your handicaps, your oppositions.
How? By victorious faith.

In Matthew 9:22 a woman touched the hem of Christ's garment. Jesus saw her and said, "Daughter. . .thy faith hath made
thee whole."

It brings peace of heart in a troubled world.

It gets you a reward at the judgment seat. It matters not the
size of your place; God is looking for faithfulness. Do you have
that victorious faith that enables you to stand in the midst of all
the vicissitudes of life? Every opposition, every handicap, every
sickness, every illness, every sorrow, every tragedy that may
come upon you?

What is victorious faith?

It is looking to Jesus, trusting Jesus. It is resting upon His
promises. God cannot lie. You can rest assured that He will see
you through to the end. Have faith in God.

God has promised to all of us: a visible faith, a vicarious faith,
a victorious faith.

I trust you are praying today for an increase in faith, more faith to believe God, to rest upon His promises. God will increase your faith when you read your Bible and rely on its promises. God will increase that faith to cause you to reach out; He will lead you through victoriously to the other side.

There was a visible faith: He saw it. There was a vicarious faith: four men were helping another. There was a victorious faith: they were led on to victory, had the commendation of our Lord and saw the performance of a miracle in the healing of this man.

Faith knows that whenever she gets a black envelope from the heavenly post office, there is a treasure in it. —Spurgeon.

39. A Commanding Faith

Now it came to pass on a certain day, that he went into a ship with his disciples: and he said unto them, Let us go over unto the other side of the lake. And they launched forth.

But as they sailed, he fell asleep: and there came down a storm of wind on the lake; and they were filled with water, and were in jeopardy.

And they came to him, and awoke him, saying, Master, master, we perish. Then he arose, and rebuked the wind and the raging of the water: and they ceased, and there was a calm.

And he said unto them, Where is your faith? And they being afraid wondered, saying one to another, What manner of man is this! for he commandeth even the winds and water, and they obey him.

—Luke 8:22-25.

Then Jesus went thence, and departed into the coasts of Tyre and Sidon.

And, behold, a woman of Canaan came out of the same coasts, and cried unto him, saying, Have mercy on me, O Lord, thou son of David; my daughter is grievously vexed with a devil.

But he answered her not a word. And his disciples came and besought him, saying, Send her away; for she crieth after us.

But he answered and said, I am not sent but unto the lost sheep of the house of Israel.

Then came she and worshipped him, saying, Lord, help me.

But he answered and said, It is not meet to take the children's bread, and to cast it to dogs.

And she said, Truth, Lord: yet the dogs eat of the crumbs which fall from their masters' table.

Then Jesus answered and said unto her, O woman, great is thy faith: be it unto thee even as thou wilt. And her daughter was made whole from that very hour.
—Matthew 15:21-28.

Christ said, "O woman, great is thy faith." What a compliment to one who was not a Jew!

She had never heard a preacher. She had certainly never held a Bible in her hand. She had never attended a church, as we know churches. She doubtless knew almost nothing about the history of the Jews; yet to this one Jesus said, ". . .great is thy faith."

She had faith in the Lord Jesus Christ and what He could do. When she came to Him, that for which she asked was accomplished.

Look at the story.

Here is the crying of a mother whose daughter was grievously vexed with a devil, a demon. She was out of her mind. Concerned for her child, she came to the Lord Jesus.

Oh, that more mothers and fathers had concern for their children, such a concern that they would bring them to the Lord! This is so needful today, with all the troubles of youth. The sin of drink, dope and immorality are working upon their hearts and minds. Here is the crying of a mother.

The compliment of Jesus. He turned away saying,

"I am not sent but unto the lost sheep of the house of Israel . . .It is not meet to take the children's bread, and to cast it to dogs."

He was in Israel, and to help the Gentiles—those not of that family—was not meet to do, He said.

That didn't bother her. She said: "Truth, Lord: yet the dogs eat of the crumbs which fall from their masters' table. Then Jesus answered and said unto her, O woman, great is thy faith: be it unto thee even as thou wilt. And her daughter was made whole from that very hour."

What a compliment—". . .great is thy faith!" He was saying, "Your faith is so great that I can only give what you have asked."

The consequence of faith. "And her daughter was made whole [healed] from that very hour."

Look at this story again. Here was one who was so concerned for her own daughter that she carried her trouble to Christ. This woman of Canaan couldn't have known much about Him, but she acted upon what she knew and brought her needs to the Lord.

Again, notice that she identified herself with her child's need: "Lord, help me." She put herself—"me"—in the place of her child.

She overcame difficulties. Here was opposition by the disciples who requested of the Lord, "Send her away."

Here was the silence of Jesus: ". . .he answered her not a word."

The fact that she was a Gentile presented a problem. But she overcame that.

Then, she manifested what can be called a "commanding faith." She obtained, she demanded His attention and the healing for her daughter. Seeing how great was her faith, Jesus made the daughter whole.

Now there are two or three things I want you to see.

I. THE SIZE OF FAITH

He said to this woman, ". . .great is thy faith" (vs. 28).

Watch carefully. In Matthew 17:20 Jesus said, "If ye have faith as a grain of mustard seed, ye shall say unto this mountain, Remove hence to yonder place; and it shall remove; and nothing shall be impossible unto you."

". . .as a grain of mustard seed. . ."—yet He said to this woman, ". . .great is thy faith."

Her faith was a pure faith, a simple faith. Nothing troubled her. Nothing distracted or distressed her. She had a quality faith, unmixed with doubt and untroubled by human effort. ". . .great is thy faith"—great in quality, undoubting.

Now Jesus always honors faith.

1. *Examine your own faith* carefully. If there are some defects, if something is hindering your faith, get it out of your life.

The human element gets into our faith. We trust in God awhile, believe His Word; but then we come back to self. We are looking to see, *What can I do? What can my family do? What can others do for me?* instead of looking to God. Examine your faith.

2. *Build your faith.* How? By faith in Him who cannot fail. By a knowledge of the Word of God and by relying upon His Word, let your weak faith become strong faith.

The size of faith: We can't say tonight just how much faith we have to have. He said a faith the size of a grain of mustard seed can remove a mountain. More faith, great faith, is certainly a maturity of that faith you have toward God.

II. THE DIRECTION OF FAITH

Christ said, "Have faith in God" (Mark 11:22). Jesus said regarding prayer, "If ye shall ask anything in my name, I will do it" (John 14:14).

The direction of your faith toward Him is it. Not toward others, not toward things, not toward situations, but toward Him.

Faith in people achieves very little. I've tried this; so have you. I've trusted people, had great faith in people over and over again; so have you. I've relied upon them at certain times, but faith in people doesn't achieve very much.

A man can make and break a promise within a few moments. He can make a promise and not mean to keep it. You may think he is sincere, but he soon breaks it. He promises to be true to his word, knowing he won't.

Scores and scores of people in all these years have gotten from our office different things, each promising to have it back in two weeks. I've never seen that loan again. I tore up the notes a long time ago.

Wait a minute! The people who borrowed were the losers. I didn't lose anything. Had I put my trust in them, had I believed their word, I would have lost. People don't keep their word very much any more.

1. *Faith in people achieves very little.* Watch it! Faith in people will surely bring disappointment. To put faith in an individual or in a family may bring sorrow.

2. *Faith in a nation can be disturbing.* Nations turn away from God. And it doesn't take long.

This winter we saw the weather change the thinking of people in many parts of our country. How easy it is for a nation to change. How easy for situations to change.

Some people believe we are a Christian nation. We have everything we want. We don't have a worry in the world. But that can change in a few hours, in a few days. We must not put our faith in a nation.

3. *Faith in so-called prosperity can humble us.* A young lad here in the school (he may be in this service tonight) came to me, saying, "Brother Roberson, a friend was going to pay my bill for the whole year so all I would have to do would be to go to school and study. But he sent a letter saying his funds are cut off; he's had a loss in his business, and so cannot pay my bill. I just don't have the money. I was trusting this man; now he cannot do what he promised."

Trusting in others, relying on others, can bring great sorrow even among loved ones, even in your own family. Build your faith upon the One who cannot fail. Build your faith upon the many promises of God. Rest upon God's Word to you and know that He never fails.

Be quick to acknowledge that you have trusted others more than you have trusted God. You've been trusting in what people promise to do for you this year or the next year, or years after that. Don't count on it! Humans fail.

Confess that you've trusted in your own ingenuity rather than in God's promises.

The Bible says, ". . .without faith it is impossible to please him" (Heb. 11:6).

Someone has said,

> Faith is the wire bringing to the soul the power of God for life and service.
> Faith is the key that unlocks God's treasure house.
> Faith is the guide that leads us into green pastures and still waters.
> Faith is the medicine that vaccinates our souls against the doubts of this world.

The question coming out of this portion we read in Luke 8 is, "Where is your faith?"

Crying, whimpering Christian, where is your faith? Lack of faith is the undoing of so many. Lack of faith causes us to drift away from God. Lack of faith causes us to say things we would never otherwise say. Lack of faith causes us to have thoughts that we would never have thought of. Where is your faith?

Don't put your faith in human appearances. "Fair-weather" Christians mean very little. They may be fair today and change tomorrow, just like the weather.

Don't put your faith in organizations. They too can fail.

Don't limit God by failing to pray and asking for what you need and by your sinful living.

Don't stop God from answering you because of sin. "If I regard iniquity in my heart, the Lord will not hear me" (Ps. 66:18).

Don't limit God by unbelief. Israel missed the Promised Land for forty years. Why? Because they did not believe God would lead them through and give them victory when they moved in the Promised Land.

Keep your direction of faith right.

III. THE RESULT OF FAITH

We can see what faith did for this woman of Canaan. She came, not having much, not knowing much; but she had faith.

She believed Him; she came to Him with a request, and her daughter was healed.

Can you imagine what happened when she went back home? Can you imagine the exclamations of joy on the part of the neighbors and friends? They couldn't understand it all, but that mother knew why she was bringing home a healed child.

Can you see this little woman going about telling others what happened? "I went to this man in Galilee called Jesus. I told Him my situation and He said, 'O woman, great is thy faith: be it unto thee even as thou wilt,' and my daughter was healed!"

The result of faith.

WHAT DOES FAITH DO?

Faith give humility. When through faith answers come, humility must be ours. We must give Him thanks. It is His work, not ours. Sometimes we ask for something and see the answer, then are guilty of not thanking God. Perhaps after much prayer about a certain thing, it took place; but instead of giving thanks to God, you go your way and say, "I worked that out pretty good! I'm doing all right!"

Faith ought to give us humility and remind us of our weakness and of His power.

Faith gives peace and happiness. In this disturbed, changing world, how we need faith in God!

I read this week from an old volume about J. Hudson Taylor, the pioneer missionary to China. It told about how quiet and peaceful he was when great matters were upon him. He was the leader of the China Inland Mission. With so many things pressing upon him, so many financial burdens, he was still serene, undisturbed, resting upon the promises of God.

It said Taylor was an object lesson in quietness, yet he was a very fervent preacher of the Word of God. Taylor said he could not possibly go through the work he had to do without the peace of God.

Faith gives peace and happiness. When we see people unduly troubled about conditions of life, it is because they are not resting upon God and His promises. When you worry, you are sinning against God. But faith will give peace and happiness.

Faith gives persistence and achievement. When we have no faith in God, we are weak and can do nothing.

This mother was persistent. She would not take "no" for an answer. She was also humble. When Jesus said, "It is not meet to take the children's bread, and to cast it to dogs," she said, "That's right, but Lord, the dogs eat of the crumbs which fall from the Masters' table. Surely I, too, can get the crumbs." He answered her with, "O woman, great is thy faith."

George Mueller, whose name always comes to mind whenever we talk about answered prayer, had mighty faith in God. Mueller could speak seven different languages. But that is not what he is known for. He is known for his faith and his prayer life. He was highly educated, trained, cultured in so many ways; yet he was like a child receiving gifts from a parent. His faith was strong. Faith gives persistence and achievement.

By faith, go on. By faith, don't quit, don't stop, don't turn aside. The Word of God says in Hebrews 6:1, ". . .let us go on." Strive on, press on, do what God wants done.

Anywhere I travel in our nation, I'll have one or two or three young people come to me before I leave and say, "Brother Roberson, I made the mistake of my life when I quit school." Or, "Brother Roberson, I made the mistake of my life when I quit the ministry." One told me that last night at 10:25: "I'm out of the ministry. I was called of God to preach. I turned away from that call. Certain things came causing me not to have the strength and power to go ahead, so I quit."

The Word of God says He'll give persistence to keep going. We can achieve if we keep driving on down the road in God's will.

Faith gives power in prayer. Acts 12 tells us that Peter was in prison. The Christians were praying. God opened the doors of the prison house, took the chains off, and set him free. He came and knocked on the door where the prayer meeting was being held. There seemed a little unbelief on the part of the one who answered the door, but not on them all. Let's not discount the prayers of those who were believing Christians in Acts 12.

In Acts 16, Paul and Silas prayed. An earthquake came; there was the release of the prisoners, the salvation of the jailer and his family. Prayer was answered. Faith gives power in prayer. When you pray in faith believing, God hears and answers prayer. Have faith in God!

This is a matter of praying with faith believing and saying, "O Lord, I'm placing this need before You. I don't intend to stop asking in sincerity and humility for what I need."

Faith gives power in prayer. We should pray for souls. We should pray for loved ones. We should pray for revival. We should pray for all our needs, both physical and material, knowing that God hears and answers prayers.

I wonder if you can see what I'm trying to say to you out of these two portions of the Word of God? Here was a humble little woman with her child who was grievously vexed with a devil and needed help. She identified herself with the child and made her appeal, then God gave the answer and healed the child.

The size of faith, the direction of your faith, the result of your faith.

Sometimes I think we forget that God wants to bless us. Ofttimes He has to chasten us and draw us back and make us wake up to see our need. He wants to bless you and me; He wants to do something for us, but we hold Him off. We don't receive it by faith. We don't extend the hand. The table is spread. He says, "I give it to you," but we don't reach out and take it.

Faith in God brings strong prayer, and it brings answers to prayer. Will you pray in faith believing?

Dr. George W. Truett was holding one of his famous camp meetings for cowboys out in the western part of Texas, which he did for many years, both as a young preacher and in his later years. Cowboys would come by the hundreds. There was one section of west Texas where no one had ever been. A lot of people there were getting old. He called them the "white-haired people of Texas." They were unsaved, and he went there to preach to them.

In the first meeting in this place, he looked around and could see many lost folks. Somebody said, "You'll see a man come in one of these nights named Big Jim. He'll sit in the back of the old tabernacle; and he'll listen to you for a while, then get up and leave and curse you. He may even come and curse you to your face. He may curse you to people outside the tabernacle. He will curse this meeting. He will curse God. He will curse the Bible. He's mean; he's wicked. Some have said he's the meanest man in all of Texas."

Dr. Truett said as he got up to preach one night he looked back and saw a big fellow walk in. At once, because of what they had said, he recognized him as Big Jim.

He sat down toward the back of the building. With a stony face he listened for awhile. After the service was going along, he got up and walked out. Dr. Truett thought, *Well, at least he was here. The people said Big Jim will never be saved because he is too wicked, too far from God.*

He finished that first service. Big Jim had gone from the tabernacle over to the cottage where they stayed. Dr. Truett walked out across the ground, in the back of a little clump of trees; and over to one side he heard some voices. As he walked along, he paused for a few moments. He said that he didn't want to eavesdrop, but couldn't help it.

Two men were on their knees calling upon God. "Now, dear Lord, you've answered prayer for us before; we want you to answer it now. We want the salvation of the worst man in all of west Texas." They began recounting all God had done for them. Dr. Truett couldn't help but listen since they were so near to him as he walked by.

They finished praying. Truett said he also prayed that night for God to save Big Jim. "If those men can believe that he can be saved, I'll believe it, too!"

The crowds came the next night. These cowboys came from all the ranches around, as did the owners of the ranches. It was some scene!

He got up to preach and looked around for Big Jim, but Big Jim wasn't there. But just about the time he was ready to give his message, Big Jim walked in, the one people said would never come back. He sat down at the back of the building.

Truett said:

When I saw him, I had to change my sermon. I said, "If you don't mind, let's have a word of prayer." I had prayer. When I finished, I felt led to turn to Luke 15—the story of the prodigal son.

I told the story of the prodigal son just as simply as you tell a baby a story. I went all the way through it, and when I came to the end I said, "Remain seated where you are, please. No song, no one standing. Sit where you are."

I turned to the audience containing so many lost people, but the main one there—known to everyone—was Big Jim.

I kept on talking and looking around the tabernacle. I said, "If tonight you want to accept Christ as your Saviour, come on down the aisle. If tonight you are tired of sin, tired of wickedness and want the safety and assurance of knowing Christ as your Saviour, I want you to come."

He said no sooner had be gotten the words out of his mouth when Big Jim stood up in the back of the house and started moving out between the people and down the row. Those big ranchers and those cowboys were all wiping away the tears. They were seeing something that they thought could never happen.

Big Jim, a cursing, profane man, hated church, hated Bibles—hated everything—came up to the platform. Dr. Truett said he bent over and said, "Preacher, I want to ask you on your honor. Will you promise me that God will take me if I'll come and believe in Jesus?"

Truett said, "Yes, sir, I'll promise you. He'll do it."

"I'm mean and tough. You mean He'll save me?"

"Yes, sir, He'll save you."

"Will He save me right now?"

"He'll save you right now, this very second."

The place was tense. Half of the audience was standing, still marvelling over the fact that Big Jim was at the front. Without a song he had walked down the aisle.

When Dr. Truett said, "He'll save you right tonight," Big Jim, a tough cowboy who had profaned the name of God so many, many times and upset so many services and done with apparent delight whatever he could to cause trouble, raised his face toward Heaven and said, "Lord Jesus, I'm the worst man in Texas. Lord, this preacher said that You'll save me. I'm coming to You just as I am, repenting and believing that You'll save me. Right now, I surrender to the Lord Jesus Christ."

When Big Jim got saved, tears were in abundance in that old tabernacle. And before Truett could do anything more, those men came rushing down the aisles, grabbed Big Jim around the shoulders and some hugged and kissed him. They were seeing something they had never expected to see—Big Jim at the altar accepting Christ!

When Big Jim came, it answered a prayer that men had prayed; and many, many others got saved. Old ranchers who had turned away from God all of their lives came forward and said, "We want to be saved tonight."

God answers prayer.

My dear friend, can you see the size of faith? To this one he said, ". . .great is thy faith."

I want you to see the direction of faith toward Him—not toward yourself or others, but toward Him.

I wonder if you're saying tonight, *My faith is so weak. I'd like to come tonight and say, "Lord, increase my faith."* If the disciples prayed that, so can you pray, "Increase my faith."

Christian people, move out tonight and confess, "My faith has been so weak. I worry so much. I fret so much instead of trusting God."

Maybe you've never been saved. Then, of course, the faith you have to exercise is faith in the Lord Jesus Christ who died on the cross to save sinners. You need Him tonight.

40. The Building of a Master Faith

And Jesus said unto them, Because of your unbelief: for verily I say unto you, If ye have faith as a grain of mustard seed, ye shall say unto this mountain, Remove hence to yonder place; and it shall remove; and nothing shall be impossible unto you.

Howbeit this kind goeth not out but by prayer and fasting.
—Matthew 17:20,21.

And the apostles said unto the Lord, Increase our faith.

And the Lord said, If ye had faith as a grain of mustard seed, ye might say unto this sycamine tree, Be thou plucked up by the root, and be thou planted in the sea; and it should obey you.
—Luke 17:5,6.

So then faith cometh by hearing, and hearing by the word of God.
—Romans 10:17.

By faith Enoch was translated that he should not see death; and was not found, because God had translated him: for before his translation he had this testimony, that he pleased God.

But without faith it is impossible to please him: for he that cometh to God must believe that he is, and that he is a rewarder of them that diligently seek him.
—Hebrews 11:5,6.

All people have some faith. Lost people have a faith—not the proper kind, but they do have a faith. Those without Christ may be trusting in good works, in church membership, in reputation; but they have some kind of faith.

All Christians have faith or they are not Christians. First, you have to have faith to know that Jesus is your Saviour. You have to look to and believe in Him. But sometimes it stops there and is a very limited faith.

This morning, I'm speaking on, "The Building of a Master Faith" for a special reason.

Christ often rebuked His disciples by asking, "Where is your faith?" They believed in Him, but their faith was weak. They had faith but not a master faith, not a faith to overcome their problems.

The Word indicates that we are to build our faith. If you are saved through faith in Christ—wonderful! But God wants you to have more. He wants you to have faith that will change and empower your daily life.

Build a faith that will give peace. There is such a lack. People are unstable, dissatisfied with life. They have no peace. The apostle said:

"Be careful for nothing; but in every thing by prayer and supplication with thanksgiving let your requests be made known unto God.

"And the peace of God, which passeth all understanding, shall keep your hearts and minds through Christ Jesus."—Phil. 4:6,7.

Build a faith that will minimize the common troubles of life. The other day I visited a lady in one of our hospitals. She is up in her eighties and is quite ill. In fact, her little body has just about wasted away. She was troubled, not about people, not about herself primarily, but about THINGS—about her apartment, who would turn off the lights, lock the doors, and so on. After awhile I said to her, "Ma'am, these are minor things." She said, "I know, but I'm troubled about them. I'd like to know how things are going."

Now she wasn't troubled about souls being lost. This seemed

not to bother her. She wasn't too worried about missionaries around the world. She was troubled about THINGS—little things.

And she is not alone. People half her age have that worry. People a third of her age worry like that, too—consumed, eaten up about little things.

Build a faith that will give a radiant testimony. You can have this without owning a house, without having a job, without money. The poorest man in our city or nation or the world, can have that kind of faith that will give a radiant testimony.

You want more than just a Sunday faith. You can have faith or profess to have it by coming to the house of God on Sunday, but don't lose it on Monday and Tuesday and Wednesday and Thursday and Friday and Saturday. Have more than just Sunday faith.

You want more than a prosperity faith. It is very easy to express faith in God when all is going well—when your home is paid for or almost; when there is money in the bank, a car to drive, and a good job. That is what I call prosperity faith. But where is your faith when all of that is taken away?

You want more than a "strong body" faith. The Apostle Paul did not have a strong body. He had weaknesses. He was weak in appearance, the Word of God indicates. He had a thorn in the flesh—no one knows what it was. But this did not diminish his faith. It was strong. A mighty faith! Paul was not building on a strong body, but on a master faith.

A man can be strong today; but tomorrow, when sickness comes, it is a different day. A man can be in public affairs and have his picture on television, hear his voice on the radio, and be written up in the newspapers; but let a few years go by and he becomes just a shell of his former self—what then?

Where is your faith? Paul said, "Most gladly therefore will I rather glory in my infirmities, that the power of Christ may rest upon me" (II Cor. 12:9). Have a faith that is more than just a strong body faith.

A master faith is not built on size. It may be like a grain of mustard seed—the smallest of seeds—yet be mighty. With a faith like that, we can speak to a mountain and command, "Be removed," and it will be removed. Or to a tree, "Be thou plucked up by the root," and it will be done.

A master faith has certain characteristics:

It is ever growing. Master faith develops and moves on. It is more than just the ordinary day-by-day faith that some people have. That kind of faith keeps on growing, keeps on advancing.

It is always stabilizing. When faith rests on the promises of God and His holy Word, then this is going to stand. "Be ye stedfast," says the Scripture. It is saying, "Steady now. Don't jump too quickly. Have faith in Me. I'll bring you through."

It is not afraid of loneliness. If you have a master faith, you may live a life of destitution, forgotten by other people; but that faith will keep you strong.

It is not afraid of crowds. Crowds bother some people. They bother me. But a master faith looks beyond them to the Saviour.

It is not afraid of weakness, physical weakness that may strike your body.

It is always satisfying. A master faith satisfies the heart.

Is is for all people—young and old—who are Christians.

It is for all countries, all centuries, all time—the master faith that our Lord speaks about.

Think with me about these three simple things:

I. MASTER FAITH IS BUILT ON A BIBLICAL FAITH

"Faith cometh by hearing, and hearing by the word of God" (Rom. 10:17). Don't try to manufacture faith by your own resources or willpower. I've tried that, and it doesn't work. I've tried to bolster my faith by association with others, to build it up by listening to certain things, by reading certain books. It doesn't work. But when you build on this eternal Word, rest assured that your faith will stand every hour!

So build on His promises, and feed on His Word. And although your faith may seem small, it will grow exceedingly. Let me give you a verse to back that up. The Apostle Paul said, "We are bound to thank God always for you, brethren, as it is meet, because that your faith groweth exceedingly. . ." (II Thess. 1:3). Faith and the Word of God.

There are twenty-four references to the Old Testament portions of the Word of God in this one chapter, Hebrews 11.

For faith to grow, one must master his own life through the Word of God, and let the Word of God master his life as he feeds upon that Word.

What is our trouble? We are oppressed by the things around us: the world, the flesh and the Devil. Here is the clamor of the world. Here is the weakness of the flesh. Here are the insidious temptations of Satan. These things trouble us in building a biblical faith, a faith that will stand in every situation and circumstance.

Satan fought the Son of God, and he will fight you. He fought the Apostle Paul, and he will fight you. Satan will make you too busy to read the Bible. He will make you doubt the Word. He will make you question God's promises. You will wonder: *Is it real? I don't know if it is real or not. I just can't see it. I pray about it but nothing happens.* My dear friend, cast aside those doubts. They come from the Devil. Believe this Bible. This Holy Word fails not. What God says, He means! What God says, He will do! The Devil will try to turn you aside. Satan sometimes deceives even good people.

I read the other day about a highly educated pastor who has decided to have all his services on Friday night. His purpose is to free people for other things on Sunday.

Now wait a minute! That may sound all right to some people; but the Lord's day is the Lord's day, the day of worship, and no one can change that.

Rest upon the Word. Build a faith, a biblical faith, upon the Bible.

II. MASTER FAITH IS A SUBMISSIVE FAITH

Christ said, "Father. . .thy will be done." And we read, "The world passeth away, and the lust thereof: but he that doeth the will of God abideth for ever" (I John 2:17).

Here is a faith that stands, a submissive faith built upon the

Bible. You cannot have a master faith unless you recognize it: First, that God has a will for your life; second, that you have to give yourself to the doing of that will, which means submission. He has a will for you, a definite thing He wants you to do. You are just one out of billions of people; but God knows you, knows your name, has the hairs on your head all counted. Yes, He knows all about you. And He has a will for you. And in order to be happy, you must give yourself to the doing of His will. That is not as difficult as it may sound.

I've answered letters this week, as I do all the time—long letters from people worried about things, troubled over tomorrow. Almost every one of their troubles could be settled if these people would do one thing: Determine to know the will of God.

God wants us to know His will. He will reveal it to us if we will determine to do and obey it.

Now here is this submissive faith: His will for your life. The master faith, submission to God, not what man says but what God says. To listen to man will get you way off center. If you listen to man, you wouldn't turn in an offering of $1,500.00 as one dear man did this morning. Man doesn't reason, doesn't think that way. But God will direct many of you to do many unselfish things if you will follow Him, obey Him.

His will brings purpose. How beautiful the peace that comes from being in His will! When we do not submit and do His will, we have unrest and trouble. These become the customers of the psychiatrist, psychologist and counsellors. Why? Because of not submitting to the will of God and turning everything over to Him.

His will brings power. Those completely surrendered have the fullness of the Spirit of God. God fills any man who is empty of self and is willing to be filled and used.

Submission means walking by faith. Genesis 5:24 tells us, "Enoch walked with God." He walked with God in a sinful day. We, too, are to walk with Him in this sinful day. Submission means walking by faith! Let people laugh, criticize, make fun of you, but stand your ground. Stand for the Word of God, and walk by faith.

I hear stories all the time of Tennessee Temple students who work downtown in some shop or office. You are right in the midst of profanity, immorality and indecent dress; in the midst of bad stories and dirty jokes—all of it. Face it. You had better determine to be submissive to God. And if the whole world crashes around you, don't change. Walk by faith.

Submission means working by faith. We haven't the time to discuss Noah, but his work was by faith. God told him to build an ark on dry ground. This was a huge task, something that had never been done before. But Noah obeyed. He worked by faith. He trusted God. He believed.

Submission means worshiping by faith. God called Abraham out of Ur of the Chaldees. He built his altars by faith. He didn't know too much about it. He had never seen a church, never seen an assembly of people; but Abraham knew God, and worshiped God. God had called him and asked him to go a certain direction. He took the way and worshiped by faith.

Sometimes God may seem far off. Sometimes when you pray, you feel nothing at all. You don't know if God even hears. But keep on praying. God has given His Word, and God can't break His Word. If you pray in earnest, He will hear you as you come with your petitions; and though you feel that you have lost touch, you can say, "But God, I am submissive. And God, I worship you. So I will keep praying for help and grace."

It may be your work is hard. It may be your family is not helpful in spiritual matters. But go on by faith, not wavering.

We have covered two things briefly this morning. We have said that the master faith is a biblical faith; we have said the master faith is a submissive faith; now let me give a third thing:

III. MASTER FAITH IS A GOD-HONORING FAITH

A life of faith honors God. It awakens others to see and trust God. Go ahead and live the life of faith. Something will happen when you do. Someone will see you, notice you. Someone will see that you have something that others don't have—a master faith that honors God. Don't be afraid of what people may say or do. You just trust God.

Men of faith were those who awakened others. In Hebrews 11 we read about Enoch and others. Their lives awakened others. Abraham and Moses awakened the hearts of those around them. God wants out of us God-honoring faith.

Coming to this third point, I tried to think of the two people who had stirred me the most as a young preacher. I thought of George Mueller. The stories I read about him when first beginning my ministry astounded me. I could not imagine a man living by faith and simple prayer. I could not imagine a man feeding thousands of children in orphanages in England—and doing it all by faith! But it was done. Here was a faith that honored God and touched others. Your faith will touch others, too.

The second man to bless me as a young preacher was Charles Spurgeon. As I have become more acquainted with some things, I may differ with him now more than I did back in those days. Then all I could see was his doing a big job for God. I saw Spurgeon preaching to thousands Sunday morning, Sunday night and Wednesday night. I read about thirty-two chapels in London at one time—extension works. That is why I began organizing chapels (ten) in Fairfield, Alabama. One was at Number Five Mine, one at Number Ten Mine (coal mines around the city where little groups of people lived). After organizing chapels for these spots, I kept on going. I did the same thing in Chattanooga. In 1942 we started the Central Avenue chapel, and kept on going. Now there are forty-five around this tri-state area.

I am saying that a life of faith honors God. It awakens others. Wives, husbands, young people, live the life of faith.

I am always a bit amused at students here in our school. If something goes wrong, do you know what they do? They call Mama. I mean they call her right away. They can stump their toe out here in front of a building and call Mama this afternoon, collect! (They always call collect.) Then if it is bad enough, Mama calls me, wondering why I don't correct the sidewalk so her boy won't stumble!

You need to turn some things over to God. Honor God by living a life of faith.

A life of faith honors the indwelling Holy Spirit. The Holy Spirit lives within, so honor Him. If you are saved, He is there to guide you, to show you His will.

A life of faith honors Christ. Some people came back from visitation this week with distressed tones in their voices. Why? They went out visiting and found some who had said, "Yes, I'm saved. I don't go to church nor read my Bible nor do thus and so; but I'm saved." Now their salvation is between them and God; but if these they visited are saved, they are certainly not honoring Christ. God wants us to live so others can see Christ in us. We are to live such a stalwart life, such a true and pure life, that no one will wonder about us, but can say, "That man, that woman, that young person, is living for Christ and honoring Him by his life."

The life of faith honors the Saviour.

The world is still crying, "We would see Jesus." My friend, they have got to see Him in us.

This nation is in a mess. This world is in a mess. We are without spiritual leadership the world over, and especially in America. We have been dishonoring Christ so long.

Some of you sitting here this morning have no intention of being in God's house tonight. You are going to sit at home and watch TV or take a trip or go visit some friend or just rest. "I must get ready for work tomorrow," is your alibi. Shame on you! You are out of touch with God. You have not even prayed over this. You just made up your mind not to come on Sunday night. Shame on you!

I even hear some people say, "I'm afraid to go out at night because of so much meanness" or you say, "I am afraid I can't find a parking place near the church." Isn't that strange? God is still alive. He still has all power. He still will reward and bless those who honor Him. He will also take care of His own.

There are many other things the Christ-honoring life does: receives Christ as personal Saviour; obeys His command; reckons itself dead to self and alive unto God; has compassion for others, etc. I do not have time to discuss each one.

Yes, the master faith is a biblical faith, based on the Word; it is a submissive faith, based on your submission to Christ and His will; and it is a God-honoring faith.

Oh, seek to honor Him!

Born Out of Faith

The men who laid the foundations and reared the soaring arches of our great republic had a vigorous, indomitable, and all-encompassing belief in God. Faith permeated their thoughts, their words and deeds.

We see Thomas Jefferson's hand guiding the quill which wrote, *"I have sworn upon the altar of God eternal hostility against every form of tyranny over the mind of man."* We see George Washington, when the fires of hope had flickered to embers, kneeling in the snow at Valley Forge. And we see wise old Ben Franklin suggesting to a Constitutional Convention, deadlocked time after time, that *"we have prayers every morning."*

This nation was born out of faith in God. It can continue to exist in freedom only as that faith remains forthright and strong. A statesman of a past age said, *"Despotism may govern without faith, but liberty cannot."*

Faith in God remains the solid rock that stands unmoved amid the sliding sands. The antithesis of cynicism, it is the dynamo which sparks the minds and actions of men who think beyond the pettiness of self. It is the tie which binds mankind in mystic unity, exalting the human creature until, indeed, he is *"little lower than the angels."* And it is the balm which salves the sting of time and death.

Faith in God has meant to me the enjoyment of those manifold *"blessings of liberty"* which the Founding Fathers sought to secure for all posterity. It is a fathomless source from which to draw strength in times of adversity. And it has helped me to catch a glimpse of the wisdom implicit in those immutable laws by which He rules His universe.—J. Edgar Hoover.

41. *The Sign of the Christian Faith*

For the preaching of the cross is to them that perish foolishness; but unto us which are saved it is the power of God.

For the Jews require a sign, and the Greeks seek after wisdom:

But we preach Christ crucified, unto the Jews a stumblingblock, and unto the Greeks foolishness.
—I Corinthians 1:18,22,23.

For I determined not to know any thing among you, save Jesus Christ, and him crucified.
—I Corinthians 2:2.

But God forbid that I should glory, save in the cross of our Lord Jesus Christ, by whom the world is crucified unto me, and I unto the world.
—Galatians 6:14.

Charles Haddon Spurgeon once said, "The heart of the Gospel is redemption, and the essence of redemption is the substitutionary sacrifice of Christ. I have found by long experience that nothing touches the heart like the cross of Christ."

Listen to this Scripture again: "But God forbid that I should glory, save in the cross of our Lord Jesus Christ."
PAUL MIGHT HAVE GLORIED IN MANY THINGS.

In his own conversion, and his was a great conversion on the road to Damascus, the story we know so well. But that was not the thing to be gloried in.

The salvation which we have is available for all men, for all sinners everywhere. He knew that. Yes, Paul was happy in his salvation, but this was not the point of glory. "God forbid that I should glory, save in the cross of our Lord Jesus Christ."

In his calling to be an apostle to the Gentiles, a great honor given to him. Even that great position was overshadowed by the glory of the cross.

In his success as a preacher, a missionary, an evangelist; but not so. He gloried in the cross of the Lord Jesus.

The sign of our Christian faith is the cross.

It is by the cross that the love of God is seen. "For God so loved the world, that he gave his only begotten Son. . ." (John 3:16). "In this was manifested the love of God toward us, because that God sent his only begotten Son into the world, that we might live through him." How much God loved us to send His Son to die for us!

It is by the cross that the love of God is seen.

It is by the cross that the love of Christ is declared. He said, "I am the good shepherd: the good shepherd giveth his life for the sheep" (John 10:11).

It is by the cross that men are reconciled unto God. "For if, when we were enemies, we were reconciled to God by the death of his Son, much more, being reconciled, we shall be saved by his life" (Rom. 5:10).

It is by the death of Christ that men are brought unto God. When we receive the atoning death of Christ as payment for our sin and receive Christ the Saviour, we are made "as one." That is the story of the great message of the atonement—made "as one" with God.

It is by the cross that men are separated from the world. Look at the text: ". . .by whom the world is crucified unto me, and I unto the world." Paul said, "The world is dead to me and I am dead to the world." Too many people profess to know Christ and want Him as Saviour, but they also want the world. Paul was delivered from the world.

How much we need this today! Too many are still tied to the things of the world. You desire the things you see around you. You are not satisfied without these things.

The cross separates man from the world. The cross makes the world distasteful.

Listen to these verses very carefully:

"Therefore let no man glory in men. For all things are yours;

"Whether Paul, or Apollos, or Cephas, or the world, or life, or death, or things present, or things to come; all are yours;

"And ye are Christ's; and Christ is God's."—I Cor. 3:21-23.

He is saying that every need is supplied, that everything you have need of, God will give you.

It is by the cross that men are saved and made ready for the future.

The sinful world is doomed. Christ is coming. The tribulation day is coming, the settling of accounts. Christ is coming to reign upon the earth. But it is by the cross that men are saved and made ready for future days.

The cross—the sign of the Christian faith. I'm not opposed to having an empty cross on the steeple of the church, as long as we know what it means. I'm not opposed to wearing a cross around the neck or on a lapel, if we understand what it means.

The cross is a sign of our faith. The cross is the sign of the Lord Jesus Christ who came and died for us. And that's what Paul was saying here: "By the cross we see these things, and they are made real to us."

I want to give you three very simple thoughts.

I. THE CROSS MUST BE UNDERSTOOD

It should be understood as much as humanly possible.

Some people who wear the cross have not the slightest idea what it means. They do not see the death of the Son of God, do not see the blood shed at Calvary.

Some churches that have crosses on the steeple know nothing of its meaning. As a matter of fact, some are modernistic. They turn away from the Bible. They are liberal. They deny the blood atonement. They deny that people are saved by the blood of

Jesus Christ. They think one is saved by his works, saved by church membership, saved by baptism or saved some other way. The cross must be understood.

THE CROSS SPEAKS OF CHRIST'S. . .

Incarnation, of His virgin birth. It speaks of the miracle of His coming to this world in Bethlehem.

Perfect life. He was God walking in the flesh. He was tempted in all points like as we are, yet He sinned not.

Vicarious death. On the cross, He died for us: ". . .Christ died for our sins according to the scriptures" (I Cor. 15:3).

Victorious resurrection. He said He would arise, and did. It is all written in the cross. He met His disciples, talked with them, commissioned them, then ascended back to Glory.

These are things we have by the cross and the teaching of the cross of the Lord Jesus.

"Forasmuch as ye know that ye were not redeemed with corruptible things, as silver and gold, from your vain conversation received by tradition from your fathers;

"But with the precious blood of Christ, as of a lamb without blemish and without spot."—I Pet. 1:18,19.

II. THE CROSS MUST BE PREACHED

1. *Paul preached the cross.* He spoke of the life of the Son of God. His death, His resurrection. But primarily, he spoke of the cross and the shed blood. ". . .without shedding of blood is no remission," no salvation. He centered on the cross.

2. *Paul preached the cross to disturbed, wayward Christians.* These Corinthian Christians were troubled. They were babes in Christ, not growing in the things of God; and Paul knew that, so he tried to help them. He speaks to them of the cross: "For the preaching of the cross is to them that perish foolishness; but unto us which are saved it is the power of God" (I Cor. 1:18). He speaks of the cross: "I determined not to know any thing among you, save Jesus Christ, and him crucified" (I Cor. 2:2). He stuck with this great theme of the cross.

The Corinthians were divided, disturbed, disobedient, sinful, away from God; yet, Paul came back to say, "It is by the cross." He declared that salvation is in the cross, that they needed to be awakened from their lethargy and sinfulness and see that by the cross they could be drawn nearer to the Saviour. Paul preached the cross.

Paul preached to the Christians in Galatia. "But God forbid that I should glory, save in the cross. . . ." What was wrong in Galatia? They were divided. Some of the Galatian churches had turned aside to a doctrine of salvation of grace and works or grace and Law.

Paul declared very pointedly and very plainly that he was offended and troubled by the matter. 'You tried to have another Gospel, but there is no such thing as another Gospel: Which is not another; but there be some that trouble you, and would pervert the gospel of Christ (Gal. 1:7). You have turned away; you have gotten away from the cross and the Lord Jesus Christ.'

He was preaching to them the cross and the blood. Paul preached the cross.

3. *Paul preached the cross as our only hope.* "God forbid that I should glory, save in the cross of our Lord Jesus Christ." He said, "This is it. One door and only one. Just one way, just one way to be saved—by the cross of the Lord Jesus."

How simple, how beautiful is salvation! To be saved you simply look up to God, look up to the crucified Son of God, look up to the Christ who died upon the cross for you. He died in your place, died that you might be saved. He offers you salvation. How? By receiving Him. "But as many as received him, to them gave he power to become the sons of God, even to them that believe on his name" (John 1:12), by receiving Christ.

III. THE CROSS IS THE SIGN OF YOUR FAITH

Jesus died upon the cross. Don't minimize that. Don't get away from it. Don't overshadow by some other doctrine, by some other teaching Jesus' death on the cross: "Christ died for our sins according to the scriptures."

1. *Salvation comes through the Christ of the cross.* He died for you. There is no other way but through Jesus Christ the Son of God.

Now I can help a lot of you, including you mothers and fathers, so please listen.

Sometimes you are prone to talk to your children about so many things. What you say is good and true, but you fail to talk about the main thing—that Jesus died on the cross for sinners.

When your children come forward, sometimes I ask them, "What did Jesus do for you?" Some look as blank as if they never heard the word "Jesus." I'm not altogether blaming you; I am saying you missed the point somewhere, since your children do not understand the plan of salvation. I do not care if the child is frightened, disturbed by coming forward or by my speaking to them; when I ask him or her, "What did Jesus do for you?" the answer always should be: "He died for me."

We are back again to Hebrews 9:22, ". . .without shedding of blood is no remission." And I Corinthians 15:3, ". . .Christ died for our sins according to the scriptures." And back to John 3:16, "For God so loved the world, that he gave his only begotten Son . . . ."

Salvation is through the Christ of the cross. See that your children know and understand that Jesus died for them. Be sure they know and understand that they are saved, not by good works, not by church membership, not by being baptized: THEY ARE SAVED BY FAITH IN THE SON OF GOD. If they miss that, then they have no real salvation. Salvation is without stability unless one can say, "I'm resting on Christ and His atoning work on the cross." Why? Because the Bible declares, ". . .the soul that sinneth, it shall die" (Ezek. 18:4), and ". . .all have sinned, and come short of the glory of God" (Rom. 3:23).

I was lost, but Jesus died for the lost. He died in my place so that I would not have to die as a sinner. He took my place when He died on the cross. I received the death of the Son of God. I trusted Christ, so I am saved.

I can take you to libraries—including our own—and show you certain books by the score with our mark in the front which says we do not endorse the things written in this book. The books are there because we want you to read and find out things. You need to find out the teaching of others. I had to find out.

You begin reading. You find no mention of the cross. The author never mentions the shed blood. He will never mention the word "blood." He will not even mention the song, "At the Cross," because verse 1 says:

> **Alas, and did my Saviour bleed?**
> **And did my Sov'reign die?**
> **Would He devote that sacred head**
> **For such a worm as I?**

Your salvation comes through the Christ of the cross. Christ died for your sins. We must know Christ through our faith in Him who died for us.

2. *The cross must be the symbol and sign of your faith.* I'm going beyond a little bit. Here is what Paul said: "But God forbid that I should glory, save in the cross of our Lord Jesus Christ, by whom the world is crucified unto me, and I unto the world" (Gal. 6:14).

Get what he said. He talked about his salvation, but talked about his life, too. "I am crucified and I died. I'm dead to the things of the world."

Listen to Galatians 2:20:

"I am crucified with Christ: nevertheless I live; yet not I, but Christ liveth in me: and the life which I now live in the flesh I live by the faith of the Son of God, who loved me, and gave himself for me."

"I am crucified with Christ" is the thing he wants you to see.

Come back to it once more, not only for your salvation, but for your success in Christian living: There must be a dying to flesh. Paul is saying, "I am crucified with Christ: nevertheless I live. I'm here, walking on the earth, witnessing, doing soul winning. I'm dead, but Christ lives within me. He guides me. And the life which I now live in the flesh, I live by the faith of the Son of God, who loved me, and gave himself for me." The cross must be the symbol, the sign, of your faith.

I read a beautiful story this week of a man in a small western city. This man lived on the back side of the street, near the railroad tracks. No one knew much about him, except that he seemed to be a quiet, loving man, a faithful Christian.

This man walked around the city and talked to people. His journey would take a long time because people would stop him to ask questions and ask for his help. Yet he had never been a citizen of any renown. He had not been a public officer nor held any big position in the city. But things happened when he was present. When he prayed in his church, some shed tears.

He was a loving, sweet Christian. Poor in financial matters, without any great educational background, but a man always on the job, living for God and letting Christ work through him.

They say that when this gentleman died, all work in the city stopped. The stores closed for a day. The people stood around talking about what he had meant to them and what he had said to them.

The undertaker in a nearby town came to say, "I want to take care of all the funeral expenses, if you will allow me. This man led me to Christ. I would not be saved today had he not stopped again and again to tell me my need of the Saviour."

A wealthy man sent a car to the widow, saying, "It's almost new, but I want you to have it. Your husband pointed me to the Saviour." On and on it went.

When the funeral was held, the man taking care of the bridge which divided one portion of that city from another said that more cars crossed that bridge in one single day than had ever gone over in any twenty-four hour period in history. These were people attending the funeral of a humble man, one who so lived for God, so manifested Christ, that he was known everywhere.

That is what Christ wants out of us. After our salvation, He wants us to reckon self dead. There is that cross again! "I am crucified with Christ. . ."; "God forbid that I should glory, save in the cross of our Lord Jesus Christ, by whom the world is crucified unto me, and I unto the world."

I am reckoned as dead, dead to this world that I might be alive unto God through Christ.

Let Christ be seen in you. Determine to show forth the Son of God. Let people know you are a child of God, born again by the power of God, redeemed by His precious blood.

The cross is the center. I am saved by my faith in the Son of God who died upon the cross for me. As a Christian I reckon self to be dead. "I die daily," as Paul said he did, that I might be alive unto God through Jesus Christ my Lord. That is what Paul is saying to us: "But God forbid that I should glory, save in the cross of our Lord Jesus Christ, by whom the world is crucified unto me, and I unto the world."

The world is out! I am on the side of Christ. I want to walk with him. I want Christ to be seen in me.

You may recall the story of Mr. Dannecker, the German sculptor who spent eight years making a marble statue of Christ. (I am not saying this should have been done; I just give the story.)

After spending the first two years on the statue, he found a little girl and asked her to come and look at his statue. She stood before it. When he asked, "Who is that?" she answered, "That is a great man." Disappointed, Mr. Dannecker led the child out of the room. He knew he had failed completely. She didn't see what he wanted her to see.

He went back to his work, laboring six more years. After finishing the work he felt he wanted to present to the world, he again went out and found a little girl about the same age as the one he had in before, brought her into his room and up before the statue, and asked, "Who is that?" She looked in silence, then with eyes filled with tears, whispered, "Suffer little children to come unto me. That's Jesus! That's Jesus!" He knew this time he had succeeded.

So be it with you. When people look at you, at me, there should be something about us that reminds them of Jesus. Paul said, "Christ liveth in me. I am crucified with Christ." There should be something about us that would make people think of Christ.

Sometimes when I get to a side road, I stop my car and think of myself. You know, I have a hard time finding anything that looks very Christlike. I feel like I fail so much, so often.

Maybe you feel the same way tonight. Maybe you are saying, "I want folks to see Christ in me. I want to so live that I exemplify to the world some of the traits of our Lord Jesus. I want others to see Christ in my life." Let Christ be seen.

What does God want you to do when you face a message like this? Is it to rededicate your life? You're a Christian. You know you are saved. You have no doubt about that. You believe in the crucified Son of God. But your life is not showing forth Christ. Then come forward tonight. Come on.

Maybe you would like to join the church by letter. Come on. Don't hold back a single second. Just walk out and say, "I want Christ to be seen in me. I'd like to join this church."

Maybe you want to receive Him as Saviour. Maybe you've never been saved. You are lost, condemned, Hell-bound. Your soul is in the hands of the Devil; without Jesus Christ there is no relief, no release.

Tonight will you take Christ as your Saviour, the crucified Son of God who died for you and rose again and ascended back to Glory? Do you want Christ? Then receive Him tonight.

A little girl in Sunday school was asked, "What is faith?" and she said, "Believing what God says without asking any questions."

42. The Personal Faith of Paul

Moreover, brethren, I declare unto you the gospel which I preached unto you, which also ye have received and wherein ye stand;

By which also ye are saved, if ye keep in memory what I preached unto you, unless ye have believed in vain.

For I delivered unto you first of all that which I also received, how that Christ died for our sins according to the scriptures.

—I Corinthians 15:1-3.

But now is Christ risen from the dead, and become the firstfruits of them that slept.

For since by man came death, by man came also the resurrection of the dead.

For as in Adam all die, even so in Christ shall all be made alive.

But every man in his own order: Christ the firstfruits; afterward they that are Christ's at his coming.

Then cometh the end, when he shall have delivered up the kingdom to God, even the Father; when he shall have put down all rule, and all authority and power.

—I Corinthians 15:20-24.

I want you to think about the personal faith of the Apostle Paul. In your Bible put a little mark under the letter "I" wherever you see it in I Corinthians 15, in the first ten verses: "I declare unto you"; "I preached" (vs. 2).

"I delivered"; "I also received" (vs. 3).

"I am the least"; "I persecuted" (vs. 9).

"I am what I am"; "I labored"; "Yet not I" (vs. 10).

You will find "I" all through the chapter—in verses 31, 32, 34, on down to the finish. Paul, Holy Spirit inspired, was expressing his personal faith in this magnificent letter to the church. He repeatedly used his own testimony. He spoke of what Christ had done for him, what Christ meant to him.

Notice: the Holy Spirit was writing a Book, a Book to be read by all people, in all countries, of all cultures; hence, you do not find some things in it you might expect. Politics are not dwelt upon. Tragedies and sorrows of the world in general are not emphasized. But the Holy Spirit is directing Paul to give a message to all people, of all times, in all places.

In I Corinthians 15, Paul talked of his experience with the Lord. He described it in many different ways, always bringing himself back into it.

We see this same thing concerning the rich fool in Luke 12:17-19, who said:

"What shall I do, because I have no room where to bestow my fruits?

"And he said, This will I do: I will pull down my barns, and build greater; and there will I bestow all my fruits and my goods.

"And I will say to my soul, Soul, thou hast much goods laid up for many years; take thine ease, eat, drink, and be merry."

This rich fool was talking out of selfishness and out of a godless life. He is a type of the evil where people talk of themselves, what they accomplish, what they do. But notice what God said to him: "Thou fool, this night thy soul shall be required of thee: then whose shall those things be, which thou hast provided?"

So Paul is saying to the world here in I Corinthians 15, "I believe in the Gospel," and he mentions the Gospel, and how Christ died for our sins. Paul is saying here:

"I believe in the death of the Son of God."

"I believe in the resurrection of the Lord Jesus Christ."

"I believe in the call of God."

"I believe in the destruction of death."

"I believe in the second coming of Christ."

"I believe in the resurrection of the saved."

"I believe in the Word of God."

Paul is advertising his faith and what he believed.

People stick up signs to show what they believe. You see them on bumper stickers, which advertise their choice of candidates for office, etc. A dignified, white-haired lady had this sticker on her bumper: PASS CAREFULLY—THE DRIVER CHEWS TOBACCO! We see signs everywhere.

Well, Paul was giving a demonstration, advertising something, broadcasting to the whole world his personal faith.

I. PAUL'S FAITH WAS IN THE CRUCIFIED, BURIED AND RISEN SAVIOUR

Here is the first great fundamental of the Faith: "Christ died for our sins according to the scriptures."

1. *Here is the message that we believe.* Thousands may claim salvation through church membership, through good works, through certain ordinances; but there is but one way to be saved and that is by faith in the Lord Jesus Christ. "Christ died for our sins according to the scriptures."

2. *Here is the message to be delivered.* Paul said, "For I delivered unto you first of all that which I also received, how that Christ died for our sins. . . ."

Paul, an educated Rabbi, was a vigorous opponent of everything Christ had ever said; yet this educated Jewish Rabbi had to receive and had to deliver this same message to the church in Corinth with its many problems, "Christ died for our sins."

This is the message that we are to deliver to people everywhere, in every place. Every nation must hear it. The Japanese, the Chinese, those in Korea, in Africa—every soul in the whole world must hear the same message: "Christ died for our sins."

My wife and I were driving along the road in Atlanta and saw on one side a number of trailers. Apparently they had been there for some time, since they looked as if they had the work of the weather upon them. On the other side of the road were houses valued from $100,000.00 to $175,000.00 each—beautiful homes right across the road from the weather-worn trailers.

The same Gospel for one side is the same for both sides. To the rich and the poor it is the same message: "Christ died for our sins."

3. *This is the message to be protected, preserved and preached.* It must be clearly given. It must not be hidden by form and ritualism, nor be concealed in denominational pride; but it must be declared with all clarity. No addition, no subtraction.

The message of the death, burial and resurrection is what I believe! That is what most of you believe, and that is what one must believe in order to be saved. Paul said, "For I delivered unto you. . .that which also I have received, that Christ died for our sins. . . ."

II. PAUL'S FAITH WAS IN THE COMING OF THE LORD JESUS

"Behold, I shew you a mystery; We shall not all sleep, but we shall all be changed,

"In a moment, in the twinkling of an eye, at the last trump: for the trumpet shall sound, and the dead shall be raised incorruptible, and we shall be changed."—I Cor. 15:51,52.

That is the same thought given by the apostle under the inspiration of the Spirit of God in I Thessalonians 4:16,17:

"For the Lord himself shall descend from heaven with a shout, with the voice of the archangel, and with the trump of God: and the dead in Christ shall rise first:

"Then we which are alive and remain shall be caught up together with them in the clouds, to meet the Lord in the air: and so shall we ever be with the Lord."

Paul's faith was fixed in the death, burial and resurrection; and Paul was convinced of the coming of our blessed Lord.

NOW, WHAT DO WE HAVE?

A living Saviour, One who intercedes for us: "If ye shall ask any thing in my name, I will do it" (John 14:14).

He is the guarding and keeping Saviour: "And I give unto them eternal life; and they shall never perish, neither shall any man pluck them out of my hand" (John 10:28).

He is preparing a place for us: "I go to prepare a place for you. And if I go and prepare a place for you, I will come again, and receive you unto myself; that where I am, there ye may be also" (John 14:2,3).

A coming Saviour. His promise has been given: "I will come again." Paul believed that and was looking for His coming.

God revealed to Paul some details regarding the Second Coming which are not given in the Gospels. One certain thing Paul brings out by inspiration is: "The dead in Christ shall rise first."

There are three resurrections to keep in mind.

The resurrection of Christ: "But now is Christ risen from the dead, and become the firstfruits of them that slept" (I Cor. 15:20).

The resurrection of the sleeping saints: "But every man in his own order: Christ the firstfruits; afterward they that are Christ's at his coming" (vs. 23). The sleeping saints are those who are "Christ's at his coming," those who are saved. This takes place when Christ comes again. When Christ comes, the graves of the saved shall be opened and the bodies of the saints shall ascend to meet the Lord in the air. The promise of God is the resurrection of the sleeping saints.

The resurrection of the lost: "Then cometh the end. . . ." (vs. 24). At the end of the millennium comes the resurrection of the unsaved. The lost will stand before the Great White Throne and be condemned to an eternal Hell. That is a fearful, awful time. But we who are saved are looking for the return of our Saviour.

The personal faith of Paul was in the second coming of Jesus Christ. He looked at this as an event to rejoice his heart:

"For this corruptible must put on incorruption, and this mortal must put on immortality.

"So when this corruptible shall have put on incorruption, and this mortal shall have put on immortality, then shall be brought to pass the saying that is written, Death is swallowed up in victory.

"O death, where is thy sting? O grave, where is thy victory?

"The sting of death is sin; and the strength of sin is the law.

"But thanks be to God, which giveth us the victory through our Lord Jesus Christ."—I Cor. 15:53-57.

Here is the faith of a man in the death, burial and resurrection, in the second coming of Jesus Christ. His faith meant a happy future—not something desperate, not dark and dingy, not something to be avoided, but something to be welcomed. Paul was ready. When his head was severed from his body, he went immediately into the presence of God.

One day Jesus is coming, and the dead in Christ will be raised and the living changed, and we will be caught up in the air to meet our blessed Lord. That is the message to shout to the nation! That is the only happy thing that we have today.

Read your newpapers. Read of the plane crashes; read of the death of people in other countries where various sects and groups are still battling and warring. We see it most in Moslem countries, in pagan lands.

Shout the message: the message of redemption and the message that means a happy future for all who put their faith and trust in Jesus Christ.

My friend, that is the best thing we have. No matter what kind of life you live, you will have heartaches, sorrows, pains, trouble, distress, disturbances and dissension.

Live the best life that you can, make all the money you can make, build your most beautiful home—still you can have cancer, T.B., a heart attack, a brain disease, and on and on we could name them. The only way for a happy future is in Jesus Christ.

While visiting in the hospital the other day, I saw so many people with various sicknesses. There was Mrs. W. I. Powell. Every old-timer here recalls Mrs. Powell. You knew and loved Mr. Powell, a Bible teacher in our Sunday school, who is now with the Lord. Mrs. Powell is barely living. Her body is wasting away. If you look at her you think, *That's terrible. That is awful.* But she is a child of God, and one day she will have a body like that of our Lord.

There is Mrs. Ernest Holt, who was here when I came in 1942. She is a very sick lady. But she is a child of God, waiting and ready. When Jesus comes, the dead in Christ shall be raised; the living shall be changed and made like Him.

Mrs. Thelma Totten is in the hospital. When I came to Chattanooga in 1942 and began my ministry here, I started visiting the home of the Tottens. Thelma Totten was sick in 1942 and 1943; she is sick today. I don't suppose she weighs 75 pounds. She has had operations on her head. She had one this week. This little thing is lying there. She has suffered for all these thirty-seven years. When I prayed today by her bedside, I said, "O dear God, encourage her heart. Let her know that this is not the end, just the beginning, that the future is marvelous. One day she will have a body like Yours—eternal and painless."

When I finished praying, she was wiping away some tears and smiling. "That's wonderful! I had just about forgotten that," she said.

Oh, the future that we have in Jesus Christ! In Him we are eternal. We will be like Him, with bodies that do not die, do not suffer the pains of this world.

I preached recently in Atlanta. At the conclusion of the service, a young fellow came up to me in his wheelchair. He said, "I want you to pray for me. I have been called to preach, and I have been preaching. I can't be a pastor, but I can be an evangelist in this chair." He had two tiny stubs for legs. The man has never taken one step, this man in his thirties. But he knows Jesus as Saviour. He knows Heaven is his home. Now he wants to tell others how to be saved! One day he will have a new body, a body like that of our Lord. Jesus promised this. There is a happy future for him and for everyone else who is saved. Whatever the suffering, whatever the affliction, you have a happy future— being with and seeing Him forevermore.

III. PAUL'S FAITH WAS IN THE CONQUEST
OF THE CHRISTIAN

"But thanks be to God, which giveth us the victory through our Lord Jesus Christ."—I Cor. 15:57.

In the dark, lonely, suffering hours in Paul's life; in the jail in Rome, shut away from all the alluring lanes of travel, closed in by dark, dingy and damp walls, surely he looked with real faith to the victorious future. He had faith that the Christian will win. "Thanks be to God, which giveth us the victory through our Lord Jesus Christ."

Paul was talking about being victorious. He saw the defeat of death; he saw the conquest of the child of God, but Paul declared victory. He knew he was on the winning side and could not lose.

We gain all of Heaven. We gain life everlasting. In Him we have victory. Paul knew that.

1. *Victory is achieved by faith.* Oh, if only there were some way that I could help you build your faith in the Lord Jesus! But I can only say this: ". . .faith cometh by hearing, and hearing by the word of God." Your faith will be built by reading the Bible and absorbing its message. Victory is achieved through faith in Him.

2. *Victory is achieved through reckoning self to be dead.* Paul said, "I die daily. I reckon self to be dead." Your victory will be achieved when you die to self, die to your own ambitions.

Many have written asking me what I meant by that. "You are taking away what we thought was so valuable." To them I say, "Your ambitions are sinful, selfish, wicked and worldly. You want gain for self."

If we are reckoning self to be dead, then all we have and are will be His. Victory is achieved through reckoning self to be dead.

3. *Victory is achieved through surrender and the fullness of the Spirit* and saying, "Lord, fill me, empower me, use me, make me what you want me to be." That is the victory we have. Paul was looking to the future and saying, "Victory is what I have in Him."

This is the conclusion of it all: "Therefore, my beloved

brethren, be ye stedfast, unmoveable, always abounding in the work of the Lord, forasmuch as ye know that your labour is not in vain in the Lord" (I Cor. 15:58).

Everything said in chapter 15, every glorious word given by the apostle, was given under direction of the Spirit. He says, "Don't worry, my beloved brethren of Corinth, you of Chattanooga, you in Highland Park Baptist Church, you people in Louisville, Kentucky, you in Atlanta, and in other places; be steadfast, be unmoveable. Don't be shaken, but always abound in the work of the Lord, forasmuch as ye know that your labor is not in vain in the Lord. Not driven into it, not forced into it, but abounding. Your labor is not in vain in the Lord."

Any time we serve God, it is not in vain. Some work we do seems to be so futile, so useless. But Paul reminds us that the Word of God will abide forever and ever.

I have a friend who works many hours at the job. He starts at seven in the morning, works until three in the afternoon. At three he leaves one business and goes to his next job. There he works from three until eleven. Everyday, eight hours in one place, eight hours in the other.

Here is a man working sixteen hours everyday at two jobs, and the most he can ever say is, "I have a paycheck."

In Jesus Christ, our work abides, and will forever and ever as we labor for the Saviour, as we pray, work, witness and try to win souls.

May God keep us busy doing what He says.

43. *How to Have an All-Weather Faith*

But after long abstinence Paul stood forth in the midst of them, and said, Sirs, ye should have hearkened unto me, and not have loosed from Crete, and to have gained this harm and loss.

And now I exhort you to be of good cheer: for there shall be no loss of any man's life among you, but of the ship.

For there stood by me this night the angel of God, whose I am, and whom I serve,

Saying, Fear not, Paul; thou must be brought before Caesar: and, lo, God hath given thee all them that sail with thee.

Wherefore, sirs, be of good cheer: for I believe God, that it shall be even as it was told me.

—Acts 27:21-25.

The Apostle Paul had an all-weather faith. In the midst of danger, and facing difficulty, he believed God. In the midst of a storm which threatened complete destruction of everything, including people, he believed God.

Our faith is nothing, my friends, if it cannot stand in the day of trial.

So I speak tonight on having faith in all types of weather, in all types of situations.

HAVE FAITH IN GOD:

When death takes loved ones. I watch many of you in the hours of sorrow. Praise God for the strength and courage some of our people have when loved ones are taken!

When friends turn away. We will lose friends. There are times when some feel they can no longer walk with us. It is at these times we must watch to keep strong.

When we have financial problems. Whether it be for you as an individual or for your whole family, this is a time to stand true.

When failure dogs your steps. It seems that some are always in the failing column. We all have our failures. It is in these times, we must stand true and have faith in God.

In lonely hours. And we all have them. When thinking on this point I thought of this Scripture. In Revelation 1, John was alone on the Isle of Patmos. The Lord appeared and stood by his side. "And when I saw him, I fell at his feet as dead." (vs. 17). He saw Christ in that lonely hour.

In suffering. Paul knew full well what it was to suffer. So do some of you. I talk to many in hospitals. I hear about the loneliness of a hospital room, the hours of suffering.

Monday night I saw a young man sitting in front of me as I preached. It seems he will never walk another step. He was in a wheelchair but smiling and singing and joining joyfully in the service. You have seen such people, some in even worse condition. What it means for them to have faith in God!

An all-weather faith means that no matter what may come, we will believe God, have faith in God, stand true to Him.

When I was a pastor in Birmingham, I bought a big, beautiful gospel tent from the National Tent Company. It cost only $200.00 in those days. I hired a company to erect it at the Pleasant Ridge Church in Hueytown, Alabama. The guarantee which I had in my pocket said the tent was both fireproof and waterproof and one of the best ever made. It had steel beams in the center for the main poles—lovely in every way.

It was paid for. I was now ready for my first revival in the tent. I was indeed happy!

It was put up in the afternoon. Before six o'clock that same day a severe storm had torn it to pieces! It bent one of the center steel poles. It tore big gaping holes in it. The guarantee in my pocket told how good, how wonderful it was.

Sometimes the best comes to ruin. Yes, sometimes things fail. But let it not be your faith. Don't have fair-weather faith when bad weather comes.

Some faith is like a good friend. When he backs you up, you feel as if you "have it made."

Some faith is a financial faith. You feel good when you have some support, some income. When all is cut off, your faith goes out the window.

Some faith is the assured record faith. In other words, you are basing it on some assured record that all is well and nothing can go wrong while you are doing God's will.

I used to ride the Incline up Lookout Mountain. I was never afraid because that thing started running about 1895; and it has been running ever since, with no wrecks. Nobody has ever gotten killed on it. But it could fail. Man fails. Machinery fails. But God never fails.

We need a faith both for good and bad weather.

How can we have an all-weather faith?

I. BY RESTING ON HIS UNCHANGING WORD

Listen to this: "The grass withereth, and the flower thereof falleth away; But the word of the Lord endureth for ever" (I Pet. 1:24,25). Not one of the promises in this eternal Book has ever failed.

It is by faith that we live victoriously, that we achieve results, that we maintain peace of heart, that we do the impossible. ". . .all things are possible to him that believeth" (Mark 9:23). By faith we please Him.

He said, "But my God shall supply all your need according to his riches in glory by Christ Jesus" (Phil. 4:19). There is another great promise in that little book of Philippians: "Be careful for nothing; but in every thing by prayer and supplication with thanksgiving let your requests be made known unto God. And the peace of God, which passeth all understanding, shall keep your hearts and minds through Christ Jesus."

All the 32,000 promises in the Bible are for us, for our comfort and peace.

Faith comes from the Bible. God's Word will not, cannot fail.

II. FROM EXPERIENCE

Has God ever failed you? No. Then risk Him. Have you ever put your trust in Him and had Him fail you? No. Then keep on believing, keep on trusting.

He did not fail Abraham. He did not fail Moses. He did not fail Joshua. He did not fail Elijah. Nor has He failed anyone else, including you and me.

Your all-weather faith will come through experience. As you trust God and move forward, you will see Him blessing, blessing, blessing you.

The future looks fearful until we recall that we endure by faith, are strengthened by faith—not by anything in this world, but by faith.

Let us go back to the text again and hear Paul say: "I believe God. I'm trusting God. I have put my faith in God." Paul looked back, and Paul could not think of one time when God had ever failed him.

For example, he was stoned at Lystra and left for dead. But he got up, walked back to the city and went on with his mission (Acts 14).

He was beaten and jailed in Philippi (Acts 16).

He was bound with chains in Jerusalem (Acts 21).

But through every trial God was there comforting him. Not one time did God fail him. Paul put Him to a test and found God did not fail him.

I thought again of what he said in II Corinthians 11:24-28. Let's read it:

"Of the Jews five times received I forty stripes save one.

"Thrice was I beaten with rods, once was I stoned, thrice I suffered shipwreck, a night and a day I have been in the deep;

"In journeyings often, in perils of waters. . .of robbers. . .by mine own countrymen. . .by the heathen. . .in the city. . .in the wilderness. . .in the sea. . .among false brethren;

"In weariness and painfulness, in watchings often, in hunger and thirst, in fastings often, in cold and nakedness.

"Beside those things that are without, that which cometh upon me daily, the care of all the churches."

Come to chapter 12 in the same book and there is the message of Paul's thorn in the flesh. He told about that, then said, "But God did not fail. I prayed three times. He didn't answer, but His grace was sufficient for me. My strength was made perfect in weakness." Paul is saying, "I've tried Him. I've proved Him. And I can assure you that God cannot fail!"

Do the same thing Paul did. Look back over your life—whether it is a long or short one—and see if God has ever failed you.

I've prayed and God has answered. His answer may have been different from the thing I asked for, but I did receive an answer from Him—the right answer for me. He has been with me in every sorrow, in every sickness, in every tragedy. And I can assure you, He did not fail me; nor will He fail you.

Let your faith rest upon your experience of knowing we serve a God who will not, cannot fail of all His promises.

Have faith in God! I will trust Him down to the last day. I will do all I can until He says, "Lee, this is all I want of you. You can stop now." But until He says stop, I'll keep on plugging, keep on believing.

As I look back on the experience of all these fifty-four years, I can truthfully say that the Lord has never failed in one of His promises. I've failed, but Him? Never!

III. BY RELATIONSHIP

It comes from the Word of God, by experience, and by relationship. I would have put this first, but I wanted to emphasize it last.

By your faith in Christ, you become a member of God's family. When you are in His family, you have His promise that He will hear and answer you and give what you have need of since you are His child.

The all-weather faith is that which stands, no matter what the weather, how you may feel, where you may go, what may happen to you physically. This all-weather faith will stand in rain or shine, hot or cold, in America or in Africa.

It is not for sinners—only for Christians. God has it for you and for me. This is ours!

By simple faith we become children of God. Think of your salvation experience: how simple it was. How plain, how simple it was for me. I listened to a Sunday school teacher, accepted what she said from the Bible, and took Jesus as my Saviour. I stood up in church and testified that I was saved. Never have I doubted since that day.

By simple faith we become children of God. "For by grace are ye saved through faith; and that not of yourselves: it is the gift of God: Not of works, lest any many should boast" (Eph. 2:8,9).

By simple faith we claim His promises. He said, ". . .my peace I give unto you." Take it. He said, ". . .lo, I am with you alway, even unto the end of the world." Believe it. He said, "But ye shall receive power. . . ." Take it. He said, "I will never leave thee, nor forsake thee." Rely on His protection. We are told, "My God shall supply all your need." Believe it. Peace, presence, power, protection, provision—all ours by faith in God, by our relationship as a child of God.

By simple faith we pray and keep on praying. Just as a child talks to a parent, just so we can talk to our Heavenly Father. Parents fail, but God never fails.

By simple faith we overcome obstacles. You say, "What can I do, Brother Roberson? I've some serious things facing me. How can I handle them?" You can give up and quit, or you can let God show you the way out. He knows the way you should go, so pray and wait for His direction (Isa. 30:21).

By simple faith we face death. For some it may seem near; for others it may seem distant.

Use all the beautiful words you wish; still death is death. When in the dark of night you face death, all have some solemn thoughts. When we stand by the side of a casket and view the body, we will have some thoughts.

I've quoted at funerals over and over again, **"Death is the**

knock that opens the door to life." I talk about release from the pain and going out to be with God. All is beautiful and true, but faith in Jesus is the release from the fears of death.

Remind yourself of this relationship; think of it, what you are. To be a child of God is an amazing, beautiful thing! Rejoice in that fact! Rest on that relationship. This is a troubled world, a nervous world, an upset world. The goings on affect most all of us. But peace can be ours when we rest on what He said.

My family can be changed. Your family can be changed. But my relationship to God will not change. He is my Father; He will stay my Father. When I received Jesus as my Saviour, I entered the family of God and will be in that family forever. He will have to correct me, chasten me when I am disobedient; but I am still in the family of God.

Rediscover the freshness of that relationship. Every day refresh your mind about what, who you are. As you pick up your Bible for your morning reading, and as you close the day with it, think: *I'm a child of God! I'm a Christian! I'm saved! I'm going to Heaven when I die!*

Faith in God brings peace of heart, growth in grace, daily happiness, and success in our work.

I don't like to mention names, but I use things I feel might speak to hearts.

This is an uncertain world, a world of sorrow, tragedy and tears. You kids have it just like others. More young people come weeping to me than older people. They tell of things that happen back at home. They tell certain things that have taken place. They tell me they have to go to the hospital. They tell me of things that go wrong. I begin wondering. It's sad.

I want you to see that God wants to help you.

In the newspaper the other day, there was a headline, "Woman Dies in Wreck a Week After Husband."

It said she was coming down Highway 153. She veered across the northbound lane and struck the guard rail head on. Thomas, the policeman, said there were no skidmarks showing that the woman had ever applied the brakes. Apparently she drove right across the main highway, straight into the guard rail.

Her husband had been killed just a week before in a car wreck; now, she, too, had been killed while driving on Highway 153.

That caught my attention when the newspaper said there were no marks, no signs of her applying the brakes.

It looked as if the dear one was so heartbroken, so lonely, so despondent that she thought she could not go on; so she went down the highway, turned the car across the road, struck the rail on the other side, and died. Maybe it was just an accident—who will ever know? Perhaps she was a Christian but away from Him and discouraged.

I'm saying tonight, Come back! God still loves you. He is waiting for your return. "But God, who is rich in mercy, for his great love wherewith he loved us" (Eph. 2:4).

Whatever your sorrow, your tragedy, your heartache, whatever emptiness you may have—look up to God! Have faith in God! Believe God! Get your head up! Keep on going!

"To learn strong faith is to endure great trials. I have learned my faith by standing firm amid severe testings."—George Mueller.

44. Are We Meeting the Need of Our City?

How doth the city sit solitary, that was full of people! how is she become a widow! she that was great among the nations, and princess among the provinces, how is she become tributary!

She weepeth sore in the night, and her tears are on her cheeks: among all her lovers she hath none to comfort her: all her friends have dealt treacherously with her, they are become her enemies.

Judah is gone into captivity because of affliction, and because of great servitude: she dwelleth among the heathen, she findeth no rest: all her persecutors overtook her between the straits.

The ways of Zion do mourn, because none come to the solemn feasts: all her gates are desolate: her priests sigh, her virgins are afflicted, and she is in bitterness.

Her adversaries are the chief, her enemies prosper; for the Lord hath afflicted her for the multitude of her transgressions: her children are gone into captivity before the enemy.

—Lamentations 1:1-5.

The book of Lamentations is a book of sorrow and tears. The people of Judah had turned away from God, so He, in love, sent chastening upon them.

The story is given here in Lamentations 1:5: ". . .for the Lord hath afflicted her for the multitude of her transgressions [her sins]."

Judah had gone into captivity, and Jerusalem was an empty city. The people sinned, and God sent trials upon them.

"The Lord is righteous; for I have rebelled against his commandment. . ."—Lam. 1:18.

The prophet knew why God was chastening them, so he said this:

"Thou, O Lord, remainest for ever; thy throne from generation to generation.

"Wherefore dost thou forget us for ever, and forsake us so long time?

"Turn thou us unto thee, O Lord, and we shall be turned; renew our days as of old.

"But thou hast utterly rejected us; thou art very wroth against us."—Lam. 5:19-22.

The city and country around that city were in desolation. The people had failed God. Now His chastening hand lay heavy upon them.

Moses gave repeated warnings to the people of Israel regarding sin and its results. Deuteronomy is full of such warnings and exhortations.

Moses knew his people, knew their danger in turning from God, forgetting God; so in Deuteronomy 6:12 He warned them: ". . .beware lest thou forget the Lord, which brought thee forth out of the land of Egypt"—the land of bondage.

Our church is in the population center of greater Chattanooga and is the largest church in the city and in the state. God is holding us accountable for a ministry of salvation and of helping others. Let us not fail Him.

Are we meeting the city's need? We know that sin is rampant. We know that truth is trampled on by many. We know our city is in great need. "But all cities are in need," you say. But we live here. This is our Jerusalem.

I. TO MEET THE NEED, WE MUST
HAVE MEN OF GOD

The Bible tells us man must be born by the Spirit: "Except a man be born. . .of the Spirit, he cannot enter into the kingdom of God." He sees himself lost and condemned and, under conviction, turns to the Lord and is saved by faith in the Saviour. The whole message is summed up in the words of Paul: "Christ died for our sins according to the scriptures." We need saved men, born-again men.

We need men who are sold out to God, separated from the world, men who hate sin and love righteousness.

We need brave men, those not afraid to stand for Christ, those who turn away from the favor of men to serve God, live for Him, do His will.

The greatest compliment anyone can pay either layman or preacher—anybody—is: "There goes a man of God." Our great need is to have men of God in leadership.

II. TO MEET THE NEED, WE MUST HAVE
AGGRESSIVE, WIDE-AWAKE CHURCHES

not just big churches, but aggressive, wide-awake churches; not just rich churches, but churches that seek God's favor.

1. *We need churches that set standards.* Neither did Israel nor Judah abide by God's standards, so they lost everything; now Jerusalem is empty after the captivity.

God set up standards; we are to abide by those standards. Churches also should have standards. These are our four standards here:

(1) Our workers must know Jesus as Saviour.

(2) They must not engage in worldly things.

(3) Each must be faithful to the services of the church—Sunday morning and night, and Wednesday night.

(4) Each must be loyal to the church, the pastors, the program.

But many churches have no standards.

While in a certain church some time ago, I asked the people to bow their heads. Then I said, "All who are saved and know it, will you please raise your hands?" Hands went up. But not seeing what I wanted to see, I asked again, "With heads bowed, I, a stranger, would like to know how many of you are saved. If you know Christ as your Saviour, will you please stand?" Most got to their feet. I could see a few still seated. When I looked behind me, I saw more than half the choir were still seated.

I did not know what was wrong. During the invitation song there was little response. There seemed a coldness, a deadness through the congregation.

Later when I asked the pastor why all those unsaved people were in the choir, he said, "Well, they enjoy singing, and we felt by having them in the choir they might get saved. Friends invited them. And they are good singers."

But how can anyone sing, "Just as I am, without one plea," and not even know Jesus Christ! How can one sing, "Jesus is tenderly calling thee home," and not know one thing about the Lord!

Standards. We must have standards. Workers in the church should be saved and following the steps of our Lord—dedicated Christians.

Don't put worldly people in leadership if the church is to help the city. To help, men must have high standards, standards which will make modernists miserable and the worldly uncomfortable. When a worldly person visits the church, he ought to get something for his need. But if he just enjoys being there, something is wrong with us. Our standards should make the compromiser unhappy.

2. *We need churches that proclaim the Word of God.* There is no way to estimate what the preaching of God's holy Word does—I mean true preaching that brings conviction.

A very splendid Christian man came to see me this week, a good preacher. He told me, "I've been pastoring for nine years, but I've got troubles. Next Tuesday I am to meet with four or five familes who do not like my preaching. They say I am not deep enough. I believe in missions. We support missions. We put missionaries around the world. I travel on mission fields. We believe in separation. I will hear their objections to my ministry next Tuesday."

I believe this man is preaching the Word of God, but he is not satisfying the worldly-minded members. He told me they wanted a pastor who would get up and speak while they held their Bibles and took notes—a teaching minister, not one who is for missions and soul winning.

The right kind of church must proclaim the Word of God. Souls are convicted when the Word is proclaimed.

This is a strange world, a very strange world. Someone handed me an article the other day saying that at the University of Missouri one can sit on campus and read Karl Marx all day, but he is not allowed to read the Bible! Isn't that weird? You can read anything you want to read *except the Bible*. To read it goes against the law on campus of that university! I have the article here before me. It allows a room for a homosexual society to meet in, but denies any Christian organization a room for their meetings. When some Christians begged for a room for some Bible study and fellowship in the Word of God, they were turned down. But the "gays" can come together. A room is assigned to them.

That story may seem strange, but it is a common happening in our nation. And this is tragic. We have such low standards. Churches have failed when a state university will let one read communistic literature on campus but not the Bible, when no room is allowed for Bible class, yet "gays" are allowed a meeting place.

Churches must declare the Word of God.

3. *We must have churches that go after souls.*

Six thousand Southern Baptist churches last year had not a single convert. Six hundred of these were in the state of Tennessee—without a convert, a baptism in twelve months. Now that was among Southern Baptists; but independent Baptists have like pathetic statistics. Many churches are not doing one single thing.

We must seek lost souls in Sunday school, in Training Union, in the preaching hours, in revivals, in prayer meetings—at every opportunity.

I held a meeting up north some months ago in a magnificent church. I was asked to meet with the men one time, with the ladies another time in special study groups. In this magnificent place where I was talking about soul winning and building a Sunday school, the members have lots of money; and the church has everything it wants or needs. When I made mention that there were people right around the church who needed to be reached, one lady immediately spoke up: "Sir, we do not visit the people around our church." She was adamant.

I asked, "Why don't you visit them?"

"They are not of our kind. We do our visiting out in the suburbs, among the nicer homes. Ours is a downtown church, and we don't visit around here."

Wait! The thing wrong was the people's attitude. They had so built into their thinking that they were an exclusive organization and could touch only a certain type people, not plain, run-of-the-mill folks who need Christ.

I made a very unkind statement which I should not have made, but made it anyway to make them think. I said, *"You know you are just like Jesus!"*

That woke them up! They knew they were far from being like Jesus. They were concerned about their name, prestige, the wealth of people, not about the down-and-outs around them, downtown.

Our job is to seek the lost, to care about a lost world, to press on people's hearts their need of Jesus.

I saw a write-up in a New York paper entitled, "WHERE THE CITY BURIES ITS POOR." It also showed pictures of Potter's Field in New York City, a plot of ground, forty-five acres of land.

A pine coffin in which to bury a poor man or woman in Potter's Field costs $28.70. The poor die; someone pays for the coffin; and they are put away in graves where two, three or four others are buried.

Since 1948, people have been buried there—I think some 700,000 in the last few years—in Potter's Field in New York City. The inmates of a nearby prison dig the graves for from twenty-eight to thirty or more a week.

The inmates built a monument thirty feet high in the middle of that cemetery. On one side of it they put a cross into the stonework. On the other side is the word PEACE.

Those inmates had more sense than some folks have. On one side—a cross; on the other side—PEACE. They had the right idea. There is no peace nor is there salvation without Jesus and the cross.

Our job is to declare the message of Christ and to emphasize the cross. A wide-awake, aggressive church is the need of the hour.

Are we doing all we can? No—and you and I know it. Our city has a desperate need, and we have a big job. We must not fail.

III. TO MEET THE NEED, WE MUST HAVE DEMONSTRATIONS OF FAITH

1. *Demonstrations of faith in God.* I continually say this to both young and old. Sometimes I point out three impeccable illustrations because there are no marks against them in the Bible.

Enoch, who walked with God;
Joseph, who suffered for God;
Daniel, who talked to God.

These human beings had difficulties, no doubt, though they are not mentioned in Scripture.

In order to be what God wants us to be, we Christians must demonstrate our faith. We must believe that God will supply our needs, that He will direct our footsteps, and will be our companion in the worst of situations.

A preacher said one newspaper editor called him and asked, "What is your subject for Sunday?"

The preacher replied, "The Lord Is My Shepherd."

The news editor asked, "Is that all?"

The preacher said, "That's enough."

On Saturday the paper came out with the pastor's subject: "The Lord Is My Shepherd; That's Enough."

My dear friend, He is enough. Demonstrate your faith. Believe God!

2. *Demonstrations of holy living.* Daniel and the three Hebrew

children refused to defile themselves. They said, "no," when asked to fall down before an idol. As a result, they were cast into a big furnace of fire. In that furnace three holy men were accompanied by the Son of God, who came down to walk with them and to bring them out to safety.

Demonstrations of holy living! Live for Christ! Live separated lives.

3. *Demonstrations of effective praying.* I know God answers prayer. I want to daily pray in faith, believing. I want to encourage others to pray. I want a strong prayer life. I want to help those who are weaker than I. We need demonstrations of effective prayer, men and women seeking the face of God, waiting before God.

The great Dr. George Truett, a man whom I knew personally, was pastor at First Baptist Church, Dallas, for forty-five years. I had not, until recently, heard this story, though I have read everything on Truett that I could find.

Dr. Truett became ill. In the last twelve months of his life he was confined to his bed, both at home and in the hospital. This mighty man suffered acute physical pain, agony. As he stood in front of his window, he looked out over the city of Dallas and cried, "O God, bring them to Christ!" This compassionate man loved others.

Dr. Louis Newton, a friend, went to visit Dr. Truett. Hearing he was spending his days and nights in bed unable to sleep, he said to Dr. Truett, "Doctor, I know you find the nights hopelessly long."

Dr. Truett spoke up: "Oh, no. On the contrary, they are too, too short."

"What do you mean, sir—too short?"

"When I find I am unable to sleep, I begin reciting names of friends and then I pray for each. I have made many friends through the years (he was then in his 80's). I recite the names one by one and talk to God about each one. Often the night is over before I have finished my list."

That is demonstrating effective praying.

4. *Demonstrations of concern for others.* How much do we

really care? How concerned are we about the lost and dying? Do we believe what the Bible says about a burning, eternal Hell? Are we concerned? Do we care? We in this church—do we really care?

Some have mentioned our new building. People drive by and look. One doctor told me this week, "I have been driving by. I want to come in and see it."

We are proud of our building and glad that people drive by. But I don't want folks thinking only about a building. I want them to know we care for their souls. I want us to show that God loves them, that He cares and will save every lost sinner who will repent and believe.

God cares. Do we?

This morning, rejoice if you are saved, then tell others about it. Let people know that God loves, that God cares, that God wants to and will save any who will repent.

Rev. Harold Dye, a pastor in Clovis, New Mexico, told me about the time his dad and mother and the children moved from the East to the West. They were poor. Their old car would barely run. He said they didn't have money for a motel, so they camped out. There were four children, mother and dad.

One night they pitched their tent not far from the highway. The four children, including himself, were put inside to sleep. The fire was burning outside. His mother and father were sitting near the fire. Harold Dye said:

> I couldn't go to sleep. I was one of the four children and should have been asleep. But I looked out and saw my mother and father sitting by the fire. I heard my father say, "Pearl, when we get to New Mexico, we won't have a thing. Our money is already gone. Our home is gone back East. We don't have a job; we don't have a thing."
>
> He poured out a very pitiful story sitting at the campfire. We children were in a little tent over to the side of the highway waiting for morning to come.
>
> I saw my mother get up and walk around the fire, then sit down beside my dad, put her arm around his neck; and I heard her say, "Harv, we have something. We have each other, and we have God."

I couldn't forget that: "We do have something. We have each other, and we have God."

Mother held Dad around the shoulders and neck as they sat by the fireside. She was comforting Dad. I cried.

We went on to Clovis, New Mexico.

Before long, our family followed a very simple gray casket out to the cemetery. The quartet sang, "Safe in the Arms of Jesus." Dirt was put on the casket. My mother was laid to rest.

Father came and put his arms around all four of us children and stood there with a lonely heart. We watched clods of dirt fall down upon the casket of his wife, our mother.

Dad said he thought as he stood there, *I have nothing left but God and the children.*

It wasn't long after that when we followed another casket out to the cemetery. It was also gray and inexpensive. This time it was our father. We stood there, the four of us, with our friends. I thought again of what Mother said that night at the campfire, *We have God; we have each other.*

We stood and watched them lower my father into the grave. At the close of the service, I thought, *We have God. He is still with us. Others may perish; others may pass on; but God is still with us.*

God is enough.

Is Christ your Saviour? Is God your Father? Is Heaven your Home? Oh, then rejoice!

Faith sees the invisble
Faith hears the inaudible
Faith believes the incredible
Faith receives the impossible.

45. *What is the Symbol of Our Faith?*

But God forbid that I should glory, save in the cross of our Lord Jesus Christ, by whom the world is crucified unto me, and I unto the world.

For in Christ Jesus neither circumcision availeth any thing, nor uncircumcision, but a new creature.

And as many as walk according to this rule, peace be on them, and mercy, and upon the Israel of God.

From henceforth let no man trouble me: for I bear in my body the marks of the Lord Jesus.

Brethren, the grace of our Lord Jesus Christ be with your spirit. Amen.

—Galatians 6:14-18.

In the cross of Christ I glory,
  Tow'ring o'er the wrecks of time;
All the light of sacred glory,
  Gathers 'round its head sublime.

When I survey the wondrous cross,
  On which the Prince of Glory died,
My richest gain I count but loss,
  And pour contempt on all my pride.

Christ died. That is history.

Christ died for our sins. That is doctrine, the most precious doctrine in the world.

The song writer says:

Beneath the cross of Jesus
  I fain would take my stand,
The shadow of a mighty Rock

> Within a weary land;
> A home within the wilderness,
> A rest upon the way,
> From the burning of the noontide heat,
> And the burden of the day.

Some friends touring the British Isles asked for directions to a town in England. A man at the roadside who knew the directions immediately said, "Keep on; don't pass the cross; and turn to the right when you come to it."

Those are good directions—"Don't pass the cross."

Dr. R. G. Lee always wore a cross attached to a chain on his lapel. He did not worship that bit of gold; but it was a symbol of the love of God, the death and resurrection of Christ, the fact of Christ's coming again.

Our text gives the message with clarity:

"God forbid that I should glory, save in the cross of our Lord Jesus Christ, by whom the world is crucified unto me, and I unto the world."

There are three thoughts that I want you to have tonight.

I. THE CROSS POINTS:

1. *The way to life.* Without Christ, we are "dead in trespasses and sins" (Eph. 2:1).

We are all sinners and are lost. There is but one Saviour!

"For there is one God, and one mediator between God and men, the man Christ Jesus:

"Who gave himself a ransom for all, to be testified in due time."—I Tim. 2: 5,6.

". . .and without shedding of blood is no remission."—Heb. 9:22.

Do not accept anything from anybody who seeks to sidestep the way of the cross. Do not accept any teaching that turns you away from the blood of the Lamb of God that was shed for you.

". . .Christ died for our sins according to the scriptures."—I Cor. 15:3.

2. *The way to victorious living.* There is no victorious living without death to self.

Romans 6:6 and 11 state:

"Knowing this, that our old man is crucified with him, that the body of sin might be destroyed, that henceforth we should not serve sin.

"Likewise reckon ye also yourselves to be dead indeed unto sin, but alive unto God through Jesus Christ our Lord."

Reckoning yourself to be dead is the toughest Christian battle. Here is where the cross comes in. The cross points the way. The cross is the symbol of death. We must die to selfishness. We must die to pride and worldly ambition.

I was preaching recently in a distant city. A man and his wife came up to me after one of the services. She said. "We're both Christians, but we're so unhappy. I am to blame. I am selfish. I make our home miserable. I am always bickering about things that I want. I know that I do not have the victory. Every day I am defeated." That lady did not have the victory.

We must die to live.

Embarrassment should not hurt me. Honest failure should not hurt me. But the self-life is so strong that little things do embarrass us. Happy the day when we can say, "The world is crucified unto me, and I unto the world."

3. *The way to service.* Christ was a servant. You will never take the "Servant place" until you come to the cross and die.

Jesus said in Mark 10:44,45:

"And whosoever of you will be the chiefest, shall be servant of all.

"For even the Son of man came not to be ministered unto, but to minister, and to give his life a ransom for many."

Follow Christ in service! That's dying. That's what you will have to do in order to be a servant. Most people want to be masters.

He was eager; we are cold.
He was enthusiastic; we are indifferent.
He wept over Jerusalem; we seldom weep over ourselves.
He had a blazing heart; we have a cold heart.
John 12:24 has the answer:

"Verily, verily, I say unto you, Except a corn of wheat fall into the ground and die, it abideth alone: but if it die, it bringeth forth much fruit."

The grain of wheat must die!

II. THE CROSS PRODUCES:

1. *Humility.*
Christ came down from Heaven's glory to die on the cross.

"But made himself of no reputation, and took upon him the form of a servant, and was made in the likeness of men:

"And being found in fashion as a man, he humbled himself, and became obedient unto death, even the death of the cross."

This is the picture for us. We must see ourselves as dying. Jesus died for us. The cross will produce humility. There is no place for pride.

2. *Awe and amazement.*
Christ dying on a cross! Christ, the Son of God! Christ, the man with all power! Yet dying the shameful death on the cross!
The song writer was overwhelmed when he wrote the words,

"Man of Sorrows!" what a name,
For the Son of God who came
Ruined sinners to reclaim!
Hallelujah! What a Saviour!

Look up to the cross with awe and amazement—the holy Saviour dying for you.
3. *Faith.*

My faith looks up to Thee,
Thou Lamb of Calvary,
Saviour divine!

Through faith I became a child of God.

The symbol of the cross reminds me of all I have in Christ. By His death the Holy Spirit indwells me. By His death I am saved. By His death I have life and victory. By His death I have His peace and the promise of His coming again. By His death I have Heaven.

The cross produces faith.

III. THE CROSS PUNCTUATES (Emphasizes):

1. *Our sin.* Christ died on the cross for our sin. He died for us. We are just as guilty of His death as anyone, in any century. He died in our behalf. This shows the awful, hideous nature of sin.

2. *Our need.* We are weak and unworthy.

"Alas! and did my Saviour bleed?
And did my Sov'reign die?
Would He devote that sacred head
For such a worm as I?"

When I was in high school, the smartest boy in the class said, "I resent that verse in the songbook. I'm not a worm! I'm a man"—boasting of his position. He had never seen himself as a lost sinner, had never understood that the cross punctuates our needs.

Listening to the news on Tuesday morning, I heard a young fellow who had won high honors in stock-car racing bragging about making $700,000.00 this past year. He concluded his interview by saying, "When I conquer the world, I am moving on to the next one."

I've got news for him! He is not going to conquer the world. He's a failure, as are all of us, until we rest in Him.

The old poem, "Invictus," by William Ernest Henley verbalizes this idea:

"I am the master of my fate:
I am the captain of my soul."

Wrong! We are needy creatures. Without Him we can do nothing.

Only Christ could say, ". . .be of good cheer; I have overcome the world." (John 16:33).

3. *Our salvation.* There is no salvation outside the cross. No one can ignore the cross. The cross punctuates our salvation. When someone seeks to escape mentioning the cross of the Lord Jesus Christ, beware.

I will never forget when I tried to lead a Jew to Christ as I sat in his office. He was a good Jew. I talked about Christ's death on the cross. He opened the desk drawer and pulled out a book. "If that's in this book, I'll accept it," he said.

The book was by Norman Vincent Peale. I tried to find something on the cross, knowing that I could not, for I had already read the book. I said, "Sir, it's not in there, but it's in here in the New Testament." That didn't please him.

He insisted, "If it's in there, I'll believe it. I've read the book and like it. I haven't read that Book (the New Testament), for I don't believe it."

How dare anyone ignore the blood of Christ! The cross emphasizes salvation by grace:

"For by grace are ye saved through faith; and that not of yourselves: it is the gift of God: Not of works, lest any man should boast."—Eph. 2:8,9.

The symbol of our faith is the cross and the Christ who died on that cross.

"But God forbid that I should glory, save in the cross of our Lord Jesus Christ, by whom the world is crucified unto me, and I unto the world."

He died to the world that you and I might be alive unto God through Jesus Christ. The cross was where He died and shed His blood so we might have everlasting life.

In the art gallery at Dusseldorf is a painting with a history, the painting of the crucifixion of Christ. It was made by the German artist Stenberg. When working on the painting, Stenberg employed a little gypsy girl to sit for a character that he was trying to sketch into the picture.

As she sat there day by day, she saw the painting and how it depicted Christ's suffering and the cruelty of the scene. She asked the artist, "What's the meaning of this? Who is this man?"

Stenberg explained that Christ was a good man, that He had lived for others and that He was dying for others that He might save them.

She was touched by the story and told the artist, "Sir, I should think that you love Him very much. If anyone did that for me, I would love Him very much."

The words of that little girl pointed Stenberg to the cross of Calvary and the Christ who died on that cross, and he accepted Christ as his Saviour.

The picture of the crucifixion was finished and placed in the art gallery. Thousands came to view that picture of the death of Christ on the cross of Calvary.

In the company of those visiting was a German count of high rank and great worldly prospects. That picture so impressed the count that it changed his whole life. As he gazed at it, it seemed to say to him: "All this I did for thee; what hast thou done for Me?" The man was Count Zinzendorf who founded the Moravian movement which became a great missionary work reaching out to a lost world.

But there is more. That little gypsy girl who had posed in the picture for the artist, came and looked at the picture. She said, "I wish He had died for me." The artist told her the story of Christ. She became a child of God and rejoiced.

A few months later the artist was called to the little girl's deathbed. She looked into his face with joy and said, "Yes, He died for me, and I am going to be with Him forever!"

"But God forbid that I should glory, save in the cross of our Lord Jesus Christ, by whom the world is crucified unto me, and I unto the world."

We have a need to know Jesus, the Son of God as our Saviour, Lord and Master, and to give our all to Him.

Are you without Christ? He died for you. If you have never accepted Him, will you do so? Make your life count for God. Die to the world. Come to the cross. Say to Jesus, "Take me and use me as I give myself to Thee, as I surrender to Thee."

I want to give my best to Christ, the One who died in my behalf.

> Jesus, keep me near the cross,
>   There a precious fountain
> Free to all—a healing stream,
>   Flows from Calvary's mountain.
>
> In the cross, in the cross,
>   Be my glory ever;
> Till my raptured soul shall find,
>   Rest beyond the river.

Sinner, come to the cross. Christian, come to the cross.

He who is small in faith will never be great in anything but failure.—Anon.

46. *A Story of Faith*

Now faith is the substance of things hoped for, the evidence of things not seen.

But without faith it is impossible to please him: for he that cometh to God must believe that he is, and that he is a rewarder of them that diligently seek him.

—Hebrews 11: 1,6.

Fifty-two years ago I made my first acquaintance with radio. I became assistant pastor of Virginia Avenue Baptist Church in Louisville, Kentucky, also director of the choir. The pastor was L. W. Benedict, a very highly educated man, graduate of a seminary, and a very fluent preacher. He came from New York City.

It was in depression days. I was paid forty dollars a month for my work as assistant pastor. I paid twenty-eight dollars a month for room and board at Southern Baptist Seminary.

Brother Benedict heard about me and about my singing in a church at the edge of town, and asked me to join with him.

The church owned radio station WLAP. The control was in the back of the choir. The engineers sat in back of the choir loft. The towers were on top of the church building. It was a strong station. WLAP stood for: We Love All People.

We had three hours on Sunday for the church, and then we had a special broadcast during the week.

Dr. Benedict told me how he happened to have the station. (I mention it on this lesson of faith, the time of faith, thinking about faith.) He began thinking about Louisville and about her great need. Radio was just getting off the ground around the nation. He believed if he could have a station, he could reach the entire city from his church; so he began to pray. As he prayed, God began opening doors for him. A man told him he could buy a station in a certain city for $100,000.00. That was a lot of money in that day, and a lot in this day, too.

Brother Benedict had no money. The church was new and poor. He prayed and asked the Lord to show him where he could get the money.

As he prayed, the Lord directed him to go to a certain building in downtown Louisville. He said, "As far as I know, I had never been there before. I walked inside the building and saw the register of the men and companies who were stationed or working out of that building. I said, 'Lord, direct me to the one who can direct me to buy the station that I want to put in my church.' " Now, this is faith!

He ran his finger up and down the list of names, and he told me, "I did not know one from the other, but as I did so, God said to me, 'If you want the money, go to see Mr. Dinwiddie.' " He knew nothing about Dinwiddie, not even what he did, but he said, "If he is the one, I will go."

Now, I am repeating his story as given to me. This university graduate, this seminary graduate, not given to fantasies, not running off on tangents, said:

> God led me. I got in the elevator, went up in the building, got off the elevator, walked down the hallway, and saw the office door of Mr. Dinwiddie, president of a certain company.
>
> I stepped inside and told the secretary I was there to see Mr. Dinwiddie. She asked if I had an appointment. I said, "No, not the formal kind. I have an appointment with the Lord. He asked me to come."
>
> She laughed. She had never heard anyone say anthing like that before.
>
> I said, "Ma'am, I am here and I want to see him."
>
> She said, "You cannot see him today nor tomorrow. I am not sure when you can see him, because he is a very busy man."
>
> I said, "I am here until I see him," and I sat down.

After a while she said, "You might as well go; you are not going to see him."

I said, "I'll stay until I do see him."

Finally, in disgust she said, "Well, I will go speak to him." She walked inside and said, "There is a strange preacher out here named L. W. Benedict who wants to see you about something, and he will not leave until he sees you."

Dinwiddie laughed and said, "Send him on in."

I walked inside the room and introduced myself. "Mr. Dinwiddie, the Lord sent me here. He told me that you would buy for me and my church a radio station where we can publish the Gospel to the people of all Louisville and to Albany and Jeffersonville, in Indiana, and the towns around."

When I said that, Dinwiddie laughed. "Why, Mr. Benedict, I have no interest in radio; in fact, I do not like it. I do not belong to a church. I am not even a Christian. I do not know a thing about you. That request is as foolish as it can be."

I settled down and said, "Mr. Dinwiddie, God sent me here. My faith has told me that you are to give me $100,000.00 with which to buy the station and establish it here in Louisville."

Dinwiddie laughed at me again. But before I left, I had the money in hand—$100,000.00 plus, given by Mr. Dinwiddie!

He bought the station. He brought it to Louisville and established it in the back of the church. He paid for the towers, for the engineers. I broadcast on the station every day for two years.

Mr. Dinwiddie paid all the bills. I went to his office with the pastor. I heard the story both from the pastor and from Mr. Dinwiddie.

Now what I am saying is this: when you have faith in God, and believe God, and know that He will stand back of you, there is no telling what can be done.

So many of us stand off. For example, I have never been impressed to do a thing like that. I have never been bold enough to ask a man for $100,000.00. I would like to be bold enough, but I never have—yet.

You may be thinking this morning, *If I just had faith enough*

. . . . God will give you what you need. "Without faith it is impossible to please God."

What we do here at the church is a matter of faith. Tennessee Temple University is a matter of faith.

The first one thousand dollars was given by Miss Verna Pullen, a missionary from Africa who is now living in Georgia. She is retired from her mission work, but still working. The thousand dollars came from her father's estate. She said, "I do not need it"—a strange thing for a woman to say! So she sent it to us. That is where we began.

From that came all the things we see around us: buildings and young people.

Camp Joy is a matter of faith. World Wide Faith Missions is a matter of faith. Everything we see, everything we have is a matter of faith in God. Sometimes our faith is so small. "Without faith it is impossible to please him." "For we walk by faith, not by sight" (II Cor. 5:7).

If you do not have faith, you are not saved. You must have faith in Jesus Christ to save your soul. "For by grace are ye saved through faith. . . ." By your faith in Jesus Christ you are a child of God.

But is faith for salvation all of it? No. God wants us to have faith to live, walk, work, serve Him, and do what He wants us to do.

I. LET OURS BE A GROWING FAITH

When I got saved at fourteen years of age, I believed God. If anyone had suggested then that at age 73 I would be doing what I am doing, I would have thought that one foolish. But by growing and developing and moving on, God will give us what we have need of.

On one occasion, Jesus asked His disciples, "Where is your faith?" There was a storm at sea, and He was asleep in the ship. They awakened Him. "There's a storm; we are perishing." He rose up and said, "Where is your faith? Don't you believe anything?" That was a sharp word of reprimand.

He is saying the same thing to us—"Where is your faith?

Where are you? What are you trusting in? What are you doing today?"

We need to pray, "Lord, increase our faith. Help us to believe and trust God."

Paul said, "So then faith cometh by hearing, and hearing by the word of God" (Rom. 10:17). Keep growing in faith. Whatever you may be, whatever your age, you have that faith that is growing every day, established upon the Word of God, resting upon the promises of God.

II. LET OURS BE A GREAT FAITH

Now, what do I mean by great faith? I mean:

1. *A faith that doesn't doubt.* Read this Word of God and believe all these 32,000 promises in the Bible.

His promise is to supply and guide our lives. Do not doubt God. Has God ever failed? No, not one single time. You know that. I know that. Has He failed anyone else that you know about? No. Then if God does not fail and we know that His Word is true, then believe Him.

2. *A faith that doesn't quit.* Some people start out strong, then fade away. That is one thing that I have watched in these forty years in this church. Many people start out strong—I mean big, active, loud, happy about it first, then fade away. Don't let your faith quit! Have a faith that keeps on going.

Demas was a quitter. He left Paul. "Demas hath forsaken me." Doubtless some little thing came up. I think Demas was a saved man, but he left the apostle.

Now, some people have a faith that just quits, just stops in the middle of the whole thing.

3. *A faith that doesn't question God.* Believe God without question! Don't be always asking, "Why?" Just take it!

There are things I don't understand. I can't explain all the mysteries of the Word of God—salvation, the greatness of what we have, and so on. I don't understand it all.

I cannot understand how God can bring people together, like He has here this morning. This is a mystery to me. In a wicked city and in a wicked nation, hundreds of thousands believe God. I hope you are one of them.

Don't question when sickness and accidents come. Just say, "Father, Your will be done."

Don't question when you have reverses. When you lose your job or your business folds, keep on trusting. Don't question God.

Don't question about your little every day problems. Everybody has problems. Abraham did. Moses did. Joshua did. There are problems throughout the Bible. The Apostle Paul had problems.

Have faith in the midst of every illness, every doubt, every sorrow. Let yours be a great faith established upon the Word of God. Without a great faith in Him, you can't be all God wants you to be.

A great faith will help you to help others. Somebody is watching you. Can you keep steady? Can you keep on going?

Two or three of you dear young people came to see me yesterday with some little bit of difficulty. Mama wrote, "Come on home." Mama doesn't mean to hurt you, but she is hurting you. When you cry and write back home, saying, "I don't have the money," she says, "Well, if you don't have the money, I'll be glad to have you back home." You stand steady! Let your faith be so strong that people can see it.

I will never forget the little mother who wrote me. Boy, she gave it to me! She had two young people in our school. They were living just two blocks away. She was upset. She said, "You go up there and tell my children that they have got to come home. They don't have any money. They are starving to death. Get them out of there and get them back home."

I wrote her, "I am not going to tell them anything of the kind."

Those two kids stayed and suffered through. They had almost nothing to eat. Lights were turned out part of the time because they could not pay the light bill. Everything seemed to go wrong, but they stood!

Later she wrote to thank me for helping them stick and keep on going.

Now, I urge you to have a faith that will help others.

Let your faith be attractive. Great men and women of God have all had faith in God.

III. LET OURS BE A GOD-GLORIFYING FAITH

God wants us to have faith in Him. Jesus said, "Have faith in God." Imagine Jesus, the Son of God, making such a statement; then He goes on to speak about prayer and trusting God. He invites us to come and trust Him.

Hebrews 11 is evidence of what God thinks of faith. These men and women listed did something because they believed God; they had faith in God.

Let your faith be so strong that God Himself is glorified. Also, you are helping someone else.

Let me point out some things.

1. *God-glorifying faith will give peace of heart when nothing else will.* He said, ". . .my peace I give unto you: not as the world giveth, give I unto you. Let not your heart be troubled, neither let it be afraid."

Glorifying God will give peace of heart. Let your faith be strong. Never doubt, never question God.

You need to talk with the young man with whom I talked last evening. It was past midnight when he called. He graduated from Tennessee Temple in 1975.

After he left here, he married a girl from this school. He set himself up in a big business.

He called me and told me the story. He is thirty years of age. He has a beautiful wife and two children. His boy Luke is twenty months old. His little girl Lydia was born three weeks ago. Business is wonderful. Money is coming in. The family is happy. But he has cancer. In November he had a little pain in his shoulder and went to the doctor, and he found cancer throughout his whole body. The doctor says he might live three months, maybe not that long.

Now, my dear friend, if you come to a time like that without faith in God, you have nothing! You are empty. That young man has a home, a wife, children, money, position and a future—but cancer that will take him shortly.

I want to say this in behalf of that young man: As far as I can tell from that telephone call last night, his faith is as strong as the Rock of Gibraltar. He told me, "God is with me. I will use these days and moments the best I can. I am not afraid. I think about my wife and children. I am going to have a video picture made. I will talk to my children in the picture, and have a tape made. At sixteen or eighteen years they can play it. I will tell them what they should do with their lives."

He is going to have this all taped. "I want them to know I am not afraid to die. I would like to live because I have everything to live for, but my faith in God is strong and I have peace of heart."

A God-glorifying faith will give you peace.

2. *God-glorifying faith will give light.* This is a dark world. Without faith you will stumble. Without faith you will fail. You will drop into the crevice of doubt and difficulty, sin and destruction.

3. *God-glorifying faith will give adventure.* To the youngest person here today it will give that sense of adventure, of doing things that thrill the heart and move you out. "Launch out into the deep," commanded our Lord. Let your faith ring out, reach out to others.

We have talked about a growing faith, a great faith, a God-glorifying faith. All of it begins with the Lord Jesus Christ.

Is He your Saviour? Have you accepted Him?

Now, Christian, let your faith expand. Let it grow. Let it develop.

If you have never accepted Jesus Christ, accept Him now, at this moment.

47. Faith Makes a Difference

And this I say, lest any man should beguile you with enticing words.

For though I be absent in the flesh, yet am I with you in the spirit, joying and beholding your order, and the stedfastness of your faith in Christ.

As ye have therefore received Christ Jesus the Lord, so walk ye in him:

Rooted and built up in him, and stablished in the faith, as ye have been taught, abounding therein with thanksgiving.

—Colossians 2:4-7.

Now when they had gone throughout Phrygia and the region of Galatia, and were forbidden of the Holy Ghost to preach the word in Asia,

After they were come to Mysia, they assayed to go into Bithynia: but the Spirit suffered them not.

And they passing by Mysia came down to Troas.

And a vision appeared to Paul in the night; There stood a man of Macedonia, and prayed him, saying, Come over into Macedonia, and help us.

And after he had seen the vision, immediately we endeavoured to go into Macedonia, assuredly gathering that the Lord had called us for to preach the gospel unto them.

—Acts 16:6-10.

I doubt if Paul ever forgot the name Bithynia. Bithynia was a province of Asia Minor. Paul decided to preach the Gospel in that place, but "the Spirit suffered them not."

How the Spirit worked, I do not know. Illness might have touched the bodies of the missionaries. Or disease might have been widespread in Bithynia. Or governmental opposition might have been raised against them. At any rate, they didn't go in.

They knew why they didn't go: "the Holy Spirit suffered them not."

God directed them to Philippi. The rest of the story you know quite well—the salvation of souls, including the jailer and his household.

Paul and Silas were men of faith. They prayed, sought the guidance of God, and followed it.

I began to think at once of all that faith does when we walk by faith.

Faith makes life exciting. Uncertain, yes, but exciting. Paul's life was exciting. He wasn't sure where the next step was going to be. No mission board back of him, no salary, no guaranteed protection on his way. Paul just went and lived by faith. Faith will make your life exciting, also.

Faith makes life flexible. Be ready for changes; they come to all of us. When you walk by faith, God is with you; and you know that everything is all right, though it may mean a big change.

Faith makes life progressive. We are moving forward. Faith in God is the one ingredient that makes life sane and progressive.

Faith makes life unselfish. Faith in God will lead you to reach out to others. George Mueller, the great man of faith in God, supported orphanages and reached out to others around him.

Faith makes life victorious. We're talking about faith in God. Faith is the victory. "For whatsoever is born of God overcometh the world: and this is the victory that overcometh the world, even our faith" (I John 5:4).

Success in the Christian life is not a matter of good luck or chance. It is a matter of faith, your faith in God.

With this as my introduction, I give two or three simple points.

I. BUILD YOUR FAITH

Salvation is by grace through faith. "For by grace are ye saved through faith. . ." (Eph. 2:8). Jesus said, "He that believeth in me hath everlasting life." Salvation is by faith in the Son of God.

Now that you know Jesus as Saviour, there should be a building of your faith. Some don't do it; hence we have a lot of baby Christians who never develop, never grow.

1. *By the Bible.* We read, "So then faith cometh by hearing, and hearing by the word of God" (Rom. 10:17). Jesus said, ". . . have faith in God" (Mark 11:22). The statements are given again and again: "When Jesus saw their faith, he said unto the sick . . ." and the apostles said unto the Lord, "Increase our faith" (Luke 17:5).

Build faith by the Word of God, for the Bible never changes while other things do.

2. *By thanksgiving.* We read in Colossians 2:7, "Abound in thanksgiving." Praise God for every blessing. Thank Him for the gift of His Son. Thank God for the gift of eternal life. Thank Him for His guidance and protection. Thank God that He is with you, that you are never alone.

Thank God!

3. *By prayer.* To neglect the place of prayer is costly. Failing to pray decreases faith. Pray in faith believing. Pray about every matter. Don't be impatient; wait on God. Pray and seek His face.

By remembering. Remember all God has done for you.

Moses recounted the miracles of God on his behalf: walking by faith, crossing the Red Sea on dry ground, the daily feeding of the Israelites on manna in the desert country for forty years.

Paul built his faith by remembering his salvation experience. He recounted what happened back on that road to Damascus and built his faith as he went back over the past.

Build your faith by remembering answers to prayer.

Build your faith by remembering His direction for your life, how God has led you.

Build your faith by remembering His chastening, when God had to correct you.

Faith makes the difference. No man is what he should be unless he has strong faith. No man is what God wants him to be without strong faith.

II. GUARD YOUR FAITH

Salvation is a gift from God. Faith is given us through our faith in Christ. Now we need to guard that faith!

Our enemy Satan will do all he can to destroy our faith. He cannot do anything about our salvation, but he certainly can weaken our faith. Hence, all the baby Christians, the complaining Christians, the wayside Christians sitting on the back row doing nothing for God. So guard your faith against Satan.

Paul said, "Put on the whole armour of God, that ye may be able to stand against the wiles of the devil" (Eph. 6:11).

Give no place to that trickster the Devil. Some, even Christians, open wide the doors of their hearts and homes to Satan. I warn you—give him no place in your life.

Guard your God-given faith. Treasure that faith. Don't allow any thought, any action to diminish it. Keep it strong. Without slowing down in fifty-five years, I have never failed to press certain convictions on people.

For example: one of the safest places is in the house of God. Whether you listen or don't listen, you are still safer here than you are out in the world. I emphasize going to church. There you sing, pray, hear the Bible expounded. There you establish your faith; there you guard your faith against the onslaughts of Satan.

I emphasize reading the Bible. You make no mistake when you pick up the Bible. Read His Word. Believe His Word. If you put it aside, the Devil walks right in and steals away that victorious faith.

I emphasize prayer, for

> **"Satan trembles when he sees,**
> **The weakest saint upon his knees."**

The place of prayer is a place of peace and power. If you have faith in God, then know that Satan hates it.

People turn away and go into the world. Oh, you think it is

smart; think you are big stuff; you think you can do as you please, go where you want, and when you want. Sure you can—and Satan will pat you on the back as you go. But don't allow him to steal away your faith.

1. *Satan will try to make you doubt this Book.* He will make an all-out effort to make you doubt the Bible, which contains the promises of God. "If ye shall ask anything in my name, I will do it" (John 14:14). The promise of prayer, the promise of His protection, the promise of His provision—these Satan will make you doubt. "Well, the Bible says it. . .but, so what?" Satan will make you doubt the Word of God until you will say, "I know the Bible says it, but it is not so." It is so! This is God's Book. Satan hates your faith in God's Word.

2. *Satan will try to turn you away from the house of God.* He will tell some of you with little puny minds, "You can worship God at home." He will tell some of you who know better, "You can watch TV and just worship God beautifully." Satan will try to turn you away from worship.

Be careful! Exercise care. He will try to use any confusion in the service, any misbehavior in the house of God, to distract you. He will try to make you say, "Well, I went to church but couldn't hear anything because of so much confusion." (We do have it, and it is going to stop.)

But that is not the issue. What counts is that you are coming to church, you are a Christian, you come to worship God, to serve God, to get a blessing from being at church.

3. *Satan makes alluring offers to lead one away from Christian service,* to get you to stop working in this church, to get you to turn away from what God wants you to do by offering something better from the outside—money, position, prestige, etc.

4. *Satan will encourage people to quit.* Quit teaching in Sunday school, quit working with young people, quit visiting, quit giving, quit singing in the choir—give it all up; all that is of Satan.

We see the dreadful success of Satan all around us. Seventy-five percent of professing Christians of America do not go to church except on special occasions—perhaps a couple of times a year. The Devil wins. Satan encourages you to quit and turn aside.

5. *Satan will encourage you to be disappointed in people.* And because of your disappointment, you quit your church and any work you are doing for God.

Preachers get disappointed and quit. I have had them come to see me often, all torn up because their church is not going as well as it should, or people have disappointed them or lied to them.

Deacons want to quit. They, too, get discouraged. They say, "I just can't make it to every service," or "I just can't go on, " and give up.

Now the Devil will encourage you to quit. He will encourage you to find disappointment in people. But we are to defeat him by loving people and keeping our eyes on the Lord. That will bring victory.

Guard your faith. I don't want anything to disturb my faith in God. Just like you, I have to fight against Satan, stand against his evil designs upon my life and ministry, in order not to fail.

Guard your faith. Young people, guard yours. Mother, dad, guard your faith.

III. USE YOUR FAITH

First, build your faith. Second, guard your faith. Third, use your faith. We are saved by faith; we are to walk by faith.

1. *Use your faith though it may be small.* Jesus said, "If ye have faith as a grain of mustard seed, ye shall say unto this mountain, Remove hence to yonder place; and it shall remove; and nothing shall be impossible unto you" (Matt. 17:20). You ask, "Do you really believe that?" Certainly. "Then why don't you get something moved?" I could if I have the faith. There is no problem getting what we need if we use our faith. Though it may be ever so small—as a grain of mustard seed—use that faith and believe God. When I have used my faith, God has answered.

You say, "I have faith, but I don't remove anything." Then that is your fault, not God's. Something hinders. Get it out of the way.

2. *Use your faith though it be ridiculed.* When we walk by

faith, some will laugh at us; some will say we are off our rocker. When we walk by faith, the world will deride. This is a mean world, a cruel world. It is: "How much is it going to pay?" "What do I get out of it?" If you do not do as the world says, then "you are not doing it right." But keep on walking by faith. Though the world laughs and ridicules your efforts, still you walk by faith and keep trusting God.

I came here in 1942. In 1943 I bought an old tent from A. C. Baker in Macon, Georgia, for $1,000.00. They shipped it here. I didn't ask any questions. Later the men said they would pay for it.

We put the tent on the Highland Park school ground. A big telephone post in the middle held it up. It was cumbersome looking. The rains made holes in it, and it split wide open.

We met in the tent for every service. The crowds came. We had Jesse Hendley for an eight-day meeting. Scores and scores were saved that week.

We wanted room for all the people, so we put up the tent, though it did look terrible. I knew that. But God was blessing, and souls were being saved.

One day while walking outside the tent, I heard voices. Inside were three preachers walking through the tent and laughing, ridiculing what I had done—taking a church out of a beautiful auditorium on the corner, over to an old tent in a field.

When I heard as much as I wanted to hear, I walked inside. Things got deadly quiet. I was angry, but that anger helped— giving me determination. They could laugh all they wanted to, but I determined to go ahead doing what God had led me to do.

I kept hammering away, kept believing God, kept trusting Him, knowing He would give the victory. You folks stood with me. We went from that old tent on the school ground to an old canvas-covered tabernacle across the street (where the dining hall is now). It, too, was a mess—sawdust floor, five old pot-bellied stoves, and a canvas roof.

Then some little boy came along, took a sack, put a rock inside it, struck a match to the sack and threw it on top the canvas roof. It burned. We didn't have a roof.

But I wasn't dumb! We had insurance. We put on another roof and worshiped there for four years. We brought in great evangelists like Herbert Lockyer and Charles Taylor. We had tremendous meetings on a sawdust floor. And though it was dirty and messy inside, we were trusting God.

The world may laugh; people may ridicule, but keep on trusting God and move ahead.

They will laugh when you come to church Sunday morning, Sunday night, and Wednesday night. They will laugh when you tithe. But honor God.

I want to stay on God's side. Satan is going to fight; the world is going to ridicule, but we must stand our ground.

I rejoiced last night when I saw our boys win the basketball game, and saw the crowds of young people attending. But I thought back to our beginning in 1946.

In 1947 the Southern Baptists didn't like what we were doing, so seventeen Southern Baptist papers carried ads saying we had no business having Tennessee Temple Schools. I mean they put it right in the Southern Baptist papers. We, too, were Southern Baptists then.

Out of that condemnation, my deacons made some resolutions. I knew all the time what we would do. We would press on and do what God had led us to do. And we are still here thirty-seven years later, and growing every year. From the beginning— with nothing at all but trusting God.

The faith that God gives, use! It may be ever so small, but use it to do His bidding.

5. *Use your faith as a testimony to the grace of God.* Every day testify to God's grace. Let people see it. Don't complain. Don't fall away. Don't criticize. Don't whimper. Don't cry. Don't bellyache. Rejoice and glorify God by your simple faith.

Faith in God will give you peace. It will give you confidence and poise, power of the Holy Spirit, and compassion to love souls and see people saved.

Ask the Lord to increase your faith, to give you greater faith, stronger faith, then use that faith.

Build your faith. Guard your faith. Use your faith. Let your faith reach out to move mountains, to turn hearts toward Christ.

I picked up the newspaper this morning and read of the death of Arthur Godfrey. Things like that bother me. We build an affection for people. We listen to them. I listened to Godfrey years ago on the radio. I liked his informality, his sense of humor. Some things about his program I did not like, but I listened. I don't suppose Godfrey knew about Christ. I don't suppose he ever made a profession of faith. He said to a friend of his who writes in the morning newspaper: "Andy, I'm going to die. Damn it! I don't like it." (I'm just reading what was written in the paper.) His friend writes, who doubtless knows no more about Christ than Arthur Godfrey knew: "He died sadly, I believe, with his love of life undiminished but with few real friends left from his audience of 80 million."

It wouldn't have mattered how he died if he had died a Christian. It matters not if a man dies rich or poor if he is saved. Without that faith, there is nothing left but loneliness, desolation, darkness, despair, and suffering for eternity.

Build your faith on the Word of God. Guard your faith against Satan's onslaught. Use your faith to the greatest advantage.

48. How to Acquire a Bold Faith

✧✦✧✦✧ ✦✧✦✧ ✦✧✦✧ ✦✧✦✧ ✦✧✦✧ ✦✧✦✧ ✦✧✦✧ ✦✧✦✧ ✦✧✦

*Now when they saw the boldness of Peter and John,
and perceived that they were unlearned and ignorant
men, they marvelled; and they took knowledge of them,
that they had been with Jesus.*

—Acts 4:13.

*And now, Lord, behold their threatenings: and grant
unto thy servants, that with all boldness they may speak
thy word.*

—Vs. 29.

*And when they had prayed, the place was shaken
where they were assembled together; and they were all
filled with the Holy Ghost, and they spake the word of
God with boldness.*

—Vs. 31.

There were many noble things about Peter and John, these
early followers of our Lord.

They were without extensive education. How much they had, I
do not know, but certainly no college, or as we think of seminary
work. They were plain men who made their living on the Sea of
Galilee as fishermen. They were human and prone to mistakes.

Then came Pentecost. The Holy Spirit came upon them, filled
them, empowered them. These men became men of boldness.
Even their enemies called them bold.

In the face of acute danger, they spoke out for the Lord. They
were not ashamed of the Son of God.

When I read this, my thoughts go to the song,

Ashamed of Jesus! sooner far
Let evening blush to own a star;
He sheds the beams of light divine
O'er this benighted soul of mine.

Ashamed of Jesus! that dear Friend,
On whom my hopes of Heav'n depend?
No! when I blush be this my shame,
That I no more revere His name.

Peter and John had a bold faith. Pentecostal power was theirs. Persecution did not deter them. Prison bars did not stop them.

LET ME SUGGEST, BY WAY OF INTRODUCTION, A FEW THINGS IF YOU WOULD ACQUIRE A BOLD FAITH.

First, read. "So then faith cometh by hearing, and hearing by the word of God" (Rom. 10:17). You cannot depend on the word of men. You cannot depend on organizations. You cannot depend on governments. But you can depend on God.

So read this Word and let God speak to your heart. Get your faith from the Word.

Second, recall. Remember what God has done for you. He has saved you. He has supplied all your needs again and again. Remember, he has many times answered your prayers. Let your memory work. It was said of the early disciples in Luke 24:8, "And they remembered his words." You, too, remember the faithfulness of God.

Third, reach—reach out for all that God has for you, and do not stop reaching. Young people, do not stop. Mothers and dads, do not stop. Grandparents, do not stop. Put out your hands and say, "Lord, I'm waiting for more blessings." Reach out. He invites you to. "Ho, everyone that thirsteth, come. . ." (Isa. 55:1). Whatever your need, He invites you to bring it to Him.

Now, some people stop reading and stop reaching. They stop believing; they stop doing.

We have a wrong impression of God. Some people have a wrong idea of how to get to God, when we only need to reach out and tell Him our need. Never stop reaching.

Fourth, rest. Rest upon the promises of God. Let nothing turn you away. Listen to the Word:

"Hast thou not known? hast thou not heard, that the everlasting God, the Lord, the Creator of the ends of the earth, fainteth not, neither is weary? there is no searching of his understanding.

"He giveth power to the faint; and to them that have no might he increaseth strength.

"Even the youths shall faint and be weary, and the young men shall utterly fall:

"But they that wait upon the Lord shall renew their strength; they shall mount up with wings as eagles; they shall run, and not be weary; and they shall walk, and not faint."—Isa. 40:28-31.

Here is the promise of God: "Come and put yourself in My hands and I will take care of you." That is the building of a bold faith.

I. GOD, GIVE US A BOLD FAITH TO STAND FOR THE SON OF RIGHTEOUSNESS

In Acts 4:8-12, when Peter had to address the Sanhedrin, he exalted the Lord Jesus Christ.

WHAT DID PETER AND JOHN HAVE THAT ENABLED THEM TO BE BOLD DISCIPLES?

An experience of grace. They had come into contact with our Lord, had received Him as Saviour. They knew that they were in the family of God, knew they could talk to God in prayer.

That is the first requirement: a bold faith, resting upon that great experience of knowing you are saved.

Memory of His miraculous and courageous life. Peter and John had walked with Him, had watched Him. They had seen the miracles. They saw Him die on the cross. They saw Him buried. They saw Him resurrected. This memory enabled them to be strong, to be bold in faith, to stand and do what God wanted done.

The fullness of the Spirit. They had been filled with the Spirit on the day of Pentecost.

The fullness depends on two things: emptiness and willingness. If you would be filled with the Spirit, you must be empty of self. If you would be filled, you must be willing to do God's will.

Emptiness and willingness, they knew. They had been filled with the Spirit of God. That made the difference. It will make the difference with any and everyone.

A command to be obeyed. The Great Commission is a serious command: ". . .as my Father hath sent me, even so send I you" (John 20:21). We must go!

A testimony to be given. It was burning in their souls. They could not rest. Jeremiah, who tried to stop giving his testimony, had to declare, "His word was in my heart as a burning fire shut up in my bones, and I was weary with forebearing, and I could not stay" (Jer. 20:9).

May God give us a boldness to speak out for Christ. I love to see new Christians begin to speak for Christ at once after conversion. But sometimes they too soon fade away. I praise God for older Christians who keep on talking about Jesus, keep on pressing the need for Christ.

II. GOD, GIVE US A BOLD FAITH TO STAND FOR THE RIGHT

"Righteousness exalteth a nation: but sin is a reproach to any people."—Prov. 14:34.

1. *Stand for the right in a day of shifting standards.* This day is not the same as twenty, twenty-five, thirty, forty, fifty years ago. This is a wicked, immoral day, a day when sin is in the open and people are almost unashamed of their wickedness. But we must still stand for what is right.

2. *Stand against sin in the home.* Make up your mind once and for all: "This is it in our house. Certian things will never be allowed here." You see that no one uses profanity or even careless speech. You determine that in your home there will never be evil talking, no drinking, no drugs, no gambling. Let nothing keep your home from being what God wants it to be. You have the authority in your home, your castle.

I am ashamed of some of you mothers and dads. You come to

me with your pitiful stories. You say you can't control certain things happening in the home. You are a weakling, a baby. You have no business with a home unless you can say, "This is how we shall operate this home," and mean it. You do not have to give in to anybody. Stand for the right and be bold.

If you do not want smoking, say so. And don't allow it.

If you do not want drinking, say so. "No one is to bring any liquor into our house. We won't have any drunks around. We don't go for that. We try to have a Christian home."

If you do not want gambling, cut it out! Tell your family, "We're not going to engage in anything that's wrong."

I tell you like I told a lady on the phone who called and said, "Brother Roberson, I've got a special burden on my heart, and I want you to pray for it."

"Yes, ma'am, tell me what it is and I will pray."

"I want you to pray that I can get the beer out of my refrigerator."

I said, "What in the world, ma'am! Are you a Christian?"

"Yes, I'm saved."

"Then what in the world are you doing with beer in the refrigerator!"

"Well, my son put it there. The thing's so full I don't have any place for food. Pray that I can get it out."

I said, "I'm not going to waste one second praying for you."

I guess I was a little bit harsh. She got mad, then cried. All women do! Then she bawled. Then she got mad again. She blurted out, "I never knew a preacher like you! Imagine a man who won't pray for a poor mother who is having trouble!"

I said, "I'm not going to pray about that beer in the refrigerator. I'll tell you how to get it out. Open the door, pick up every can, carry them out into the alley, take an axe and chop them up!"

You know what she said to me on the telephone? "I couldn't do that; that would make my boy mad."

3. *Stand against sin in school.* Don't contribute to it but stand against it!

I am a little bit weary of you high school kids—in our high

school and in other high schools. Sometimes you need to stand on your two feet and declare, "This is the way I believe, and I'm not going to move or be shaken." But instead, you let the wicked crowd push you around. Why don't you take your stand and not move? But, no, you just mess around with them. You are sometimes so babyish in your actions. You act scared to death.

If you are on the Lord's side, you are somebody; and you have no reason to be afraid, whether you are in high school, college, business college or wherever it may be.

They will call you names. Don't let that bother you, just so they know what you are, and whose you are. If you are a child of God, let them know where you stand in the school.

You kids in Tennessee Temple, listen. We can have a dormitory full of kids, ninety-nine percent of whom are as honest as they can be; but let some dirty little rascal walk in the dormitory, and he has you boys afraid. Shame on you! Kick him out!

I will say the same for you girls. Ninety-nine percent of you are as fine and sweet as can be found in America. Yet you will allow some little half-wit to criticize the churches, preachers, and the Bible. When she runs off at night and goes out and acts wild, she thinks she is smart. But you tell her what you believe! You lay it down and you say, "I'm going to live right. I'm not going to do wrong things." Stand against sin.

May God give us a bold faith. When young people do wrong, stop them and say, "That is wrong. We're going to pray that you will get this straightened out." Don't write home and say, "Mama, we've got a terrible girl in our dormitory. She came in very late the other night. She does thus and so." Don't write Mama. Come to see me! We will straighten things out. We don't have that. What I say is for all of our schools.

Now stand against sin in your home, in your school—every place.

4. *Stand against sin in your business.* Don't give way to sin, wickedness, evil, and wrongdoing in the business world. Make up your mind to live for Christ and be righteous, honest, and holy no

matter where it be in the business field. If you cannot be that, then get out of it.

Some of you recall the Sunday morning years ago when one of our ushers came forward, one of our best men, asking prayer. He knelt down front in tears. After the service I brought him over to my office and asked, "Sir, what in the world is wrong with you?"

He said, "A very simple but awful thing. I have been stealing. It is not uncommon in our business—a lot of men steal; but I am a Christian. I have been stealing out of the cash register five dollars, ten dollars, fifteen dollars every day."

From my office in the Phillip's Chapel building, I dealt with him. I said, "We will call your boss." I called the boss. He sat there. I said, "Sir, I have a man sitting in my office who came forward in church this morning and confessed to stealing from your cash register."

The boss said, "I do not know of anybody doing that. What is his name?"

I gave his name.

"Why," he said, "that is one of the best men I have!"

I said, "You had better talk to him."

The usher got on the phone and said, "Sir, I have been wrong. I have been a robber, a thief. I have taken hundreds of dollars from the cash register, a little at a time. I want you to forgive me. I am a child of God, and I want to be right. I am miserable, so miserable I cannot live. I want to straighten it out."

I talked to his boss again. He agreed to keep him on. He kept him until the money was all paid back, then this member of our church volunteered to move to another city. He left Chattanooga and Highland Park Baptist Church, and went elsewhere. But I commended him for confessing his sin.

Stand against sin. Make things right. Be holy in your life.

5. *Stand against sin in your social life.* What a wicked day this is for young people! There is sin, evil of every kind. There is indecency in many places. But young people, stand! Fasten your eyes upon the Lord Jesus Christ. Have faith in Him. Please Him. Seek to so live that others can see and know that you are on the side of Christ.

Do not joke about evil. Do not laugh at dirty, evil jokes. If I happen to hear something that I do not like, I do not crack a smile. Somebody will say, "You do not think it is very funny." I say, "No, I do not." That sure does cause quietness! They don't like that. People want you to laugh at them and with them. But you stand.

Now, that is my second point. Let God give you courage to stand, a bold faith to stand amid difficulties.

III. GOD, GIVE US A BOLD FAITH TO LIVE IN PEACE

I said, "Live in peace," not in fear. Listen to the words: "Peace I leave with you, my peace I give unto you: not as the world giveth, give I unto you. Let not your heart be troubled, neither let it be afraid" (John 14:27). To the troubled disciples, Jesus said, "Fear not."

God, give us a bold faith, a faith that will give calmness in the midst of trials—money trials, family trials, health trials, or any other trial we may have to face. Faith gives calmness in the midst of these trials of life.

Have a faith that does not fail when sad news comes of the death of a loved one. Have a faith that will be with you when you yourself are facing death. It may not be far away, but keep looking to God. Have faith in God.

Have a faith that stands steadfast. When men are slipping away, when friends and loved ones slip away from the right path, let this not shake your faith. I see people such as that all the time in this church—shaken by other people's failures. Because someone else failed, they get discouraged and quit. That is certainly not God's way. When others *fail*, make up your mind to *stand*. When others fail, determine to be faithful and true to the last mile of the way.

Without faith there comes worry, weakness, uncertainty, fear and failure. With faith there comes peace, rest, direction, usefulness and power. Pray to God for a bold faith that cannot be shaken.

When people saw the boldness of Peter and John, they knew

they had been with the Lord. Have you been with Him? Have you been in touch with God? Have you let the Lord God control your life? If you will let Him, He will give you strong and courageous faith.

IV. GOD, GIVE US A BOLD FAITH TO OBEY THE SON OF GOD

"Then Peter and the other apostles answered and said, We ought to obey God rather than men."—Acts 5:29.

Obedience gives stronger faith. This matter of living right today is not easy. But if you will tithe your income faithfully and honestly, God will give you a blessing.

1. *Obey Him in the way you live.* Live a separated life. Have faith. Have a bold faith to live separated from the world. A worldly, careless life dishonors Christ and hurts others. Live to help others. "For none of us liveth to himself, and no man dieth to himself" (Rom. 14:7).

I began preaching at a church in Memphis, Tennessee. I had a good time. I preached and tried to hold up the standards. It was not too difficult.

I came to my second church up in middle Tennessee. I did not have much trouble there, either. It was very nice, and the people responded. They were separated from the world. Many of them were very good people.

But when I went out for two years in evangelism in different meetings, I saw different things.

Then forty-five years ago, God put me at the First Baptist in Fairfield, Alabama, where I stayed for five years. When I first walked in, I knew things were not right. But I knew God had put me there. The people were not responding to what I was saying.

I soon discovered that a man who led the choir (he had a beautiful tenor voice) drank liquor. He drank wine every night at his table, and on other occasions he drank. I had to go to him and say, "Sir, we cannot have that."

"Oh," he said, "I never get drunk. I just take a little sip every day. I enjoy it. It is good for me."

I said, "Sir, we cannot have that." But when he refused to quit it, I said, "You are out of a job." I got rid of him right away. It was not easy. He was popular. He was a big man, but he had to walk out. It was tough going. This standing for separation was a tough thing, but I knew I had to do it.

Soon after that I discovered something about the superintendent of the Sunday school. He was head of the whole school system of the entire city. He was educated. But in his home, they played cards. I had to go and talk to him and his wife.

He said, "Brother Roberson, we play with regular playing cards, but we are not actually gambling."

I said, "Yes, you are. And there is a shadow on your life." Young people, mothers, dads, get all the cards and burn them. I said to my superintendent, "We will have to settle this. Either you will have to quit playing cards, or give up your position in the church." When he refused, then I had to say, "You are no longer superintendent of our Sunday school."

That was not easy for a young preacher twenty-seven years old. But I had to take a stand. I had to obey.

The Sunday school which had been averaging 120, averaged 850 the last year I was there.

My dear friends, you have to obey Him in the way you live. You must have convictions and stand by those convictions.

2. *Obey Him in the matter of baptism.* Baptism is to follow salvation. If you are saved, then you are to be baptized. You need to obey the Lord in baptism. Do not question, just obey. Do what God says.

3. *Obey Him when chastening comes.* The Lord puts the rod upon us. "For whom the Lord loveth he chasteneth, and scourgeth every son whom he receiveth" (Heb. 12:6).

You might well investigate every trial of your life, then ask, "God, is this Thy chastening hand?" If it is not, He will make it known to you. And if it is, you had better do something about it.

Obey Him when the chastening comes, whether it be sickness, death, sorrow, or some conflict or something else. Stop and listen. Hear Him speak to you.

I know He has chastened me; I know that He has had to deal

with me in different ways I did not like. I do not like chastening. The Book says that it is not pleasant, but I know it is right. God has had to bring me back so I could straighten out some things in my life. Obey Him when the chastening comes.

4. *Obey Him when you are sharing the Good News of salvation.* In Acts 3, we find Peter and John going up to the Temple. When a lame man asked alms of them, Peter said, "Silver and gold have I none; but such as I have give I thee: In the name of Jesus Christ of Nazareth rise up and walk." They shared what they had with this one. God, give us a bold faith.

When threatened, the Sanhedrin "saw the boldness of Peter and John" (Acts 4:13). And in Acts 4:29 we read, ". . .now, Lord, behold their threatenings: and grant unto thy servants, that with all boldness they may speak thy word." The word "boldness" also occurs in verse 31, ". . .and they spake the word of God with boldness."

There has to be a bold faith that doesn't tremble, doesn't shake, doesn't fade in some hour of difficulty. Stand your ground.

Do not build your faith on superstition or on some talk of your ancestors or on what they did. Build your faith on the Word of God. Ask the Lord for that bold faith that will stand, a bold faith to stand for the right, a bold faith to live in peace, a bold faith to obey the Son of God.

On this past Wednesday, a tragedy happened in Birmingham, Alabama. A little nine-year-old boy came home. His mother, Mrs. Peters, had become ill; and Mr. Peters had taken her to the hospital.

The grandmother put the child in a tub of water and went to do something. When she returned, she found the little fellow had drowned. He was a beautiful child. I have his picture on my desk.

They had to carry the sad news to his mother and father at the hospital. It was very hard on them.

The parents were left alone for awhile in the room. They talked and prayed.

Later, they took the body of the boy to the funeral home. Dr. Bruce Peters, the father, walked into the room. They closed the door and left him alone with the boy. He knelt by the side of that casket and prayed.

What did he pray? I have stood beside the casket of my baby, two months old. I know how I prayed. What did he pray? Perhaps he asked, "O God, why? O God, why did this take place? Why did my baby die? O God, why?" Or, perhaps it was, "Dear God, now I am ready to do Your will, whatever it may be." Maybe God had been dealing with his heart about something. I do not know. Perhaps he said, "Dear God, now." Or maybe he prayed, "Dear God, what? What do You want me to do?" Whatever it may have been, there were questions coming from his sad heart. I'm sure there must have been a submission of his own life by the side of that casket.

My dear friends, no matter what it may be, have a bold faith, a faith that is strong enough to meet any emergency of life. You need to say tonight, "I don't know what's going to happen tomorrow. I don't know what's going to happen to my business, my home; but I want that faith in God, that bold faith! A faith that will stand every trial, every shadow, every explosion that may occur, every turn and circumstance. I want to have a faith that will stand. I want God to deal in my heart and life. I want a bold faith to live for Him."

IT IS NEVER A QUESTION WITH ANY OF US OF FAITH OR NO FAITH; THE QUESTION ALWAYS IS, "IN WHAT OR IN WHOM DO WE PUT OUR FAITH?"—Anon.

49. *Victorious Living*

Now faith is the substance of things hoped for, the evidence of things not seen.

—Hebrews 11:1.

And Jesus answering saith unto them, Have faith in God.

—Mark 11:22.

So then faith cometh by hearing, and hearing by the word of God.

—Romans 10:17.

And the apostles said unto the Lord, Increase our faith.

—Luke 17:5.

A hundred sermons could not adequately deal with this subject of victorious faith. It is by faith that we receive the gift of everlasting life and become the children of God. It is by faith that Christians live victoriously.

Illustrations of faith in action are seen in Hebrews 11. God has placed in this Hall of Fame the names of men and women of victorious faith.

Exhortations to have faith are given by the Lord Jesus. In the Sermon on the Mount, Jesus told His disciples to trust God for the needs of every day.

To a father whose son was ill, He said, ". . .If thou canst believe, all things are possible to him that believeth."

In Mark 11:22, Jesus told Simon Peter to have faith in God.

Appeals for victorious faith were often made by the powerless disciples in the hours of failure. A cry to God for living, victorious faith is going up now from many of your hearts.

The sin of unbelief and lack of faith is one that we should shun as we would a dreaded disease. Many Christians have given up everything to Christ with the exception of unbelief. May that be given up in this hour.

First, remember that it is only by faith that we are saved. Notice a few verses:

"That whosoever believeth in him should not perish, but have eternal life."—John 3:15.

"Verily, verily, I say unto you, He that heareth my word, and believeth on him that sent me, hath everlasting life, and shall not come into condemnation; but is passed from death unto life."—John 5:24.

"Therefore being justified by faith, we have peace with God through our Lord Jesus Christ."—Rom. 5:1.

"That if thou shalt confess with thy mouth the Lord Jesus, and shalt believe in thine heart that God hath raised him from the dead, thou shalt be saved."—Rom. 10:9

"For by grace are ye saved through faith; and that not of yourselves: it is the gift of God:

"Not of works, lest any man should boast."—Eph. 2:8,9.

Friend without Christ, the essentials to salvation are that you see yourself a lost sinner and see Jesus as the only Saviour. As the gift of everlasting life is offered, you are to take it by faith.

Second, remember that our lives can only be victorious through continued faith in our God. "Without faith it is impossible to please him. . . ." Whatever else we may accomplish, it will not bring pleasure to God if it is done without faith.

I. THE RESULT OF WEAK FAITH

Weak faith hinders the Lord in His working. Jesus could not accomplish much in His own town because of the unbelief of the people.

When Jesus walked upon the earth, He looked for faith; and when He found it, marvelous things happened. Blind men received their sight. The lame were made to walk. A paralytic was raised from his bed of affliction when Jesus saw the faith of the men who brought him to them.

1. *Weak faith deprives us of many great blessings.* Many of the Israelites who came out of Egypt did not enter into the Promised Land. The reason is given in Hebrews 3:19: "So we see that they could not enter in because of *unbelief.*" Lack of faith to take the Promised Land caused them to wander about almost forty years.

2. *Weak faith fills our hearts with worry and care.* This causes many Christians to have a clouded countenance. Care and worry choke the development of the spiritual life. Growth in grace is hindered by worry. The cares of home life will choke the grace of patience. The cares of business life will choke the voice of prayer. The cares of social life will choke the plant of holy separation to the Lord.

Care and worry are a direct disobedience to the Lord's Word. The command of Christ is, "Take no thought. . ." Paul said, "Be careful for nothing." Be not anxious about material affairs. Seek the kingdom of God and His righteousness and know that all things will be added to us.

Worry is a thief, stealing time which should be given to the Lord. If all the time spent in worry were given to prayer and study of the Word of God, the world would be filled with notable Christians.

Worry shuts the Lord out of our lives. We are invited to come and cast our cares upon Him. If we do not do this, then we have turned our faces away from Him, have disregarded His invitation.

3. *Weak faith deprives others of blessing.* Our lack of faith will hinder the effective working of God through us. Jesus often reproved His disciples because of their weak faith. Again and again we read of the Lord blessing others because of those who came to Him in faith.

The palsied man was healed because Jesus saw the faith of the four men who brought him to Christ.

The centurion's servant was restored because of the faith of the centurion.

The daughter of the Syrophenician woman was blessed because of the faith of her mother.

The nobleman's son was cured because of the faith of his father.

Now, since faith brings blessing, then it stands to reason that lack of faith will keep back the blessing. If we are to help others, then we must have faith in God.

II. THE RESULT OF STRONG FAITH

We have noticed what weak faith does. Now let us think of the result of the strong faith.

1. *Faith in God gives courage.* What else but faith gave Gideon courage to wage war against the Midianites with only three hundred men?

Cowardice has never accomplished anything. It dissipates our love. It kills our zeal. It cripples our testimony. It stifles our prayer life. It grieves the Holy Spirit. It cause men to disobey God.

Faith in God gives courage so that we need not be afraid of man.

2. *Faith in God gives peace.* The great goal of the average Christian is peace. We desire to be free from worry and anxious care. There is no way to have peace except through a strong faith in God.

Faith will bring a song in the darkest night. When everything seems against you, when every support has been taken away, faith will still bring peace of heart.

Faith overcomes all obstacles. We worry about many things which never come to pass. Faith in God will let us live a day at a time and peacefully trust everything into His hands.

3. *Strong faith brings to pass great things.* Yes, the Lord tells us that even the impossible can be done when we have faith. Hebrews 11 is a record of what can be done by faith.

"By faith, Abel offered unto God a more excellent sacrifice than Cain."

"By faith Enoch was translated that he should not see death."

"By faith Noah. . .prepared an ark."

"By faith Abraham. . .went out, not knowing whither he went."

By faith Moses led the children of Israel "through the Red Sea as by dry land."

"By faith the walls of Jericho fell down."

What mighty things can be accomplished when we have faith!

George Mueller is an outstanding illustration of simple, child-like faith in God. For sixty years he fed two thousand orphans without an appeal for money. He made his needs known only to God, and every need was supplied.

4. *Strong faith glorifies God.* Our heavenly Father is trustworthy. Whenever people believe Him, manifest that faith to the world, the name of the Father is glorified. A weak faith dishonors Him.

III. THE WAY TO HAVE VICTORIOUS FAITH

The way is simple. There is no magic word. There is no mystery about it.

D. L. Moody, the great evangelist, said:

> I prayed for faith and thought that some day faith would come down and strike me like lightning. But faith did not seem to come. One day I read in the 10th chapter of Romans, "So then faith cometh by hearing, and hearing by the word of God." I had closed my Bible and prayed for faith. I then opened my Bible and began to study, and faith has been growing ever since.

Know the Word of God. There is no way to build or develop a victorious faith aside from the Bible. This is God's Book, God's Word to us. The first requirement for faith is to know what He has said.

Believe the Word. Faith is taking God at His Word. If you are a doubter and a skeptic regarding the Bible, then do not expect to have any faith. All the Word must be read and believed—not a part, but all of it.

Step out on the promises. Stand on them. Rest on them. What a marvelous sensation it is when we find ourselves standing on the substantial, unchangeable promises of God!

Many months ago I visited the great Okefenokee Swamp. The Indians call it, "The land of trembling earth." I do not think that anyone would want to live in the midst of such an uncertain place. What appears to be solid ground becomes a place of death when one steps upon it.

We need have no fear as we step out upon His promises. They will not fail, will not tremble. They will hold us up.

This audience is composed of two kinds of people—the saved and the lost. There are many here who are conscious of a weak faith which has been a great handicap to your lives and has deprived you of many blessings. In some cases, although you know the Word of God, you have refused to launch out upon the promises.

Still again, there are those who have never accepted Christ as Saviour. Your great need is to have faith in His Word that He will save all who come to Him. His promise is, ". . .him that cometh to me I will in no wise cast out." In all the annals of history, never has anyone been turned away who has come to Christ in simple faith.

Will you come now?

50. Prayer, Anointing With Oil, Faith, and Divine Healing

Is any among you afflicted? let him pray. Is any merry? let him sing psalms.

Is any sick among you? let him call for the elders of the church; and let them pray over him, anointing him with oil in the name of the Lord:

And the prayer of faith shall save the sick, and the Lord shall raise him up; and if he have committed sins, they shall be forgiven him.

Confess your faults one to another, and pray one for another, that ye may be healed. The effectual fervent prayer of a righteous man availeth much.

—James 5:13-16.

Many things are more important than physical health.

It is more important to know your soul is saved and your name written in the Lamb's book of life.

It is more important to be in fellowship with Christ and walk and talk with Him daily.

It is important to live righteously so that others might see and know that you are a child of God.

It is more important to be on praying terms with God.

But physical health is important and should be considered in its proper place.

James 5:13-16 has been greatly misunderstood and misinterpreted, mainly because of failure to take the verses at face value.

Under four headings, I will summarize the thought given in these verses.

I. THE REALITY OF SICKNESS

The Bible speaks of sickness as real. We read of Jacob's sickness, the sickness of David's child, the illness of Hezekiah. In the New Testament "a certain man was sick, named Lazarus."

Christ went about healing the sick. Not once did He tell these people they weren't sick; rather He healed them of their sickness. Today we find those who say that sickness does not exist, is not real. Jesus never said that.

Paul spoke of sickness as real when he wrote regarding Epaphroditus, "For indeed he was sick nigh unto death: but God had mercy on him; and not on him only, but on me also, lest I should have sorrow upon sorrow" (Phil. 2:27).

Paul also had an infirmity of the flesh. He prayed much about it, but it was not God's will to remove it. Instead, the Lord told Paul, "My grace is sufficient for thee."

Sickness comes:

1. *From Satan.* This was true in Job's case and also with many other Christians. Satan is back of much of our sicknesses and sufferings. Christ spoke of the woman with an infirmity of eighteen years as one bound by Satan.

2. *From the natural breakdown of the body.* Sometimes this may be hastened by evil or sinful living. Yet we are declining creatures. As we grow older, the body loses its strength and becomes more susceptible to disease and weakness.

3. *From the Lord.* There are certain Bible cases which plainly say the sickness came from God. For example, Miriam was smitten by God with leprosy. David's son was smitten by the Lord. Don't forget that God can send sickness for disobedience.

II. IMPORTANCE OF PRAYER

We must note the emphasis placed by the Holy Spirit on prayer. To understand this passage, we must see that fervent, earnest prayer is the key to any healing.

Who can pray? Any child of God. James says, "Is any among you afflicted? let him pray. . . ." "Afflicted" means suffering hardship. In prayer, we find relief from afflictions, from sicknesses, from hardships.

We are to lay our burden before the Lord. This was true with Jonah when, down in the great fish's stomach, "I cried by reason of mine affliction unto the Lord, and he heard me."

In the Psalms we often find David crying to the Lord.

In the Philippian jail, Paul and Silas prayed in the midst of trouble.

Any child of God should make prayer a major part of his life.

We are exhorted to pray for self and for others. When elders of the church are called, they are to come and pray with the sick. This Scripture says we are to pray one for another.

Who are these elders mentioned by James? He seems to take for granted that every church had elders. Paul and Barnabas ordained elders in every church they established. For instance, in Titus 1:5 Paul said, "For this cause left I thee in Crete, that thou shouldest set in order the things that are wanting, and ordain elders in every city, as I had appointed thee."

In Acts 15:2 Paul and Barnabas were sent to Jerusalem to see the apostles and the elders about a matter. So it seems that the early church had pastors or bishops and elders and deacons. Today deacons take the place which seems then to have been held by elders.

An elder was experienced in things pertaining to the Lord, a person with real Christian character. We note also that "Elder" is always used in the plural form. The churches then had a number of elders in each.

The sick called for the elders to pray. The invitation was from the sick, not from elders. Notice what they were to do: ". . .let them pray over him, anointing him with oil in the name of the Lord."

The elders were not doctors; therefore, the oil was not medicine but a symbol of the Holy Spirit. Anointing was a symbolic act, such as the washing of feet in John 13, the washing of the body in Hebrews 10:22.

Now when the sick get well, who is it that does the healing? The next verse answers that: "And the prayer of faith shall save the sick, and the Lord shall raise him up. . . ." No credit given to the oil; all given to the Lord. The prayer of faith heals.

Should this be carried out today? Was this right only for the early church? There are some strong arguments that this was addressed only to the Hebrew Christians. However, I believe this word is for all people of all ages.

If today a sick person calls for elders and asks them to pray over him and anoint him with oil in the name of the Lord, it should be done. But we need to be careful to understand from whence comes the healing.

We come to a third important matter:

III. CONDITIONS LAID DOWN FOR EFFECTIVE PRAYING

1. *Faith is essential.* ". . .the prayer of faith shall save the sick. . . ." In James 1:6 we read that we are to "ask in faith, nothing wavering." The prayer of faith is the main condition required for the raising up of the sick. If there is a doubt in our faith, there will be a doubt in our healing.

2. *We must be right with others.* "Confess your faults one to another, and pray one for another, that ye may be healed." If there is to be healing, confession of sin is necessary. We cannot pray in faith as long as there is sin in our life. The Word says, "He that covereth his sins shall not prosper: but whoso confesseth and forsaketh them shall have mercy."

We are told that we must confess our sins one to another—that is, when it is between individuals. There are some sins known to the Lord alone and against Him alone; therefore, these can be confessed to Him only. But many sins are against people, so confession must be made before forgiveness is obtained. We cannot expect the blessing of God when we are harboring ill feelings toward others.

3. *Effective prayer depends much on a righteous life.* "The effectual fervent prayer of a righteous man availeth much." This verse tells us how we are to pray—fervently; this verse tells us who can offer an effectual prayer—a righteous man. James is

surely speaking of one who has been made righteous through the blood of Jesus and living a life well pleasing to Him.

To illustrate, James chose Elijah and told of his power in prayer.

"Elias was a man subject to like passions as we are, and he prayed earnestly that it might not rain: and it rained not on the earth by the space of three years and six months.

"And he prayed again, and the heaven gave rain, and the earth brought forth her fruit."

Elijah had the common faults of men, but he was righteous; he prayed earnestly, so God heard him.

Oh, that we might see the importance of prayer! Five times in these verses in James 5 prayer is mentioned and emphasized. In our extremity, we are to turn to the Lord.

Let us pray earnestly when our loved ones are sick. It is all right to see a doctor, but first ask for Divine help. Unbelievers may make their first appeal to humans, but not believers.

IV. THE LOVE AND POWER OF GOD

1. *Our Heavenly Father is concerned about us.* Doubt not for a single moment that the Lord has loving compassion for His children. "Like as a father pitieth his children, so the Lord pitieth them that fear him," says Psalm 103:13. Because of His love, we can make known to Him our every need: relief from pain, healing of body, wisdom to help us in making right decisions, courage to face a wicked world.

2. *He has the power to help us.* ". . .the Lord shall raise him up." Such power belongs only to God. Not only does He have power to raise the sick, but if that sick one has committed sins, he can receive forgiveness by God's power.

3. *He has made a way for us to come to Him.* The veil has been rent in twain, making it so we can come directly into God's presence through Jesus Christ, our High Priest, holy, harmless, undefiled and separate from sinners, now at the right hand of the

throne of the Majesty in Heaven—a High Priest touched by the feeling of our infirmities. Herein is the love of God.

Now, summing up: First, our God is interested in us, and He answers the prayer of faith. There are certain conditions to answered prayer: we must pray in faith, be right with others and live well pleasing to Him. If there is something that hinders prayer, confess it, forsake it.

But the state of your soul should be your first concern. Are you saved? This is the all-important question. If you are not, then repent of your sins and believe on Jesus Christ now.

Faith is the wire that connects you to grace, and over which grace comes streaming from God.

51. *Food, Fire and Faith*

. . . the multitude came together. . . .
—Acts 2:6.

. . . and it was noised that he was in the house. And straightway many were gathered together. . . .
—Mark 2:1,2.

The lament of pastors and churches today is about the same.
"This is a hard day in which to work."
"No lost people in the services."
"Evangelism is dead in my church."
We blame the confusion of today for our church difficulties. It is good to have something to blame it on.
What are we to do? If we are sincere, we want to reach the lost. But how?
With the message of Christ. There is no command in the Bible for the lost to come to church. They do not discern spiritual things. But Christians are commanded to go to them. We may not be received well, but our part is to GO.
By a going of the church. Next spring we are making plans for our church to sponsor tent meetings. We want one large tent up all spring and summer, then about three 40' x 60' tents. We will buy them outright, or rent them, and equip each for use in needy places.
We must go. On that we all agree. But now back to the lament—"The lost are not coming to the church services. Once they did, but not now." Now, I believe many of the lost would still come if the churches were right with God—ours and others. Face it: we are not right with God.

I. MEMBERS MUST ATTEND CHURCH

We will never get the masses coming as long as so few of our members are attending.

It has been found that in America, only eight percent attend Sunday morning church services, and only two percent at night. And in our Baptist churches, less than twenty-five percent of the members ever come inside the church. That means seventy-five percent are dead timber.

The other night at Pike Avenue we counted the members present in the last night of the revival. The building was well filled. But there were only 273 members out of 1,200 in the membership. Some special effort had been made to get them out, but less than twenty-five percent of the members, on a special night, with a special drive! Tragic!

Our own church is as bad, perhaps worse. Think what would happen were fifty percent of our members to attend. What a powerful influence we would have! You say, "If they did, there would be no place for them. And no room for visitors." Brother, we would build for larger crowds, build auditoriums large enough to challenge the membership, and large enough to care for the lost.

Members need to attend church. When great crowds of Christians start toward the house of God, the unsaved will follow. The multitudes would be coming together if we saw the importance of coming to God's house.

What is attractive to the lost in a church where only ten to twenty-five attend prayer meeting? Nothing. But they will get excited when they see friends and neighbors heading toward church. When we show as much interest and enthusiasm in attending church as we do in attending places of amusement, then the lost world is going to sit up and take notice.

II. WE MUST DEMONSTRATE THE
CHRISTIAN LIFE

Cars are sold when salesmen demonstrate. Sewing machines are sold when demonstrated. So with the vacuum cleaner. Just so, we must give a real live demonstration of what it means to be a Christian.

We need a regeneration of the church membership. Even many church members are not saved. The poor, deceived, deluded ones need Christ. They must know the meaning of repentance and faith.

We must unite on spiritual things and give a demonstration of our zeal. Show the world you mean business. Most of us follow until the way gets hard. But make a sacrifice. Oh, no! This is the day of "no sacrifice." We sing, but don't mean

> **"Jesus, I my cross have taken,**
> **All to leave and follow Thee."**

There must be a distinct difference between the Christian and the lost sinner. The lost look for it. He is not going to attend church where all the folk look, act, speak and live just as he does. He is looking for something higher, better.

There must be a demonstration of our love for the Lord and the lost.

III. OUR CHURCHES MUST CENTER AROUND CHRIST

When Christ is the central figure, we will have a repetition of that which happened in the time of Christ: ". . .and it was noised that he was in the house. And straightway many were gathered together." A great multitude came to hear and see Jesus.

The unsaved will still come if Jesus is there. He is still the world's greatest attraction. But Jesus is not present in all of our churches, nor in all of our programs. He is not present in all of our denominational "shindigs." Too much talk about the Kingdom and too little talk about the King.

Christ is hidden by formality, rituals and ceremonies. Christ is hidden by high brow music. Sometimes He is hidden by irreverence. Sometimes by degrading music.

Make Christ the center. He will attract. Centering around Christ, our churches will then be full of:

Food for hungry souls. Jesus fed the people with the bread that came down from Heaven. "This is that bread which came down from heaven: not as your fathers did eat manna, and are dead: he that eateth of this bread shall live for ever" (John 6:58).

As God gives us guidance and grace, we will want to give this life-giving bread to the lost. More than that, we will want to try to feed the Christians. We will want more Bible classes and Bible conferences.

The world is starving for the Bread of Life.

Fire of the Holy Spirit. Fire attracts. Crowds will come to see a fire. When the fire of the Holy Spirit comes upon our churches, the lost will come and something will happen.

A true New Testament church is a spiritual church, and her work is carried on by the movings of the Holy Spirit. We must follow the Holy Spirit. When anything else is substituted, then He is grieved and our churches become cold and desolate places.

Pray for spiritual fire to fall upon this church.

Faith. There will be faith when we center around Christ, a working faith, a doing faith, a faith that steps out on God's promises.

Doing things by faith may seem foolish to the lost, but even they like to see it. Men are attracted by the adventurous and the romantic. The world watches to see if we believe God. Faith is one of the most attractive things in the world.

Our business is winning souls. One soul is worth more than all the world.

52. *"Have Faith in God"*

And Jesus answering saith unto them, Have faith in God.

—Mark 11:22.

This statement of the Lord Jesus needs to be written upon all our hearts.

As we rise to face each new day, we should "have faith in God." As the day comes to a close and we review what we have tried to do, again there should be that sense of committing everything to God. Whether in sunshine or rain, it will help us to have these inspired words before us: HAVE FAITH IN GOD.

Notice that Jesus did not say, "Have faith." All about us there are would-be advisors who tell troubled people to have faith. The statement is incomplete unless it reads, "Have faith IN GOD."

I trust that in this simple message I can help you to lift up your eyes unto the Lord from whence cometh our help.

A traveller in southeastern France was told if he would climb a certain hill, he could see the Alps several miles away. He did, but could see nothing but the mists rising from the plains below. Then someone said, "Look higher." He did so, and towering within his delighted vision were the snow-white peaks.

Let us, too, heed such a command and look higher unto the hills and beyond for our help.

Faith is made up of belief and trust. Many people believe God, but they do not trust themselves into His keeping and care; consequently, they are filled with worry and fear.

Worry is nothing but practical infidelity. The person who worries reveals his lack of trust in God and that he is trusting too much in self.

Let us learn today that in all true faith there is complete committal to God.

This story illustrates our need of committal.

A party of visitors going through the national mint was told by a workman in the smelting works that if the hand were dipped in water, the ladle would pour its contents over the palm without burning it. "Perhaps you would like to try it," said the workman to a man standing nearby.

The gentleman said, shrinking back, "No, thank you. I prefer to take your word for it."

Then turning to the man's wife, he said, "Perhaps, madam, you would like to make the experiment."

"Certainly," she replied. And suiting the action to the word, she bared her arm, thrust her hand into a bucket of water, and calmly held it out while the metal was poured over it.

Turning to the man, the workman quietly said, "You, sir, believed, but your wife trusted."

Now, let us consider this text in the light of God's past performances and His promises for today and the future.

I. HE DID NOT FAIL MEN IN OLDEN DAYS

Sacred history points out to us that no man who had faith in God was ever disappointed.

Turn to Hebrews 11—the great faith chapter. That word "faith" occurs some twenty-five times in this chapter alone. Some seventeen people are mentioned as examples of what faith in God accomplished. I wish that we had time to consider every one of these names in God's "Hall of Fame."

In Abel, we have the worship of faith.

In Enoch, the walk of faith.

In Noah, the witness of faith.

In Abraham, the wandering of faith.

In Sarah, the waiting of faith.

In Moses, the work of faith.

In verse 32, we have the success of faith as exemplified in Gideon's life. The song of faith given us by Barak, the supplications of faith by David, the sweet singer of Israel, and the singleness of faith as made known in Samuel. Through flood and fire, stones and swords, destitution and death, affliction and torment, God delivered His people.

I like to read about Elijah and his faith. First, God answered his prayer and brought fire from Heaven, consuming an altar of wood, stone, sacrifice and water, then answered his faith by sending a downpour of rain upon a parched and destitute country.

What a joy to read about Daniel, a young man whose faith towered above all others, just as Mt. Everest towers above all other mountains in the world. Nothing was able to daunt the faith of Daniel. The threatening of an enemy could not shake him; the prospect of the lion's den did not move him from his course. Daniel had faith in God. Sacred history records that God did not fail him.

Nothing but encouragement can come to us as we dwell upon the faithful dealing of our Heavenly Father in centuries gone by. Faith in God has not saved people from hardships and trials, but it has enabled them to bear tribulations courageously and to emerge victoriously.

Foxe's Book of Martyrs tell us that men and women with faith in God faced every conceivable torment and death without faltering. In the early centuries when persecution was meted out without mercy, men were known to sing and smile as the fires consumed their bodies.

Doesn't your very heart burn to have such faith in God as the spiritual giants of the olden days had?

II. HE IS ABLE TO WORK MIRACLES TODAY

Let us read the verses which follow our text:

"Have faith in God,

"For verily I say unto you, That whosoever shall say unto this mountain, Be thou removed, and be thou cast into the sea; and shall not doubt in his heart, but shall believe that those things which he saith shall come to pass; he shall have whatsoever he saith.

"Therefore I say unto you, What things soever ye desire, when ye pray, believe that ye receive them, and ye shall have them."— Mark 11:22-24.

These words are shocking to our modern, materialistic minds; but Jesus said what He meant and meant what He said. Nowhere in this Bible do we find a statement cancelling this prayer promise. On the other hand, the Bible is full of promises supporting this statement by Jesus.

When George Mueller began his mighty work of prayer, he based his faith upon this promise. At first he prayed, then waited for God's answer, then gave thanks. But as he read and re-read these words, "What things soever ye desire, when ye pray, believe that ye receive them, and ye shall have them," he began thanking God for His answer even at the time the request was made. If we pray in faith believing, this is as it should be.

It gives me unusual joy to shout out these words, "God answers prayer!"

This is a faithless old world. Men and women are hardheaded, pleasure-mad, money crazy. They write up their successes and say, "The power and might of my hand have done these things." God has been ruled out; consequently, the thrill and romance of true living are gone for most people.

If you are a child of God, know that every promise in the Bible is yours. The Bible is a gold mine, waiting for someone to take out its riches.

Most of us are too much like the woman who received a letter, but in her distress, went to a friend to try to secure some money before opening it. The friend said, "Why, I sent you money yesterday!" "Dear, dear," replied the poor soul, "that must be the letter I put behind the looking glass."

There are people putting God's letter to mankind in some hiding place and failing to make use of the promises meant for them.

What is your need? Take it to the Lord in prayer.

III. HE WILL TAKE CARE OF THE FUTURE

A Salvation Army girl said, "I don't know what's in the future, but I know the Lord is, and I know I am in Him."

It is true that most of our worries are about things that never happen. We anticipate trouble. We cross bridges before we get to them. We spend sleepless nights thinking about things which will likely never come to pass. People become chronic worriers. Even Christians worry until it becomes a habit.

Are you worried about the future? Then listen to these Scriptures.

"Commit thy way unto the Lord; trust also in him; and he shall bring it to pass."—Ps. 37:5.

Are you a Christian, yet worry about provisions for the future? Then hear these words of the psalmist:

"I have been young, and now am old; yet have I not seen the righteous forsaken, nor his seed begging bread."—Ps. 37:25.

Jesus said,

"Therefore I say unto you, Take no thought for your life, what ye shall eat, or what ye shall drink; nor yet for your body, what ye shall put on. Is not life more than meat, and the body than raiment?

"Behold the fowls of the air: for they sow not, neither do they reap, not gather into barns; yet your heavenly Father feedeth them. Are ye not much better than they?"—Matt. 6:25,26.

Paul says to us,

"Be careful for nothing; but in every thing by prayer and supplication with thanksgiving let your requests be made known unto God.

"And the peace of God, which passeth all understanding, shall keep your hearts and minds through Christ Jesus. . . . But my

God shall supply all your need according to his riches in glory by Christ Jesus.''—Phil. 4:6,7,19.

Another kind of faith that I want to tell you about today is saving faith. Without this saving faith, man looks into the future and cries, "Where will I spend eternity?" Without saving faith, all that I have said this evening avails nothing.

What is this faith that is the foundation of time and eternity? It is faith in Christ, God's Son. Phillips Brooks' definition of faith has been helpful to many people: F-A-I-T-H means Forsaking All, I Take Him.

Yes, to be saved there must be an acceptance of Jesus and a committing of oneself to Him. This done, salvation is sure and eternity is settled. We can then say with the Apostle Paul, "I know whom I have believed, and am persuaded that he is able to keep that which I have committed unto him against that day."

The blessed thing about this salvation is that we can have it at the very moment we receive the Lord Jesus. After possessing it, fear of a dark future is taken away and peace comes in.

When Cannon Wilberforce was in this country, he told how a miner, having heard the Gospel, determined that if it promised his immediate salvation, he would not leave the presence of the preacher until he was in possession of that salvation.

After the meeting was over, he addressed the minister in his rude speech, "Didn't ye say I could have the blessing now?"

"Yes, my friend," answered the preacher.

"Then pray with me now, for I'm not going away without it."

And they did pray, both the minister and the man. Waiting before God until the miner heard silent words from the still small voice of the Spirit and knew that he was saved. Then he started up, saying, "I have got it now!" His face was all aglow as he repeated, "I have got it now!"

The next day a terrible accident occurred in the mines. When the preacher reached the scene, the dead and dying were on every side. Searching among them, he came upon this big, brawny fellow whom he had seen the night before. He was dying, also. But when he recognized the minister, his eyes flashed with their new light as he said, "Oh, I don't mind to die, for I have got it! I have got it! It is mine!"

Friend, is salvation yours today? If not, make up your mind that you will not leave this building until you know Christ as your own personal Saviour.

If you stand on the mountain of faith and look down, things will seem easy to you; but if you are in the valley of doubt, they will look like giants. What the church wants and what it is looking for are men and women of faith. —Moody.

53. *Famous for Your Faith*

For from you sounded out the word of the Lord not only in Macedonia and Achaia, but also in every place your faith to God-ward is spread abroad; so that we need not to speak any thing.

For they themselves shew of us what manner of entering in we had unto you, and how ye turned to God from idols to serve the living and true God;

And to wait for his Son from heaven, whom he raised from the dead, even Jesus, which delivered us from the wrath to come.

— I Thessalonians 1:8-10.

Now faith is the substance of things hoped for, the evidence of things not seen.

—Hebrews 11:1.

"By faith Abel. . . ."
"By faith Enoch. . . ."
"By faith Noah. . . ."
"By faith Abraham. . . ."

I have a beautiful five-page letter from a friend in another state. A mother is writing about her daughter and her husband who are here in school. The young couple has been living by faith and believing God. The husband is out of work, so the letter says. His wife is five months pregnant. They are often without electricity or gas or food.

The mother writes, "We found them walking close to the Lord and in no mental stress. Their faith was strong. We helped them all we could; so did the young husband's parents. They give and give and keep on giving."

When both sets of parents endeavor to help them, they reply, "The Lord will take care of us." The mother wants me to show them that they are wrong, but I can't do that. Now the mother closed the letter by saying, "We're the ones in mental stress because of this situation."

Congratulations to that young couple! For many years I have been preaching on living by faith. If some of you don't believe one can live by faith, that is your loss. This couple believes it.

What is my opinion of these young people she mentioned?

First, I'll risk my life, my reputation and all I have *they will never starve.* Yes—they are giving a lot, and the mother is upset about it. She sends them money; they give it away, trusting God. I know you are saying they don't use good sense. I am saying they will never starve to death.

Then, by trusting God, they are helping others who are obsessed by THINGS.

Next, they will be used of God mightily to glorify Him. God will not forsake His own.

He wrote to the church in Thessalonica to congratulate them on their faith, saying, ". . .your faith to God-ward is spread abroad." Others talked about their faith.

If you recall, the Thessalonian church began in the face of furious opposition (Acts 17). A few were converted under Paul's preaching; but Paul and Silas had to leave there by night and go to other places, such as Berea, Athens and Corinth.

This church was, doubtless, small. Even when Paul wrote the letter, perhaps there was only a handful in the church. No Sunday school building, no office staff—nothing. They may have had a handful of books.

Then it was a sorrowing church. They had lost loved ones, and they were looking for the coming of the Lord. They felt that perhaps Paul had missed something somewhere. They thought the Lord was coming and they wouldn't die. But they did die. So Paul wrote his letter to them, inspired by the Holy Spirit, to show that the Lord is coming.

Read I Thessalonians 4:13-18 which tells of the second coming, how the dead in Christ will be raised and how the living will be changed. This was written to comfort those of Thessalonica and us. Paul admonished them not to worry.

It is evident it was a hungry church, hungry for the way of God.

One more thing: they were the object of Paul's affection and concern. Look in chapter 5, verses 6 to 8:

"Therefore let us not sleep, as do others; but let us watch and be sober.

"For they that sleep sleep in the night; and they that be drunken are drunken in the night.

"But let us, who are of the day, be sober, putting on the breastplate of faith and love; and for an helmet, the hope of salvation."

Then we read:

"Rejoice evermore. Pray without ceasing. In every thing give thanks. . . . Quench not the Spirit. Prove all things; hold fast that which is good. Abstain from all appearance of evil."—Vss. 16, 19, 21, 22.

Because of the apostle's love for them, he wanted to encourage them in every way he could.

These folks in Thessalonica were famous for their faith.

In Hebrews 11 we have the Westminster Abbey of Faith. It says of these men: "By faith. . .by faith. . .by faith." Here is the parade of God's faithful as they moved on.

SOME PEOPLE ARE FAMOUS FOR DIFFERENT THINGS.

Some are famous for their sin. We have too long glorified the sinner. There are those who boast and brag about stars in Hollywood who are deep in sin, immoral in life, drunkards, and unfaithful. Some even glorify the fact of their sin.

When in Jacksonville, Florida, a few weeks ago, someone gave me a clipping which told of a certain famous eating place and how the food is served in an atmosphere of sin. You can guess what type place that is, but it was advertised in the paper.

Some are famous for their foul speech, speaking evil, dirty, filthy words. Some men have even been so foolish, so infantile as to brag about their profanity! How dumb can one get!

Some are famous for their boasting, their lying. It becomes a part of their lives.

Some are famous for their procrastination, delaying, putting off until tomorrow or next week or next year. This type never accomplishes anything.

Some are famous for their cheating. Sometimes it is open; sometimes it is subtle, covered.

Some are famous for gossip, always ready to relate some story which might hurt another.

Some are famous for their criticism. Anyone can criticize.

Some are famous for their doubts, doubting anybody and everything.

But see the story of these people famous for their faith. To me, the dear young folk in this letter I mentioned are famous—famous for their faith in God, for their trust in God, for believing God.

Oh, determine tonight not to be famous because of having money or a big reputation or popularity. But determine to be famous for your faith in God.

I. MAY YOUR FAITH SHINE WHEN THE
NIGHT IS DARKEST

These Thessalonians had had adversity, trouble; yet they kept on shining.

The shadows may come, but let your faith keep on glowing. When others are failing and dropping by the wayside, let your faith continue bright and shining and glowing.

To these Thessalonians, Paul wrote, 'I know you have had trouble, but your faith is still shining. Everywhere people talk about you.'

That was also true of these valiant ones of Hebrews 11. In spite of dark shadows, they kept on shining. Their faith kept on showing. They were graduates of University of Hard Knocks—Abel, Enoch, Noah, Abraham, Isaac, Jacob, Joseph and Moses.

Oh, let your faith shine!

Let your faith be steadfast—in season, out of season.

Let your faith be seen—don't hide it under a bushel. Let not modesty hold you back. Let people know of your faith, why you believe God, why you trust Him.

Let your faith help others—reaching out to those all around you.

II. MAY YOUR FAITH SHAPE YOUR LIFE

Some people believe in God, believe in Christ, believe the Bible, yet remain babes in Christ. They never grow. They stay the same size. They never develop. Let faith shape your life.

1. *Let faith shape your giving.* I like what the mother said in her letter: "They give and give and give." We can't say that of many, can we? Most give when driven to give. Most give when embarrassed into giving. The young people tithe and go beyond their tithe.

Be a tither, yes—but more. Let faith direct your giving.

It is strange how we work. Here in this church there is a big difference in your giving a dollar and five dollars, or five dollars and ten dollars, or ten dollars and twenty dollars. But newspapers don't talk in terms of dollars but in terms of billions. If America is in debt, she is in debt billions of dollars. This year we can add billions more to those billions. Next year billions more. Government deals in BIG figures.

I read about an astronaut carrying a golf ball on his historic journey to the moon! He took the golf ball for a tee shot on the lunar surface!

A statistician toying with numbers came up with a bit of information that made the news. Analyzing the weight of a golf ball against the total cost of the mission, he calculated the cost of transporting that ball to the moon was forty thousand dollars!

Giving is important. Everyone should give to the Lord. Everyone should be a tither, then giving, as God directs, above the tithe.

2. *Let faith in God direct your separation from the world.* Live a separated life because you believe God, because you are not afraid to stand for God, for you know God will stand with you.

Being a separated Christian frightens some, even frightens some pastors. One pastor told me point blank, "Brother Roberson, I would not dare—I would be afraid to say in my church what you say and do in your church." When I asked, "Why?" he said his people didn't believe in separation: in appearance, in dress, in actions, and so on. He was frank to say, "I'd be afraid to come out against these things."

Faith must direct your separation. Be bold in your stand, knowing God will be with you and direct you.

3. *By faith get a vision of a lost world.* Such a vision will affect your prayer life, will change your habit of giving; and it may call you out to some foreign field.

These are simple things; I pray your faith will shape your life.

Selfishness shapes a lot of lives. It causes one to do certain things. Buying a home, or clothing, or a car, or eating a meal, or whatever it may be—all enter into the realm of selfishness.

Faith guides and shapes our lives without regrets, without excuse, without rebellion.

III. MAY YOURS BE A FAITH THAT SPEAKS

Among the seven deacons in the early church was a man named Philip. In Acts 8:5 we read, "Then Philip went down to the city of Samaria, and preached Christ unto them." Then he went to the desert country and led a man of Ethiopia to Jesus. Philip, a quiet deacon humbly speaking of Christ.

Let yours be a faith that speaks, whatever may be your position in church: Sunday school teacher, BTU leader, deacon, usher, choir member, orchestra member. Remember—you will do your best when you have faith in God, when you feel God standing near. Then you can share that faith by telling others what Christ means to you, what He has done for you.

Share with others. Does your life reach out to others? That's why Camp Joy. That's why our Union Gospel Mission. That's why our 45 chapels. In everything we try to share what we have.

This week I read a beautiful story about a boy who got in trouble. He stole a car. The police caught him. He was standing before the judge awaiting sentence. A picture of the courtroom and the judge on the stand was shown. The lawyers were there, along with his parents and others. The mother was crying. Her boy had failed.

The attorney stood up and testified that the boy was a nuisance to the community. Then the judge, cold-eyed, looked down upon the boy and spoke harshly. The boy stood there without a single motion—rebellious. Finally the judge spoke. "I think I'll give you six months in reform school."

The boy answered back, "Sure, go ahead. Do whatever you want to"—that rebellious attitude.

An officer standing by said, "He's hopeless." Another said, "He needs a horse-whipping."

The judge on the bench was cold in spirit about the whole ordeal. Looking out over the courtroom, he saw a man by the name of Mr. Weston, known for what he had done to help others. His faith had gone out like these people of Thessalonica. When the judge saw Weston, he asked, "Mr. Weston, what do you think about this boy?"

This quiet, dignified, Christian gentleman walked to the front and answered, "Judge, that boy isn't tough. He's just scared. Judge, that boy's not mean like you say. Oh, he's got a bad streak in him, but he's scared half to death. He needs help. If he had a chance—just a little chance; if he had a friend—someone to stand by him, someone to give just a little opportunity to develop what he's got—he could amount to something."

As Mr. Weston talked, the people listened intently. When he got through, the courtroom was quiet. All of a sudden there was a stifled sob. All looked around. This time it was not the mother but the boy. He had bowed his head where he had been standing so rebelliously; and at the kind words by Mr. Weston, he began to cry like a baby.

The judge said, "Mr. Weston, you think you can help him?"

"Sir, I'll do my best."

This good man put him in a home where he could care for and

watch over him. The story goes that the lad of sixteen grew to be a fine, stalwart Christian, led to the Lord by Mr. Weston and directed by him along the way.

Wait a minute! That led me to think of this matter of our faith in God and showing forth that faith. I've had some of you to ask, "The money we spend in running a downtown mission and having a building and fixing it up—is it worthwhile?"

Worthwhile if just one soul gets saved!

We have Camp Joy and three thousand kids. Many thousands of dollars have been spent there every summer since 1946. Is it worthwhile?

Worthwhile if just one boy is saved—if he is your boy, or my boy.

Everything we do has to come back to this.

Give expression to your faith by your living. If almost every one else on the plane is drinking liquor, I'll continue to sit there with open Bible, studying or praying, giving my testimony.

Someone is watching you and me. We must give expression of our faith in our living. Live a clean, growing, fruitful life.

Give expression of faith in waiting for His coming. "Be patient therefore, brethren, unto the coming of the Lord" (James 5:7).

Give expression to your faith in witnessing. This is the greatest single need of our churches today. Let ours be a witnessing faith.

Ask God to increase your faith.

O God, help me to be famous for my faith in the eternal, loving God!

54. *A Demonstration of Faith, Love and Obedience*

And all the tithe of the land, whether of the seed of the land, or of the fruit of the tree, is the Lord's: it is holy unto the Lord.

—Leviticus 27:30.

Thou shalt truly tithe all the increase of thy seed, that the field bringeth forth year by year.

And thou shalt eat before the Lord thy God, in the place which he shall choose to place his name there, and tithe of thy corn, of thy wine, and of thine oil, and the firstlings of thy herds and of thy flocks; that thou mayest learn to fear the Lord thy God always.

—Deuteronomy 14:22,23.

Bring ye all the tithes into the storehouse, that there may be meat in mine house, and prove me now herewith, saith the Lord of hosts, if I will not open you the windows of heaven, and pour you out a blessing, that there shall not be room enough to receive it.

—Malachi 3:10.

Woe unto you, scribes and Pharisees, hypocrites! for ye pay tithe of mint and anise and cummin, and have omitted the weightier matters of the law, judgment, mercy, and faith: these ought ye to have done, and not to leave the other undone.

—Matthew 23:23.

We're beginning today a week of emphasis on faith, love and obedience. We will pray that this thought for these days will stir the hearts of our people. And we need stirring.

We pray that this demonstration will be of such sincerity and meaning that it will stand at the judgment seat, when one day we give an account of ourselves to Him.

We pray that this heart-felt demonstration will speak to a lost world and will show our love for Christ and lost men.

The Lord touches every part of our lives. Our homes—husband, wife, children—all should be directed by the Saviour.

Our civic life is touched by the Lord. The problem is, men try to conduct government affairs without God's leading and help.

Our business life is touched by Christ. The Lord shows us that all is sacred—home life, civic life, business life.

Our giving is directed by the Lord. Giving is God's way of conducting His work. Our Lord tells us to:

"Bring ye all the tithes into the storehouse, that there may be meat in mine house, and prove me now herewith, saith the Lord of hosts, if I will not open you the windows of heaven, and pour you out a blessing, that there shall not be room enough to receive it."—Mal. 3:10.

This is God's way for you and for me. If church members tithe, then everything can be handled right, both at home and abroad.

In our mission work, tithing is the right way. The Bible asks, "Will a man rob God? Yet ye have robbed me. But ye say, Wherein have we robbed thee? In tithes and offerings." A nontither has robbed God!

One very wealthy man, a good man, said, "I cannot give my tithe to my church. It is not doing all I think it should be doing. I give the church a certain number of dollars, but the rest I put where I want to." No! I believe a tither is to tithe into his local church. Though the local church may not always be right, it is still the honest way for you and me, and should have been for that man.

Why did I mention this fellow and his giving? Because of this: he has passed away now, and his business is suffering great loss. I believe the suffering is because of his failure to be honest with God when he was still living.

The simple, loving way is to bring the tithes every Lord's Day. By this God-given plan all needs are supplied.

Tithing proves we are trusting God, proves that when God speaks, we are willing to obey. It means we believe Him and know He will supply our needs.

Tithing proves that we are grateful. God has given each of us so much. How can we not express our gratitude for all He has done! For these marvelous, magnificent gifts from God daily— salvation, life, peace, joy, direction, the indwelling Holy Spirit, the promise of Heaven, the second coming—are we grateful?

Dr. Angel said he had a very fine man in his church one time who took jobs just anywhere, did anything he was called on to do. Usher, teach a class, visit people—always busy was this man. Dr. Angel was surprised at the way he worked and how willing he was to do anything.

One day Dr. Angel stopped him and said, "Sir, I want to thank you for the way you work and how willing you are to do anything."

The man replied, "Please, Sir, don't thank me. I'm serving God out of gratitude. One day my little girl became sick, and the doctor informed us she couldn't live. I went aside and prayed for the healing of my daughter. God healed her! And the Lord has let me have her for all this time. I told Him I would do anything He asked, serve Him in every way I could. I'm just keeping my promise."

Tithing proves our concern for others. By tithing I have a part in 544 missionaries stationed in every part of the world; in works all over this city; I have a part in this church, the mission downtown, the 45 chapels, Camp Joy. My tithe has a part in all that. Your tithe has a part in all that.

God blesses us and will keep on blessing us when we stay concerned for His business.

A small church out in Texas started out with big problems. They had a building and some land they couldn't pay for. They had big troubles.

After awhile they started to declare bankruptcy to see if they could get out of it and turn it back to somebody else. But one of the deacons said, "Friends, we are going the wrong direction. If we will begin now to give emphasis to the tithe and to missions, God will take care of our needs."

Taking his advice, they enlarged their missionary work. Today that church is giving more than two and a half million dollars per year to the cause of Christ, and much of it goes to missions! It is now a big and great church.

God blesses when we do right about giving.

I. TITHING DEMONSTRATES OUR FAITH

By tithing we show our faith week by week. By tithing we are showing we have faith in God, our Father, and the Lord Jesus Christ, our Saviour.

It is by faith we are saved. It is by faith that we are stabilized. It is by faith that our hearts are satisfied.

Tithing is a concrete demonstration of our faith in God.

I began tithing at age eighteen. I would have started sooner had I been taught to. At this age I was called to preach, so I began to do some studying. It was then that I discovered the Bible teaching about tithing and decided it was for me. I wanted to do that for the rest of my life. I began before I read any books on it. I knew what the Bible had to say, and I knew what I wanted to do. God has supplied. He has kept His promise to supply my every need.

Tithing is a demonstration of our faith in God.

When I went to my first church in Germantown, Tennessee, my total salary was fifty dollars a month. Two millionaires were in the church. One sat on one side, one on the other. They each give fifty dollars a year! But I was a tither and gave my tithe every Lord's day.

I drove an old Ford car that would barely get through the streets of Memphis. I told the Lord, "Lord, unless some miracle happens, this car is not going to make it."

I had a little room in the attic in a home on Snowdon Circle which cost me then only a few pennies a week. However, I was having trouble. I told the Lord my problems, but I said, "Lord,

You know I am a tither. And You know I am going to continue to trust You."

The next morning after I had prayed, I started out the door, and stuck under it was a white envelope. I picked it up. It was sealed. Nothing was written on the outside. I walked out in the hallway, held it up and asked, "Did somebody lose this?" Nobody said anything. I said to myself, *Then it must be mine.*

I walked back in the room and opened it. There was a dollar bill. Then a dollar looked like a thousand. I thanked the Lord and told Him, "I'll take out my tithe and use the rest."

I tell people that I ate all my meals in the White Hamburger Stand! They were 5¢ each. That day I ate two!

But wait a minute! Just the fact of that envelope coming under the door established my faith. I knew the Lord was answering prayer and supplying my needs.

For nineteen mornings in a row I picked up the dollar from under the door. I didn't bother again to go out in the hall to ask if anybody had lost it! It was under my door!

Wanting to find who was doing this good deed, I put a little trap up to the door and thought, *When somebody touches the door, it will shake the trap and that will wake me. I can then see who is placing that dollar there.*

At two o'clock in the morning I heard a noise, jumped up and opened the door. A little lady, Mrs. Kate Barker whom I didn't know then, was standing at the door with envelope in hand. She said, "Son, here's your money. And if you ever tell a soul about this, I'll never give you another penny."

Mrs. Barker was the wife of Judge Henry Barker, the president of the University of Kentucky. She knew of my need and wanted to help me. That dollar a night helped me in many ways for a number of years, when the going was rough.

Mrs. Barker was doing what God told her to do. And I was the recipient of that leading. God had promised to take care of all my needs. He will take care of yours, too.

Tithing is a demonstration of our faith in God.

After I married, I took my first church in Birmingham, Alabama. This was in the Depression days. We were having it a little hard. Actually, we didn't have any money; and I was paid a very small salary.

When we came down to not having a penny, I said, "We will have to do something." Unwisely I said to my wife, "We will go downtown and check with a loan office to see if we can borrow some."

We went downtown. I walked up to the counter. In the back stood the operator of the loan office. I tapped on the counter but he paid me no attention.

As I walked away, I said, "I'm not going to ask for a penny. I'd rather starve. I will trust God!"

We drove back home and looked in the mailbox. There was a check, a check that we had never expected. God sent it. I've never faltered another day!

I am saying that tithing is a demonstration of our faith. "Have faith in God."

II. TITHING DEMONSTRATES OUR LOVE

We know that God loves us.

"For God so loved the world. . . ."—John 3:16.

"But God commendeth his love toward us, in that, while we were yet sinners, Christ died for us."—Rom. 5:8.

God loved us so much that He gave His Son to die for us. Christ loved us and left Heaven's glory to die on the cross. The Word of God is established.

What can I do to show my love? I can read my Bible. I can be faithful in church attendance. I can pray, looking to God for all my needs. I can witness for Him. I can give to His work, giving my tithes and offerings that the Gospel might be sent out to others. What a glorious, happy thought that we can give and know that around the world people hear the Gospel because of it.

Rejoice that you belong to a church that reaches out to the whole world. Give with enthusiasm and joy, knowing God will take care of your needs. Tithing is our expression of love.

Somebody said we ought to express ourselves with enthusiasm.

I believe we ought to give, as well as sing and preach and pray, with enthusiasm and love.

I was reading about Sam Scantlan, who was saved in his twenties. He felt God wanted him to preach, so he went to high school for the first time at age twenty-eight, finished, then went on to college. Then he became an outstanding pastor in an Oklahoma town. He was head of a mission program in his state for about twenty-five years.

At seventy he was made president of the whole State Convention. Now at seventy-nine he is pastor of a big, thriving, country church in that state. Sam Scantlan, a man of faith and enthusiasm, believing and trusting God!

While Sam was walking down the street one day, he saw a little fellow selling newspapers. He was standing there rather meekly, not saying much, just motioning to the people to buy a newspaper.

Sam watched, then walked up and took all the papers from the boy, got in the middle of the street and began shouting, "PAPER!" and calling out the headline. "HERE—GET YOUR PAPER—NOW!" Sam sold every one in just a few minutes.

After he had made his last sale, he walked to the boy, handed him the money with this admonishment: "Son, whatever your hand finds to do, do it with all your might! Put enthusiasm into what you do!"

I doubt that boy ever forgot that. And what a good lesson for us all!

Tithing demonstrates our love. And if we love God wholeheartedly and with enthusiasm, we will want to serve Him with our tithe. It may be a penny a week, or a thousand dollars. Every person can be a tither, even if it is just 5¢ or $500.00. Enter into your giving with enthusiasm!

Now some things we do are not wise. For example:

When I was pastor in Germantown, I was paid fifty dollars a month, as I have already mentioned. When I got there, I found that the former pastor had not received his salary for three months. He, too, had gotten fifty dollars a month. Now they owed him $150.00. They said to me, "You will not get your money until he gets his."

That bothered me. He had to have his pay before I could get any of my fifty dollars a month. And I was just beginning my pastorate there and was in great need.

Seeing my predicament, they said, "We will help you out a little. We have decided to put on a womanless wedding. (I had never heard of such a thing!) We will charge 15¢ a person. We will have it in the high school uptown. We will make some money for you this way."

They advertised it well.

Now a womanless wedding is just that. No women—all men, all dressed like women. The bride—a man dressed like a woman. The bridesmaids—men dressed like women.

I never thought much about it, except "it will pay that fellow's salary and I will get mine." So I was in favor of it!

The night came for the big womanless wedding in Germantown, Tennessee. I will never forget it. I walked in the back door of the schoolhouse to see the performance. I didn't have to pay the 15¢; they let me in free. But as I came in the door they said, "Pastor, we want you to take part in this."

I said, "Not on your life! I'm not getting into a thing like this!"

"You've got to. Either you participate or we won't be able to pay your salary."

"Well," I said, "in that case I'll consider it."

I was led inside. You would not have believed it! They said, "Put on this dress." I weighed a little more than 200 pounds then.

I said, "Nothing doing!"

"Either that or you don't get paid."

After I got the thing on, I was told, "Now go out there and play the piano." (Back then I did play the piano, but I quit playing about fifty years ago.)

With a dress on, I, the pastor, walked in for a womanless wedding to a packed schoolhouse. The bridal party was ready to march in. I played, "Tramp, Tramp, Tramp, the Boys Are

Marching," as they came down!—the only thing I could think of, and I played it loud, in the key of B flat.

They performed the wedding. At the Recessional I played what I thought of: "The Fight Is On," in the key of C!

I told you this just to show you that this is not God's way of doing God's business. That was of the world, and it was wrong. God's way to raise money is by tithing. And the tithing way is the way of love.

III. TITHING DEMONSTRATES OUR OBEDIENCE

Faith, love and obedience—a demonstration to our God. "To obey is better than sacrifice," says I Samuel 15:22. And Acts 5:29 tells us, "We ought to obey God rather than men." We are to give our love and devotion to Him only. "No man can serve two masters. . . ."

This means uniting with a New Testament church. We are to go where we can best serve God, such as a church like this which stands for the fundamentals and preaches and teaches the Truth, and sends missionaries around the world.

This means following Christ in believer's baptism. If you are saved and have never been baptized, then don't let another day go by without settling this. Obey the Lord!

This means studying the Word.

This means attending services of the church.

This means being faithful in your giving.

Demonstrate your *faith* in God; your *love* for God; your *obedience* to God.

We had in our church years ago one of the best men I have ever known. He is now with the Lord. This gracious, good man would be known to ninety percent of you here, were I to call his name.

One Sunday morning there came a knock at the door of my office just before church time. I went to the door, and there stood this man in tears. I asked, "Sir, what in the world is wrong?" (I thought there may have been a death in the family.)

He told me this:

Brother Roberson, I've been a liar and a cheat. I promised

God I would tithe. But six months ago I decided the church didn't need my money, so I quit tithing. I kept it in a separate bank account thinking I would use it for something else besides giving it to this church. Here I was, working as an usher and known to all the people, keeping back the tithe and failing God.

Now for six months I haven't prayed a single prayer. I lost my prayer life when I lied to God and began to cheat God. I haven't any joy in reading the Bible. I haven't tried to witness because I am so ashamed.

I have discovered what is wrong, and I have asked God to correct it. Here is my tithe.

He pulled out his check and said, "That will cover those six months. I want to apologize to you and to my church."

I said, "God bless your heart! That is between you and God. I'll not say a thing about this." I put the check in the offering. That dear man then was faithful to God through the rest of his life. It wasn't long before he died. He asked me to come to see him. The one question he asked me was, "Have you forgiven me?"

I said, "Why, certainly, Sir. That wasn't in my line anyway. That was between you and God."

"But," he said, "I failed." It had made that much of an impression on his mind and heart.

O my dear friend, today let God make you what He wants you to be—an honest, sincere Christian. Tithe of your income to the Lord's service.

Our business in this church is to preach the Gospel, to send the Gospel around the world, and to tell people about Jesus and His power to save.

55. *The Result of Great Faith*

And the apostles said unto the Lord, Increase our faith.

And the Lord said, If ye had faith as a grain of mustard seed, ye might say unto this sycamine tree, Be thou plucked up by the root, and be thou planted in the sea; and it should obey you.

—Luke 17:5,6.

Above all, taking the shield of faith, wherewith ye shall be able to quench all the fiery darts of the wicked.
—Ephesians 6:16.

Yea, and all that will live godly in Christ Jesus shall suffer persecution.
—II Timothy 3:12.

It is my prayer that questions on great faith can be answered.

Some of you may wonder about great faith. Does it provide ease of life? Take away suffering? Promise an abundance for daily living?

Some would have you believe that this will be accomplished and, more simply, by having faith in God. Some say that all we need do is to take a stand for God, believe His Word; then our problems and heartaches will be solved. Let me answer three questions.

I. WHAT MUST THE CHRISTIAN EXPECT IN LIFE?

If one stands for God, what should he expect? If he is firm in faith, believes the Word of God, and is willing to follow wherever the Lord leads, what should he expect in life?

1. *Peace of heart.* I say this with assurance. The result of real faith in God will be peace. It will straighten out the difficulties of life; hard places will seem easy.

Paul endured trouble beyond anything we have known, yet he had deep peace. Philippians 4:6,7 tells us how to have this same peace:

"Be careful for nothing; but in every thing by prayer and supplication with thanksgiving let your requests be made known unto God.

"And the peace of God, which passeth all understanding, shall keep your hearts and minds through Christ Jesus."

It is the Christian's right to expect peace. Though the world be against him, he can still have perfect peace within.

2. *Opposition and adversity.* Nowhere does the Bible promise freedom from difficulties simply by our believing in Jesus Christ. On the contrary. We are to expect adversity.

The Bible gives us one illustration after another of those who endured great hardships for the sake of Jesus Christ.

Many of the greatest Bible leaders died the martyr's death because of their faith in God. Did ever more noble men than Peter, John and Paul walk upon this earth? No. But what great suffering they endured because of their faith in God.

3. *Heartaches.* Paul endured great difficulties, tremendous heartaches; yet he had peace. He desired to see the conversion of his own brethren according to the flesh. He had upon himself great heaviness and continual sorrow. He did not try to escape these things, but bore them because he felt that they were a part of the Christian's life.

4. *Deceivers.* Did such a noble man as Paul have deceivers, enemies? Yes, in many places. Men turned against him. He was stoned, cast out of the city, and left for dead. We read in II Timothy, the last writing of the apostle, how many turned against Paul. He was deserted by friends in Asia. Demas forsook

him and returned to Thessalonica. Alexander the coppersmith did him much evil. But in the midst of it all, the apostle had a sweetness of spirit, a devotion to God, a dedication of life which was never shaken.

The Christian can know that he is saved, can enjoy the peace of God; but he must be conscious that when he identifies with the people of God, he will have adversity, heartaches; and men will deceive him.

II. WHAT MUST THE CHRISTIAN DO?

1. *We must stand for God.* "Put on the whole armour of God, that ye may be able to stand against the wiles of the devil." We have an opponent who fights against us at every turn. Though we must not expect to be free from his onslaught, yet we can and must stand.

Certain things will help us in our standing. One is prayer. This is one reason the apostle said, "Praying always with all prayer and supplication in the Spirit. . . ." Prayer will give us faith to stand against the wiles of the evil one.

Not only prayer, but the Word of God. Without reading our Bibles, we may get some false ideas. We may feel that after accepting Christ, all will be well. But the Bible reveals how God's people have suffered since the beginning of time, and will continue to suffer until we get Home to Glory.

2. *We must be willing to suffer.* One of the texts for this message says, "Yea, and all that will live godly in Christ Jesus shall suffer persecution." That is as true today as it was then. If we live for Christ, then we can expect suffering. I challenge you to find one noble man or woman who has ever walked this earth who did not suffer. Suffering has been the part of every great Christian. Do not seek to escape it. Do not deliberately put yourself in difficult situations—they will come of themselves— but be ready to face whatever may come.

3. *We must live consistently.* The Bible condemns compromise. There is no place in life for weakness, for selfishness, for self-centeredness. We are to forget self and be strong in Christ. It was for this reason Paul wrote Timothy:

"Thou therefore, my son, be strong in the grace that is in Christ Jesus.

"And the things that thou hast heard of me among many witnesses, the same commit thou to faithful men, who shall be able to teach others also.

"Thou therefore endure hardness, as a good soldier of Jesus Christ."—II Tim. 2:1-3.

The temptation to compromise is ever before us. The world seeks to lead us into estrangements which would take away our power, our ability, and the presence of God. Therefore, the Christian must live consistently. His faith must enable him to face every difficulty, to stand against every foe.

4. *We must speak out for Christ.* This is not the type sermon which every person will follow, but some will. Some noble believers will know this is the Christian's obligation. Others will take salvation, but they will not engage further in the work of Jesus Christ.

The Christian life is far from easy. It is fraught with many difficulties. But we are nevertheless to speak out for Christ, letting others know whose side we are on.

Every command of our Master, after His ascension, incorporated this command: "Go ye therefore, and teach all nations . . . ." It was in obedience to this that the disciples scattered everywhere, telling the story of Jesus Christ.

We have briefly enumerated some things that we must do: Stand for God, be willing to suffer, live consistently, and speak out for Jesus Christ.

III. WHAT WILL BE THE CHRISTIAN'S REWARD?

We are discussing the result of great faith: faith that works—faith that speaks—faith that launches out into the deep.

1. *The satisfaction of a right stand.* The Holy Spirit who dwells within gives sweet peace when we take our stand for right. Peter had it. The Apostle John had it. Paul knew what it was. A reading of any one of these letters by these men will reveal their

satisfaction, their consciousness of the presence of God.

Listen to Paul as he speaks in II Timothy 4:17:

"Notwithstanding the Lord stood with me, and strengthened me; that by me the preaching might be fully known, and that all the Gentiles might hear: and I was delivered out of the mouth of the lion."

Paul had peace and satisfaction because he had obeyed God and had done what God had saved him to do. To you will come, also, satisfaction when you take a right stand.

2. *The solution to many problems.*

Have faith in God and see how many things take care of themselves! Trust in God and see how brightly the sun will shine again. But worry and fret, and see how the problems increase.

The solution is putting them in the Lord's hands. This takes faith.

It is only human to try to work things out for ourselves, but faith will see us through every difficulty.

3. *The joy of helping others.* It is difficult, if not impossible, to be of any help to others unless we have faith in God.

An interesting story is given in Luke 7:1-10. A certain centurion's servant was near death. Certain elders of the Jews were sent to Jesus, asking Him to come and heal this servant. Jesus went with them; and when He was yet far from the house, the centurion said, ". . .trouble not thyself: for I am not worthy that thou shouldest enter under my roof."

The centurion went on to say that he did not think Jesus would come but would simply speak a word and the servant would be healed.

When Jesus heard these things, the Word tells us that He marvelled at the centurion and turned to the people around Him and said, "I say unto you, I have not found so great faith, no, not in Israel." When the people returned to the house, they found that the servant had been made well from that very hour.

Others are always blessed by our great faith. It is impossible to exercise faith in God without giving a blessing to others.

In a sickroom, a blessing is imparted by our faith. A man going through trying times will be helped and blessed by your faith.

We think we must have money to help others or be able to give them what they need. We usually imagine that all needs can be supplied by material things. Not so. The greatest need is faith in God. When we have faith, we can best help.

Yes, we are helping others through faith in the blessed Saviour.

4. *Our reward will be complete* at the judgment seat. Here our works and service will be judged, as well as our faith.

It is at the judgment seat that our stand for Christ will be judged. If our works and service are found worthy, we will receive our reward. "If any man's work abide which he hath built thereupon, he shall receive a reward" (I Cor. 3:14).

Let us so labor that when we stand before Christ, He will be able to say, "Well done, thou good and faithful servant."

What is the result of faith? First, peace of heart; second, opposition from others; third, an eternal reward when we stand before Christ. Jesus said, "Have faith in God."

It is faith that wins victories day after day. It is faith that gives assurance and peace. It is faith that presents to us the victories of this sinful day.

With this story I close. It is the story of a girl who gave her heart to Jesus while young. She afterward married a young man who was a sinner. In this she did wrong; but to the credit of the Lord and her own faith, she lived for Jesus every day.

The years passed. The husband still cared nothing for Christ. Though he would not attend worship, the heartbroken wife was true to her Lord. Several children were born, and the sweet mother taught them to love and worship Jesus.

Finally, she was taken with that awful and dreaded disease, tuberculosis. She lingered for awhile, then died. Just before her death, she called her husband to her bedside and said to him, "My dear, I have tried to be a faithful wife. I do hope you will change and receive Christ as Saviour, and rear our little ones so that all of you will meet me."

To the children she said, "I have taught you to look to Jesus and have trained you to walk with Him." She then became very weak and soon died.

A few hours later her body was carried to the lonely cemetery. The husband stood by and saw the last clod fall upon the coffin that held the remains of his precious wife.

Soon he was back with the children in their lonely home. He gave them a cold supper, tucked them in bed, and sat down before the fire to think.

Soon he heard sobbing. He called, "Johnny, are you hungry?"

"No, Papa."

"Are you thirsty?"

"No, Papa."

"Well, what is the trouble, son?"

The little fellow broke down and said, "Papa, Mama used to get all of us children around her knee at night and read to us about Jesus, then put her hands on our heads and pray with us. You have sent us to bed without our prayers."

That father, in giving his testimony, said, "I could stand it no longer. I got my children up and, reaching up on the shelf, got my dead wife's Bible. I read a few verses, then knelt and told God that I would give Him my heart and life, and that I wanted Him to take and use me to train my children so all of us could meet her in Glory."

There is power in living for God. There is power in great faith. Some of you may have gone through such sorrows as this one. May I urge you to let your light so shine that others may see your good works and glorify your Father which is in Heaven.

Christian, live for God. Let Jesus Christ be all to you.

Sinner friend, the need of your life is threefold. First, the knowledge that you are lost and undone without Christ as Saviour; second, a knowledge that He can save you; third, repentance and faith toward the living Son of God.

56. *The Touch of Faith*

And a certain woman, which had an issue of blood twelve years,

And had suffered many things of many physicians, and had spent all that she had, and was nothing bettered, but rather grew worse,

When she had heard of Jesus, came in the press behind, and touched his garment.

For she said, If I may touch but his clothes, I shall be whole.

And straightway the fountain of her blood was dried up; and she felt in her body that she was healed of that plague.

And Jesus, immediately knowing in himself that virtue had gone out of him, turned him about in the press, and said, Who touched my clothes?

And his disciples said unto him, Thou seest the multitude thronging thee, and sayest thou, Who touched me?

And he looked round about to see her that had done this thing.

But the woman fearing and trembling, knowing what was done in her, came and fell down before him, and told him all the truth.

And he said unto her, Daughter, thy faith hath made thee whole; go in peace, and be whole of thy plague.
— Mark 5:25-34.

If I were an artist, I would paint a picture of Christ in the midst of a great crowd such as thronged about Him on the day He went on His way to heal the daughter of Jairus.

Christ in a crowd! Untouched by criticism, scoffing words, or hard looks. Untouched, unhindered by the world's opposition. Walking as a giant among men. Unafraid of all that men might do to Him.

Christ in a crowd! Touched by the needs of all mankind. A kind, compassionate and loving Saviour, gentle, approachable, anxious to serve others.

Christ in a crowd! Untouched, yet easily touched. Untouched, yet willing to be touched by a poor soul in need.

When Christ had finished His ministry on the eastern side of the Sea of Galilee, He crossed over to the Capernaum side where a great crowd gathered as soon as His ship came to land.

Out of the crowd came a ruler of the synagogue, Jairus by name. Falling at the feet of Jesus, he besought Him to come and heal his daughter. It is written that Jesus went with him, and "much people thronged him."

As He went His way, a certain woman, who had been sick for twelve years, drew near Him. In spite of trying many doctors and spending all she had, her health had steadily declined.

When she heard of Jesus, she decided to get in touch with Him. Getting through the crowd, she gently touched His garment. She thought: "If I may touch but his clothes, I shall be whole."

As her faith, so was it unto her. When she touched the hem of Jesus' garment, she was immediately healed of her plague.

Jesus knew that someone had touched Him; but in order to bring out the woman, He asked, "Who touched my clothes?" The disciples, very ordinary and practical men, said unto Him, "Thou seest the multitude thronging thee, and sayest thou, Who touched me?" But when Jesus looked around to see her, she came and fell down before Him and told Him all the truth.

The word of Jesus to her was, "Daughter, thy faith hath made thee whole; go in peace, and be whole of thy plague."

Now, permit me to emphasize three wonderful words which stand out in this scriptural account.

I. SALVATION

The woman had heard about Jesus. She knew that He could do something for her, that if she could just touch the garment of Christ, she would be made whole.

She came to Christ in spite of her weakness. Remember, for twelve years she had been plagued with her trouble. Doctors had failed to help her. Though her body was weak, she determined to come to Jesus.

Remember also that the crowd was gathered around Him. She might have decided: *"The crowd is so great. I cannot get to Him, so I had as well go back home";* but instead, she worked her way through the pressing throng until He was in touching distance.

Great blessings come to those who are not turned aside by weakness of body or thoughtless multitudes. Blessings come to those who do not wait for a more convenient season but take hold of the present opportunity to reach Christ and get His blessing.

Perhaps her faith was weak, but she touched a mighty Saviour, and straightway she was healed. Faith brought the victory and the healing.

How suddenly the Lord works when we touch Him!

She was completely healed. The Word tells us that she was made whole at once. There was no period of convalescence. It was an instant cure. She felt in her body that she was healed of that plague.

I wish that I might get you to see that salvation comes through simple faith in Christ. Simple, childlike faith touches the all-powerful Lord and is sufficient to bring salvation.

1. *Salvation is sudden.* There is no such thing as a gradual salvation. At the moment of believing faith, the sinner passes out of darkness into light, out of death into life. We are not almost saved; we are either saved or lost.

2. *Salvation is complete.* Just as this woman was completely healed of her illness, so is salvation a complete salvation. No halfway work for our Lord.

3. *Salvation brings joy.* Feeling always comes after faith. Some desire to have the feeling before they touch the Lord and believe on Him, but feeling is not first.

There are three "F's" to keep in mind: first, FACT—the fact that man is a sinner, lost and condemned, and the fact that Jesus is able to save to the uttermost; second, FAITH—faith in the crucified, risen and living Lord; third, FEELING—the joy of the Lord flooding the soul.

Let's not make salvation more or less than what we find in the Bible. It is a serious thing to add or take away from the Word.

Now, what saith the Word of God on salvation? "Believe on the Lord Jesus Christ, and thou shalt be saved." That sounds nothing like some of the preaching we hear on the radio, nor like some of the vague and rambling writings of past and present false prophets.

Some people have the idea that a man cannot be saved unless he can quote practically the entire Bible. He must be able to give the story of creation, the fall of man, Noah's flood, Abraham's call, Israel's backslidings, Christ's birth, and other Bible events.

Some churches think a man is not saved unless he looks a certain way. If he appears happy, he is frivolous. If he is too sad, he lacks the joy of salvation. If a man doesn't have an expression halfway between crying and smiling, he doesn't have it.

O friends, let us come back to the Word of God. How simple, how plain, how wonderful it is! Here we read in John 1:12, "But as many as received him, to them gave he power to become the sons of God, even to them that believe on his name." How plain is John 3:36: "He that believeth on the Son hath everlasting life: and he that believeth not the Son shall not see life; but the wrath of God abideth on him."

Yes, some believe one cannot be saved unless he has heard the Word of God over a long period of time and has gradually come to conviction and a place of decision.

Surely the Word teaches that anyone who recognizes himself as a lost sinner and will, in simple faith, look to Jesus Christ in repentance and faith, can be saved.

Children can come to the Lord and, by the touch of faith, be saved. The poor, the uninformed, the untaught, the ignorant can all be saved by faith in Him.

It is certain that among the three thousand saved and baptized on the day of Pentecost many could not pass the entrance examinations given in some churches today.

Come near to Christ; yes, touch Him by faith, receive Him as Saviour. He will not turn you away.

II. CONFESSION

This is the second word from the story. Christ was certainly content with the simple faith of this woman, but He was not content for her to go away without an open confession of her faith. Therefore, He asked, "Who touched my clothes?" This question was designed to bring her to public acknowledgement of the blessings she had received.

Jesus was not trying to embarrass her, but trying to help her. He had a definite purpose in asking for her confession. He wanted her joy to be full. He wanted to strengthen her own faith. She had believed in her heart; now the Lord is asking for a confession from her mouth.

"That if thou shalt confess with thy mouth the Lord Jesus, and shalt believe in thine heart that God hath raised him from the dead, thou shalt be saved.

"For with the heart man believeth unto righteousness; and with the mouth confession is made unto salvation."—Rom. 10:9,10.

This woman had already been healed; now the Saviour is calling for a confession.

Gratitude demands that we confess the Lord Jesus Christ as Saviour. Have you been saved? Do you love the Lord Jesus Christ? Then come out and with a grateful heart confess Him as Saviour.

An interest in others calls for a confession. Secret disciples cannot be greatly used—if they can be used at all. If we are to help others, we must openly confess our faith in Christ.

Has God blessed you? Then tell others. Speak of His salvation. Let others know its wonder and majesty. Have you received victory over temptation? Then tell some friend or loved one about it. Give God the glory. Has the Lord given you comfort in time of sorrow? Then do not hesitate to testify of this. Let your gratitude of heart speak that others may know what Jesus can do.

The need of the hour is for more people to come out of the crowd and speak for Christ. The number of soul winners in any church is exceedingly small. The masses of people stand in the multitude and say nothing. Speak out for Christ. Let others know what He can do.

Medical doctors do not advertise. A doctor's advertisements are his patients, one patient telling another until he has built a large practice.This is the way the Lord Jesus, our Great Physician, intends souls to be won—each Christian witnessing to someone else.

If the Lord is sufficient for all of your needs, then tell that needy person about it. No Christian should be content until he has helped someone else to know the Lord. Ofttimes your testimony is worth more than a thousand sermons.

Speak out for Christ. Confess Him in the church. Follow Him in believer's baptism. Confess Him daily before others.

III. CONFIRMATION

"And he said unto her, Daughter, thy faith hath made thee whole; go in peace, and be whole of thy plague."

Her confession brought His confirmation.

She was saved by faith. She was assured by the Word. Had this woman slipped in the crowd without confessing what the Lord had done and receiving His assurance of complete healing, she might have had serious doubts that all was well. But when Jesus spoke to her, she knew that her body had been completely healed.

Christ not only saves, but He wants to give us complete assurance of our salvation by His eternal word. Many portions of the Bible were written to give a Christian assurance.

One such is I John 5:13:

"These things have I written unto you that believe on the name of the Son of God;. . .that ye may believe on the name of the Son of God."

Look back a few verses in this same chapter at further assurance:

"If we receive the witness of men, the witness of God is greater: for this is the witness of God which he hath testified of his Son.

"He that believeth on the Son of God hath the witness in himself: he that believeth not God hath made him a liar; because he believeth not the record that God gave of his Son.

"And this is the record, that God hath given to us eternal life, and this life is in his Son.

"He that hath the Son hath life; and he that hath not the Son of God hath not life."—Vss. 9-12.

You cannot have joy unless you have the assurance. A doubting soul is not a happy soul. The uncertain believer will be a critical, fault-finding, doubting believer. We must have assurance for joy, and this assurance is in the Word of God.

Last, we must have assurance if we are to help others. Not only must we trust in our Lord; but we must have His word of confirmation that all is well, if we are to be a blessing to those around us.

Lord Guthrie was on his way to church in London when he passed a preacher addressing a crowd in the open air. The speaker said, "I have not been to college, but I have been to Calvary." Lord Guthrie said, "That day I heard three of the world's greatest preachers in the city of London; but after a lapse of many years, I find myself unable to recall a single sentence uttered by the celebrated preachers; but I still remember the words of the earnest lay preacher in the open air."

Yes, it is when we are saved and know that we have received eternal life that we can bring blessings to others.

D. L. Moody said, "Nothing disqualifies us for doing God's work more than a doubt as to our salvation."

He used to illustrate it in this way: "If I were in the river and didn't have a firm grip on something, I could not help anybody. I've got to get a good hold for myself before I can help someone else. There's no liberty, peace, rest, joy, or power until we have assurance."

See the woman going her way with the words of Jesus ringing in her ears, "Daughter, thy faith hath made thee whole; go in peace."

Salvation, confession, confirmation are strong, important words.

Christ is passing by today. Will you press forward and touch the hem of His garment? Will you in faith come and receive Him as Saviour?

Perhaps you have been saved but have never confessed Him openly. If this be the case, may gratitude compel you to do so. May your burden for the souls of others bring you to an open confession of faith.

Christ is passing by. Will you come, hear, and touch Him in faith?

TAKE ALL THE BIBLE YOU CAN ON REASON AND THE REST BY FAITH.—Abraham Lincolon.

57. *The Adventure of Faith*

> *Now he that hath wrought us for the selfsame thing is God, who also hath given unto us the earnest of the Spirit.*
>
> *Therefore we are always confident, knowing that, whilst we are at home in the body, we are absent from the Lord:*
>
> *(For we walk by faith, not by sight:)*
>
> *We are confident, I say, and willing rather to be absent from the body, and to be present with the Lord.*
>
> *Wherefore we labour, that, whether present or absent, we may be accepted of him.*
>
> *For we must all appear before the judgment seat of Christ; that every one may receive the things done in his body, according to that he hath done, whether it be good or bad.*
>
> —II Corinthians 5:5-10.

These are beautiful words, with preaching in every verse. But I am going to use verse 7: "For we walk by faith, not by sight."

The cry of my heart is for a wholehearted faith: a faith that stands in the darkest night, a faith that endures when all else fails, a faith that gives a song when the shadows gather, a faith that never wavers when storms appear.

We walk by faith, not by sight. Have faith in times of illness, in times of tragedy, when there are financial reverses, an accident.

I want the faith of God's choosing for me.

I have read and re-read Hebrews 11. All these great men and women had a distinct job, a definite task to do. To each, faith was given.

I want God to give me faith needed for my every task. I know you want that also. Your task is different from mine, but we all have work to do for Him. In spite of their sufferings, each of those in Hebrews 11 succeeded.

In thinking on this sermon, a host of outlines came to me.

1. *The call of God is an adventure.* He called Abraham, Moses, Joshua, Gideon, Elijah, Paul and others. He called me. I did not see it all then—it's a good thing I didn't. From the very beginning it has been an adventure.

2. *The preaching of the Gospel is an adventure.* Standing here preaching to you this morning is an adventure. I do not know what will happen in this service. I pray some will turn to the Saviour. It may be that some Christian will be encouraged, inspired and sent out to do more for God. It may be that some despondent person, at the point of ending it all, will say, *Today I see something for me in life.*

3. *The daily life of the believer is an adventure.* It will profit you if you will see this. Every day is an adventure of faith to a child of God.

We face mysteries. We do not know what may happen next. Every day strange things do happen—plane crashes, car wrecks, shootings, home accidents; yes, for a child of God, every day is an adventure. There are mountains to climb, rivers to cross for each of us.

4. *The end of life is an adventure.* Paul said, "I am now ready to be offered, and the time of my departure is at hand." Then he added, "I have fought a good fight, I have finished my course, I have kept the faith" (II Tim. 4:6,7). Paul was now a prisoner in Rome. The day of his execution was drawing nigh. Timothy had to know what this faith would do in such a time as this, so Paul wrote the above to young Timothy and, of course, to us.

". . .the time of my departure is at hand." Departure means to unloose. Paul was near the time of his unloosing, leaving the shoreline for a better place.

Here we have bonds of the flesh, but there comes an unloosing time, and here is the picture of death. We now live in frail bodies, hedged in by obstacles and limitations. Being bound by the shores of time, we can go just so far. Our fondest dreams fail here on earth. Our noblest ambitions are not now realized. We are bound.

But there will come an unloosing, and that was what Paul was talking about and waiting for. One day we are going to be with our Saviour; then we will realize these fondest dreams of life.

How do we face today? By faith. How do we face tomorrow? By faith. The future? By faith.

Now to my outline. Whence comes faith?

I. FAITH COMES FROM REGENERATION

Jesus said, "Ye must be born again" (John 3:7).

Paul said, "For by grace are ye saved through faith" (Eph. 2:8).

Faith for life and for meeting obstacles comes from regeneration, from the Christ who saved me. If I am wise, I will use this God-given faith. If I am to be happy, I will use this God-given faith.

1. *By faith I can pray.* Through regeneration I became God's child; as God's child, I can call upon Him for all of life's needs. Recognizing my weakness and seeing my desperate need, I must call upon Him.

Listen to the words of John:

"And this is the confidence that we have in him, that, if we ask any thing according to his will, he heareth us: And if we know that he hear us, whatsoever we ask, we know that we have the petitions that we desired of him."—I John 5:14,15.

2. *By faith I can have peace of heart.* Jesus said:

"Peace I leave with you, my peace I give unto you: not as the world giveth, give I unto you. Let not your heart be troubled, neither let it be afraid."—John 14:27.

In Acts 12 is a marvelous picture of peace. Simon Peter was in prison. The guards were watching him. He was bound, chained. James had already died; now Peter was the next one to lay down his life. But we read that he was sleeping! Sleeping like an infant in his crib. The guards, the chains, the cell, the blocks—all were there. Nevertheless, Simon Peter, having committed his life, including his future, to the Lord, had gone to sleep.

Now when your troubles are heavy and your anxieties many, think of this man, then ask God to give to you the peace, the submissiveness that Peter had.

Peter believed Jesus who said, "Be anxious for nothing." Peter believed the Son of God who said, "Your father knoweth what things ye have need of" (Matt. 6:8). Peter was resting on Romans 8:28.

Claim this peace for yourself.

3. *By faith I can rest on every promise of God.* Whence comes our faith? From regeneration. Have you been born again? If you are saved, then He has given faith whereby you can live and move and exercise your talents in the service of Christ.

II. FAITH COMES FROM THE RECORD

The Bible is a record of faith. The Word of God says, "So then faith cometh by hearing, and hearing by the word of God" (Rom. 10:17).

1. *Build your faith on the infallible Word*—not upon man, not upon man's ideas, but upon the infallible Word. Here is the foundation for your faith. God never fails. The Bible never changes. "Heaven and earth shall pass away, but my words shall not pass away," says Matthew 24:35.

I saw a beautiful building up north which was built on the bank of a river, a lovely building some five or six stories high. The one taking me around said, "This building is sinking. The foundation is laid down on the rocks on the side of that river. It is sinking an inch, maybe two inches every year. Eventually they will have to move out, and it will have to be torn down."

The things of this world are continually sinking, always failing; but God never fails. He will give you what is needed.

When you don't know what to do and when you are nonplused by the affairs of life, then build your faith on the unchanging Word.

2. *Guide your life by the unchanging Word.* By the Word and by the indwelling Spirit of God one finds guidance.

3. *Gain inspiration from the eternal Word.* Inspire your heart. Difficult times will come. Opposition will be yours. The adventure of faith will not be easy. You are wondering, *What can I do?* Read from the Word; be inspired from the Word.

Read the writings, the epistles of the Apostle Paul. He could suffer and be victorious even to the end of life. So can we.

Read of David and his trials. Let the Psalms encourage you.

Read about the Apostle John and his writings, what he endured even in old age, how he was kept to the very close of his life. Say! If it could mean so much to him, maybe it could mean the same to me! Gain inspiration from the eternal Word.

Adventure means excitement, always.

Adventure means uncertainty, always.

Adventure means danger, always.

Read your Bible. Let the Word speak to your heart. Surrender yourself to His commands. Meet His requirements. Whatever He says do, do. Begin that walk of faith. Walk like Enoch walked; walk like Joseph walked; walk like Daniel walked. I pick these three names in whom you can find no criticism, men who walked with God.

III. THIS FAITH COMES BY REMEMBRANCE

The emphasis in the Word of God is on remembering. The Bible says, "Remember."

Moses said to the people of Israel, "Beware lest thou forget the Lord, which brought thee forth out of the land of Egypt" (Deut. 6:12).

"Remember" is written about the Lord Jesus and the disciples who forgot—"And they remembered his words" (Luke 24:8). Faith comes by remembrance.

1. *Remember your regeneration*; second, remember to rest upon the Word; and third, God calls upon you to remember what

He has done and will do for you as you rest in Him.

2. *Remember what God said to you.* Remember His unfailing promises. In the darkest hour, rest upon those promises. I can recall very vividly the day I laid hold of Romans 8:28.

3. *Remember what God has done for you.* Look back: how amazing and wonderful all of it is!

I remember my first church. I went to my first pastorate in Memphis, Tennessee, many years ago. The salary was $50.00 a month at this big and beautiful church. The crowd was small, and it was spiritually dead.

I remember my other pastorates at Germantown, Greenbrier, Fairfield, Chattanooga, and how God led all along the journey.

I remember feeling His divine hand upon me in times when I thought it was all over.

I remember how I felt when the doctors at Mayo's Clinic said I would never preach again. I remember how I felt when the doctors, who had gathered around in conference at Oschner's Clinic in New Orleans, said I was through preaching. One asked, "How old are you?" (I was then sixty-three.) He said, "That's long enough to preach. Now enjoy life." "But," I said, "I've something else I want to do. There are a few more things to be accomplished."

In spite of all they said and thought, God has given me about ten more years to do the things I felt I had to do. And I'm still doing them, still preaching.

Look back over your life and remember what God has done with and for you: how He has directed you, helped you in the past days, answered your prayers, kept your loved ones, supplied every need.

Maybe you have been through some difficult times. Maybe you have faced opposition. Maybe people have turned their backs on you, ridiculed you. Maybe you have fought many battles. You have been standing alone. But if God be for us, who can be against us! One with God is a majority. Remember what God has done for you.

Whether friends, family, finances or health fail, you remember what God has done for you.

4. *Remember what God will do in the future.* He will never leave you nor forsake you.

He is sending His Son back to get us. Jesus said, "I will come again" (John 14:3). He is going to bring us unto Himself. That promise of God we can rest upon.

Let your memory work. Keep these things in your heart. We walk by faith, not by sight. We don't have to see at all what will happen next year or ten years down the road; we just need to take life one day at a time.

Where does your faith come from? Faith comes from your salvation. When Jesus saved you, He gave you faith. I hope you are using that faith. Faith comes from God's Book. This is the record of faith. Reckon on that. Faith comes from remembrance. God said to the children of Israel, and He exhorts everyone of us, to remember what He has done.

Unless you abide by these simple things, then you will face more tragedies, more sorrows, more heartaches. You will go around wondering, *Just what can I do? What is my next step?* You will stay puzzled, confused unless you start walking by faith.

Young people, walk by faith. Don't come to me and say, "I've got to see where I'm going for the next few years. I've got to have a money guarantee." No! Walk by faith.

Husbands, wives, walk by faith. In any financial crisis, walk by faith. We read of suicides and tragedies every day committed by those not walking by faith.

A good friend of mine, one of our stronger preachers, lived in Nashville. I knew him when he was in his fifties. Every sermon he preached was just about perfect. He studied hard, worked hard. He stayed with it night and day. He wrote books. He never had a note in front of him at the pulpit; all was memorized.

I've listened to him preach. I've had him with me in revivals. I've been with him in several campaigns. I thought he was one of the strongest of men. But somewhere, somehow, he slipped.

He preached on Sunday evening at the First Baptist Church in Nashville. Many were saved. He shook hands with the people in front of the church, then got in his car and drove home. He walked to the kitchen, picked up a revolver and ended his life.

He failed. Was he saved? That is in God's hands. He had preached for years, a mighty preacher of the Gospel, a great scholar; but he failed somewhere. Somewhere along the line he failed to listen.

Was he mentally off? He didn't seem to be. He preached at the First Baptist Church on Sunday night. But something happened. He failed to remember all God had promised to give.

You take hold today and say, "Praise God, I'm saved! Lord, let me walk with You, talk with You. Let me be revived and be all You want me to be. I will read and follow this Book. I will remember what You have done. I will remember Your goodness in saving me, in keeping me, in calling me into Your service."

Do you know Christ? Have you received Him? If not, come now. If you wish to unite with our church, coming on promise of a letter, we invite you to come. If God is calling you into full-time service, come forward. If He is speaking to you this morning about any matter, quickly walk down the aisle. You may wish to rededicate your life. This invitation is for you, too. Come when the others start down toward the front.

FAITH STEPS UPON THE SEEMING VOID AND FINDS THE ROCK BENEATH.

For a complete list of books available from the Sword of the Lord, write to Sword of the Lord Publishers, P. O. Box 1099, Murfreesboro, Tennessee 37133.